PRINCIPLES AND TECHNIQUES OF EDUCATION

PRINCIPLES AND TECHNIQUES OF EDUCATION

O.P. Dhiman

KALPAZ

Published by

Kalpaz Publications
C-30, Satyawati Nagar,
Delhi – 110052

Distribution Network
gyanbooks.com
India, USA, Canada, UK, Australia, France

ISBN: 9788178355573 (HB)

15 impression 2019

Printed at: Goyal Offset Printers, Delhi.

To
those who live
for
the cause of school education
and
teacher education

Preface

When I was a student of M.Ed class at Govt. College of Education, Jalandhar during the session 1963-64, I realised that students and teachers in College of Education experienced a dirth of good books on the subject. Soon after doing my course, when I joined M.G.N. College of Education, Jalandhar as a Lecturer in Education to teach this subject to B.Ed. class. I started writing a book, 'A Textbook of Theory and Principles of Education', which was published by the Panjab Kitab Ghar, Jalandhar in 1965. This was my first attempt at writing. Being very ambitious, the book became very voluminous having 650 pages. The book, though very popular proved to be somewhat, above the standard of B.Ed and M.Ed students.

Later, when I joined Govt. College of Education, Patiala in 1965, I started teaching both B.Ed and M.Ed classes. After having taught this subject for about a decade, I felt it necessary to reshape the said book in the light of my experience so as to make it more handy and useful for students. The new book of 392 pages appeared under the title "Principle and Technique of Education" in the year 1973.

This book found wide circulation and appreciative comments from several authors on the subject and was recommend as 'Text Book' for B.Ed by various universities. Four editions of this book were published. As there was a great demand for this book, my colleagues of different colleges and universities suggested me to get this book re-published. But, because of my various other engagements in the field of education, I could not do so. I retired from Govt. College of Education in 1991 and immediately joined Multani Mal Modi Post-Graduate College as Principal. So I could not find time to reshape this book and get it published.

Still there is a great demand for this book from students and teachers-educators and I have to bend before these demand. So after teaching M.Ed and B.Ed classes for 27 years, now I decided to reshape and get this book published under the title of "Principles and Techniques of Education". The book is an endeavour to provide the readers with a comprehensive but comprehensible study of various aspects of Education—theory as well as technique. I have tried to present very analytically all the aspects of education in a simple, lucid and intelligible manner. This book unfolds all that a teacher must know in order to be able to teach in the schools or to become a good teacher-educator.

I do not claim any originality either in selection of the title or subject-matter. I only seek to examine, analyse and present the Principles and Techniques of Education in a simple, lucid and intelligible way in the light of present day educational theory and keeping in view the standards and limitations of our students. I hope that this compact text book will cater to the needs of M.Ed. and B.Ed students and teacher-educators.

I a knowledge the co-operation extended to me by several friends and colleagues in the preparation of this book. However for the entire text and opinions expressed and also for whatever short comings that may be there, I alone am responsible.

Formal though it may look, I must express my grateful appreciation to my wife, Mrs. Manorama Dhiman, formerly, Head of the Department of Home Science, Govt. College for Women, Patiala without whose encouragement, devotion and sacrifice the publication of this book would not have been possible.

I take this opportunity to put on record my deep sense of gratitude to all the principals with whom I have worked who always inspired me despite my habit of being critical and independent in my views.

I should not complete this preface without thanking my students who were instrumental in clarifying some of my thoughts and in stimulating me to think anew on Philosophy of Education. They taught me more than they realise.

Last though not the least, I am grateful to my publishers, especially Amit Garg for his enthusiasm in the publication of this book.

March 6, 2007 **O.P. DHIMAN**

Contents

1

The Meaning and Nature of Education

We often think ourselves to be educated. We use the word 'Education' in our daily life. But we seldom try to understand the real meaning of education. We sometimes regard education as mere collection of information. Sometimes we think that getting 'Education' means getting degrees or diplomas. In this chapter, let us ponder over the real meaning of Education.

ETYMOLOGICAL EXPLANATION OF EDUCATION

The first step in any systematic attempt to understand the nature of education should be clarification of the precise meaning of education-what its derivative meanings are. Thus, our first approach to this problem should be etymological.

Education as bringing up process

Different derivations of the term 'education' have been given by educational thinkers. According to some of them, it has been derived from the Latin word *'educare'* which means *to bring up*' or *'to raise'*. According to this view, education is a process of imparting to an individual certain information and knowledge which society deems necessary. Education implies modification of the behaviour of the individual by imposing standards of society upon him. Thus, education is a process of external imposition rather than growth from within. This derivation gives us the concept of teacher-centred rather than child-centred education.

Education as a drawing out process

There is a group of thinkers who believe that the term education' has been derived from the Latin word *'educare'* which means to *'lead out'* or *'to draw out'*. Education, they think, means to draw out something and not to put in something.

Some theorists who hold that education is a drawing out process give a slightly different explanation of the word 'education'. They believe that the term education has been derived from two Latin word–*'e'* meaning *'out of'* and *'duco'* meaning *'to lead'*. Education, therefore, means to lead out or to draw out the best in man. It is the process of 'drawing out from within' rather than 'imposing from without.'

Education, from this point of view is considered as a process of the development of what is innate in the child. It is an agency of, or an instrument for the transformation of the potential into the actual. This explanation presumes that all knowledge is inherent in children. Education, therefore, implies growth from within rather than imposition from without. Education is a process of the development of talents inborn in the individual and not conveying to an individual a body of information or knowledge. A large number of eminent educators and philosophers have endorsed this interpretation. By education", says **Gandhiji**, "I mean an all round drawing out of the best in the child and man—body, mind and spirit."

Education as a bringing up as well as drawing out process

The two view points of education discussed above cannot be isolated from each other. The view that education is a drawing out process can be accepted with a pinch of salt. In this interpretation an important aspect of education has been disregarded. Can it be possible that every thing which forms part of education was already inherent in the child's mind ! Is it possible to draw out everything? Can it be established that everything—ideas, ideals, beliefs, opinions and attitudes—was potential in the mind of the child? It is true that certain inherent capacities do form part of the natural endowment of the child, but the factual knowledge acquired, skills learnt or the habits and sentiments developed, during life time, were not innate in the child's mind. Therefore, it can be said that in the absence of poured in knowledge or suitable foundation laid through learning under environmental influences, drawing out will be out of question. Unless knowledge or experience is given to the child, we cannot draw out the best in him. Education, therefore, is not only a drawing out, but also a bringing up process, whereby the educand is trained for certain types of social behaviour—democratic living, worthy citizenship, international understanding and is developed into a full man or woman with a well integrated personality.

BROAD AND NARROW MEANINGS OF EDUCATION

Despite its various interpretations, the term 'education' is generally used in the following two meanings.

Broad Meaning of Education

The word 'education' makes it clear that this process is very broad in itself. From birth upto death we come in contact with many things, persons, institutions and ideas. Every moment we gain new experiences. These experiences and traits bring change in our behaviour. These experiences are of varied forms. Education is the process of gaining these experiences. Hence, education is a very wide process.

In the broad or non specific sense, education means the process of development from infancy to maturity. In other words, it is the process whereby a human being gradually adapts himself in various ways to his physical, social, and spiritual environments. Thus, education is a life long process. "It is really life that educates", says **T. Raymont**. "One is educated by one's vocation, by home life, by friendship, by marriage, by parent hood, by recreation, by travel, and so forth."

Lodge in his book "Philosophy and Education", explaining the nature of education in the wider sense, says, "In the wider sense, all experience is said to be educative. 'The bite of a mosquito, the taste of a water-melon, the experience of falling in love, of flying in an aeroplane, of being caught in a storm in a small boat—all such experiences have a directly educative effect on us. The child educates his parents, the pupil educates his teachers... Everything we say, think or do, educates us no less than what is said or done to us by other beings, animate or inanimate. In this wider sense, life is education and education is life. Whatever broadens our horizon, deepens our insight, refines our reactions, and stimulates thought and feeling, educates us..."

Narrow Meaning of Education

"In the narrower and more definite (or specific) sense", says **T. Raymont**, in which the term is used in common speech and in legal enactments, education does not include self-culture and the general influences of one's surroundings, but only those special influences which are consciously and designedly brought to bear upon the young by the adult portion of the community, whether through the family, the church, or the State." These influences or modes of influences are deliberately planned, chosen and employed by the community for the welfare of the members of the rising generation. The purpose of these influences is to modify the behaviour of the child in such a way that he may become different from what he would have been without education. It is to effect change which makes possible a better adjustment of human nature to surroundings and to change the surroundings so as to harmonise with human nature. It is restricted to that function of the community which consists in passing on traditions, its back-ground, its knowledge and its attitudes to the members of the rising generation through specialised people, instruments and methods.

FORMAL AND INFORMAL EDUCATION

Education may be formal or informal. Informal education is incidental—the education which a person receives from living with others. It is important and natural but it is not deliberately planned.

Formal education is consciously and deliberately planned for the purpose of training the child. It consists in direct schooling or tution. Its need increases with an increasing development in society. In undeveloped social groups there are no special agencies for imparting education, hence, there is little formal education. Schools are the specialized agencies for imparting formal education in socially developed groups. Dewey warns us against an inherent danger of formal education. In its extreme form its subject-matter may be divorced from life experience. It may become rigid in its contents.

EDUCATION AND OTHER TERMS

Education is generally confused with literacy, instruction, schooling and training. In the interest of clerity, therefore, education should be distinguished from these terms, though a distinct line of demarcation is ruled out. A brief explanation of the meaning of each of these terms will, however, give us a better insight into the real nature of education.

Education and literacy

We often hear people saying, "He knows reading and writing," "My wife, is not educated." In both of these sayings education means reading and writing. Thus, we have not made distinction between reading, writing and education. A literate wife may be less educated than an illiterate wife. There is a difference between education and literacy. Knowledge of reading and writing is literacy. No doubt literacy is a part of education, but it is not education. "Literacy", says **Gandhiji**, is not the end of education nor even the beginning. It is one of the means whereby man and woman can be educated. Literacy in itself is no education."

Literacy lays more emphasis on the subjects and tools rather than on the personality of the educand, which is the main concern of education. Education is an all-round harmonious development of all the aspects of human personality—body, mind and spirit.

Education and Instruction

Sometimes the term education is used to indicate the day-to-day teaching of lessons in school. The process of imparting knowledge and skills in the class room or laboratory may be called instruction, but not education. Whereas, instruction is the process of conveying to an individual a body of information or knowledge, education is a process of development of the powers which are inborn in the child, at a rate and in a manner determined by the capacity of the child. Whereas instruction implies external imposition, education implies growth from within. Thus, instruction is only one of the means of education and not education. Education is the complete development of the student's personality.

Education and schooling

Education is sometimes confused with schooling. The concept of schooling is similar to that of instruction, but it is a wider concept. It includes academic activities and programmes, other than class-room instruction. Co-curicular activities, community work, hobbies, educational trips and social service camps form part of school, though they are excluded from the limited sphere of instruction. The venue of schooling may be the school or its neighbourhood—even environment taken as a whole. If education is considered as schooling it means that the child is educated, only for five or six hours a day and not for the remaining time. Again, this means that he is educated only for six days a week and not on Sundays and other holidays. Perhaps he is educated more when he sees movies, listens to radio, chats with friends and members of his family. Education is more comprehensive than schooling which is confined to a certain function only. Education is life-long and continuous process.

Education and Training

In the opinion of some thinkers, education is an act of training meant to enable a person to take his proper place in the life of the community. Man is basically animal. Hence, he needs training in emotional adjustment, in controlling his impulses and aspirations and in modifying his behaviour so that he may not face maladjustment when he participates in a group. Education, no doubt, provides training for adult life. But training itself is not education. Animals are also trained by imitating the action of others, but in their training the purpose is neither conscious nor well designed. In education, on the other side, the purpose is clear and well designed. Education is a conscious process to train the individual so that he should make correct responses to the problems of life. If a child bows automatically while he is in the company of others, his response is physical and he may be called a trained child. If the child bows out of respect, he may be called educated because this is a mental response. In training, the desired outer action is secured ; in education, the desired inner attitude, the mental and emotional disposition of behaviour are secured. True education means training the individual to discriminate between good and evil, both on the level of physical response as well as mental response. However, in popular sense, training is associated with preparation for professional career, or technical education. Education is a very comprehensive term and training is only a part of it. It is only because of this distinction between education and training that the names of all the Teachers Training Colleges in the Punjab and Haryana States have been changed into colleges of Education.

Education cannot be equated with literacy, instruction, schooling, or training

In the light of above discussion we can say that education cannot be equated with literacy, instruction, schooling, or training. It is more comprehensive and continuous process. It is planned as well as unplanned, formal as well as informal. Literacy, instruction, schooling and training, however, are confined only to planned and organized enterprises. Education, no doubt, does include literacy, it does have instructional aspect, it implies schooling and it involves training of body and mind. However, education is growth from within rather than an imposition from without. Education is related to life, it is life itself.

IMPORTANT FEATURES OF 'EDUCATION'

The best way to understand the nature of a thing consists in enumerating some of its important features. Let us now try to understand the nature of education by describing its salient features.

Education is a human enterprise

Education, it is clear, has to do with human beings and not with inanimate objects, plants, or animals. We may train a dog but we cannot educate it. Educative capacity of man distinguishes him from other objects—animate or inanimate. It is only man who can be educated. Therefore, education is a human enterprise.

Education is a process and not an object

Education is not an object which persons possess or which is a part of them. One does not have education in the same way as one might have a thousand rupees or brown hair. Even knowledge or skill or good character are not in themselves education, but only an evidence that one has been educated. Education is not an object ; it is a process, a kind of activity in relation to human beings. To educate is to engage in a process, and to 'have an education' is to be someone who has undergone a process.

Education is a purposeful process

Education is a deliberate process undertaken by the teacher and the taught for reaching a definite destination. It is inspired both by an immediate and remote goals. The central problem of education is educational aims. Methods and curriculum are determined in conformity with the educational aims. Aims are relative to a number of variables—socio-economic structure, political ideology, philosophy of life etc. The interpretation of educational aims by educational thinkers has varied from one thinker to another and from age to age. However, the individual and the social aims are the two broad categories under which the various aims can be subsummed. These aims are complementary to each other and not contradictory.

Education is a continuous process

Education is not a process which after starting at a time comes to an end at a definite time. We often say, "He has finished his education" or "he has now started education." In fact, education commences at birth and continues upto death. There is no end to this process. It goes on throughout life without any break or barrier. Education comes not only from the school, but also from the educand's participation in his environment-physical and social, especially through the informal agencies of home, the play group, the profession, the community, the church, The state, the press, cinema, the radio, the television etc. Thus, education is a comprehensive, life long and continuous process.

Education is a triangular process

Education was considered in the past a uni-polar process. It was Adams who first pointed out that education is a bi-polar process. "Education" says **Adam,** "is a conscious and deliberate process in which one personality acts upon another in order to modify the development of the other by the communication and manipulation of knowledge." In the bi-polar process two persons are involved. At one pole we have the educator and at the other, the educand. The one speaks, the other hears ; the one teaches, the other learns ; the one directs, the other follows. Their activities are inter-related and interdependent. If the educator does not come down to the level of the educand and if the educand is not stimulated to rise to the level of the educator, the work of imparting and receiving education cannot proceed. Thus, it is a conscious and deliberate process in which there is subject-object relationship.

Unlike Adams, Dewey considers education as a tri-poler or triangular process. **Dewey** recognises the importance of psychological side of the process which includes the study of the child's needs, interests, capacities and talents, and which forms the basis of this process. Yet he lays a greater stress on the sociological side. "All education" he says, "proceeds by the participation of the individual in social consciousness of the race." Thus, Dewey believes that society plays a very vital role in the process of education. Therefore, we can say that education is not a bi-polar, but a tri-angular process. It involves inter-play of three elements—the educator, the educand and the social forces. The social forces provided by the social environment or society supply the material to the teacher and they are taught in the form of curriculum. The curriculum is framed in the light of the needs and demands of society. Hence, we can say that education is a tri-polar or tri-angular process. It is a social process with social functions.

Education is conservative as well as dynamic

The social aspect of education includes cultural aspect. Education creates social order and it also stablises it. It ensures and facilitates the continuity of social life, by preserving and transmitting the cultural heritage from generation to generation. Education is the instrument whereby culture is transmitted—from the adult section of the community to the younger section, from one generation to another, and from one period of history to another.

Culture is not only transmitted but also preserved and developed further. Conservation and further development are implied in the process of transmission. We do not inherit culture in the way we inherit parents property. Culture is not static, it is dynamic. It is always in constant-flux Thus, education which acts as an agency for the transmission of culture, also serves as the means by which it is not only conserved, but also reconstructed, re-organised, transformed and expanded. Education is, thus, both a conservative as well as a dynamic force.

Education is both a science and an art

In the past education was considered as an art. We thought that a man having perfect knowledge of his subject and interested in teaching turns out to be an efficient teacher by practice of teaching. This is true to some extent. It is said that teachers are born and not made. It is also said that doctors and engineers are born, and not made. But that does not mean that medicine and engineering are arts. These are, undoubtedly, sciences. Education is undoubtedly an art, but it is also a science. Education like other sciences, undertakes a systematic study of certain facts and principles. It employs the usual scientific method of observation and experimentation. It classifies its data into certain categories, makes use of the analytico-synthetic method, proceeds from particular to general, and tries to explain facts and discovers principles underlying the various educational problems and finally establishes a number of generalizations about its methodology, motivation, learning, curriculum construction and evaluation. Education is a science in itself, and it has established its own existence, as an independent subject.

In 'education' we discuss subjects like Educational Principles, Educational Psychology, Educational Administration, Teaching Methods, Guidance, Evaluation etc. But, while we are saying that education is a science, we are not forgetting that education is an art also. In spite of the knowledge of educational science, one cannot become a successful teacher unless one puts it into practice. We have to put the principles into practice which is the artistic feature of education. Thus, education is both, a science and an art.

SOME DEFINITIONS OF 'EDUCATION'

A general survey of the field of education reveals to us a multiplicity of definitions of educations.

1. "I mean by Education that training which is given by suitable habits to the first instincts of virtue in children."
   —Plato
2. "Education is the creation of a sound mind in sound body."
   —Aristotle
3. "Education is a natural, harmonious and progressive development of man's innate powers." —Pestalozzi
4. "By Education I mean the influence of the environment upon the individual to produce a permanent change in his habits of behaviour, of thought, and of attitude.
   —G.H. Thomson
5. "Education is the development of good moral character."
   —Herbart

6. "Education is the complete development of individuality so that he can make an original contribution to human life, according to his best capacity." —T.P. Nunn
7. "Education is a conscious and deliberate process in which one personality acts upon another in order to modify the development of the other, by the communication and manipulation of knowledge." —Adams
8. "Education is the development of all those capacities in the individual which will enable him to control his environment and fulfil his possibilities." —John Dewey
9. "Education is the influence of a person who holds the vital belief brought to bear on another person with the object of making him also hold that belief." —Ross
10. "Education is the manifestation of perfection already in man." —Vivekanand
11. "The highest education is that which does not merely gives us information but makes our life in harmony with all existence." —Tagore
12. "By education, I mean an all-round drawing out of the best in child and man—body, mind and spirit." —Gandhiji

2

The Aims of Education

Education, as we have already discussed in the previous chapter, is a purposeful activity. It is undertaken both by the educator and the educand for the sake of a clear-cut objective. Therefore, every system and process of education, in order to be worth anything, must have some aim which should reflect the philosophical aim of human life. If there is education without an aim, the educator does not know where he has to lead his pupil to and what the learner has to become as a result of his education. Unless there is a clear-cut aim before education, it would be impossible to measure the achievement of the educand. Therefore, the first consideration in any discussion on education must be a statement of its aims.

NATURE OF THE AIMS OF EDUCATION

In order to know the aims of education, it is necessary to understand the nature of these aims. Are the aims of education fixed, final, eternal and universal or are they flexible, adaptable, changeable and relative? Let us discuss this problem in the light of two distinct philosophies of education—Idealism and Pragmatism.

Idealism on Aims of Education

Idealism stands for superiority of mind over matter and it conceives the nature of ultimate reality in terms of mind or spirit rather than in terms of matter. The idealist believes in the existence of absolute, eternal and unchanging values and consequently defines the ultimate aims of education in terms of these values. According to Idealism, the aims of education are spiritual in nature and they are pre-determined, absolute, unchanging and universal. The values of life are not man-made, but pre-existing. The aim of education is realization of these pre-existing, absolute and universal values.

According to some idealists, there are two types of educational aims—immediate and ultimate. Whereas the immediate aims are changing, flexible and adaptable, the ultimate aims are eternal, absolute and unchanging. In determining any hierarchy of values the immediate objectives must occupy a subordinate position.

Pragmatism on Aims of Education

Pragmatism believes that the nature of reality is not fixed. What is true today, may not be true tomorrow. Pragmatism, therefore, does not believe in absolute and eternal values. Values are man-made and constant experimentation is needed to test their validity. Thus, pragmatism requires an individual to be creative so that he should formulate values of life on the basis of his experiences.

THE DETERMINANTS OF EDUCATIONAL AIMS

Even a casual survey of the history of education will reveal that there have been different aims of education in different countries in the past. Even in the same country the aims of education have been different at different times. For example, in India the aims of education during Ancient Period were not the same which were during British Period. Again, the aims of education in the Modern India are different from those which were prevalent in British India. The aims of education in a democratic country like England or America are not the same as they are in Communist countries like USSR and China. The important determinants of the educational aims which have led to their diversity are discussed below.

The Philosophies of life

The philosophy of life in which the people of a particular society or time believe goes a long way in determining the aims of education. In a materialistic society educational aims are based on the materialistic outlook of the people. In such a society there is no place for moral ideals and spiritual values and the aim of education is self-gratification or self-expression. On the contrary, for the idealists who believe in the spiritual basis of the universe, the aim of education is self-realization or exaltation of personality. A pessimistic attitude towards life fashions pessimistic aims of education, whereas an optimistic philosophy of life determines optimistic aims of education. In short, the different philosophies of life give rise to different aims of education.

The Socio-political Ideologies

Socio-political ideologies, too, determine educational aims. For example, different social philosophies—views about the Individual-society or Individual-state relationship had led to different concepts of educational aims. According to totalitarianism, the state is considered as an end in itself. The individual is regarded only as a means for the good of the state. Evidently, the educational aim under such a regime is to train the individual for blind obedience to the state and there is a rigid, state-controlled and stereotyped system of education. On the contrary, according to the individualism or pluralism the individual is regarded as an end in himself and the state as a means to the good of the individual. Accordingly, the aim of education is considered as self-expression or self-gratification and the state adopts "Hands off" policy in the sphere of education. Democracy strikes a balance between individual freedom and social obligations. The authoritarian and dictatorial attitude of the state is replaced by parental one. The aim of education under democratic regimes is considered to be social efficiency or citizenship.

Again, education in any country and at all periods reflects values of the ruling class. All forms of governments—democratic, fascist or communist—formulate their own aims of education to serve their purposes. In a democracy educational aims are not fixed, absolute or eternal. They change with the changing aspirations and demands of the society. Man, in a democracy, is considered as an end in himself and not as a means to an end. Therefore, educational institutions cater to the diverse abilities and aptitudes of children. The child is educated for a life of freedom, for the fullest possible realization of his capacities and their service to the community. In a Fascist regime, the Individual exists for the state. Thus, in a Fascist state the individual must bow to the demands of the state and the aim of education is to inculcate values like service, sacrifice, duty and obedience. The educational aims in a communist state are formulated quite differently from those in a fascist or democrate state. As labour is the cardinal ideal of the communist society, it forms the central pivot of the educational aims. The student must feel himself a worker in a labouring society. Educational institutions are considered as deliberate instruments of State Policy. To ensure the victory of communist ideals, educational aims stress the need of virtues like bravery, loyalty, steadfastness and discipline.

Hence, we can say that different socio-political ideologies give rise to different educational aims.

The Socio-economic problems

Sometimes social and economic problems of a country also influence the educational aims of that country. For example, India is a country of various castes, creeds and religions. Social stratification has been rigid. This has created special social problems. Education, therefore, must fight the caste-barriers. Similarly, in determining its educational objectives every country has to take into consideration its economic conditions. We can take the example of Denmark. About half a century back the country faced economic crises. Traditional occupations did not yield income to support all the people of the country. A survey of national sources and man-power was made. The country had meagre resources, but it was close to a steady market for certain food articles. For the economic advancement of the country, it was advised to start dairy products, even though the food for the cattle was to be imported from other countries. Denmark educated its generation to meet the new requirements. The result was that Denmark not only increased the per capita income and her national wealth, but also captured the markets of England and several other countries.

Similarly, India of today, has low economic standards of living. As a large majority of the people in India have to live at an economically sub-human level, one of the most important functions of education is to improve productive efficiency, to increase national wealth, and to bridge the gulf between the rich and the poor so that the dream of socialist society may become reality. Thus, we can say that social and economic conditions of a country also determine the, educational aims of that country.

Exploration of knowledge

Educational aims are also influenced by exploration of knowledge. Because of rapid exploration in sciences, education today has become science oriented all over the world. In India also educationists are stressing the need for science-oriented education in the schools, colleges and universities. More and more stress is being laid on the study of modern sciences. The government is giving liberal grants and scholarships by way of providing incentive for the study of science. This clearly shows that the spreading of new knowledge is an important factor in determining aims of education.

DIFFERENT AIMS OF EDUCATION

We have already discussed the important determinants of educational aims which have led to their diversity. We shall confine our attention to some important ones and discuss them here.

The Knowledge Aim

Since, the time of sophists (400 B.C.) down to the present day, knowledge has almost been universally considered as the aim of education. There are some educators who hold the acquisition of knowledge to be the only aim of education. They emphasise the cognitive or the intellectual side of personality. Forgetting that knowledge is merely an instrument for achieving other ends, they exalt it into an end by identifying it with education. The acquisition of knowledge of different subjects is regarded as the test of successful schooling and success in examination is regarded as the criterion of such acquisition. The only aim of education is 'complete knowledge' or 'knowledge, more knowledge and yet more knowledge.'

Those philosophers and educationists who hold the knowledge aim of education, offer a justification for their view. They argue that knowledge is indispensable for all right action and it alone is the source of all power and happiness. Before one could feel either pleasure or pain in respect of any object, or could make any response with regard to it, one has to know what it is. Thus, knowledge is not an idle or merely ornamental possession ; it is a source of complete living and progress. For example, if education is intended to help individual-environment adjustment, the individual must have the knowledge of his environment, before he can think of adjusting himself to it. Again, if education is to help the child to realize moral values, he must first have a knowledge of those values. Thus, knowledge alone is power ; knowledge alone is happiness ; knowledge alone is virtue ; knowledge alone is progress.

The knowledge aim of education has been criticised by many educators who put forward a number of arguments against this aim. They argue that over-emphasis on the knowledge is likely to reduce all schools to mere 'knowledge-shops' and the teacher to the mere information monger'. Schools are infact agencies to bring about the all-round, not merely intellectual development of pupils. They believe that knowledge is not the only aim of education. They argue that no amount of factual knowledge can make a person truly educated. True, we cannot be wise without some basis of knowledge ; but at the same time we may remain devoid of wisdom, even after acquiring much knowledge. True, we should have knowledge of moral values to become virtuous, but we may remain immoral, even after having knowledge of all moral values. Education is partly information and partly formation. The knowledge aim ignores the latter part. The knowledge aim is unpsychological because it emphasises the study of subject-matter rather than the child. It reduces the child to the position of a passive learner and places the teacher on a very high level.

If we weigh the arguments advanced for and against the knowledge aim, we arrive at the conclusion that knowledge, though, is not the only or supreme aim of education, yet it is one of the important aims of education. Knowledge is an indispensable means for any suitable and comprehensive aim of education. But knowledge should be a 'means to an end' and not an 'end in itself.' It should be acquired for human happiness and social welfare.

The Vocational Aim

Whenever we ask any parent the question : "Why do you send your children to schools and universities?" The answer will always be: "so that they may get some good vocation in life." No one can deny this concern of parents for their children. Man has three basic needs—food, shelter and clothing. If education does not fulfil these, it does not fulfil its aims. The long stride taken by industrialization and mechanization in the modern age of science gives priority to vocational aim over all other aims. Every man, unless he is born with a silverspoon in his mouth, has to search out a living for himself. It is this aim which enables an individual to solve the problem of his livelihood. If education fails to do this, it is not worth its name. Therefore, the main aim of education should be to train the child for a vocation, profession, business, calling or trade. This aim is also called as, 'bread and butter aim' or 'utilitarian aim'.

The supporters of this aim maintain that education for vocation makes use of the habits and instincts of the educand : appeals to his interest and aptitude : stimulates his thought, skill and observation ; and trains him for social efficiency. They argue that man cannot live without means of subsistence : his economic needs will have to be satisfied. If an individual is not able to earn his own living and that of the children dependent upon him, he is a parasite upon others. He misses for himself one of the most educative experiences of life. Therefore, no scheme of education can afford to neglect such basic consideration. Moreover, the vocational aim is an integral part of the general aim of education. For example, from the idealistic point of view 'Exaltation of Personality' is regarded as the aim of education.

The vocational aim in education has not been spared criticism. It is argued that man, after all, is born not only to eat and drink but also to gain knowledge, acquire culture and develop personality. Therefore, the vocational aim is not a complete aim by itself. Earning one's bread is only one part of man's life, not the whole of it. Moreover, if vocational aim is over-emphasised, education is reduced to nothing but commercialism. It ceases to be a refining and enabling influence. It may make an individual a good doctor, a good teacher, or a good engineer, but it does not necessarily make him a good man. It does make him rich, but does not inspire him for the ideals of life. It does not prepare him for complete living.

In the light of above discussion it may be said that there is a considerable justification for the vocational aim of education. But the fact remains, that most of the evils that have crept into the life of the modern man are because of an over-emphasis on this aim.

The Moral Aim

There are some educationists, generally belonging to the idealistic school, who think that the ultimate aim of education should be character building or moral development. Character means an inner consistency or unity of personality. It means consistency, steadfastness, dependability and stability. A man of character acts as he does because of principles or ideals within rather than from expediency or because of pressure from without. They believe that a man of character—a man endowed with a strong will, virtuous conduct, noble ideals—is the only man who can be said to be really educated. On the contrary, one who lacks these qualities, however learned or cultured otherwise, is a person on whom education has been completely lost. Therefore, knowledge, culture, physical development, vocational efficiency, all are secondary to moral training. The formation of sound moral character should be the primary and only aim of education. Education is the process of modifying the child's original behaviour.

True, character-building is a very laudable aim of education, but it has its other side also. Morality, as pragmatists believe, is never fixed, absolute or predetermined. It is relative. Moral ideals change with a change in time and social values. Ideals valued today may not be given any importance after the lapse of a hundred years. As such, it is not possible to interpret and trace moral ideals which can be considered effective in a particular situation. Moreover, undue emphasis on moral aim throws the other aims of education to a lower level. The physical and intellectual development of the child is as necessary as his moral progress. Therefore, we can conclude that only character-building cannot be the aim of education. Not only good moral qualities, but qualities like intelligence, creativeness, health and vigour are also needed for the welfare of man and society.

The Complete Living Aim

Some educational theorists insist upon the need of an aim in education which will be all-comprehensive. This view point has led to the emergence of two aims—'the complete living aim' and the harmonius development aim'. The former has been formulated and brilliantly expounded by Spencer. Education, according to this great thinker, should acquaint us with the laws and ways of complete living. He has given a list of activities and suitable subjects. According to Spencer training of activities of self-preservation, indirect preservation of life, rearing of off-springs, social preservation and leisure can be imparted through Hygiene, Physiology, Physics, Language, Mathematics, Geography, History, Child Psychology, Home Science, Music etc.

The emptiness of this aim can be shown with the help of certain questions. What can determine the completeness of life? Is the aim completeness of life an unchanging thing? It should be noted that no mention has been made of art, literature and religion in the above list. Therefore, it can be said that the aim of complete living put forth by Spencer in too vague to be held and carried out by any educator.

The Harmonious Development Aim

One serious objection to the various aims of education discussed above, is that they all are one sided or incomplete. In the opinion of some thinkers harmonious development of mental, physical and aesthetic powers is the aim of education. According to them every child is born with certain powers and capacities—physical, mental and intellectual powers, spiritual moral and aesthetic capacities and social tendencies. The aim of education is to help the development of all these powers and capacities hidden in the child. If some of these capacities are developed while others are neglected, the result would be an unsystematic and irregular development of personality. Therefore, the advocates of harmonious development aim urge that education should aim at the development of all capacities and powers of the child, rather than that of only a few of them and neglect others.

Gandhiji is a strong advocate of the harmonious development aim. For him, the aim of education is the development of full man and woman. However, since the essential nature of man is spiritual, Gandhiji advocates the aim of all round development of the physical, intellectual and emotional aspects of personality under the guidance of spiritual self. Lop-sided development of personality is the product of modern education which neglects the spiritual aspect of human personality.

The harmonious development aim deserves credit for its comprehensiveness. This aim embraces all other aims discussed above, because all these together aim at the harmonious development of personality. In fact, no aim is worth persuing unless it contributes towards such development. But the critics of this aim maintain that man is a unit and this division of his personality in different aspects is impossible. And, even if we take this division to be true, what would be the measure of definite quantities of harmonious development. In their opinion this harmonious development is an imaginary ideal which cannot be applicable in life.

The Leisure Aim

Science has revolutionized human life. It has shown us how we can do a greater volume of work in shorter time and with less physical labour. It has placed at our disposal innumerable labour-saving devices. The type-writer, the computing machine, the telephone, the motor-cars, the electric fan and light, the refrigerator all these and many others show how much work we can do with minimum labour. They save us from the mechanical drudgery of manual work. At the same time, they create plenty of leisure. Hence, the aim of education in the modern time should be to teach people a proper utilization of leisure so that they add to the achievements of man in art, architecture and literature, and thus, develop their culture. Teachers and organisers should pay their attention to education for leisure. For doing so, reasons are not far to seek.

Education for leisure brings out the hidden talents of children and thus helps them to find their proper place in life. It trains them to participate in creative activities leading to their development and the progress of society. It makes their life richer, their tastes refined, their minds occupied. Hence, schools must make a provision of co-curricular activities, hobbies, games, sports, music, painting, dancing etc.

All this sounds well.

Synthesis of different Aims

Since, the aims of education discussed above are epigrams rather than real definitions, they do not take us very far and quite naturally leave us unsatisfied. They are half-truths, one sided or incomplete statements, for obviously it is impossible to compress in one small sentence the whole meaning and aim of an important human activity as education. But, inspite of their lack of agreement and their inadequacy, one-sidedness or incompleteness, the various aims are complementary rather than contradictory. Instead of contradicting each other, they supply each other's deficiencies. There is no real antithesis between them, but merely a difference of stress. They overlap, although they do not coincide. Since, they are complementary and overlapping in nature, they can be reconciled with one another.

INDIVIDUAL VERSUS SOCIAL AIMS

We have discussed in brief some of the important aims of education. The main emphasis of each of them is either on the individual or on the social aim. Thus, they are ultimately reducible to only two major aims—individual and social—which appear to be opposed to each other. Before we see whether they are opposed or compatible, let us discuss in brief the nature of these two aims.

The Individual Aim

The exponents of the individual aim in education assert that the individual should be in the fore-front of the picture. This concept is based on the socio-political philosophy that social institutions, such as the family, the church, the school and the state, exist only for bettering and improving the life of the individual. The individual is the end and these social institutions are the means. Therefore, they justify their existence only if they are conducive to the promotion of the individual's welfare. The school as one of the important social institutions exists for the educand, and not the educand for the school. Therefore, the school should offer an environment and atmosphere which will be conducive to each child's development. Rousseau, the father of naturalism is the greatest supporter of individual aim in education.

Some of the supporters of the individual aim in education are extremists. They are against all sorts of restrictions and they advocate untrammelled and unrestricted freedom for the educand. According to them, the aim of education is self-expression. It implies unrestricted freedom for the individual to act according to his own nature, even if that action is objcctionable to others. They are against discipline, religion or morality. The purpose of educational efforts, according to Sir Percy Nunn, is to secure conditions conducive to the complete development of individuality and to help him to make his original contribution to the variegated whole of human life as fully and as truly characteristic as his nature permits. Although Nunn supports his contention by an appeal to biology, his conception of individuality is a philosophic one. It is an ideal which has to be yet attained, "a spiritual perfection that is possible to each individual." In other words, Nunn's conception of individuality is synonymous with what self-realization stands for.

Self-realization is not the same thing as self-expression. Self-expression as a meaning of development of individuality entphasises the play of self-assertion. It implies unrestricted freedom to act as nature prompts, even if that action is objectionable and undesirable. No doubt, self-realization does necessarily imply a certain amount of self-assertion, but only if it is not undesirable for society. Moreover, in self-expression, the self is taken as ready-made, merely waiting to express itself. The self in the ideal of self-realization is not the undisciplined self which is ready-made but one that is a bundle of possibilities and potentialities. Self-realization does not always need freedom from restraint. According to Adams, the self in the ideal of self-realization cannot realize itself against society, it realizes itself in society through social interaction.

The Social Aim

The supporters of the social aim of education believe that society or state alone is the real, and the individual is only a means. They hold that an individual should be educated for the good of the society. The social aim of education, they believe, will produce social cohesion and a sense of co-operation which is necessary for enjoying the amenities of life. Its supporters cannot conceive of an individual living and developing in isolation from society. As **Raymont** says, "The isolated individual is a figment of the imagination." As long as a human individual is a social animal, living in society and developing through social contacts, there will be some subordination of individuality to public or social needs of society and the curbing of individuality will go on consciously or unconsciously.

The social aim, however, is not as simple as it seems. It has two meanings. In the first sense, by social aim we mean purposes of the state. The function of education in relation to that aim is to cater consistently for the welfare of the state, subordinating the welfare of the individual to that of the state. This is a narrow interpretation which is given by certain extremists. They think that the state is an "idealised metaphysical entity over and above the individual citizen, superior in every way." The state or society alone is the reality and the individual is only "a throb in the social pulse." The state is the embodiment of reason, justice and morality and the individual is inferior to it in all respects. Hence, the state is to control and direct every affair in life including education which is but a means of shaping its citizens to a certain mould. It is the state which is to decide the mode and type of education or training which an individual is to receive. The curriculum and methods of education are also the complete monopoly of the state and the individual has no choice to develop his powers in his own way. He is only to obey what the authorities dictate. His needs, urges and nature are completely ignored. The exponents of this school of thought believe in imparting education through social control and their watch-words in the educational process, are discipline, obedience, regimentation and authority.' The interpretation is best illustrated in the Spartan system of education in ancient times and by the more recent Japanese and Nazi systems of education. These systems crushed individual initiative and enterprise and brought for the misery of man such cataclysms as those of 1914 and the world war of 1939-1945.

Another interpretation given to social aim' in education is the one which is applauded in Great Britain, America and other democratic countries. It finds expression in such slogans as 'education for social service' or education for citizenship', and aim at the good of the community laying stress on teaching citizenship in schools directly and indirectly, through various subjects in the curriculum and through various social activities. Such virtues as co-operation and self-abnegation are to be cultivated. It is true that the demands of society are to be given priority against the inclination and wishes of an individual but the dictatorial or authoritarian attitude of state will be replaced by paternal attitude. The function of education according to this ideal is to enable the individual to develop himself fully according to means compatible with the interests of society.

Professor Bagley and Dewey think that social aim in education attempts to bring about 'social efficiency'. According to Professor Bagley social efficiency stands for :

(i) 'economic efficiency' or ability 'to put his own weight' in economic life ;

(ii) 'negative morality' or willingness to sacrifice those of his desires the gratification of which would interfere with the economic efficiency of others ;

(iii) 'positive morality', or the willingness to sacrifice his own desires when gratification would not contribute directly or indirectly to social progress.

In a broad sense social efficiency means cultivation of one's powers and capacities to join freely, intelligently, and fully in the shared activities of the community as a whole. Education should make each individual socially efficient and must secure social efficiency by the positive use of individual powers and capacities in social occupations and 'not by negative constraint' or imposition from without. A socially efficient individual is able to earn his livelihood. He is not a drag or parasite on any other member of society. He is a good citizen and as such possesses knowledge and intelligence enough to understand and appreciate the world. He is ready to sacrifice his own desires if their satisfaction is harmful for others or if their gratification does not contribute, directly or indirectly, to social progress. 'A socially efficient individual conforms to a certain standard of conduct known as the moral standard.

Synthesis of the Individual and the Social Aims

How far is it possible to strike a balance between individual and social aims in education? At one glance it seems that they are poles apart and that no synthesis is possible.

If social aim in education means education for 'good of the state' and individual aim in education means 'self expression', there cannot be any synthesis between the social and individual aims in education.

However, a synthesis is possible if the social aim in education implies the encouragement of social service, social efficiency, ideals of good citizenships and the individual aim in education means 'self-realization' rather than self-expression'. As a matter of fact, there is no real antagonism between the rival claims of the state and the individual. The interests of the state can be promoted by the development of good qualities in the individual, and the individuals can make the best of themselves in and through state. The individual has no meaning apart from society. Man by nature is not self-sufficing; and he is a social creature. He must live in a social environment, and have social contacts if individuality is to be fostered and personality is to be elevated. **Ross** has summed up the whole controversy as follows: "Thus individuality is of no value and personality is a meaningless term apart from the social environment in which they are developed and made manifest. Self-realization can be achieved only through social service, and social ideals of real value can come into being only through free individual who have developed valuable individuality. The circle cannot be broken." **Gandhiji** also believes that self-realization can be achieved only through social service. He says, "Willing submission to social control and restraint for the sake of the well-being of the whole society enriches both the individual and the society of which the former is a member."

To sum up we can say that there is, in fact, no conflict between the individual and social aims of education. Individual as well as society has the same claim on education. Hence, a synthesis of the two aims is essential.

3

Educational Aims in India

We have already discussed in the previous chapter, the nature and determinants of educational aims in general. In this chapter, we propose to discuss the same with reference to Indian conditions. Every society evolves its own system of education meant to prepare individuals for a particular end. In India the aims of education have been changing with changing philosophies of the people from time to time. Let us have a brief historical retrospect of educational aims in India.

A HISTORICAL RETROSPECT

In the Brahmanic system of education, the religions and moral aims dominated. Education was regarded as a means of inculcating such moral habits as strict obedience to elders, truthfulness, honesty and temperance. It enjoined on the pupils the tenets of the all comprehensive Dharma which included the ideas of sacred law and duty, justice, religious and moral rectitude and the established practices and customs of caste and community. Later on, when the caste system became rigid, a vocational aim in education also came into being. Each caste was to be given a certain type of education which would fit its members for a certain profession or vocation in life.

Buddhistic education was primarily monastic in its outlook and contents. It aimed at the religious development of the individual. Later on, Buddhistic education underwent change in ideology and practice. It became secular in content and was given a vocational bias. Education was to pave way for royal appointments and other lucrative jobs.

Early Mohammedan education did not depart from the ancient religious ideal. The chief function of the 'Maktabs' which were invariably attached to some mosque was to instruct the boys in those portions of the Holy Quaran which were to be memorised and was to be used by them in performing their daily devotions and at other religious functions and ceremonies.

During the Mughal period, educational aims were reshaped for the better. The emphasis was shifted from the religious aims in education as such to moral aims. Such moral virtues as equanimity in the face of success or failure, the ability to adjust to the surroundings and the ability to earn one's livelihood were looked up in an educated person.

The educational system implanted by the British in India, was designed only to prepare Indians, for taking certain subordinate positions, in government offices ; it was not intended to develop among the people capacity to take leadership and initiative in different walks of life. The aims of education were not based on the broad foundations of national culture and did not derive their inspiration from the achievements of the past or the pre-occupation of the present or the hopes of the future. Hence, after her independence when India transformed herself into secular democratic republic and declared the establishment of the socialistic pattern of society, it was inevitable that the existing education system should be reviewed and a new comprehensive system of education responding to the challenging needs of the country be devised.

To evolve such a national system of education, the government of India appointed from time to time three commissions, namely the University Commission (1948-49), the Secondary Education Commission (1952-53) and the Indian Education Commission (1964-66). The Secondary Education Commission has formulated the aims of Secondary Education. The Indian Education Commission has also given a list of national objectives, of education.

Now let us discuss the aims of education as given by these two Commissions.

SECONDARY EDUCATION COMMISSION ON EDUCATIONAL AIMS

From a careful analysis of the dominant needs of India, the commission formulated the following aims of Secondary Education.

Developing Democratic Citizenship

The adoption of the goals of Democracy and Socialism necessitates the development of habits, attitude and qualities of character which will enable its citizens to bear worthily the responsibilities of democratic citizenship. Among these qualities which are to be fostered through curricular and co-curricular activities in secondary schools are :

1. The capacity for clear thinking (allied to which is the capacity for clearness in speech and writing).
2. The scientific attitude of mind.
3. A receptivity to new ideas.
4. A respect for the dignity and worth of every individual.
5. The ability to live harmoniously with one's fellow-men through the cultivation of discipline, co-operation, social sensitiveness and tolerance; and
6. A sense of true patriotism.

Vocational Efficiency

India is rich in potential resources, but at present she is actually a poor country. Therefore, one of the urgent problems of the country is to improve productive efficiency and to increase the national wealth and thereby to raise the standard of living. In this respect the Commission recommends fostering dignity of manual labour and promotion of technical skill for the advancement of industry and technology. Thus, our Secondary Education must be ridden off the purely theoretical instruction, and must lay greater emphasis on craft, productive-work and diversification of courses. This will certainly result in equipping educated youngman psychologically and practically with better vocational efficiency, whereby they will help in increasing the national wealth and in improving the general standards of living.

Education for Leadership

Since, the youth of today will assume leadership in different walks of life tomorrow, special function of the secondary education is to train persons who will be able to assume the responsibility of leadership in social, political, industrial and cultural fields' in their own small group of community or locality. To achieve success in this work, the qualities of justice, courage, discipline, tolerance, wisdom, sacrifice, initiative, resourcefulness, understanding of social issues, civic as well as vocational efficiency should be developed in the young men and women of our land.

Development of Personality

An important aim of democratic education is the all-round development of every individual's personality. This requires that education should take into account all his needs—psychological, social, emotional, and practical—and cater to all of them. It should release in him the sources of creative energy so that he may be able to appreciate his cultural heritage, to cultivate rich interests, which he can pursue in his leisure, and contribute in later life, to the development of this heritage. Hence, education should be so organized that subjects like art, craft, music, dancing, and the development of hobbies should find a place of honour in the curriculum. Only when education is organized on the basis of freedom and its scope is widened to include new subjects and new activities, the pupils will go out with more sensitive and quickened minds and will respond readily to the numerous stimuli in the world of Art and Nature. At the same time, they will be able not only to enjoy their cultural heritage more keenly but also help in its enrichment.

THE INDIAN EDUCATION COMMISSION ON EDUCATIONAL AIMS

The latest and the most authentic report on Indian Education has also given a four-fold aim of our national education. According to it education should aim at :

1. Increasing productivity.
2. Achieving social and national integration.
3. Accelerating the process of modernization.
4. Cultivating social, moral and spiritual values.

The Commission has also given suggestions for the achievement of these aims. Let us now discuss those suggestions.

Increasing Productivity

For the promotion of productivity the Commission emphasises that :

1. Science education should become an integral part of school courses.

2. Work-experience should be introduced as an integral part of all education.

3. Every attempt should be made to orient work-experience to productive processes including agriculture, technology and industrialization.

4. Secondary education should be increasingly and largely, vocationalized.

Achieving Social and National Integration

It is an important objective of education. The following steps should be taken to strengthen national consciousness and unity.

1. The common school system of public education should be adopted as a national goal and effectively implemented in a phased programme spread over twenty years.

2. Social and national service should be made obligatory for all students at all stages. It will prove an effective instrument for building character, improving discipline, inculcating a faith in the dignity of labour and developing a sense of social responsibility, if it is organized concurrently with academic studies in schools and colleges.

3. The development of an appropriate language policy can materially assist in social and national integration.

4. A re-evaluation of our cultural heritage is needed. For this, there should be well organized teaching of languages, literature, philosophy, religion, history of India, Indian architecture, sculpture, painting, music, dance and drama. Camps, summer schools etc. should be organized without any barrier.

5. The educational programme in schools and colleges should be designed to inculcate democratic values.

Accelerating the Process of Modernization

There has been a great explosion of knowledge during the last few decades. Education in a modern society, is no longer concerned with the imparting of knowledge or the preparation of finished product, but with the awakening of curiosity, the development of proper interests, attitudes and values and the building up of such essential skills, as independent study and capacity to think and judge for oneself, without which it is not possible to become a responsible member of democratic society. The progress of modernization will be directly related to the pace of educational advance. And the one sure way to modernize quickly is to spread education, to produce educated and skilled citizens and to train an adequate and competent intelligentsia, coming from all strata of society, whose loyalties and aspirations are deeply rooted in the Indian soil. This also involves a radical change in the methods of teaching and in the training of teachers.

Cultivating Social, Moral and Spiritual Values

The expanding knowledge and the growing power which it placed at the disposal of modern society must be combined with the strengthening and deepening of the sense of social responsibility and a keener appreciation of moral and spiritual values. For this purpose, active measures should be adopted to give a value-orientation to education.

1. The Central and the State Governments should adopt measures to introduce moral, social and spiritual values in all institutions under their control (or under local authority) on the lines recommended by the University Education Commission and the Committee on Religious and Moral Instruction. The privately managed institutions should also follow suit.

2. Departments of Comparative religions and philosophies of the Universities should be specially concerned with the ways in which these values can be taught widely and effectively and should undertake preparation of special literature for use by students and teachers.

3. The Commission observed that a multi-religious democratic state like ours, should also promote a tolerant study of all religions so that its citizens can understand each other better and live amicably together. For this purpose a syllabus, giving well chosen information about each of the major religions, should be included as a part of the course in citizenship or as a part of general education to be introduced in schools and colleges upto the first degree. It would be of great advantage if common text books are prepared at the national level by competent experts in each religion.

INDIAN SOCIO-POLITICO-ECONOMIC SITUATIONS AND EDUCATIONAL AIMS

We have achieved freedom after centuries of slavery. This freedom cannot be preserved and the vision of a socialistic pattern of society, that we have held before us, cannot be built unless we improve the quality of our education.

We have adopted Democracy, Socialism and Secularism as our national ideals. We should keep in our mind that democracy in India has evolved in a society which, to a very great degree, is rural and agrarian, also in a society in which vast majority of the people are ignorant, where many superstitious and rigid ways of behaviour prevail ; where people are victims of many prejudices, and social maladies ; where there are wide diversities in their modes of living, in their methods of speaking, in their customs and manners, and loyalties ; where people have got political freedom without having necessary resource to defend it. Therefore, no system of education borrowed from other countries can be grafted to flourish in the Indian soil. No doubt, there has been a marked progress in education in many states ; the literacy figure has risen, many more schools have been opened, the number of technical and professional schools and colleges has increased, there has been a rapid growth of University Education and much has been done to promote scientific research, many plans—both at the union as well as states level—have been carried into execution and many of them are still on. Yet it seems that things have not progressed in the way and in the direction in which they were intended.

What is needed now? We need a system of education which is geared to the needs of the country, which is practicable within the resources in men and material which we have , which is based on country's traditions and social behaviour and ; which assures all those efficiencies to the youth.

To achieve these national goals our education must inculcate among the pupils such qualities as respect for the opposed views, respect for freedom, respect for the dignity of man, respect for rule of law, and respect for constitutional change. It must develop among them optimistic out look, positive attitude towards work and dignity of labour, scientific and objective thinking and critical judgement. It must teach them to utilise their leisure time in a proper manner, and above all it must promote among them Emotional and National Integration, National Pride and International Understanding.

4

Philosophy and Education

Fichte in his 'Address to the German People' observed that the art of education would never attain clearness in itself without philosophy; there is an interaction between the two, and either without the other is incomplete and unserviceable. Fichte's contention will become clear if we examine the meaning of philosophy.

THE MEANING OF PHILOSOPHY

Etymologically, the word Philosophy is derived from two Greek words *Philo (love)* and *sophia (wisdom)*, means *love of wisdom*, Wisdom is not the same thing as knowledge. It includes knowledge, but goes beyond it to find relationship and to discover implications. Philosophy means 'mature reflection' about any problem in its complete perspective.

In the ordinary sense of the term 'philosophy' means the sum of man's beliefs. Technically it is 'the sum of man's reasoned-out beliefs.' What are these beliefs about? They are about the most fundamental question, the nature of reality. What is this universe? What is Man and what is his relation to the universe? Philosophy is a search for a comprehensive view of nature, an attempt at a universal explanation of the nature of things. It is a continuous seeking of insight into basic realities : the physical world, life, mind, society, knowledge and values. According to **Dr. Radhakrishanan** "It is a logical inquiry into the nature of reality." It explores the basic sources and aims of life. Thus, philosophy means beliefs or points-of-view concerning purposes and values according to which man tries to live. He raises, questions about reality, universe, nature of man, his origin and his destiny. He tries to answer these questions and forms a reasoned-out point of view on these fundamental matters. These answers come from his philosophic attitude towards life or his philosophy according to which be lives, "Men live," says **Huxley**, "in accordance with their philosophy of life, their conception of the world." It is impossible to live without a metaphysics. if this metaphysics is vital enough. it is bound to urge its possesser to live in accordance with it. A philosophy always results in a certain way of life. According to **Dewey**, philosophy signifies "a wisdom that would influence the conduct of life."

The three great religious teachers of the world—Buddha, Christ and Mohammed—had their own philosophy resulting in different ways of life. So was the case with Gandhiji, Hitler and Omar Khayyam. Buddha preached the philosophy of renunciation and personal salvation ; Christ advocated the philosophy of love and charity ; Mohammed upheld the doctrine of brotherhood ; Gandhiji believed in the philosophy of non-violence ; Hitler supported a militant philosophy; Omar Khyyam extolled the Epicurean philosophy. All these philosophies, based on different beliefs, resulted in different ways of life.

Thus, every philosophy of life is based on a certain belief. And a belief, if it is vital must lead to an educative effort. As such philosophy is inseparable from education.

RELATION BETWEEN PHILOSOPHY AND EDUCATION

The common subject for both philosophy and education is 'man'. Education, concerned with the modification of the natural man, looks to philosophy for the ideal to which to lead him. the two notions—philosophy and education like the two sides of a coin present different views of the same thing, and one is implied by the other. Education is the dynamic side of philosophy or its active aspect while philosophy is the contemplative side of it. In other words, education is the practical means of realising the ideals of life.

It is impossible to come across a philosopher without a blazing urge to propagate his beliefs and metaphysics among others and educate them to follow his way of thinking and living. It is equally impossible to imagine a system of education completely divorced from any philosophy. Philosophy provides the aim of life and thereby the aim of education, and education provides the vehicle for carrying out that philosophic aim in practical life.

Education means a planned modification of the natural behaviour of the child. At birth the child is not what his community would ultimately wish him to be. Therefore, he has to be shaped.and reshaped into a socially desirable individual. He has to be changed accordingly. Change presupposes a direction which is chosen consciously and deliberately, and along which the change has to be effected in the child. Before, the child's native behaviour begins to be modified, the agency attempting the change has to be clear regarding the direction along which the change has to be made, and this direction of modification is to be defined by the aim or purpose of the change. The aim and direction of the modification to be attempted in the child's behaviour through education are supplied by philosophy. This is what education owes to philosophy.

Dependence of education on philosophy is clearly seen by the fact that great philosophers of all times have also been great educators and their philosophy finds reflection in their educational schemes. In the words of **Rusk**, "We need only cite Plato's Idealism and his cultural scheme of education ; Rationalism and formal training ; Empiricism in philosophy and Encylopaedism in education ; Rousseau's anti-social philosophy and his negative or natural education ; Spencer's Hedonism and his discipline by natural consequences ; and American Pragmatism and Project Method in education."

Dependence of education on philosophy is further realised by the fact that in view of modern developments in the field of education, we need 'a co-ordinating if not determining principle,' which will give meaning to our whole educational endeavour. Only the philosophy of the subject can furnish us with such a principle, We need an ideal life to which education should aspire.

The relation between philosophy and education is proved still more clearly by the relation between education and politics. No political system can do without evolving a suitable educational policy and practice. For instance, the educational system in a democratic country cannot escape the influence of democracy ; its educational methods and institutions can not but be democratic, to a large or to a small extent. Infact, every philosophy has both a political and an educational system following closely in its wake. The educational system has to find its guiding principles in the aims of social order for which it prepares. Education is a sustaining, progressive and purposive endeavour, and its strength comes only from the moral and political values of the community, the only source of which is philosophy.

Therefore, we can say that without philosophy, education would be nothing but a blind effort ; and without education philosophy would be no better than a cripple. In the words of **Adams**, "education is the dynamic side of philosophy, the practical means of realizing ideals of life." Divorced from philosophy, education would become an aimless endeavour, a hopeless waste of time and energy ; philosophy gives its point, its target, its goal. This is how philosophy and education are inter-related.

IMPACT OF PHILOSOPHY ON THE THEORY AND PRACTICE OF EDUCATION

Having established the fact of a fundamental relation between Philosophy and Education, we should now discover what concrete form this connection takes with reference to different aspects of education. Philosophy exercises its influence on education in all its aspects. "From every angle of the educational problem," say **Rusk**, "there comes the demand for a philosophical basis of the subject. There is no escape from a philosophy of life and of education." Philosophy determines the practical aim of educational effort ; it determines the content of curriculum ; it influences the discipline in the school ; it exercises an effective influence on the methods of teaching and it defines the place of the teacher in the educational set-up. Let us now discuss the impact of philosophy on these different aspects of education.

Philosophy and Aims of Education

Philosophy has an effective bearing on the aims of education. It is philosophy which determines whether the aims of education are universal or relative ; whether the aims of education should be intellectual development or moral perfection ; whether education should be vocational or liberal; whether education should be for the development and happiness of the individual or for the good of the society? Such conflicting opinions regarding the aims of education are reconciled in the light of philosophy.

The aims of education have a reference to the aims of life. The aim of life is determined by the philosophy that prevails at a certain time. Thus, educational aims depend on the philosophy that prevails among the people living at a particular time. That is why aims of education have been changing with the changing philosophy of life. They have varied in different countries in accordance with their respective philosophy of life.

In ancient Sparta, for example, the ideal was understood as dedication of the life and property of the individual to the cause of the state. It was ingrained in the mind of the educand that the country's honour must be vindicated at all costs. Hence, the aim of the Spartan system of education was to prepare citizens to be soldiers and patriots. On the other hand, the Athenian system of education aimed at the cultural development of each individual in conformity with the Athenian philosophy of that time. Rousseau learnt much from nature and received hard rebuff from society. In due course of time he developed a philosophy of education which was anti-social, negative and naturalistic. The British Public Schools, the Folk High Schools of Denmark, the American High Schools—all aim at producing good citizens in accordance with their democratic philosophy of life.

The German system of education illustrates effectively how philosophy determines the aims of education. In pre-war Germany, the philosophy of life that prevailed 'was based on the idea of Kultur—the great achievements and creations of the German mind; its language, literature, art, science, history—the nation was regarded as the chief factor for determining the aim of life. This philosophy which emerged in accordance with the needs of times created an ideal of education that deliberately instilled the spirit of national egoism, crushed individuality ruthlessly, and cultivated in individual citizens unquestioning loyalty and obedience to the Nazi regime by means of a rigid, militarised system of education deliberately planned for the purpose. Thus, we can conclude that philosophy is the determining force for laying down the aims of education.

Philosophy and Curriculum

Choice of means depends on the ends which they are required to realise. Ends determine the means. Curriculum is only a means for realizing the aims of education. So it is bound to be determined by educational objectives. The objectives of education, as has already been discussed, are derived from the general aim of life which is determined by Philosophy. Thus, the curriculum to be followed in schools has to conform to the prevailing philosophy. For instance, if the philosophy of life accepted by the people of a country is Naturalism, the curriculum followed in her schools cannot allow any place to humanities subjects that have only a cultural value. The curriculum naturally will consist only of those subjects which would enable the pupils to secure a better adjustment with their environment. Natural sciences are, therefore, bound to form an integral part of the naturalistic curriculum. According to the naturalists the present experience, activities and interests should be the guiding factor in framing the curriculum ; while to the idealists, the experiences of the human race as epitomed in science and humanities, should provide the primary consideration in deciding a curriculum. In fact, the idealists attach great importance to the spiritual perfection to which some subjects are abundantly conducive. The pragmatists emphasise the principle of utility as the main criterion for determining the nature of the curriculum. The realists think that a bookish, abstract or sophisticated curriculum is useless. They want to concentrate on realities of life and emphasise the importance of subjects that fall within the range of natural science.

The above discussion indicates that the problem of curriculum construction is tackled and solved in terms of the philosophical beliefs held by a group of people. The same is true of text book as well.

Philosophy and Methods of Teaching

Even the choice of methods is ultimately a question of philosophy. **Kilpatric**, realizing the ultimate relation between philosophy and methods of education, introduced the significant term 'philosophy of method.' It is through this method that the teacher is going to establish and maintain contact between the child and the subject-matter. The nature of the method of teaching is determined by the aim, which is sought to be realised by the method in question. Since, the aim of education is determined by philosophy, the method of teaching also is determined by the prevailing philosophy. If the philosophy prevailing at the time is that of Rousseau and the system of education is naturalistic the method naturally would be to follow nature, and 'learn by experience'. The child's nature being basically good, he must be left entirely to his natural inclinations and all external impositions and interference must be avoided. In the naturalistic scheme of teaching, the method of teaching has to be the "method of experience, and not the 'method of telling". On the other hand when the prevailing philosophy is idealism, the child has to understand and realise certain ultimate values and ideals, the method of teaching will be teacher-centred. Pragmatism holds that the most effective and lasting learning is possible only around a problematic. situation of practical life. Consequently, method of education consists in the creation of a practical problem or a project and in inducing many-sided learning through it.

Philosophy and Discipline

The nature of discipline is always determined by the philosophy one holds. Naturalism stands for unhampered freedom for the child.

It emphasises self-assertion of the individual, as against blind obedience to authority. Idealism relies much on the personality of the teacher for the maintenance of discipline. With the help of such a discipline, idealism advocates the development of a transcendental or a spiritual self which is liberated from the fetters of a merely physical, reality. Pragmatism does not believe in the employment of external discipline as a means for the adequate performance of educational functions. It gives complete freedom to the child and stresses the educational value of interest. We, thus, see that the problem of discipline is closely related with philosophy and the conception of discipline as held by a teacher or educator will always be influenced by his philosophical beliefs.

Philosophy and the Teacher

Lastly, let us consider the teacher himself. He must have a definite outlook on life, optimistic or pessimistic ; positive or negative', materialistic or idealistic. This vital belief of his will effect the various problems of education—the educand, the aims and its realization, the type or nature of discipline to be maintained, social organization in school, its general tone, the method he employs, the matter he emphasises in each subject and the conclusion he cherishes as his ideal.

A typical Indian teacher with a negative, fatalistic and other worldly philosophy cannot possibly help the child in the realization of such an aim as 'complete living' or 'harmonious development'. He cannot but place the virtues as self-denial, self-sacrifice, and renunciation on a high, but false pedestal. Imbued with ideas of other worldiness or personal salvation, he can not cultivate a social sense. On the contrary, he is likely to create in the young minds an attitude of pathetic indifference to the real problems of every day life.

CONCLUSION

We have looked at the problem of relation between philosophy and education from several angles and have found education to be completely in the grip of philosophy. From every angle of the educational problem comes the demand for a philosophical basis of education. The determination and formulation of aims, the choice of suitable curriculum or even text books, the employment of proper methods and devices, the decision about the type of discipline to be maintained and how to maintain it, the creation of a general tone in school by school organization : nay, even the problem of examination and mental testing are ultimately questions of philosophy. "Education," as says **Adams**, "is the dynamic side of philosophy. It is the active aspect of philosophical belief, the practical means of realizing, the ideals of life." There is no escape from a philosophy of life, and of education. In the words of **Ross**, "Philosophy and education are like the two sides of a coin ; the one is implied by the other ; the former is contemplative side of life, while the latter is the active side," Philosophy is wisdom that education transmits and disseminates it. Philosophy represents a system of thought which education embraces in the content of instruction ; Philosophy offers an outlook on life ; which is fostered or developed through education in the young. Philosophy presents a way of life, education is an understanding of and a preparation for it Both of them go together. They are allied in origin, inter-dependent and work jointly. Hence, we would end the chapter with Fichte's words with which we began it, that the art of education would never attain clearness in itself without philosophy. The next few chapters dealing with the different schools of philosophy in education will further support our contention.

5

Idealism in Education

Idealism takes many and varied forms, but the underlying principle is that "ultimate reality" is spiritual in nature rather than physical, mental rather than material. Idealism does not deny the existence of the world around us—the physical world which science and our senses acquaint with us. It maintains that real as it is, it is not ultimately real. It is manifestation of some more fundamental reality, a universal mind, which is all-embracing, all-knowing, all-rational. This spiritual reality may be either personal or impersonal.

Since, the ultimate reality is spiritual in nature, it is to be found in man's mind rather than in his material nature. Therefore, all knowledge is from within rather than from without. Idealism attaches more importance to knowledge that is acquired through the activity of mind than to the knowledge that is acquired through the senses. It contends that the material universe known to science is only an incomplete manifestation of reality ; it is subordinate to a higher type of reality—a spiritual universe of ideas and values. Ideas are of ultimate cosmic significance. They are the ideals, moulds, patterns or standards by which things of senses are to be judged. These ideals or values are eternal, unchanging, and absolute in nature. These values are not man-made, they pre-exist, the chief of them being Truth, Beauty and Goodness.

BASIC PRINCIPLES OF IDEALISM

Below are given some of the basic principles of Idealism, which will make the concept of Idealism' more clear.

(i) Ultimate realty is mental or spiritual in nature. The material world is nothing more than an outward manifestation of ultimate reality.

(ii) The material world is mortal and changing. Ultimate reality which consists of ideals, purposes and values is eternal and unchanging.

(iii) On this basis, body is false as it is mortal ; soul is true as it is immortal.

(iv) Man is essentially a spiritual being and his spirituality alone distinguishes him from animals. His spirit alone enables him to control his environment.

(v) Man is a free agent, free in the choice of his ends and means to realise them.

(vi) Values are pre-existing, ultimate, eternal and unchanging. Man cannot create values, but the aim of his life is realization of ultimate values—Truth, Beauty and Goodness—for their own sake.

IDEALISM IN EDUCATION

The idealistic school in education is represented by such thinkers as Plato, Comenius, Pestalozzi and Froebel and others. We are indebted to idealism more for the aims and objectives of education than for its devices and methods. In as much as idealism believes that reality is spiritual rather than material in nature, that the world of ideas and experience is more important than the physical world, it lays more emphasis on the study of the humanities than on the positive sciences. Man, it asserts, is an important subject of study while the human personality and its dignified expression is the important, function of education.

Some general principles of idealism have been mentioned above. Now we shall discuss the aims of education, curriculum, methods of teaching, concept of discipline and the role of teacher in the light of these principles.

Idealism and Aims of Education

Idealism believes that man has two natures—original and spiritual. The aim of education is to convert the original nature into spiritual nature. It must make him a man in the true sense of the word. It has been rightly remarked that man can become man by education only. In other words, we can say that the divine in man is to be unfolded and brought to his consciousness by means of education.

Rusk as well as Ross have given us the aims of education associated with Idealism. The aim of education, says **Rusk**, "is the enhancement or enrichment of personality, the differentiating feature of which is the embodiment of universal values." "The aim of education specially associated with Idealism" say **Ross**, "is the exaltation of personality or self-realization, the making actual or real the highest potentialities of the self."

Hence, according to Idealism the foremost aim of education is to exalt personality. The exaltation of personality implies the realization of the highest potentialities of the self in a social and cultural environment. The educand has to be provided with suitable environment and conditions that will be conducive to the realization of his self.

Idealism and Curriculum

Idealism believes that goal of human life is exaltation of man's personality. Education has to achieve this aim. The school curriculum accordingly, consists of those subjects which are conducive to this goal. The curriculum must reflect the capitalised knowledge and experience of the race. So it must primarily consist of 'humanities' or 'cultural studies'.

Plato, a great exponent of Idealism, conceives of the curriculum from the point of view of ideas. He believes that the highest idea of life was the attainment of the highest good or God, hence, the curriculum. ought to impart inherent values in order to enable the educand to attain his highest good. The inherent or spiritual values, according to him are truth, beauty and goodness These three values determine three type of activities, intellectual, aesthetic and moral. Each type of activity is represented by studies and should form a part of the curriculum. Intellectual activities are represented by subjects as languages, literature, science, mathematics, history and geography; aesthetic activities will be possible through the study of art and poetry and moral activities through the study of religion, ethics and metaphysics.

Interpreting the idealistic conception of the curriculum, Ross talks of two types of activities which would be represented by it. On the one hand, we have physical activities, and on the other spiritual activities. Physical activities draws our attention to such subjects as health and hygiene and to subjects that foster bodily skills such as gymnastic, and athletics. These subjects will lead to good health and fitness, thus making the pursuit of spiritual values possible. Spiritual pursuits imply the intellectual, aesthetic, moral and religious studies.

Hence, such subjects as history, geography, languages, fine arts, morality, ethics, religion, sciences, mathematics and others should be included in the curriculum.

The idealistic scheme of curriculum may be represented, with **Rusk**, by means of the following table :—

- Education
  - Physical activities
    - 1. Care of body
    - 2. Skills
  - Spiritual activities
    - 1. Intellectual
    - 2. Moral
    - 3. Aesthetic
    - 4. Religious.

Sir Percy Nunn recommends that the school should make a provision for these activities that are of greatest and most permanent significance in the wider world and are the grandest expression of the human spirit—those that are essential for maintaining the standard of individual and social life and those that represent the lofty attainment of civilization.

Idealism and Methods of Teaching

Idealism has exercised more influence on the aims and objectives of education rather than on methods of teaching. It speaks of general nature of teaching methods. It does not specify any method to be adopted. The great Greek Idealist Plato, however, advocated the Socratic method—Dialectics. Many educational philosophers advocated many other methods—the didactic method, the inductive method, the analytic method and so on. Idealism is not much concerned with the choice of methods so long its essential objective is fulfilled, which is the enrichment of personality of the pupil. To educate a child as to lead him to discover and develop what is within him rather than that which is beyond him is the real goal of education and with a good teacher any method can work well to realise that objective.

Idealism lays stress on instruction, activity and experience. The word instruction has been used in the wider sense, meaning "educative instruction," not 'order' or 'repression.' It implies sympathetic guidance by the teacher. Emphasising the need of such instruction, **Herbart** says, "I have no conception of education without instruction and do not acknowledge any instruction which does not educate." Instruction does not let the mind become a store-house of vague and undesirable ideas. It chisels and chastens them.

Another factor which Idealism emphasises in the methods of teaching is activity or learning by doing. The normal child should learn through activity. Idealism does not decry questioning, discussion, and lecture method of teaching, but it extols the method of creative and spontaneous mental activity. It does so because creative activity leads to self-expression and realization of the highest potentialities of the child. Mental activity leads the child to learn with pleasure and love and this love exalts his personality and introduces him systematically and deliberately into a wholly new order of things.

Experience has a significant place in the Idealistic method of teaching. The truly educative acts are those which go on within the private experiences of the learner and are comprised of the student's own self-activity, never of the artifices of the clever teacher. The duty of the teacher is to develop in him an insight into deeper experiences than he already possesses. In addition to it, the teacher should endeavour to unfold his potentialities 'by providing him stimulating experiences.

In short, the essense of Idealistic method of teaching is activity and freedom, freedom which is regulated and guided.

Idealism and Teacher

The naturalist would do without the teacher at times, he positively resents his interference in the development of the child and would like this development to be unchecked, unrestricted and unmodified by any sort of suggestion, guidance or direction. According to him, there is no place for the teacher in his natural, autonomous process of development towards perfection or rationality. The idealist does not be-little the importance of the teacher. In the Idealistic system of education, the teacher is indispensable.

The immature pupil cannot be expected to be able to understand by his own intelligence the real nature of the eternal values he has to realise in his life. It is only under the enlightened advice and able guidance of some individual of mature understanding and seasoned experience that the child can have such a knowledge. Thus, according to Idealism, there can be no teaching without a teacher. The immature learner can never be able to perfect his personality unless there is someone to teach him the methods of becoming perfect.

The universe is a rational system of which the teacher forms one part and the pupil another. The two are related to each other by the bond of a common purpose—the purpose of perfecting the personality of the child. This purpose is known clearly to the teacher but only vaguely to the pupil. The teacher has to make this purpose clear to the immature pupil. He has to explain it and also devise methods of enabling him to realise this purpose. The teacher is thus necessary for advising, directing, and even controlling the conduct of the pupil in order that he may be able to ensure the perfection of his personality.

The Idealist teacher can guide and help his pupils in three ways. Firstly, he can influence them by his personality i.e. by associating with them personally. Secondly, he can suggest questions and problems to them and encourage them to think for themselves. Thirdly, he can enable them to understand the problems by following the scientific methods of analysis and synthesis.

According to Ross, in the Idealistic scheme of studies the teacher is needed "to assist the educand, who is developing according to the laws of nature, to attain levels that would otherwise be denied him." The teacher is needed to draw the attention of the pupil to the 'formative' side of his education as much as a garden requires a gardener to tend the tiny and young.

According to idealism, education is a process in which "the educator as well as the educand is working out his salvation", and both are achieving self-realisation by inter-action with one another. The pupil is as much a necessity for the teacher as the teacher for the pupil. The teacher needs the pupil for his own spiritual growth and salvation.

Idealism and Discipline

Freedom is the cry of the Naturalists, while discipline is that of the Idealists. The latter believe that the child cannot attain his complete development unless he submits himself to a process of discipline. It is only through this process that self-realization and spiritual attainment can be made possible.

The idealists, however, do not favour rigid discipline. In fact, their theory of discipline is based on their concept of freedom. Their chief concern is "to harmonise freedom with subjection to authority and discipline, to unite submission to the necessary restraint with the child's capability of exercising his free-will". It is this process of discipline that will enable the educand to understand the great values of life—the inherent spiritual values. As such, the teachers' guidance is necessary. He will present ideals of conduct for the educand to follow and will see that his environment is conducive to the realization of his spiritual potentialities. The idealists look askance at the free discipline, and at the same time they are against the discipline that amounts to external restraint and supperssion of spontaneous activity. Froebel, for example, advocated complete absence of physical constraint for the sake of developing the pupil's powers of self-expression through self-realization. Self-realization recognizes the importance of teacher's guidance. Froebel, however, resented the imposition of the arbitrary will of the teacher. Control over the child was to be exercised through a knowledge of his interest and by expression of love and sympathy.

Some Idealists go to the extent of recommending direct moral instruction as an agent of maintaining discipline. Discipline according to them, implies cultivation of moral virtues such as humility and obedience to the elder.

CRITICISM OF IDEALISM

Some thinkers have criticised Idealism in education on the following grounds.

(i) Though Idealism is very eloquent about the aims and ideals of education, it says very little about the methods of teaching.

(ii) Idealism advocates a rigorous discipline which is altogether out of tune with the modern conception of education. The educationist of today believes in applying little or no authority at all. He wants to reduce the imposition of rules of work and conduct on the pupil to the minimum. He wants the entire activity and process of education to be purely spontaneous effort on the part of the pupil.

(iii) Idealism allows and assigns an exaggerated role to the teacher when it makes him an indispensable instructor and disciplinarian. This conception of an educator seems to be too primitive. In the modern times such a teacher would be simply a back number. It is extremely doubtful, if such a teacher can ever win the confidence of his pupils and inspire them to learn. The modern teacher does not aim at teaching the pupil but at teaching the pupil 'how to teach himself'.

(iv) The ideal of education—the attainment of the ultimate and absolute values, is too abstract to be grasped and appreciated by the immature pupil. The aim of the child's education may thus be clearly known to the educator but it cannot be understood by the young pupil. How can there be a thorough co-operation between the teacher and the pupil in this circumstance, is a matter of extreme mystery.

CONTRIBUTION OF IDEALISM

Idealism has exercised a great influence on education and has largely inspired educational thought in respect of the ultimate goals of education.

(i) So far as aims of education are concerned, no other thought can stand the light of Idealism. It is the unique contribution of Idealism in its having given a clear definition of the goals and aims of education and having drawn a pointed attention to the cultural and spiritual side of man's life and education.

(ii) Idealism has laid an invaluable emphasis on the dignity of the individual and on the personality of the child. It has rightly stressed the importance of aiming at the training and perfection of the educand's personality. Character-building is the most laudable among the aims of education.

(iii) Idealism has rightly stressed the need and importance of discipline in education. The immature pupil can not be expected to be able to discriminate between good and evil. So there can be a danger of his committing blunders which may quite often involve a great risk for him. Thus, some set rules of conduct imposed by the experienced personality of the teacher are a necessity, at least in the initial stages of the pupil's life and education.

6

Naturalism in Education

Naturalism is a type of philosophy which takes Nature as the whole of reality. According to naturalism the material and physical world is the only real world. It denies the existence of spiritual universe—the universe of ideas and values. This material world which is the only reality, is being governed by a system of natural laws. And man, who is the creation of the material world, must submit to it. Naturalism has regard for the observable facts, for the realities, and for the actual situations of life. It does not believe in spiritualism or supernaturalism. Therefore, it does not believe in any spiritual values or absolute truths. For it, nature is everything. It is the whole of reality. It denies the existence of anything beyond nature, behind nature, or other than nature. It believes that everything comes from nature and returns to nature. Nature, according to this philosophy, is a self-sufficient entity ; it contains its cause within itself. It is self-determined ; it has been created and is moved by natural forces only. Nature is governed by its own laws.

Naturalism does not believe in the spiritual nature of man. It takes recourse to such concepts as appetites and emotions which are regarded as the only motive of all our activities—biological, psychological or social. According to it, moral instinct, innate conscience, other world, miracles. providence, power of prayer, freedom of will, are illusions and there is no absolute good or evil in the world. Values of life, according to it, are created by the human needs. Man creates them, when he reacts to, or interacts with his environment. He must adapt himself to environment.

Naturalism believes that mind is an accident in the process of evolution and it can be explained in terms of matter. Mind is the function of brain which is material in nature. Mind is not the source of knowledge, all knowledge is acquired from without and sense organs are the gate-ways of all knowledge.

BASIC PRINCIPLES OF NATURALISM

Below are given some of the basic principles of Naturalism. The understanding of these principles makes the concept of naturalism clearer to us.

(i) Nature is the final reality. All things have originated from matter and all are ultimately to be reduced to that. Matter combined in different proportions takes different forms.

(ii) Mind is the brain functioning and brain is matter.

(iii) Experience, imagination, thinking, reasoning etc. are all processes of mental activity, which is the function of the brain.

(iv) Laws of nature are unchangeable and the entire universe is governed by them. Science reveals the mysteries of nature; hence only that knowledge is true that is derived from science.

(v) Real knowledge comes through our senses. All matter is within the ken of human senses and therefore, the final truth can be known through senses.

(vi) There is no God or Spirit. Therefore, there is no religion. There are no higher or eternal values. There is no spiritual ideal or aim or goal of human life. Man himself creates values in interaction with the environment in which he is placed.

(vii) Divine inspiration, revelation, strength of prayer, power of soul, other world—these are illusory conceptions and mislead human mind.

FORMS OF NATURALISM

Naturalism exists in many forms. The outstanding forms of naturalism are discussed below.

Naturalism of Physical Sciences

This type of naturalistic philosophy lays emphasis purely on physical nature. It believes, only in the reality of material objects and the laws of mass and motion. Mind, as something other than the body, has no existence at all. Man also is only one of the objects of physical nature, a creature of mass and motion. One is apt to agree with them, when they say that this universe of ours is governed by natural laws. However, their assertion that these very laws are applicable in their entirety to man and his experience, material, rational or spiritual, is indeed a bitter pill to swallow. It believes that scientific laws govern not only the facts and events of external world but also the behaviour of animals and conduct of man. Too much emphasis is, thus laid upon the external nature and the inner and the spiritual nature of man is more or less neglected. These facts make it perfectly clear that this form of naturalism can have little bearing on education and has little to contribute to its theory or practice, because education is a mental rather than a physical activity.

Mechanistic Naturalism

Mechanistic Naturalism or Mechanicalism regards the whole universe as a big complicated machine, working according to the laws of Mechanics. Man, too, is a machine, only a little more complicated and intricate than other objects of nature. His life, too, is subject to the laws of mechanics ; it is governed by mechanical laws of motion and causation. Though this form of Naturalism has made some contribution to education in the form of 'Behaviouristic Psychology', yet its contribution is not of much significance.

Biological Naturalism

Biological Naturalism believes that the nature and process of universe cannot all be explained in terms of physical science or mechanical operation. In the realm of living creatures the sole basis of explanations is evolution. All creatures have an urge to live and life evolves from lower to higher levels. The process of evolution is continuous, and all life is involved in that process. The process of evaluation is, however, the same for all living creatures.

The basic standpoints of Biological Naturalism are two : (i) each creature has an urge to live and (ii) he struggles to exist. In the struggle to existence those that are fit, survive, and those that are not, die. The theory is known by the comprehensive term, 'survival of the fittest'. According to Biological Naturalism self-preservation is the first law of nature.

Charles Darwin and Lamarck were two great scholars who advocated and interpreted this theory. Let us take note of their views briefly.

(i) The species of animal (and man, to George Bernard Shaw) are not unchanging. According to Darwin some sudden changes take place in germ cells, which create physical changes also. According to Lamark it is external environment that creates physical changes.

(ii) According to Darwin only the changes, which are sudden, are transmitted according to the law of heredity. But to Lamark changes, instead of being sudden, are according to desire and need, and traits changed by efforts may be transmitted.

(iii) According to Darwin organ is created first and used by activity afterwards whereas according to Lamark creation or attraction of need or activity comes first and then organ is created for its fulfilment.

Thus, there is a similarity between the instincts of man and animal according to Naturalism. This school holds that man is continuous with animals ; he has, infact, grown or 'evolved' out of his 'pre-historic' ancestors. Consequently, even now he has much which is common with animals and that common nature is the real man, and it is inherently good. Man's primitive impulses, instincts and emotions are an unerring guide to his conduct. They are more dependable than reflection or capitalised experience of the race. This school emphasises the original nature of man and declines to place much faith in his spiritual nature. It believes that all forms of moral conduct and character can be evolved in man by a proper modification, training and sublimation of his instincts and emotions. Mc. Dougall, the well-known psychologist, is the chief exponent of this view.

This form of Naturalism has a great bearing on the theory and practice of education. It maintains that real education lies in the modification and training of man's instincts and emotions. This is the view most acceptable to the modern educators.

NATURALISM IN EDUCATION

Naturalism as a philosophy of education was developed in 18th century., It exercised a great influence on the theory and practice of education. It decries all external restraint in education and it condemns all unnecessary formalities in education. In the naturalistic system of education there is no place for class-rooms, text books, time-tables' curricula, formal lessons or examinations. The chalk and talk' method has no scope. The teacher has no significant role to play. External discipline is altogether out of place ; the only discipline applied in this system is the discipline of natural consequences. Naturalism believes that formal education was the invention of society which was artificial and as such vicious. Good education can be had only by a direct contact with nature.

On the positive side, Naturalism in education stands for the doctrine of follow nature in education. It wants all education to be in strict conformity with the nature of the child. It stands for complete freedom to be given to the child in learning. He is so be left alone, absolutely free, face to face with nature, permitted to learn undisturbed anything he likes and by any method he likes. He is to be thrown into Nature as an explorer and discoverer, to make experiments with any objects of nature that appeal to him and to learn from them whatever he can. Even if he takes a wrong track, he is to be allowed to go on until his mistake is brought home to him by its unfavourable or unpleasant, consequences. Thus, the whole of the child's learning will come from his own experiences and their natural consequences. His whole education will be according to the natural laws of human development.

In the beginning, Bacon and Comenitics were associated with Naturalism. But much of the Naturalistic movement finds its root in the pages of Rousseau, who brought it to its zenith. He brought the child into the foreground of the educational arena and impressed on the people that educational material should be the facts and phenomena of nature.

Naturalism and Aims of Education

Of all the forms of Naturalism, it is the biological naturalism which has exercised the greatest influence on education. The influence of Physical and Mechanical Naturalism is practically nil in education, specially that of the former which seeks to interpret the entire universe in terms of physical science.

Views of Mechanical Naturalism

According to Mechanical Naturalism, the individual is also like a machine and consequently, the aim of education should be to make the machine work with as much perfection and efficiency as possible. According to this view, all activities of human beings originate on receiving some stimuli from the environment and hence they are functioning in the form of conditioned reflex actions. The process of education should be to improvise the stimuli in such a way that desired activities proceed from them. This form of Naturalism has given birth to Behaviouristic Psychology which has also influenced education.

Views of Biological Naturalism

Biological Naturalism interprets educational aims in several ways.

(i) Spencer, affirms that preservation of the self is the main consideration and self-satisfaction constitutes the highest good in human life. It is self-satisfaction on which is based the present and future happiness of life. Hence, the aim of education should be to make an appeal to the primitive instincts and natural impulses of the child and assist him in securing self-preservation and self-satisfaction.

(ii) MacDougall, the famous exponent of the Naturalistic School of Psychology, does not accept the Hedonistic view (presented by Biological Naturalists) that all our actions spring from the pursuit of happiness and avoidance of pain. He believes that pleasure and unpleasure are not goals, but by-products of our activities : The aim of education is the sublimation of the native instincts and energies of the individual—the redirection, co-ordination and harmonious working of the native impulses.

(iii) The Neo-Darwinians base their aims of education on the notion of man's evolution from lower forms of life. They hold that the living-creature has to struggle continuously against the environment for existence, resulting in the survival of the fittest. The aim of education, therefore, should be to equip the individual for the struggle of life and thus ensure his survival.

(iv) Like the Neo-Darwinians, the Neo-Lamarkians believe in the theory of man's evolution from lower forms of life, but they offer another explanation. They maintain that evolution to higher forms of life is based on "the power of the living creature to adapt itself, its habits, and its bodily structure to the circumstances in which it finds itself." As such they see education as the process of adjustment to environment. In other words, the aim of education should be to enable the individual to be in harmony with and well adapted to his surroundings. It will be through the process of adjustment that an individual will grow physically and mentally. The ideal is a well-adjusted, happy being, with no discontent, divine or otherwise.

(v) Nunn regards the 'autonomous development of the individual' as the central aim of education and insists that an education which aims at fostering individuality is the only education according to nature. The term individuality is misinterpreted. It may be identified with mere self-assertion or selfishness. The individual may disobey all authority and may acknowledge only his own will and disparage all other individualities or wills. But Nunn does not imply all this from the use of the word ; for him it means self-realization. He seeks to establish a harmony between individual and social claims in education and does not believe that there is any dichotomy existing between the two.

Of all the Naturalists, Rousseau's statement of aims, in accordance with his Naturalistic Philosophy, is the most comprehensive and lucid. Education, he holds, should aim at the development of the child in conformity with his nature. Normal and natural development enjoins on the teacher and parents the need of the bodily health and vigour. it implies a respect for physical nobility and regard for individual differences among children. It impresses on the parents the need of observation of the child's natural tendencies, their origin, growth and decline.

Naturalism and the Curriculum

Naturalism emphasises scientific studies on a laboratory basis. For such studies, they recommend subjects like physics, chemistry, biology etc. As regards language and mathematics they opine that only so much knowledge of these subjects should be acquired as is essential for scientific studies. It believes that the pupil should not be plunged into poetry and literature. Naturalism assumes that the nature of man is that which he shares to some extent with the animals, that it consists of his instincts, appetites and primitive emotions ; it therefore, damps down, it does not altogether ignore man's spiritual nature. As such, Naturalism gives a very insignificant place to spiritualism in the curriculum. At the same time it does not include classical music and painting in their curriculum. In its support, it says that children have no interest in them.

Almost all the Naturalist have expressed their views about the curriculum or the subjects to be taught. Let us make a brief mention of them.

Spencer, an extreme Naturalist, thought that human nature is strictly individualistic and that self-preservation is the first law of life. Accordingly, he advocated the inclusion of those subjects which would subserve self-preservation. He attaches no importance to cultural subjects or those which enhance the value of man's social and cultural inheritance. This was in strict conformity with his hedonistic philosophy.

Rousseau's curriculum for Emile in the first two stages especially, and in the following stages generally, was illustrative of the principle of negative education which is typical of the naturalistic philosophy—the subordination of the child to the natural order and his freedom from the social order. The doctrine of negative education, as applied to physical education, demanded the greatest possible "freedom for the child in his movements and exercises, simple diet, loose, scanty and light clothing, etc." Intellectual education would amount to absence of verbal lessons, books or any positive studies. The Naturalists in general, contend that the child's present experiences, interests and activities should determine the choice of studies.

The Naturalists, in general, contend that the child's present experiences, interests and activities should determine the choice of studies. He should be allowed to grow up in a free atmosphere, his natural inclinations finding a suitable outlet. Knowledge for its own sake is not an aim worthy of emulation or worth striving after.

Naturalism and Methods of Teaching

In methods of teaching, Naturalism is a revolt against the old, traditional and stereotyped methods. It condemns learning by rote and passive drill work, and emphasises activity and learning by doing. It advocates that education should provide real experiences to the child and help him to learn with his own personal experiences. He should take his lesson from nature, not from man. Hence, there should be no formal schools and text books. The best thing is to let him 'follow nature' because it supplies all the laws of learning. Direct experiences from nature, men, and things form the basis of instruction, according to naturalism. **Rousseau's** advice was, "Give your scholar no verbal lessons ; he should be taught by experience alone. Teach by doing whenever you can ; and only fall back on words when doing is out of question. Book knowledge should be as little as possible." Emile, for example, was to discover things for himself in learning science, he would make use of rough experiments performed with the help of apparatus self-made and self-invented. He was to adopt the heuristic attitude and to apply it in the first hand study of natural phenomena. The same principle is to work in learning mathematics, geography and history. Thus, the direct method of learning languages, the heuristic and laboratory methods of learning sciences and mathematics, the observational method in geography, etc.—all illustrate the naturalistic attitude.

The Naturalists believe that every child's ability to acquire knowledge and to benefit thereby is individual. Hence, those class methods which assume a uniform speed of learning for every child are discredited by them. The naturalistic methodology has been aptly described by **Ross** when be says, "The naturalist educator rightly thinks less of his own exposition much more of the learning experience of the pupil." In other words, they advocate the use of paedo-centric methods which stress the importance of the educand in the process of education more than the subject-matter or the educator himself.

To cut short, the Naturalists advocate such methods of teaching which offer the child an opportunity for self-education, self-expression, creative activity and integrated growth in an atmosphere of unrestrained freedom. In the words of **Ross**, "The naturalist educator allows the child to follow the lines of his natural interests and to have free choice of activities with no interference or thwarting."

Naturalism and the Teacher

In an educational system based on the Naturalistic Philosophy, the teacher has a peculiar place and duty to perform. Neither is he to interfere with the activities of children, nor is he to provide any ideals or ideas in order to form their character. He must not impose himself on them and must see that their education is the free development of their interests and motives rather than an artificial effort made by him. He has to provide them with suitable opportunities for, and create conditions which are conducive to, natural development. He is not to expect any undue difference from the pupils he teaches, nor does he try to look superior. He tries to understand them, loves them and approves of their behaviour. He is on the side of the child. Rousseau and Fichte are in favour of such non-intervention of the teacher on account of the child's nature. It is contended by them that the child's nature is essentially good, and any intervention, is, therefore harmful. Montessorie deems the teacher's interference as unjustifiable since the specially constructed environment through the use of the didactic apparatus can evoke the right type of response from the children and thereby perform the function of a teacher.

According to Ross, the teacher in a naturalistic set-up is only a setter of the stage, a supplier of materials and opportunities, a provider of an ideal environment, a creator of conditions under which natural development takes place. He has to be simply a non-interfering observer. He has only to understand the tendencies and capacities of the child, and arrange suitable conditions for their free development, and then he must retire into the back ground.

Naturalism and Discipline

Naturalists have no faith in discipline based on external force. They condemn corporal punishment as it represses the impulses, and instincts of the children and forms in them undesirable complexes. They uphold the theory that the child's conduct is based on impulses or instinct, which should not be repressed either by force or punishment.

Naturalism stands for a "hands-off " policy in education. The only discipline to be applied is the discipline of natural consequences. The child should be left perfectly free to act in any way he likes and then face the consequences of his actions. If the consequences of his action turn out to be pleasant and favourable, it would be repeated and therefore learnt. On the contrary, if the consequences of an action are found to be unpleasant, it shall be given up. Thus, the forces of pleasure and pain will effectively teach discipline to the child ; his behaviour and moral conduct will ultimately be shaped by these forces.

Rousseau is of the opinion that children should never be punished. If they commit a fault its unpleasant natural consequences will inflict enough of punishment on them. Nature spares none. Every action is inevitably followed by its natural consequences. All immoral or undesirable actions will result in unpleasant consequences and these unfavourable results will make the individual avoid the repetition of such actions in future.

Herbart Spencer also supports the doctrine of natural discipline. He wishes the children to be left to suffer the natural unpleasant consequences of their wrong actions and learn from them. The punishment for their actions should come from their natural consequences rather than from the rod of any supervisory agency. **Spencer** writes, "when a child falls, or runs its head against the table, it suffers a pain, the rememberance of which lends to make it more careful; and by repetition of such experiences, it is eventually disciplined into proper guidance of its movement." Spencer, however, admits that his principle does not apply without exception, and that during infancy it would be unwise to apply it. He says, "A three-year-old urchin playing with an open razor, cannot be allowed to learn by this discipline of natural consequences, for the consequences may be too serious."

CRITICISM OF NATURALISM

The Naturalistic Philosophy and its application in education is open to the following objections :

(i) Naturalism altogether ignores the spiritual and moral sides of man's nature. While aiming at the natural development of the child, it omits the mention of his moral development—the development of his will, his conscience, his moral motives, his sense of good and evil and the moral law.

(ii) Naturalism pays attention only to the present needs of the child and ignores his future needs and the ultimate ideals and purposes of man's life.

(iii) Naturalism leaves the child purely to the 'discipline' of natural consequences.' But this discipline quite often involves grave risks, may be to his very existence. For instance, it would be extremely risky to allow the child to go near the fire and burn himself in order to enable him to learn that fire should be avoided.

(iv) Naturalism throws the teacher completely into the background. He is not to impose either his knowledge or his personality on the child. This is bound to cause a serious loss to the pupil of the value which the teacher's knowledge and the seasoned experience of his mature personality can supply him. Every pupil shall begin with the scratch and a big zero.

(v) Naturalism allows complete freedom to the child from the very start of his life, even when he has not yet learnt the right use of freedom. This is a very risky experiment. In some cases the pupil may completely lose himself in this freedom, lose himself beyond any recall or redemption. In the early stages, some guidance and authority are altogether necessary.

(vi) Naturalism attaches too much importance to the animal nature of man—his instincts, impulses and emotions, and completely ignores his spiritual and moral nature and culturals ideals.

(vii) Naturalism banks too much on the heredity of the child and ignores the influence of environment on 'raw' nature. This is a serious under-rating of the school environment.

CONTRIBUTION OF NATURALISM

Naturalism in education has resulted in the following educational principles :

1. Follow Nature

'Follow nature' is the most significant slogan of Naturalism in education. The natural development of the child, the naturalist believes, takes place in the natural environment rather than in the artificially designed atmosphere of the school. In the domain of education, the term 'Nature' is used in two senses. It stands for 'physical nature' in one sense and the 'inner nature' of the child in the other sense.

2. Instincts as basis for Education

According to Naturalism there is animal in man, that is, his instincts and impulses, his apetites and primitive emotions are more valuable than his rational or spiritual nature. The Naturalists would even go so far as to assert that these very instincts. which are not plastic or prone to any great modifying influence, are the chief dynamics behind the entire behaviour of the child. The instincts or life-urges of the child should constitute the basis of all education. Thus, according to the Naturalists, instincts should be the main instrument of education.

3. Paedo-Centricism

In the educative process the pivotal position is that of the child whose nature must be fully understood, before he can be helped to grow naturally, and harmoniously. As it, has been already stated above, "It is the child himself rather than the educator, the school, the book or the subjects of study that should be in the fore-ground of the educational picture." Unnecessary. interference on the part of the parents or teachers should be avoided. Children should be treated as children and not as adults in miniature.

4. Freedom for the Child

The conviction of the Naturalist in the efficacy of self-activity and his bias for Hormic Psychology naturally Prompted him to advocate child's freedom as another important feature of naturalistic education. Freedom is indispensable, for only through the exercise of freedom can the child grow in a natural way. Freedom should be the pivot round which the educational programme should be planned. Education is merely the fostering of natural development, and true education takes place when the nature, powers, and inclinations of the child are allowed to develop freely with a minimum of guidance.

5. Senses the Gateway to Knowledge

According to **Rousseau,** "Education should prepare the way for reason by the proper exercise of the senses." He says that from the age of five to twelve, the child's senses are to be exercised. As such, naturalists consider the training of senses very important. They believe that senses are the gateway to knowledge. Hence, if effective learning is desired, the child must be provided sensony experiences.

CONCLUSION

To conclude, we can say that Naturalism has secured freedom for the child and has further succeeded in freeing the child from the tyranny and rigidity, interference and strict discipline. Naturalism has given an impetus to new Psychological methods in education. Self-expression, follow nature, self-education, play-way, and self-discipline are some of the main characteristics of naturalism in education.

7

Pragmatism in Education

Pragmatism is a mid-way between Naturalism and Idealism. It criticises the impersonal interpretation of existence as forward by naturalism, and rebels against the academic and orthodox as forwarded by Idealism. Pragmatism holds that whatever fulfils one's purpose and develops his life, is true. Only those theories are true which work well in practical situations. There are no absolute ideas. All ideas are relative to the situations in which they arise and they are subject to continuous verification by consequences.

Pragmatism is a typical American school of philosophy. It represents the American life and mind and has arisen out of the history of the American nation. The Puritans who came to settle in the unknown land of America had to continually face difficulties and new problems of life. They had no ready-made solutions for such problems. They had to plan out an ideology that would help them to meet novel situations. They had to think of solutions that would enable them to make their headway in life. Consequently, they built up a philosophy of life through experiences instead of being guided any established theory. This philosophy denies the existence of any fixed eternal values and by revolts against absolutism. It is humanistic in as much as it is concerned more with human life and things of human interest than with any established tenets. It arises out of actual living.

The chief principle of this philosophy is that man creates his own values; there are no fixed, eternal truths. Truths, if any, are man made. Reality is still in the making. It is never complete. Our judgment happens to be true if it gives satisfactory results in experience, i.e. by the way it works out. A judgment in itself is neither true nor false. There are no established systems of ideas which will be true for all times. All systems of ideas are relative to the situation in which they arise and the personalities they satisfy and are subject to continuous verifications by consequences. The Pragmatists lay emphasis on man's power to shape his environment to his own needs and to create by the successful solution of problems, fairer and better environment for himself. The chief exponents of pragmatism are William James, Schiller and John Dewey.

FORMS OF PRAGMATISM

There are three forms of pragmatism—humanistic, experimental and biological. Humanistic pragmatism conceives of the true as that which best satisfies human nature and welfare as a whole. Whatever fulfils man's purposes, desires and develops his life, is true. According to experimental pragmatism, the true is that which can be experimentally verified or whatever works. Biological pragmatism stresses the human ability of adaptation to the environment and that of adapting environment to human needs.

BASIC PRINCIPLES OF PRAGMATISM

Below are given some of the basic principles of Pragmatism, which will make the concept of Pragmatism more clear.

(i) There is no ultimate unchanging reality. Reality is that which is 'experienced' by man. Since, the experience of man is constantly changing, truths and reality are also changing constantly.

(ii) Man's life is an unbroken series of experiments, and through, these experiments he creates values. He is constantly creating and recreating values of life. Therefore, values are man-made, changing and relative.

(iii) Man is a social creature. That is why, the quality of social efficiency in man is necessary. Man's life may be successful in a society. Man outside the society is a thing of imagination.

(iv) It is only in and through a democratic society that the individual can fulfil his purposes and perfect himself.

(v) Thought is only a means to life. Man should think only to live. Action, not mere contemplation is the aim of life.

PRAGMATISM IN EDUCATION

William James and John Dewey are the two outstanding pragmatic educators. Education for them is not the pursuit of knowledge for its own sake. It may have its intellectual, aesthetic, moral, religious and physical aspects, but they are to be regarded as modes of activities through which the child has to create his values. These activities are to be produced by the child because they will satisfy aid subserve human needs or because they are useful. According to pragmatism education is not the dynamic side of philosophy as it is advocated by idealism. It is philosophy which emerges from educational practice. Education creates values and formulates ideas that constitute this philosophy. Philosophy is, thus, the theory of education in its most general phases.

Today this philosophy occupies the most dominant place in the United States of America. Those who build their educational theory on Pragmatism call themselves. Progressivists and their education, progressive education. Their approach to the theory and practice of education is based on two main principles, viz (i) education should have a social function, and (ii) education should provide real life experience to the child.

Pragmatism and Aims of Education

Pragmatism does not lay down any aims of education in advance. It believes that aims of education cannot be fixed. They must be revised with the changing times and needs. Aims towards which educative effort has to be directed or values which the educational practice has to realise, are to be created by man himself in the light of his own experience. The only aim of education, according to pragmatism, is to enable the child to create values in his life. As stated by **Ross**, "the general aim of education is just the creation of new values; the main task of education is to put the educand into a position to develop values for himself."

Education is intended to direct the desires, impulses and interests of the child in such a way that he may be able to satisfy his wants in adjustment to his environment and solve his present-day problems. What pragmatism wants to achieve through education is the cultivation of a dynamic, adaptable mind which will be resourceful and enterprising in all situations—the mind which will have powers to create values in an unknown future. It is such minds that will reconstruct society in which the human wants will be fully satisfied through a social medium consisting of co-operative activities.

Pragmatism and Curriculum Construction

Pragmatists lay down the following principles for curriculum construction :

(i) Principle of Utility

Practical utility is the only watch-word and the guiding principle of Pragmatism. Therefore, whatever is likely to help the pupil in his practical life deserves to be taught and what is not likely to serve any purpose in the day-to-day life of the child should be omitted from the curriculum. As such, language, hygiene, physical training, history and geography, mathematics, sciences, domestic science for girls and agriculture for boys, should be incorporated in the school curriculum. The utility criterion requires direct training for a vocation in the later stages. It also demands that different studies should be viewed from the stand-point of their usefulness in dealing with life situations rather than as a disinterested pursuit of knowledge. But the utility principle should not be adopted in the narrow sense. The main aim of knowledge i.e. human progress should not be overshadowed by it.

(ii) Principle of Child's Interest

According to the Pragmatic system of education, the only aim of education is to prepare the child for a successful and well-adjusted life. He must be fully adjusted to his environment. The school curriculum has, therefore, to be guided by the natural tendencies, impulses and interests of the child at the various stages of his growth. So nature study, elementary arithmetic, drawing, reading and writing should be conspicuously present in the elementary school curriculum. This curriculum shall be expanded at the later stages according to the growing needs and interests of the child. According to Dewey, the child has four kinds of interests. Firstly, he is interested in conversation or communication. His second interest lies in inquiry or finding out things.. In. the third place he is interested in construction, or making of things. Lastly, he is interested in artististic expression, Curriculum should be constructed on the basis of these interests.

(iii) Principle of Child's Experience

According to Pragmatism all education is 'learning by doing'. So it must be based on the child's experiences as well as occupations and activities. In addition to the school subjects, free, purposive, and. socialized activities should be included in the curriculum. If these activities take the character of the activities of the community of which the school is an organ, they will develop moral virtues, result in attitudes initiative and independence and will give training in citizenship and promote self-discipline.

(iv) Principle of Integration

This principle assumes the unity of knowledge and skill., Such an integration will be secured if the subjects are presented as modes of activities which are purposive and connected by a common end. The Pragmatist, it must be noted, does not want to abolish the division of curriculum into subjects. The scheme of dividing it into subjects is convenient and useful. Moreover, subjects are the capitalised experience of the race. But the pragmatist warns us against the water-tight compartments between one subject and another.

To sum up, we can say that Pragmatists have an idea of curriculum which is useful, flexible, dynamic, and well integrated. They offer an "Activity Curriculum", because they maintain that activities are necessary both to make education life-like and to make life yield the truth.

Pragmatism and Methods of Teaching

Pragmatism has to its credit an important contribution that it has made to the methods of teaching. While answering the question of the methods of teaching, Pragmatism places in the forefront the view-point of practical necessity and utility rather than logic. According to this Philosophy, it is the problem to be solved which determines the method rather than any dogmatic and predetermined concepts and views.

Pragmatism advocates the elimination of all formal aims, predetermined values, dogmatic principles, and stereotype practices employed in teaching. It only wants the child to be prepared for his practical life. Therefore, it gives the first place in school teaching to practical problems and real situations of man's life. The problem must come first and the learning should be incidental to its successful solution. The pupil should acquire principles, skills and methods as he experiences the need for them. Thus, the method employed by the pragmatist teacher is the experimental' method or the method of "trial and error".

The methods of teaching should be related to the practical life of the child—his desires, impulses and purposes. His learning should be thoroughly purposive. He should learn purely to fulfil the purposes of his life. He should be provided opportunities to indulge in purposeful activities. Action, rather than contemplation, is to figure conspicuously in the Pragmatic Education. Not books but practical activities, can and would provide knowledge of real value. Therefore, he should 'learn by doing' rather than by thinking. A child according to Dewey, learns not by reading books or listening to explanations, but by burning himself and feeding himself, that is by doing things.

The child has an inborn love for activity—action and construction. The Pragmatic system of education aims at providing opportunities for the development and free-play of this tendency of the child. He has to be placed in real situations which he has to tackle ; he shall learn from the process of tackling these problems.

The pragmatist does not, however, fix up his methods once for all. His methods of handling his pupils vary from time to time according to the total situation—the situation regarding the teacher, the students, and the equipment.

The most general method of Educational Pragmatism, according to **Ross**, is "to put the child into situations with which he wants to grapple, and provide him, at the same time, with the means of dealing with them successfully". And these conditions are satisfied by the Project Method introduced by Kilpatrick, a follower of Dewey. The Project Method consists in initiating a "whole-hearted, purposeful activity proceeding in a social environment".

Pragmatism and the Teacher

Pragmatism neither treats the teacher merely as an on-looker as Naturalism does, nor regards him as an indispensable necessity as Idealism does. It takes the middle course. According to Pragmatism, teacher is useful, even though not indispensable, for creating life-situations for the immature child, and placing him in them to learn by making attempts to tackle them. He would make independent experiments to solve his problems and learn from them. The position of the teacher is of a guide and adviser. He has to make his pupils to think and act for themselves, to do rather than to know, to originate rather than repeat. He is considered a social environment. With his sympathetic and personal contact with the children, he is expected to develop in them social habits, social interests and social attitudes. His importance lies in the fact that he has to place his students in suitable problematic situations and to motivate their interests in such a way that they may solve the problems with tact, intelligence and co-operation.

The Pragmatist teacher is a Pragmatist first and a teacher afterwards. He is essentially an experimentalist, a trial and error man, who tackles and solves problems as they arise in the class-room and outside. He aims at teaching his pupils to do rather than to know, to originate rather than to repeat, to think and act for themselves.

Pragmatism and Discipline

Pragmatism does not believe in external discipline enforced by the superior authority of the teacher and the award of punishments. It advocates that discipline to be beneficial should be based on the principles of child's activities and interests. In fact, it deprecate all forms of individual and personal discipline. It uphold discipline based on social understanding. It believes in engaging the children in free and purposeful real activities. They are not only permitted but positively encouraged to undertake real activities of the human life and learn through their performance. This process is bound to inculcate in them permanent attitudes of initiative and independence. It gives him a discipline which is acquired in every kind of real and creative work, as a very natural consequence of the activity itself. Thus, the discipline in Pragmatic system of education is to be self-discipline—the discipline of the pupil's own work and activity.

In the pragmatic scheme of education the children are expected to work in co-operation with one another. They are to take up a "project", or a real problem, and to work at it as a team. These co-operative activities impart to them very useful qualities of social life—sympathy, give and take, fellow feeling, spirit of sacrifice and tolerance, which constitute an invaluable moral training for them.

The school of the Pragmatic conception, is a reflex of the community to whom it belongs and whom it represents. Its pupils have ultimately to take their places in the community and live in accordance with its point of view. Therefore, the school has to provide for all those activities which constitute the normal life of the community. It has to provide for the socialised, free and purposive activities. These activities provide the pupils a very useful training in citizenship.

Since, in the Pragmatic system of education, external restraint and imposition are altogether absent, the entire discipline that the pupils are to learn, will come from their work and self determined activities. Their discipline would be a self-discipline. Imposed discipline and a strict and rigid discipline can have no place in the pragmatic school.

CONCLUSION

To conclude, we can safely say that Pragmatism has contributed much to the theory and practice of education. Its opposition to formalism and artificiality, its emphasis on practical results, its bias towards social efficiency, its questioning spirit and perpetual re-evaluation of traditions, all have greatly revolutionsed education. It has accelerated the pace of democracy in educational institutions. Its humanistic and social approach in education ensures better citizen. To conceive education as a life-long process of reconstruction and re-institution of experience, puts education on a progressive pedestal.

8

Realism in Education

Realism is not a Philosophy of life like Idealism or Naturalism, but like Pragmatism it is an attitude of mind, a mode of thinking and an attempt to explain the nature of things. It is the doctrine that the objects of our senses exist independently of their being known or perceived by mind.

BASIC PRINCIPLES OF REALISM

Realism is an epistemological school. The basic principle of realism is the 'principle of independence'. If we put a question like this : Can a thing exist without being humanly known? Or, can a thing exist independent of our knowledge? The realist would say, Yes". Whereas the answer of Epistemological Idealism will be in the negative. Now one who holds that an object known is independent of the knowing mind may still hold that independent object is spiritual in nature. Hence, he would be Epistemologically a Realist, but Metaphysically an Idealist. Plato was Metaphysically an Idealist bat Epistemologically a realist. Most of the modern Realists are either materialists or dualists or neutralists.

Realism, like Idealism, admits of various types and degrees, because the object, may be held to be either wholly independent of and distinct from the mind or to be partly so, and that to different extents. Therefore, the maximum of Realism is the pre-supposition that there is such a thing as knowledge ; in other words, the perception and thought refer to some object, not the mere experience of perceiving and thinking. The maximum of Idealism, on the other side, would be the assurance that everything ever perceived or thought of existed apart from apprehension and exactly in the form in which it is believed to exist. In other words, there is no such thing as error.

REALISM IN EDUCATION

Coming into the field of education Realism has acquired different meanings and even contradictory ones at different periods of history. Today Realism is a reaction against the book-centred academic, intellectual, liberal, literary or humanistic education. It favours child-centred, practical, specific, scientific and psychological education. Applied to education realism manifested itself in three different forms, namely (a) Humanistic Realism, (b) Social Realism, and (c) Sense Realism.

Humanistic Realism

Although Realism is a reaction against humanistic studies today, yet it expressed itself through humanism during the Renaissance when it was believed that the ancient classics dealt with man's life more richly than the formal grammarian education of the middle ages. Thus, Humanistic Realism represented the survival of the idea of the Renaissance, but it did that in a different way. While, the classical humanists placed emphasis on form and style, the humanist realist opposed it in favour of content and ideas. This humanistic Realism was not only a rebirth of the ancient classical studies, but also a revolt against the prevalent traditional system of education. Medieval scholasticism was mere study of books and linguistic forms, while the purpose of the Humanistic Realist was to master his own environment through knowledge of the life of the ancient. It places substance before form, thought above words and practical efficiency in life above show accomplishments. The Dutch international scholar Erasmus, the Frenchman Rabelasis and the English poet Milton were the most prominent representatives of humanistic realism.

We may review the ideas of Milton to have a clear understanding of Humanistic Realism, as Milton's 'Tractate on Education' remains one of the best expressions of Humanistic Realism. In the beginning Milton exposes the folly of the traditional curriculum and methods. Then he goes to analyse the work of the school and gives a scheme of education from 11 to 21 years. This course covers a variety of subjects such as Latin, geometry, 'moral training in the first stage ; agriculture, architecture, natural philosophy, medicinal and mathematical science, poetry in the second stage ; and ethics, economics, politics. history, theology, logic, public speaking in the third stage. It was a complete and general education which fits a man for all offices both private and public, of peace and war. Criticising this scheme of education, Monroe points out that the course was too heavy and meant for a College of Milton only.

The influence of Humanistic Realism was very little because it was not characterised by any external difference from the dominant formalism of those times, particularly in method, organisation and administration. Whatever influence it had, was through individual teachers only. Its spirit flourished more in the Universities, though they were artificial, formal and traditional. Yet, by its opposition of form and its placing emphasis on the realities of life, it directly led to sense realism that soon found a place in organised educational work.

Social Realism

The same force of revolt that gave birth to Humanistic Realism during Renaissance gave birth to Social Realism during the 17th and 18th centuries when the humanistic education turned into an extremely rigid formalism and ceased to be a progressive force. Social Realism was the natural reaction of practical men of the new world against a type of education that tended to perpetuate the pedantry of an earlier age, by devoting its energies to the production of the scholar and professional man to the neglect of the man of affairs. The exponents looked upon humanistic culture as insufficient for producing a man of the world. Montaigne was its chief representative. He would advise his scholar to spend his time at tennis, if education could not develop social qualities in him and made him only a book-worm. He takes a utilitarian view of education and interprets it as a preparation for the life of the man of the world. Social Realists were practical men and were against existing routine curriculum. They pleaded for direct contact with men and things particularly through travel. Consequently, it included a study of heraldry, genealogy, riding, fencing, and gymnastics, and a study of modern languages and the customs and institutions of neighbouring countries.

The idea of education through travelling was meant for aristocracy because travel involves expenditures. It is more a method of educational practice rather than a philosophy of education. Social Realism is not a completely distinct trend from other forms of Realism. It is, therefore, that Montaigne is confused as a humanist, a realist and a naturalist. He was against Humanistic Realism because he rejected book-learning and second hand knowledge. He was not a Sense Realist because things to him included thoughts as well, which Sense Realists neglect. He was not a Naturalist because the latter emphasised isolation while he emphasised society and contact with men. To Rousseau one's own experience mattered while to Montaigne the experience of others as well was significant. Social Realism has influenced modern Pragmatism for both are philosophies of life rather than of thought and both have narrow utilitarian end in view.

Sense Realism

In the 17th century through this very spirit of Renaissance, the individualistic attainment and religious, social and reformative influence gave way to the idea of reality comprehended through senses. Sense Realism contains the germs of modern education.

The aims of the sense realists were the following :

(a) to apply inductive method formulated by Bacon for his science in the field of education, with a view to organize and simplify the instructional process, and

(b) to replace the instruction in Latin, by instruction in vernacular and to substitute new scientific and social studies in language and literature.

The Sense Realists emphasised the training of the senses. They held that senses are the conveyers of knowledge, and learning takes place through the operation of the senses, This movement may be called the precursor of scientific tendency in education. The rapid growth in the knowledge of man regarding the world convinced the Sense Realists that Nature is the treasure-house of all knowledge and that this knowledge can be obtained through the training of senses. Their belief led to the formulation of a rudimentary science or philosophy of education and also a tendency to assign linguistic material a secondary place in the curriculum and attach greater importance to the material chosen from natural sciences and contemporary life, This attempt of theirs led to the formulation of Educational Psychology. Though the knowledge of child's mind was very meagre in those days, yet the Sense Realists could assert convincingly that all studies should be adopted to suit the needs and interests of the child, and that "the child should acquire the idea rather than the form and should understand the object before the word, or the word through the object. This led to another change—that of the necessity of the use of vernacular which produced a practical and everlasting form.

The work of the Sense Realists corresponded to the spirit of the day. Distinguished with the futility of the classical learning in the cause of social betterment some people had started a movement, called the "Pansophic Movement" by turning to the new sciences and new methods for finding out a cure for social evils. The new ideals and new methods of the Sense Realists who tried to unify and systematise all knowledge and impart it in very simple inductive way had a great appeal. The use of vernacular in the teaching process made knowledge look comparatively simpler. By means of the new methods a man could master with in a very short time that amount of knowledge which put him to tremendous suffering and cost a considerable amount of time. The new writers placed emphasis on rationality rather than authority.

This attempt to simplify the instructional process led many thinkers in different lands to find out a way whereby education could be simple and easy to be imparted. The German historian Karl Von Raumer called this group of thinkers, 'Innovators'. Their chief pedagogical ideas were as follows :

(i) Education to proceed from simple to complex and from the concrete to the abstract.

(ii) Things before rules and words.

(iii) Students to be taught to analyse rather than to construct.

(iv) Each student to investigate for himself rather than to accept things dogmatically.

(v) Only clearly comprehended things to be memorised.

(vi) Restraint and coercion to be replaced by creation of interest in studies.

(vii) Vernacular to be the medium of instruction.

(viii) The order and course of nature to be discovered and a method based on this to be applied.

BASIC PRINCIPLES OF REALISM IN EDUCATION

Like Idealism and Naturalism, Realism also manifested in different forms in the field of education, but like Idealism and Naturalism it today has a broad meaning and it has also exercised a potent influence on education by emphasising the following basic principles :

(i) Since, we live in a world which is rapidly changing, it is necessary that we remain prepared to adjust ourselves to any psychological, intellectual and social changes that occur at any time.

(ii) A philosophy of education should be based on the realities of life and it can prove its worth by being practical.

(iii) No Ism' can solve problems of education. To be useful, education must be organized by harmonizing values—past and present.

(iv) Things and objects exist independently. Human experience is limited. Truths of science are more reliable.

(v) The surest way of acquiring knowledge is the scientific way, but this does not mean that science has discovered all truths. There might be many truths which have not yet been discovered.

(vi) Curriculum should be many-sided and it should present to the children a rounded view of the universe.

(vii) Like Naturalism, Realism also lays emphasis on sense training, study of science, diversified curricula, catering education to varied interests, making methods of teaching interesting and basic theme on psychological principles.

(viii) Realism places more emphasis on curriculum and contents of studies than on behaviour training like Pragmatism. Education may be defined as behaviour training, but according to realism there is no possibilities of behaviour training without regard to the content of experience.

(ix) By emphasising the independence of objects Realists outlook is more balanced than the Pragmatic view which over estimates the worth of human experience.

CONCLUSION

Realism has exercised a very potent influence on modern education. The movement was not popular in the beginning but gradually it gained momentum and spread to different parts of the world. The increased interest in scientific studies, preference to the study of things before words, faith in the truths of science, enthusiasm for making curriculum broad-based, making methods of teaching interesting, sense training, direct experience—all these bear out influence and contribution of realistic trends of education. Realism places a great emphasis on curriculum and content of studies. As a philosophy it holds our attention while determining the contents of studies and as an educational trend and attitude it influences our thinking with regard to methods of instruction.

9

Eclecticism in Education

We have discussed four major philosophies of education—Idealism, Naturalism, Pragmatism and Realism. Education being a dynamic process, has to conform to the changing norms and ideals of life. Instead of following Certain beliefs and ideologies rigidly, it has to get inspiration from all the philosophies, borrow from each what we feel as functional in the prevailing circumstances and fuse them into a new philosophy suiting the higher values of life. The harmonious blend of different philosophies is called Eclectic Tendency or Eclecticism. It means putting together of various view-points from different philosophies into one comprehensive whole.

NEED FOR ECLECTICISM

Even a casual study will reveal that no educational thinker is exclusively an Idealist, or a Naturalist or a Pragmatist or a Realist. It is only in general sense that an educational system is influenced by a particular school of philosophy. In the words of **Ross**, "most educational systems draw their sustenance from more than one school of philosophical thought, they are to a greater or less degree, eclectic." That is, the educational systems are borrowed freely from various philosophies and not from one philosophy. No one philosophy can be comprehensively complete and correct in every way. There are always trends of education, which call for one label or the other. Rousseau, who was characterised by Adams as perhaps the most prominent Naturalist was labelled by Rusk as an Idealist. While his methods, especially in the early stages of education, were decidedly Naturalistic, his aims were Idealistic. Gandhiji's philosophy of education is, in the words of **Dr. M. S. Patel**, "naturalistic in its setting, idealistic in its aims and pragmatic in its method and programme of work."

Diversity of thought is inherent in human civilizations and cultures, but the unity in diversity is to be found in eclecticism. One ideology can hold true for sometime, some aspect of an ideology can hold true for all times, but no one complete ideology can hold true for all times. Therefore, synthesis and the fusion of diverse ideologies is essential. it is the fusion of the useful, from various sources, that we call eclecticism.

THE CONSENSUS

Consensus means an agreement of some sort which neither sacrifices one's ideology nor leans one to anothers' ideology too much. This type of consensus is essential at all levels, only then we can solve problems successfully. Paradoxical though it may seem, we must agree in order to disagree. In the words of **Brubacher**, "A civilized community is one where people learn to disagree without being disagreeable."

The task before us is to find out certain common points or areas of agreement among the warring philosophies. Without minimising the importance of differences in the basic principles of the four schools of educational philosophy—Idealism, Naturalism, Pragmatism and Realism discussed earlier, we can safety says that these schools have certain areas of agreement as well. There is a consensus of different philosophies in the specific aspects of education like aims, curriculum, methods and discipline.

Aims of Education

While in the ultimate aims of education, the schools of philosophy differ from each other, in the proximate aims they have no variance. All of them endorse the Seven Cardinal Principles of Education as laid down by the Commission on the Re-organization of Secondary Education constituted by the National Education Association of America (1918) The Commission listed the objectives of education as health, command of fundamental processes, worthy home-membership, vocation, citizenship, worthy use of leisure and ethical character. While there is a complete agreement on these objectives, there is a divergence of opinion on the details and the means through which these objectives are to be realised.

None of the school, of educational philosophy denies the child education for individual development and education for social efficiency. While they concede to the child 'self-discovery' and 'self-realization' through 'self-expression', they don't expect him to grow in social vaccum. They visualise him as social individual, enjoying individual freedom and at the same time integrating himself with the general pattern of society. He has to be a 'good man' as well as a 'good citizen'. If the objectives of philosophy are to interpret 'life as it ought to be' and if education is the means to make life fuller and richer, then the educational philosophies can't rebel against 'education for complete living.' In the aim of 'education for complete living' all other aims subsume. No philosophy runs away from this aim. The point of difference among them is on the connotation of the phrase fuller and richer life.

Curriculum

In the matter of curriculum all the philosophies support life-centred education, of course each one of them differing in the Summum Bonum of life. According to them if there can be one 'subject' for education, that subject is life.

In curriculum construction, there is a complete agreement regarding certain fundamental subjects. Nearly all the philosophies recommend humanities, history, geography, sciences, art and various activities. Their ultimate concern is to provide a better sense of human relations, personal adjustment and command of fundamental processes. For this, certain basic subjects form the basis of curriculum construction. All the philosophies of education condemn verbalism and recommend different activities to supplement it.

Methods of Teaching

All the philosophies base their methods on the interest of the child. Education through direct experience has been enuciated by all. Moreover all the philosophies believe in freedom. No philosophy supports the idea of external and strict discipline.

Discipline

With regard to discipline none of the schools of philosophy supports 'repressionism'. 'Freedom' or free discipline is their key word. They espouse 'emancipationism and impressionism.' For them, example of the teacher to regulate the conduct of children is better than precept of the teacher. Conviction rather than coersion, free-discipline rather than imposition, inner urge rather than intimidation to do a thing sum up their theory of discipline. All of them wish the mature children to play their part in making decision about the affairs of the schools. They should not be pushed around against their consent. 'Discipline through knowledge and knowledge through experience' is the under-current of all educational philosophies.

CONCLUSION

In the end we can say that no philosophy stands out exclusively. They are interdependent. Instead of contradicting each other, they complement each other in the interest of the development of the 'whole child', who must grow into balanced, integrated and co-ordinated personality. Therefore, maximum attempt ought to be made to have synthesis among various philosophies. In other words these philosophies should be studied, viewed, interpreted and applied together in a unified manner. The best approach in eclecticism. But the dominant characteristic of each one of these philosophies should not be taken separately. They should be fused into a 'Unity', giving rise to the theory of education which would suit the needs of the day and satisfy loftiest aspirations of the human soul.

10

Jean Jacques Rousseau (1712-1778)

Rousseau was a revolutionary. "Without him," said **Napoleon**, "there would have been no French Revolution." It may equally be admitted that without him there would have been no Social Revolution : at least it would not have come so soon. Rousseau was a revolutionary not only in politics, but he was also a revolutionary in education. A study of Rousseau's educational ideas is, therefore, very much significant for a student of education.

ROUSSEAU'S PHILOSOPHY

Rousseau's philosophy was a reaction against the contemporary social and political set-up which was saturated with formalism, despotism and hypocricy. Rousseau condemned the contemporary systems and denounced civilization in most unequivocal terms. He held society responsible for all evils, religion for all superstitions, and social life for all snobbery and hypocricy that pervaded all around. All governments he declared, were despotic and tyrannical, and man was a victim of prejudices and conventions.

The key-notes to his philosophy are his concepts of 'State of Nature', 'Natural Man' and 'Natural Civilization.' Rousseau has a profound faith in the original goodness of human nature. "Everything", he believes, "is good as it comes from the hands of Author of nature, but everything degenerates in the hands of man." Thus, according to Rousseau, Nature is the only pure, clean and enabling influence. Human society is thoroughly corrupt. Therefore, man should be freed from the bondage of society ; and he should be enabled to live in the "State of Nature." The only civilization he should learn is natural civilization. Human nature is essentially good, and it must be given fullest opportunities of free development. His native tendencies, his instincts and emotions and his inborn capacities must be permitted to be developed freely. The child must be enabled to grow in a free atmosphere.

ROUSSEAU'S EDUCATIONAL PHILOSOPHY

Rousseau's philosophy of education is Naturalistic. He is against a system of conventional and formal education. For Rousseau, education does not mean merely imparting information or storing knowledge. It is not imposition from without, it is development of the child's natural powers and abilities from within.

Doctrine of Negative Education

The essence of Rousseau's philosophy of education is that, since human nature is essentially good, an attempt should be made through by education to preserve its natural goodness ; and it can be done by keeping the goodness of child's nature away from evil. This important thing is not to implant virtue but to preserve the soul from the vices which society puts in the child. It is Rousseau's concept of 'Negative Education'. The doctrine of negative education meant in realm of physical education, a grant of freedom to the body and limbs, simple diet, no medicines and open-air life. In the realm of intellectual training it stood for no formal instruction and 'no reading'. Childhood, he said, is the sleep of reason. So far as moral training is concerned, Rousseau advocated the theory of 'Natural Consequences'.

The Theory of Natural Consequences

The theory of Natural Consequences means that a child should suffer the natural consequences for his mistakes and follies. "If the child is slow in dressing for a walk, leave him at home ; if he breaks a window, let him sit in the cold ; if he disobeys and gets wet, let him have cold ; if he over-eats, let him be sick. In fact let him suffer the natural results of the contravention of the laws of nature." This theory of Natural Consequences has been further discussed under the heading, Rousseau's concept of discipline.

Rousseau's Conception of Educational Aims

According to Rousseau the process of education should facilitate the development of the child's innate powers and capacities. It should not confine the child to the acquisition of knowledge only or prepare him for a particular vocation in life. It should prepare him for life itself. It should make him a man.

Besides this general aim of education, Rousseau, in his book 'Emile', has given specific aims for different stages of education. Emile is divided into five parts. The first four parts contain education for infancy, childhood, boyhood and manhood. In the fifth part, he gives a plan for the education of women.

Education for Infancy (1 to 5 years)

For the period of infancy, Rousseau advocates physical education. He says that since 'all wickedness comes from weakness, the child should be made strong so that he will always keep a restraint upon himself and will not be led into evil ways." He condemns all checks on freedom during this period. The child has a desire for physical activities. His spontaneous growth and training can be facilitated if he is placed under simple, free and healthy conditions. Rousseau regards habit as contrary to impulse. He therefore, insists that child development should not be arrested by any fixed patterns. The child should not be made to talk prematurely. Moreover, plain and simple language should be used with him. The Education of Emile during infancy is to be purely negative and physical. All that the educator is to do, is to protect his instincts and impulses from vice and afford him opportunity for his natural activities.

Rousseau believes that education does not emanate from without infact, it springs from within. The first education should be the free and unrestricted expression of the natural activities of the child in his natural environment.

Education for Childhood (5 to 12 years)

During the period of infancy, attention should be concentrated upon building up good health. No other training is to be given. When the infant grows into a child, he has different needs and he has also acquired some control of his limbs. Hence, during this period attention should be focussed on training the senses and providing opportunities for the exercise of his limbs. No intellectual training during this period is to be given but moral training is to be given by example and through the theory of natural consequences. Education during childhood should be exclusively directed towards the training of senses.

Education for Boyhood (12 to 15 years)

This stage is the pre-adolescent period. So far Emile has been prepared for reviewing knowledge, his organs and powers have been perfected and exercised. He has gained surplus energy which is to be utilized by keeping him busy in instruction, labour and study. Hence, the aim of Education at this stage is to enable Emile to acquire useful knowledge which would satisfy his wants and stand the test of 'practical needs'.

During this period the child should be instructed in Natural Science. But the boy should discover science himself rather than learn it from others. Geography and astronomy should not be taught through maps, globes and other misleading representations. The spirit of inquiry should be stimulated in the child. He should be encouraged to observe the rising and setting sun and the moon during different seasons and draw the inferences himself therefrom. Let him understand the various problems of topography and neighbourhood and find out the solutions. To Rousseau, text books are of no importance for the boy. All valuable knowledge may be acquired most clearly and naturally through one's own experience.

Education for Manhood (15 to 20 Years)

It is during the period of manhood that Emile is to receive moral training. Hitherto his body has been developed and his senses have been trained. During manhood he needs training in human relationships. His sex instinct makes its appearance and it is necessary that he is given proper training in social and moral relationships. Rousseau advocates direct experience with regard to this training as well. For inculcating qualities of sympathy and social sensitiveness Rousseau says that Emile should be taken to infirmaries, hospitals, and prisons because there he can observe the example of human wretchedness at all stages.

He is to observe concrete examples of miseries in all stages, but not so often as to make him hardened. Care, however, is to b taken to ensure that the youth does not become cynical and hyper-critical. For this he should be given lessons in history. History is a study where one sees man simply as a spectator without feeling or passion. No formal instruction in moral education is to be given. Placed in the proper environment Emile would learn things through direct experience. But only contact with concrete things may not produce the desirable sentiments in the youth. Hence, his conduct should be directed on the reward and punishment level through the use of fables and stories ; for by censuring the wrong doer under an unknown mark, we instruct without offending him. If he displays vanity, let him be exposed to flatterers, spendthrifts, and sharpers and allowed to suffer the natural consequences of his acts of omissions and commissions.

Female Education

In the fifth part of Emile, Rousseau has detailed out an education for Sophie who is to become the wife of Emile. By doing that, he expresses his views regarding the education of women.

To him, woman must not possess any individuality of her own. She should be regarded only as subordinate to the nature of man. He says, "The whole education of women ought to be relative to men. To please them, to be useful to them, to make themselves loved and honoured by them, to educate them when young..." The woman should undergo hardships at the hands of man, as the latter should suffer at the hands of nature. She should acquire physical charm by bodily exercise. Woman should be taught sewing, embroidery, lace work and designing so that they may decorate themselves to please men. The wives should be obedient and must be prepared to suffer injuries at the hands of their husbands without any complaint. They should be given religious training at an early age. "Every daughter should have the religion of her mother, and every wife that of her husband." Rousseau does not want that women should learn philosophy, art and science. She is only to learn the technique of pleasing man and to that end she should try to acquire a psychological insight into the nature of man.

Thus, we find Rousseau most radical, naturalistic and individualistic in the education of the boy, but hopelessly traditional throughout in the education of the girl.

Rousseau's Views on Curriculum

Although Rousseau has not set forth any principles underlying the teaching of different subjects in the different stages of Emile's education, yet his discussion of the value of various studies is quite suggestive. Describing the details of education in the first stage, Rousseau maintains that Emile will not be taught the usual subjects, for those do not fulfil the needs of childhood. Children are not capable of learning things which the adults can learn. Their ways of seeing, thinking and feeling are different from those of the adults. So, during the first period of the child's education, parents should pay little attention to positive instruction in the usual subjects, but should see that the child develops physically, has good health, his senses are properly exercised and he gets a chance of cultivating natural habits.

In the second stage, Emile's education is to be primarily negative. There will be no verbal lessons for him, no lessons in languages, history and geography. Emile is to learn by his own experiences. "No book should be used, for Reading is the curse of childhood." There is no place for moral instruction or positive education from five to twelve years, because these require the exercise of reasoning power on the part of the learner and this is not present in an active form during this period. "Childhood is the sleep of reason." Positive education in this stage, consists in imparting physical education through a set of gymnastic exercises and exercises for the training of senses. Rousseau attaches great importance to sense training. He thinks that if the senses are not trained properly, independent reasoning and judgement are impossible.

With his bodily organs and senses trained, Emile is now prepared to receive knowledge in the third stage. Accordingly, he will be taught physical sciences, language, mathematics, manual work, a trade, social relations, music and drawing. The purpose of teaching drawing is to train his eye and muscles, while that of teaching sciences will be to inculcate a heuristic attitude. Some manual work or trade will be taught to develop his powers of judgement, reasoning and cultivate in him habits of neatness, precision and work. Rousseau recommends carpentry and the making of scientific instruments. Social relations will be taught with a view to impressing on him the reciprocal duties of men, the need of co-operation in life and the economic dependence of man on man.

With the beginning of the adolescent period, begins the moral and religious education of Emile. Moral education consists in Emile's learning about his relations with his fellow men and such moral qualities as benevolence, kindness, service and sympathy. Moral education, says Rousseau, is to be preferably given through activities and occupations and not through lectures on Ethics. Besides, moral education, history, religious instruction, aesthetics, physical culture, and sex instruction are to constitute the curriculum in the fourth stage. History will be utilized in the service of moral instruction. Rousseau recommends the study of biography for Emile. Aesthetics is included in the curriculum for the development of taste. Physical training is to be recommended for keeping Emile busy, diligent and hard work. It will keep at bay for a little longer the more dangerous passions. Sex instruction is to consist of direct moral exhortation on chastity and an explanation of the mysteries of creation in the world of plants, animals and men in a dispassionate manner.

Rousseau's Views on the Methods of Teaching

The methods of teaching as suggested implicitly by Rousseau, reflect his Naturalistic Philosophy. He lays stress on direct experience of things and on the principle of 'Learning by doing'. He says, "Teach by doing whenever you can, and only fall back on words when doing is out of the question." Rousseau is a great exponent of the theory of 'self-teaching'. He is deadly against didacticism. He says, "I like not explanations given in long discourses. Young people pay little attention to them and retain little from them. The things themselves ! I shall never repeat often enough that we attach too much importance to words. With our chattering education, we make nothing but chatterers." The teacher is very often inclined to didacticism and moralising. The child can never feel interested in theoretical things. He wants activities. He hates all explanations and lectures from the teacher. He does not like abstract talks. He wants to manipulate concrete objects. Lecturing is the most unscientific and unpsychological method of teaching the young child. Rousseau has done a great service to education by making the school conscious of this wrong method. He advocates the adoption of the Heuristic Attitude which places the child in the position of a discoverer. Emile, for example, is to learn Science in a practical fashion by means of simple experiments performed with apparatus self-made and self-invented. The same principle is to be followed in teaching Mathematics, History, Geography, Social Relations and Morality. While discussing the method of imparting moral instruction to Emile in the fourth stage. Rousseau remarks that the practice of virtue is to count far more than lectures on Ethics. "It is by doing good that one becomes good... occupy your pupil with all the good actions that are in his reach ; let the interests of the poor always be his ; let him assist them not only with purse, but with his personal attention ; let him serve them, protect them, and consecrate to them his person and his time ; let him be their advocate ; he will never have nobler employment." Similarly, Emile will learn about social relations by his actual visits to shops and factories where people engaged in industrial and mechanical arts, will be shown working together, but according to their talents and opportunities. Rousseau, like a modern educator, thinks less of teacher's exposition, much more of the learning experiences of the pupils.

Although Rousseau has not named any principles and methods as such, yet his scheme of education for Emile has furthered and stimulated thought in this direction with the result that we have now such methods as the Laboratory Method, the Heuristic Method and such principles of teachings and learning as those of learning by doing and learning through sense experience.

Rousseau's Concept of Discipline

Rousseau's cry is "freedom" and "absence of restraint" for Emile. It is only in an atmosphere of freedom that Emile can develop his innate powers spontaneously. Impositions are of no use Punishments have no value as the child has no conception of right or wrong or of the 'why' of punishment awarded to him. The child's reasoning power is not so developed. He wants children to have their own way and suffer the unavoidable consequences or inevitable reactions of their conduct. He believes in discipline according to natural consequences. He says, "Allow the child to suffer the natural results of his own acts, without the intervention of human being to protect or to punish." The child is thus to suffer the consequences of his actions and he will set himself right. If he breaks a window-pane, let him sit in the cold wind that gushes in as a result of his folly. If he climbs a tree, let him fall and learn not to attempt it." Rousseau goes to this extent if the child puts his hand into fire, let him burn his hand and learn by the natural consequences of his fault not to do it again. Thus, according to Rousseau, "Children should never receive punishment as such, it should come as a natural consequence of their fault." Rousseau advises the teacher not to intervene in matters of moral guidance as a means of disciplining the child. He contends that the child's nature is essentially good, and any intervention is, therefore, harmful.

ROUSSEAU'S CONTRIBUTION

Rousseau's contribution to the theory as well as practice of education is indescribable. There is hardly any side of education which his philosophy did not affect. He challenged traditionalism in education on all fronts. He questioned the traditional aims of education, the traditional curriculum, the traditional methods of teaching and traditional concept of discipline.

Rousseau rendered a great service to the educand, by psychologising education. He emphasised that the education of the child must be based on the study of his nature and organized in conformity with it. He rightly stressed that traditional aims, rigorous discipline, and telling method can never produce good educational results. Full and free development of the child's inner powers alone should be the aim of education.

Rousseau stressed the fact of individual differences between the child and child, as also between one stage of development and another in the case of same child. This concept exercised a marked influence on the determination of the curriculum and methods of teaching at different stages.

Movement for learning by direct experiences of things and heuristic teaching have been the contribution of Rousseau. It is he, who awakened the educator to the need of introducing physical activities and sense training in the education of the children.

Rousseau emphasised the goodness of the child's nature and as such advocated complete freedom for him. This attitude virtually laid the foundation of all later and modern movements for self-education. He gave a death blow to authoritarianism in education.

Thus, one of the most important contributions of Rousseau is his assertion that the child is a positive factor in education. The function of education is to ensure his proper development at each stage of his growth. Rousseau's ideas inspired the thinking of Pestalozzi, Herbart, Forebel and many other educational thinkers of the 19th Century, who expanded them further and adopted them for class-room practices.

It may be summed up in the words of **Ross**. "Rousseau was decidedly contrary in his attitude towards established institutions... Certainly he has irritated many people, but, like Socrates, he has been a gadfly stinging his contemporaries and his successors into thought. He was the fore-runner of so many, who have followed in the trails he blazed through the forest, until now they have become the broad-highway of common travel." Certain it is that the educational ferment he started has not died down even yet.

11

Fredrick August Froebel (1782-1852)

Froebel follows Rousseau when he wants to take shelter in 'nature' but with a different motive. While, Rousseau considers nature as a great teacher, Froebel wants that man should become intimate with it, not so much with reference to the outer forms of her phenomena as with reference to the spirit of God that lives in her and rules over her.

FROEBEL'S PHILOSOPHY

Froebel's philosophy is a philosophy of Absolute Idealism. He assigns high place to Spiritual Education and the inherent worth of the individual. The key-point in his philosophy is that there is a fundamental unity of existence of nature and man in the absolute which is Self-conscious Spirit. He believes that the purpose of all existence is to reveal God.

The two great ideals that he preached are "Unity in Diversity" and "his theory of development."

Unity in Diversity

Froebel views the whole universe as a unity emanating from the Absolute or God. He remarks, "In all things there lives and reigns an enternal law. This all—controlling law is necessarily based on all pervading, energetic, living, self-conscious and hence eternal unity. This unity is God. All things have come from the Divine Unity (God), they have their origin in the Divine Unity. The Divine affluence that lives in each thing is the essence of each thing." Within this all-inclusive unity, Froebel includes every existing thing viz. man, animal, plant, inanimate object and human society. Each one of these is an individual and also a unity. All of them are bound into one great cosmic unity, which may be called God or a Spiritual Being. He says that "in everything there works and stirs one life, because to all, one God has given life. Every creature, every object is matter informed by spirit... God is the pre-supposition, the condition of their existence. Without God they would not exist. God is the one ground of all things. God is the all comprehending, the all sustaining. God is the essential nature, the meaning of the world."

From this follows his principle that there is unity in man, nature and God. "Nature and man," seem to him "mutually explaining each other through all their numberless various stages of development." Man should become conscious of the Absolute Unity of the universe. He should also know the diversity of things and appearances which are perpetually unfolding them selves within that unity. The varied phenomena in man's life, work, thought and position, he believes, can be summed up in the unity of man's existence. Therefore, the purpose of education, according to him is to expand the life of the individual until it should comprehend this existence.

Theory of Growth

His theory of development is very clear and consistent. Froebel says that there is an Absolute goal towards which all things are growing. This Absolute is present but only implicitly in every existing thing. Development or growth of anything consists in making this Absolute explicit by a gradual unfolding process. The absolute goal, he says, is realised through the presentation of symbols which represent the various aspects of the Absolute. Without such symbols the conception of the Absolute is not possible. Those symbols, he calls "gifts", a reference to which would be made later.

His doctrine of development is that everything develops according to a universal or creative force. May be animal, vegetable or mineral, they have a drive to develop along those lines suited to their characteristics. By development he does not mean "an increase in bulk or quantity (though it may include this), but an increase in complexity or structure, an improvement in power, skill and variety in the performance of natural function". To him, "a thing appears fully developed when its internal organization is perfect in every detail and when it can perform all its natural actions or functions perfectly."

Applying the theory of development to mind, he says, that mind is developed when it has the power, skill and variety in dealing with knowledge and putting knowledge to all its natural uses. To Froebel mental growth is organic. In order to make a plant grow, we induce it to become active in its own natural way. We may seek shortening the duration of time needed for its growth, but we have to stimulate the plant's own activity. The activity of a thing's own self is self-activity. Knowing, feeling and willing are the three major activities of the mind. Exercises directed towards mental development must be in complete accord with the process of knowing, feeling and willing, and at the same time proportionately balanced according to their strength. We find the result better, if the activity is that of the whole mind.

To Froebel, the soul itself is an activity. To be active is inherent in our nature. With our birth, we bring certain tendencies which always prompt us to action. Thus, mind is a purposive activity. Froebel believes that mind is a unity, just as life is also a unity. Mind has no independent faculties. All its powers and forces are organically related like branches and leaves of a tree. For sound mental growth of the child, Froebel suggests that there should be no gulf between home and school. The influences of the two should be organically connected. Otherwise, the purpose of education is sure to be defeated.

Froebel contends that the unity between the various stages of mental growth—infancy, childhood, youth, manhood—should not be lost sight of, otherwise education would be of no avail. There should be a connection between the various activities of the mind and the various aspects of life. Froebel calls this relation between the two "inter-connectedness." The realization of this inter-connectedness should constitute one great aim of education.

FROEBEL'S PHILOSOPHY OF EDUCATION

Froebel's philosophy of education is the direct outcome of his general philosophy.

Let us now discuss his Educational Philosophy.

His Concept and Aims of Education

Education, he says, is a development by which the individual realizes that he is one unit of the all-encompassing unity. It is "a development by which his life broadens, until it has related itself to nature, until it enters sympathetically into all activities of society ; until it participates in the achievements of the race and aspiration of humanity." Education, he advocates, is but the realization of the evolutionary process in its highest stage, which the individual should attain. Such development takes place "in accordance with eternal, self-governed and self-developing laws. Thus, he believes that development proceeds through the divine self. The aim of education should be that the child should develop according to his natural and systematic course of development. Education has failed, if it has neglected or prevented the development of certain aspects of the child's nature or if it has caused 'the distortion of originally good human powers and tendencies by arbitrary interference. If the child's nature has somehow been marred, it should be redirected into the original course of development. If the child displays activities contrary to the true principle of growth, they must be recognised and corrected in order to keep the development progressing along the right lines. Thus, according to Froebel education should be a 'Controlled Development'.

Instruction, he commends, should lead the child's spontaneous activities and native interests to some tangible expression of the knowledge. "Education seeks neither to eliminate nature, nor to leave it severely alone." It helps nature and guides it to attain higher ends.

Stages of Development in Education

Like Rousseau, Froebel recognises in education, the stages of development and desires that each one of the stages—infancy, childhood, boyhood and youth—should be fully exploited to prepare the pupil for the succeeding stages. While in infancy, be emphasizes the sensory development, in childhood his emphasis is on play. While childhood is characterised by making the internal external, in boyhood the process is reversed. Education in boyhood has to be determined by environment and not by endowment as in childhood. Feeling now gives way to thought and play to instruction. It is now to be curriculum-centred and not child-centred. The characteristic activity of childhood is play, but that of boyhood should be work. The child takes interest in the process, the boy takes interest in the product. The range of the pupil's environment in boyhood is considerably widened. This provides him with new patterns of activities in the shape of vocational occupations to be imitated and learnt through training. Of course, this work is not those of adults. Learning of some vocation should still be dominated by the spirit of play and not work. The only difference between the two stages is that in childhood the pupil intended domestic activities, in boyhood he imitates neighbourhood occupations. His activities, now, are Projects—practical problems, demanding co-operative effort and giving intellectual and moral training.

The Curriculum

All-round development being his aim, of education, Froebel wants that the curriculum at the boyhood stage should consist of four main divisions : (a) Religion : religion he says, should be the basis of all education. No other knowledge is possible without it. (b) Natural Science : nature, he has often repeated, is the manifestation of God. Its study will mean the contemplation of outer facts, while religion requires inner contemplation. Therefore, both are necessary to have a complete man. Insight into nature, reveals the laws that govern human life. This creates a sense of the reign of law. "From every object of nature and life there is a way to God." In this study of Natural Science, he also emphasises the importance of Mathematics. In his opinion this subject is a connecting link between the mind of man and the natural world. Mind and Mathematics, he says, are inseparable as the soul and religion. (c) Languages : these help in establishing the inner living connection among the diversities of things and thus complete the work of education. (d) expressional work : Froebel believes that there is need for the expression of the soul in outward forms. This expression may take the form of singing, drawing, painting and modelling. The school does not aim at "making each pupil an artist in some one or all of the arts but to secure to each human being full and all-sided development."

Importance of Play

Play of childhood is of paramount importance. It is a nature's device for directing the growth of the child according to the social pattern. Childhood is a period of play and not of work. Play, says **Froebel** is "the highest phase of child-development—of human development at this period ; for it is self-active representation of the inner impulse. Play is the purest, most spiritual activity of man at this stage... It gives, therefore, joy, freedom, contentment, inner and outer rest, peace with the world. It holds the source of all that is good."

Play, if it is to have any educative value, should not be motivated by any ulterior purpose. However, it needs to be organised and controlled by suitable materials in order to harmonise the feelings and the activities of the children while engaged in activities. "Without rational conscious guidance", **Froebel** says, "childish activity degenerates into aimless play instead of preparing for those tasks of life for which it is destined."

Value of Hand Work

According to Froebel all constructive work should be the beginning and the end of the educational process. Rousseau recognises industrial training on social and economic grounds. Pestalozzi introduced manual activities for developing sense perception. Froebel emphasizes the manual and industrial training because, it gives expression to some of the most dominant urges of the child. All constructive work, he believes, manifests outwardly what the child feels inwardly. Such manifestation of ideas is the basis of the higher power of expressing the intellectual, moral and spiritual life in action.

Nature Study

Similarly, he commends the introduction of the Nature-study in the school curriculum. By prescribing this study, he is the least concerned with the facts about nature. He desires that the child should "have moral improvement, religious uplift and spiritual insight", by coming into contact with nature. Nature-study affords the child opportunities for varied activity. It suggests material for reading, 'language work', constructive work and number work. He does not want nature to be analysed and dissected. He wants to study nature as life the plant as development, the animal as acting, the organ as functioning.

Froebel's Theory and Practice of Kindergarten

Froebel, in his conversation with the teachers under-training at Burg-dorf, learnt that the pre-school age of the children was entirely neglected. His conception of harmonious development led him to attach great importance to early years and his work, "The Education of the Man", chiefly deals with the education of children. It became obvious to him that all school education was yet without a proper initial foundation and he realised that until the education of nursery years was reformed nothing solid and substantial could be achieved. It was at Burg-dorf that he began to think over the training of children and prepared for them a gradual course of exercises, modelled on the games in which the children were interested.

Chief Characteristics of Kindergarten

The chief characteristics of Froebel's method are

(a) Self-activity.

(b) Creativeness.

(c) Social participation.

1. Self-Activity

By self-activity, Froebel means that the child should not be forced to indulge in any activity which is suggested by parents or teachers, but in those, whereby he can satisfy his own impulses and fulfil his desires. Education, he believes, is a process of individual growth which is directed by inner forces in the child. This growth differs from that of a plant, as the child has perception and reason. He can be made conscious of the working of God within him. Froebel believes that the divine spirit reveals itself in the activities of the child, if these activities are spontaneous.

The teacher should provide appropriate experiences for such purpose. But, while directing the process, he must follow nature ; never thwart it, for he is but nature's assistant. "Education" says **Froebel**, "should not be prescriptive, categorical or interfering. It should provide for "free self-activity and self-determination on the part of man—the being created for freedom in the image of God."

Self-activity arises out of one's own interests and is sustained by one's own power. It alone can lead to the evolution of mind and can secure the aim of education. It is, therefore, essential that all processes of educational instruction must originate with the interests of the child. The child must be stimulated to achieve certain ends through spontaneous activities if they are properly directed and influenced by the teacher. Fuller harmony between the inner and outer, between the thought and the external world cannot be created, if the child is not aided by the teacher. Self-activity manifests in the child, a desire to enter into life around it, the desire to help, to find out, to discover and to participate in the affair of daily life. Froebel believes that there is no conflict between theory and practice and no discrepancy between ideas professed and the actions performed.

2. Creativeness

With self-activity, is connected Froebel's principle of 'creativeness'. Through creativeness, new forms and combinations are made and expression is given to new images and ideas. He says, "plastic material representation in life and through doing, united with thought and speech, is by far more developing and cultivating than the merely verbal representation of ideas." Man, he says, is by nature an active and dynamic being. He is not a receptive and passive observer of events. He must create something. Thus, according to Froebel, the result of education consists in what the child gives out from within himself. It does not consist in what the child learns from outside. Each child has a tendency to make new forms and combinations which suggest the new ideas and images arising in him. The child produces something which may appeal to the adult as absurd and meaningless. But the divine principle is active in the child as well as the adult. So whatever he produces follows from some ideas connected with his creative urge. Thus, Froebel concludes that the best development of self-activity is essentially creative. He devotes special attention to this attribute of creativeness in the child.

3. Social Participation

Whereas Rousseau advocates isolated and un-social education for 'Emile', Froebel lays great emphasis on the social participation. He believes that increasing self-realization or individualisation through self-activity comes through a process of socialization. The social instinct being a primary instinct of man, the individual can be truly educated only in the company of other human beings. Man's life is bound up with participation in institutional life. The home, the school, the church, the vocation, the state—all are the medium for individual activity and a means of social control. The school, says Froebel, is an association for the child, wherein he discovers in a,simplified and idealised form the relations of society. It is a means of social progress and individual development. Similarly in the society a child receives the development and also prepares for the future life. Through imitation of co-operative activities in play, he obtains not only physical but also intellectual and moral training. His growth, therefore, should be in harmony with the unity and purpose of humanity to which he belongs.

A New Method of Teaching

According to Froebel the child expresses his feelings and ideals through singing, gestures and constructing objects. He, accordingly, believes that everything to be taught to the child must be expressed to him through singing, gestures and construction. This is a unique device which Froebel most remarkably invented. He recommends that history should be taught through dramatization or through songs. Froebel aims at stimulating the child's imagination and thought by placing concrete things before him.

However, the teacher should be very careful in the selection of songs, games and pictures, because the child feels very much amused by them and tries to express himself while he is in their association. Froebel does not regard songs, gestures and construction as isolated means to educate the child. He thinks of them as three co-ordinate forms of expression in the child. He saw an organic relation between them. The whole process becomes one organic whole. For example, when the story is told or read, it is first expressed in song, then it is dramatised in movements and gestures and finally it is illustrated by constructive work from blocks, paper, clay or other material. In this way ideas are given, "thought stimulated, the imagination verified, the hands and eyes trained, the muscles co-ordinated, and the moral nature strengthened." In the Kindergarten all efforts are put into concrete objective forms. The higher motives and, sentiments are aroused.

Gifts and Occupations

Gifts and occupations are the other means which Froebel used in the Kindergarten system. The gifts suggest to the child some forms of activity. They are arranged in an order to be determined by the principle of development. Occupations are the activities suggested by the gifts. The very order and arrangement of the gifts lead the child from the activities and thoughts of one stage to those of another.

The First Gift

The first gift consists of a box of six woollen balls of different colours. The child is to roll them about in play. Rolling is the occupation. These woollen balls are meant to give to the child an idea of colour, particular stuff, form, motion and direction.

The Second Gift

In the second gift there are a cube, a sphere and a cylinder of hard wood. In occupation with these things the child marks the difference between the movements of the different articles. He sees that the cube is stable and the sphere is unstable. He also notices that the cylinder is stable in certain positions and unstable in others. Thus, the cylinder is noticed as possessing the quality of both the cube and the sphere. It is a concrete example of harmony of two opposite things in one.

The Third Gift

In the third gift there is a large wooden cube divided into eight equal parts. These cubes are meant to make the children understand the relation of part with the whole. From these cubes the child may make a number of objects such as chairs, tables, benches, and stairs etc.

The Other Gifts

Among the other gifts are included sticks and rings. While playing with these gifts the child gets the ideas of lines, surface points and their inter-connections. The child has to engage himself in making a number of constructions with papers, sand, clay, wood and other materials.

The Role of the Teacher

In the Kindergarten one should not think that the teacher is to remain entirely passive. As a matter of fact, his responsibility is not lessened in any way. While the children are offered gifts, the teacher has to suggest the occupation connected with them. He has to demonstrate certain activities to them.

Froebel's socialistic and liberalizing tendencies were not liked by governmental authorities during his days and the Kindergarten system of education was banned.

CRITICISM OF FROEBEL'S EDUCATIONAL THEORY AND PRACTICE

The following have been the chief points of criticism raised by some educators against Froebel's educational theory and practice.

(1) Many critics hold that Froebel's law of evolution does not explain definitely how to proceed in the development of child's life.

(2) Froebel's emphasis upon play in education cannot be acceptable because it detracts the child from serious learning.

(3) Froebel's insistence upon play, constructive work, and many other subjects has under-rated the importance of true knowledge and leads to a disrespect for learning.

(4) Some criticise Kindergarten methods because of over-emphasis on form and mathematical knowledge. He presents the gifts. He sings a song connected with them and thereby tries to help the child to form appropriate ideas. The songs and pictures used by Froebel are crude and rough.

FROEBEL'S CONTRIBUTION

No educational theory has been followed more faithfully in actual practice than that of Froebel. Therefore, modem education will ever remain indebted to him. Almost all modern tendencies in education can be traced back to what Froebel stood for a century ago. We may not agree with many educational procedures outlined by Froebel, but it was he who first drew the attention of the society towards the education of very young children. The formalism of the Kindergarten system may be subject to many criticisms. But its methodical arrangement of plays and occupations invited the active interest of many who lack the spirit of the master to give 'play' a place into school.

We admit that the songs and pictures used by Froebel are crude and rough, but he never meant that they should not be improved upon. He gave direction to the teacher to modify songs and pictures suiting the needs of the time. The underlying principles of Froebel's philosophy may not be intelligible at times, but his doctrines are of immense practical use. Just as Jesuists and Comenius introduced a systematic methodology of instruction, similarly, Froebel gave a methodology of play to be applied in educational procedure.

The educational ideologies of Froebel were deeply coloured by the philosophy and scientific principles of his time. The essence of his contribution to education may be put in the words 'self-activity' and 'creativeness'. The meaning of these words is being understood more and more as time passes on. Froebel stood for the recognition of the child's individuality in the school. Now the school is being regarded as a place where the teacher should try to discover the individuality of the child and devise means to develop the same activities, such as, play, songs, and making objects etc. have been given an importance in the learning process of the child. Needless to say that all these tendencies in modern education may be traced back to Froebel's fundamental doctrines.

Froebel's permanent contributions to education may be summarised in the following :

1. Inner self-activity directs the development of the child.

2. The natural course of evolution of the child's activities should be the main guide in the education of the child.

3. Early education should be organised around play.

4. The child's physical, mental and moral powers should be developed and harmonized through constructive activity.

5. Spontaneity and social control may be harmonized through creative activity.

6. The curriculum should be based on activities and interests of children.

7. The education of women should be regarded as essential for the development of the human race.

8. Education can ensure the future evolution of mankind.

9. Knowledge should not be considered as an end in itself. It should be evaluated in terms of the activities of the individual.

CONCLUSION

In conclusion, we may say that it was Froebel who said that education is a natural process, that the child is an organic whole in itself, is an integral part of the society and that the whole universe is an organism of which all smaller organisms are members. His faith in man's relationship with nature, his advanced scientific thought, his belief that human life should be in harmony with the universal spirit are his greatest contributions. He was the first modern educator who stood for spiritual evolution. Education to him is the process by which the race and the individual evolve to higher and higher levels. His emphasis on 'Play', 'Self-activity' and 'Creativeness' have gone a long way in changing the concepts and practice of educational theory.

12

John Dewey (1859-1952)

While Rousseau stressed the original nature of the child and Froebel idealised his spiritual nature, the social aspect of education was left to Dewey who stressed that education is a process of living in society. John Dewey, the American philosopher, psychologist and great teacher, challenged the old static cold-storage ideal of knowledge; he brought education more in accord with the activities of the present day life ; brought fusion of psychological and sociological aspects of education.

DEWEY'S PHILOSOPHY

Dewey is a Pragmatist, holding that all thought is subordinate to action. Philosophy is only a means to guide the individual to live his practical life successfully. No opinion, belief, hypothesis or principle is worth anything unless it works—that is, serves some practical purpose. No philosophy is true in its own right, unless it helps man in solving the practical problems of his life. Truth is thus nothing eternal, absolute or unchangeable ; it is purely purposive, changeable, relative and practical.

Dewey emphasizes the importance of science and of scientific methods as central in determining approach to human affairs of all kinds. In the scientific method, he found principles and procedures that gave him the concepts of experience. According to him, knowledge and thinking are closely associated with action. People ordinarily believe that knowledge arises apart from action and regard it as an independent existence. Dewey does not agree with this point of view. He believes that knowledge can never arise apart from action. It is only as a result of action that knowledge is acquired. For Dewey the only reality is one's experience of objects, physical and social surroundings around him. It is through experience that true knowledge increases and the modification of one's behaviour takes place. Such modification determines and modifies his subsequent experience.

Dewey believes that "all knowledge has come as a result of activities of individuals in their struggle for existence. The struggle for shelter, food and clothing resulted in certain activities which ultimately formed certain tendencies as instincts, impulses and interests which are inherited by each individual and transmitted from generation to generation." These inherited tendencies are not as fixed and definite in human individuals as they are in the animals. These tendencies are general urges which prompt the individual to respond to the various stimuli present in the environment. It is through the play of these tendencies or general urges that human intelligence has developed to its present level. Therefore, Dewey thinks that the natural play of these tendencies should be considered as the starting point of the educational process of the child.

Dewey was convinced of the organic relationship between the individual and the society. He wants the individual to commune not with nature alone hut with his fellow-beings and to understand and appreciate their achievements. The environment of the individual is both natural and human. He should value the one as much as the other. The self, he believes, cannot grow in solitude. Nor can it grow in the mere contact with nature. For the growth of man, it is essential that he should live with the rest of mankind. This is a natural condition. The make up of individual includes reflections of a multitude of man ; his thoughts are their thoughts. Just as the knowledge of the physical world has led man to control the physical world to some extent, similarly the understanding of social inter-relationship brings about maximum human development.

DEWEY'S PHILOSOPHY OF EDUCATION

Dewey defines education as the "development of all those capacities in the individual which will enable him to control his environment and fulfill his possibilities." It is a process that begins with the very birth of the child, and goes on throughout the whole life. It is a process which has two sides—one psychological and the other sociological. Of these two, the psychological is the basis.

The Psychological Factor in Education

Dewey regards the child as the core of the whole educational process. He says, "Education must begin with a psychological insight into the child's capacities, interests and habits. We must know what they mean. They must be translated into terms of their social equivalents—into terms of what they are capable of in the way of social service." Dewey looks at the child's capacities and interests in a social context, thinking that it is in the social context alone that they can be developed. Dewey speaks of four instincts or fundamental interests of the child, viz., (i) the interest in conversation, (ii) the interest in inquiry or finding out things, (iii) the interest in construction, (iv) the interest in artistic expression.

Dewey thinks that the child's interest in conversation is the greatest of all educational resources. But all these four interests may be accepted as the basis of the curriculum of the school, because these represent the great racial activities, such as communicating each other's thoughts procuring food, obtaining shelter, and making clothing. Dewey believes that if education is conducted on these lines, the child will develop into a healthy personality and will acquire such traits as will help him in reconstructing new experiences.

The Social Factor in Education

Dewey can not conceive of an individual apart from the society. To him, both the individual and the society exist at the same time. It is only by living in a society that the individual becomes human and acquires the necessary modes of responses and conduct which make him an individual. If the individual is dependent upon society, the society, too, is an organic unity of individuals. The activities of the individual centre round social inter-course, relations and interactions. Whereas, Dewey starts with psychological basis—child's instincts and innate powers, the sociological side to him is equally important, perhaps more. The knowledge of the social conditions is essential for the proper appraisal and assessment of the child's powers. "All education proceeds by the participation of the individual in the social consciousness of the race." The social consciousness continually shapes and modifies the individual's powers and personality. Dewey maintains that the child is to live in and for the society to which he belongs, hence the stimulation of the child's powers, through the social medium, constitutes true education. The social medium is educative because it affects every fibre of one's character and mind, forms habits of language and enlarges vocabulary, cultivates social manners and conduces to good taste and aesthetic appreciation. At birth, the child's capabilities are undeveloped. They are developed as he begins to take increasingly greater interest in home and other social activities. In the beginning, the activities of the child are self-centred. Therefore, he must be helped to realise the ends and purposes of society. For this, it is necessary to organise the school for co-operative activities. Thus, Dewey has emphasized the need of reorganizing the school programme for promoting community work. This idea of socialization is Dewey's educational contribution of the highest importance.

Dewey's Concept of the Aims of Education

Dewey does not believe in an 'ultimate aim of education'. In his 'Democracy and Education' writing on education he says, "It has all the time an immediate end, and so far as activity is educative, it reaches that end—the direct transformation of the quality of experience. Infancy, youth, adult life—all stand on the same educative level in the sense that what is really learned at any and every stage of experience constitutes the value of that experience..." Thus, Dewey finds the aim of education in the process itself. The aim of education is not to reach any pre-fixed final goal. In fact, the aim is the immediate end that attracts and engages the learners' attention. Education is to re-make experience. Hence, it always tends to move further towards new activities and reorganisation of experience. As **Dewey** says, "The process of education is a continuous process of adjustment, having as its aim at every stage an added capacity of growth." The individual has always to re-adjust himself to the environment. So long as such process of re-adjustment is continued, education goes on. Since, this readjustment never stops, and the individual is always in the process of learning things, education never stops in life. Evidently, no such final goal or end of education can be conceived at which education can be considered to have been completed. Further more, the aim of education is not to be determined by the teacher. It is the child himself who has to determine or choose his own aim.

Dewey emphasises that education is life itself, and not preparation for life. A remote aim of education can not be appealing to the child. It is only an immediate aim that can be interesting to him. The whole process of education becomes discouraging to the child, if he is required to put in efforts for an aim which is not immediate, pertaining to his felt need. The child lives in the present. The future is meaningless to him. Hence, it is absurd to expect him to do things for some future preparation. As the child lives in the present, the educative process will be naturally based on the present needs and interests of the child.

Functions of Education

Discussing the functions of education Dewey holds that education is a necessity of life. It is needed for living a socially desirable life. It is that power which bridges the gulf between the innate nature of the immature child and the social standards and demands made upon him. It gives him social consciousness through the school as a special environment. The school as a special environment has been deliberately planned with a view to realizing some social purpose. The ordinary environment of the child is too complex to be assimilated properly or to influence the mental and moral disposition of the child. The school will simplify this environment by eliminating its unworthy features and "will co-ordinate the diverse influences of the various social environments into which the child enters—family, street, workshop, religious associations etc." The school as a special environment will cultivate, within the young, the attitudes and dispositions which are necessary for a continuous and progressive life in society.

Not only does education perform the social function through the school as a special environment, it directs, guides and controls the inborn propensities of the child. These propensities have to be directed in socially desirable channels or sublimated. The undesirable expressions of these innate propensities have to be controlled. But this control or restraint, according to Dewey, should not be alien to the child's nature ; it should not amount to repression.

Education helps the child in the process of growth by enabling him to form habits and sentiments wherewith the child can control his environment and his native impulses. This growth is not a accretion or storage of ideas from without, it is the unfolding of the innate powers from within. Thus, education is, as **Dewey** says, growth and all one with growing. This is so because the child is an ever-growing and changing personality.

Besides these functions, education constantly re-organises or reconstructs the human experience. It preserves that much of the experience which is valuable and re-weaves it in the light of present needs and demands. This function of re-weaving and re-vitalizing the social fabric or heritage is performed through special agencies like the school. The child who is an ever-growing individual, too, takes part in this function of re-construction. The growing child selects and reorganises his cultural heritage according to his own needs in a changing and new world. It is for this reason that his creativity needs to be encouraged.

Dewey's Conception of an Ideal School

Dewey regards school as an institution, essential to social life. To him, school is an absolute social necessity. The school is not a place where some knowledge is imparted and an attempt is made to develop certain habits in children. For Dewey, the school is a place where the child learns by his own experiences. At the school the child will make many experiments in life, in order to learn how his life is directly dependent on the continued growth of the society. As a social institution, the school will try to develop a social consciousness in the child. So that he may be able to derive the maximum benefit from what the society has to offer him. The school should try to develop in the child powers which he can use for furthering the ends of the society as a whole.

The school is to be a representative of the society outside it. As already mentioned in a different context. According to **Dewey**, "The school is to be a reflection of the larger society outside its walls, in which life can be learnt by living. But it is to be a purified, simplified and better balanced society."

Dewey's ideal school will not cut the child off from the home. It will gradually grow out of the home life. It will preserve, continue and rebuild the activities with which the child is familiar in the home. It should reflect the ideal home and its conditions, should re-touch them if needed, in order to give them more perfect form and scientific garb. Dewey would like his school to be a genuine community like the family where the pupils are engaged in common pursuits and educative experiences. "The school, in fact, should be an enlarged family, in which discipline the child receives more or less accidentally at home is continued in a more perfect form with better equipment and more scientific guidance."

Dewey's school will be a place where moral education is provided not in the form of separate lessons, but through its social and conjoint activities. He thinks that "the best and deepest moral training is precisely that which one gets through having to enter into proper relations with others in a unity of work and thought."

The school should try to make the society conscious of its own needs, by giving the people a clearer conception of the needs and problems of the modern life. As such, the school is to provide ideals in the light of which these needs will be determined. But these ideals will not be divorced from the life of the community ; they will arise out of it.

The Place of the Teacher

What is the place of the teacher in the ideal school? Dewey has answered this question in his own way. Unlike Rousseau, Dewey gives an important place to him. He is a social servant whose duty is to maintain a proper social order and to see that the children grow in a social atmosphere. The teacher is not to impose his personality or his ideology on the child. His business is to select the influences which should enrich the child's experience and to help him in properly reacting and responding to such influences. Even in the matters of discipline, he is to simply guide the child on the basis of his richer experience and riper wisdom.

Dewey's Conception of the Curriculum

We may infer from the above account that Dewey has no sympathy with the traditional curriculum. Dewey does not like the division of knowledge into isolated branches. He says that "we violate the child's nature and render difficult the best ethical results, by introducing the child too abruptly to a number of special studies, of reading, writing, geography etc." To Dewey, it is the child's own activities, around which the school subjects should be organised, and not around science, literature, history or geography. It is with the 'activities' that the child has participated in the home that the school should begin its work, and not with the teaching of reading, writing and arithmetic **Dewey** says, "the beginning is made with child's expressive activities in dealing with the fundamental social material—housing (carpentry) ; clothing (sewing) ; food (cooking) ; these direct modes of expression... bring out the factors of social communication—speech, writing, reading, drawing, modelling etc." Thus, the curriculum in the primary school should be organised according to the fourfold interests of the child—in conversation, inquiry, construction and artistic expression.

According to **Dewey**, the curriculum should consist of "educative experiences and problems". The aim is to enrich the experiences already gained by him. The problems should be so organised as to inspire the pupil to add to the existing knowledge and ideas. It should be noted that Dewey uses the word 'educative experiences' in a special sense. According to Dewey, only those experiences are educative which pay due regard to the natural inclinations of the child in the context of the social, political, physical and economic conditions of the community. According to him, "an educative experience is creative and leads to further experience. It has the power of modifying the experiences and the modification thus effected, affects the subsequent experiences." An educative experience subordinates books teachers and apparatus to the natural inclinations of the pupil and takes into consideration the social, economic, political, physical and occupational conditions of the community.

Besides laying down the general principles of the choice of subjects,in the school, Dewey has advised us as to how to organise the curriculum. He suggests that it develops critical discrimination and the ability to reason. But this will be possible, Dewey says, if different subjects are taken from the materials of day to day life, the subject-matter of each subject links the present with the past and they are taught in such a away that their usefulness in the immediate present is emphasized. Moreover, different subjects should be naturally correlated and, therefore, they should not be presented as distinct studies, but as types of the process by which society keeps itself going.

Dewey's Conception of the Methods of Teaching

Dewey's views on method of teaching are in line with his pragmatic philosophy. He emphasises that direct experience is the basis of all method. To him, knowledge should arise from concrete and meaningful situations. Hence, spontaneous activities of the children should provide the natural condition for the growth of knowledge. This means that learning should be the result of doing. Nothing should be learnt directly for its own sake. According to Dewey, the method of teaching should be based on the principles of learning by doing, activity, purpose and connection with the life of the child. It is to integrate the various subjects, his activities and experiences. Kilpatrick, one of the most famous of Dewey's followers, is of the opinion that Dewey had in mind the following rules when be conceived of the project technique.which was later on developed into Project Method by the former.

1. The pupils must propose what they actually wish to do.
2. They should be allowed to do only those things which build up certain attitudes.
3. All learning should be done only, if it is necessary for what the pupils have actually proposed.
4. What the pupils are allowed to do, should be guided so as to enrich the subsequent stream of experience.

Thus, the Project Method of teaching is different from the method employed in traditional schools. It utilizes the child's interests for teaching the various subjects. In the Project Method the child's interests and purposes are the important things, and the various subjects are regarded merely as means for satisfying those interests and purposes.

Dewey's Conception of Discipline

Dewey believes that discipline should be social through and through. The natural impulses of the child ought to be directed and disciplined through the co-operative or conjoint activities of the school. "Out of doing things that are to produce results, and out of doing in a social and co-operative way, there is born a discipline of its own kind and type." It is such a discipline that will lead to character training, not the discipline that is the result of force, imposition or authoritative instruction. Dewey believed that the child's activities—intellectual, social, moral and physical, are disciplinary in their effects if they are carried out in co-operation with others and are directed towards the realization of certain purposes. Discipline is inherent in the relation of members of the school society in pursuit of common ends.

The teacher's duty is to provide the right type of physical environment that will enrich the child's experience and will direct his activities in a co-operative manner. The individual will thus develop social attitudes, social interests and social habits. Even his will will be socialised. Thus, according to Dewey, the main purpose of school discipline is the cultivation in the pupils of social attitudes, habits and ideals of conduct through the conjoint activities of the school,which has been organized as a community.

DEWEY'S CONCEPTION OF DEMOCRACY IN EDUCATION

According to **Dewey**, democracy means "equality of opportunity for every one ; it means freeing intelligence for independent effectiveness, the emancipation of the mind as an individual organism to do its own work." It does not simply mean freedom of action. The freedom of action must be preceded by freedom of thought.

Dewey wants that education should reflect democratic principles on all sides. Teachers, in a democratic system of education, will have some regular say in matters of school organization, selection of text books and others. The school authorities, managers and supervisors are not expected to dictate to them in determination of educational methods. Dewey deprecates the minute and close supervision which is exercised on the teacher at present. This will mean restriction of his intelligence and imprisonment of his spirit. It is contended by some critics that teachers, on account of their incompetence and inefficiency, should not be given such powers. Dewey characterises such an injuction as undemocratic.

Dewey disapproves of a system of education which subjects the mind of the child to outside and ready-made material. A democratic system will aim at the development of moral, self-directing individuality. It will encourage his emotional as well as intellectual freedom by providing outlets for his growing intelligence. It will not train children for docility or obedience, but they will be trained to think, to act and to develop qualities of initiative, independence and resourcefulness—qualities of an intelligent citizen in a democracy.

Dewey advocates the employment of methods that give much scope to the child's participation in the process of learning and those which emphasise the child's view-point. The curriculum will undergo change and will stress the subjects that are vocational in character. It is these subjects that will conduce to individual efficiency so necessary for good citizenship in a democracy. Discipline in a democratic system of education will be free and through self-government in the school.

DEWEY'S CONTRIBUTION

Dewey was a great educationist and a great philosopher. He is more for change than for permanence, more for practice than for theory, more for experimental enquiry than for speculation, more for contemplation. One could remark that Dewey under-estimated the action than for significance of ideas. Ideas are more powerful and lasting than actions, the influence of which is limited to a particular time and place.

But whatever the limitations of his philosophy or the way of trying to do without philosophy, we cannot but be grateful to Dewey for his service to education. He emphasised the importance of including activity in education. In fact, he wished activity to be made the medium of all teaching and learning. His contribution to the 'activity movement' in education can never be exaggerated. He stressed learning by doing.

Dewey emphasised the necessity of relating education with the practical life of the child. No lesson can be as useful as the one learnt in the course of an attempt to solve a practical problem of life. Education divorced from the real situations of life is no education at all. To Dewey we owe the credit of stressing the utility or practical value point of view of education.

Dewey emphasised the necessity of studying the capacities and interests of the child, for educating him successfully. He thus stressed the psychological point of view in education. At the same time, he did not fail to emphasise the social sanctions that govern education. He rightly stressed that education is intended to be a means of preserving, transmitting and advancing the culture of the community, and realising its standards and ideals. For the fusion of these two stand points in education, we owe the credit to Dewey.

By denying the existence of any eternal and absolute values, and characterising all values as man-made, Dewey emphasised the need for developing the creative powers of the children. The credit of emphasising the development of the creative powers of the educand, goes to Dewey.

One of the gifts of Dewey is the Project Method. In the Project Method the child's interests and purposes are the important things, and the various subjects are regarded merely as means for satisfying these interests and purposes.

Dewey has rightly stressed the need for devising education in such a manner that it may train the pupils in co-operative activities and democratic living in their community. Training for citizenship forms an integral part of education, and training for citizenship essentially involves training for a vocation.

To sum up, we can say that Dewey challenged the old static cold-storage ideal of knowledge ; he brought education more into accord with the activities of the present day life. **Rusk** remarks, "The general principle underlying the developments in his philosophy and his applications of these in education appears to be that both philosophy and education should reflect the main currents of contemporary thought and incorporate the techniques that have so signally contributed to modern, industrial and social progress." In the words of Russel, Dewey has an outlook which is in harmony with the age of industrialism and collective enterprise.

13

Swami Dayanand Saraswati (1824-1883)

Swami Dayanand Saraswati was a great social and religious reformer of modern India. He was the champion of Arya Samaj movement and its founder. He revived the ancient Vedic Wisdom of India and worked for the upliftment of ignorant masses of his motherland. Truly, he was the saviour of Hinduism and maker of Modern India.

SWAMI DAYANAND'S GENERAL PHILOSOPHY

A thorough protagonist of the Vedic culture and religion, Swami Dayanand Saraswati was shocked to see the apalling condition of his countrymen who leaving his own ancient faith were gradually embracing Christianity and were under the sway of Western Culture. Being pro-Vedic and holding that the life in the Vedic ages had reached its highest level in culture and illumination, and himself being an ardent scholar and a seeker after the ultimate truth, he devoted his whole life in reviving the Vedic studies and discipline in India. He founded the Arya Samaj, because social reform formed an important part of his religion. He laid emphasis on the Vedic knowledge as a means of attaining emancipation, the highest end of life. He tried to revive the Vedic Culture through educational centres. He also laid down the Vedic Scheme of Education.

Swami Dayanand fought against the superstitions, the Pauranic Hinduism and the Dharma Shastras which were largely responsible for leading the masses towards darkness, idol-worship and disunity. To him, the Vedas are the source of all knowledge and character. Character or righteous living as taught by the Vedas, and Smritis is the highest virtue. This is the end-all and be-all of human existence. Let a man, therefore, always take the path of righteousness.

His Concept of Religion

Swami Dayanand regards religion as the true conduct of life. The central doctrine of religion, according to him, is the worship of God by means of prayer, meditation and the daily Havana. There is no place for idol-worship or pilgrimages and even for a priestly class.

His religion is the religion of a common man. He believes in the equality and brotherhood of man and believes that it is the obligation of all human beings, to work for the welfare of all human beings. In brief, the essence of his religious doctrine is that a religious and God loving man is not only to make his own life noble and beautiful ; he is also to devote himself to helping other people to live virtuous and happy lives.

His Views About God

Swami Dayanand believes in the oneness of God. According to him God is one and the various names such as Agni, Vayu, Surya etc., are the different names of the same God-head. God is pureUniversal Spirit. God has no form. Dayanand does not believe in the finite and human form of God. According to him, the assumption that the infinite, all-pervading and eternal Lord can take on a human form, is the height of illogical thinking. He holds that God permeates the whole Universe. He is personification of Sat-Cit-Ananda. He creates, sustains, and dissolves the Universe.

His Ideas About Transmigration of Soul

Swami Dayananda believes in the doctrine of transmigration of soul. He holds that the soul is immortal and eternal. Death of the body does not mean the end of the body. Due to ignorance the soul is in bondage in this world. This ignorance is the cause of sin. Salvation lies in the emancipation of the soul from pain and suffering.

SWAMI DAYANAND'S EDUCATIONAL PHILOSOPHY

Swami Dayanand attached great importance to educational institutions and felt a necessity of their establishment. It would serve as permanent means of enlightenment for the public and in the work of reform and regeneration. He established about seven schools at various places in U.P. His educational thoughts and principles as contained in Satyartha Parkash, are in accordance with the Vedic Philosophy interpreted in the light of contemporary socio-political and religious conditions of India. In order to understand his educational assumptions we refer to certain basic points.

Education as a Life-long Continuous Process

Swami Dayananda believes that education is a life-long continuous process. Though formal education of a child begins after his 'Upnayana ceremony,' education informally begins from the time of conception. As mind is the product of food, Dayananda recommends Sattvik food to the parents : such a food, besides producing health, strength, energy and intellect, also produces mental tranquillity and good temper.

Therefore, a pregnant mother must be particular about this fact. The parents must have a selective environment for themselves and must remain in close commune paving the way for the advent of a blissful life. During the whole period of pregnancy the mother has to be on her guard against all sorts of distractions and evil effects. According to **Swamiji**, "No other person can equal a mother in her love for her children, and in her anxiety for their welfare. **Swamiji** has given details how education has to be imparted in accordance with each period of the child's physical and mental growth. Summing up, we can say that the character of the mother influences the character of the child in the womb. Therefore, the upbringing of the child begins not at its birth but at the conception.

Education for all

Swami Dayananda considers it a sacred duty of the parents to look after education of their children. To give their children the highest education possible, to instruct them in the ways of truth, to make them refined in character and manners, in short, to devote all their wealth, body and mind for this objective. To accomplish this objective, is the paramount duty, the highest virtue, and the glory of the parents.

Apart from this duty of the parents, "both state and society should make it compulsory upon all to send their children (both male and female) to school after the fifth or the eighth year. It should be made a penal offence to keep a child at home after that age."

To have the society in perfect order, **Swamiji** asks the teachers not to neglect the education of classes other than Brahmanas, viz., Princes and other Kashatriyas and intelligent Shudras "Because, if Brahmanas only were to acquire knowledge there could be no advance in knowledge, religion and government, nor increase in wealth, for, Brahmanas, whose sole duty is to acquire knowledge and disseminate it, depend for their living on Kashatriyas, etc., to whom they are lawgivers. Brahmans would be relieved of all restraint and fear from Kashatriyas, who, being uneducated, would be quite incapable of judging the soundness or unsoundness of their teachings. They would thus gradually use their powers for their own selfish ends, drift into hypocricy and do whatever they like, and their example will be followed by other classes. But when Kashatriyas, and other classes are also well educated, Brahmanas study still harder to keep ahead of other classes, and walk in the path of righteousness. They could never then falsely teach and lead selfish, hypocritical lives. It follows, therefore, that it is in their own interest, as well as that of community at large, to try their best to teach the Veda and other true Sciences and Philosophies to Kshatriya, etc. It is Kashatriyas, and other classes, that are the real cause of advance in knowledge, religion, and government, and of increase in wealth, etc. They never live on alms, they, therefore, can have no reason to be partial in religious or scientific matters. When all the classes are well educated and cultured, no one can set up any false, fraudulent, and irreligious practices.

All this goes to prove that it is the Brahmanas and sanyasins, who keeps Kashatriyas, and others in proper order, and vice versa Therefore, all persons of all classes should be given good, sound education and be well instructed in the principles of true religion.

Gurukula or Acharyakula

At the age of eight after Upanayana ceremony has been performed boys and girls should be sent to their respective schools. The schools should be situated in a lonely place and must not be within five miles of a town or village. The boys' school should be at least three miles away from that of the girls'. The tutors and other employees should in the boys' schools be all of the male sex and in girls of the female sex. Not even a child of five years of one sex be allowed to enter the school of the other sex.

Tutors should see that the students perfect their knowledge, cultivate amiable dispositions and manners, and gain in strength, both of body and mind thereby grow in happiness. All the scholars should be treated alike in matters of food, drink, dress and seats. Be they princes and princesses or the children of beggars all should practise asceticism—severe bodily and mental discipline. Simple living and high thinking should be the motto of the students. They should not be allowed to see their parents or hold any communication whatever with them. Being thus freed from all worldly worries and cares, they should devote themselves heart and soul to their studies. Their tutors should accompany them in all their recreations, so that they may not fall into any mischief, get indolent or naughty.

Period of Studentship

Twenty-five years is the minimum period for the observance of Brahmacharya. If any one wants to remain celebate till death, he may do so, but this is possible to those whose knowledge is perfect, who have full control over their minds and senses, and who are perfect yogis, free from all vices.

After their entrance into school, the second Upanayana ceremony should be performed and Gaitri Mantra, though given at the first Upanayana ceremony at home, should be taught to the children along with its meanings. After that Sandhyopasana (सन्ध्योपासना) along with its accessories and the techniques of Yajna performance should be taught to him. This forms part of daily worship.

Scheme of Studies

Swami Dayananda suggests a scheme of studies through which one can be master of the Vedas, the Upavedas, and other sciences within twenty or twenty one years. The following subjects have to be studied in the order given below :—

1. Phonetics (shiksha) by Panini.
2. Grammar.
3. Nighantu and Nirukta.
4. Chhandograntha.
5. Manusmriti Valmiki Ramayana, Vidur Niti etc.
6. Six Shastras.
7. Four Vedas with their four Brahmanas.
8. Upvedas-which are four in number :—
   (a) Ayurveda.
   (b) Dhanur Veda.
   (c) Gandharva Veda.
   (d) Artha Veda also called Shilpa Vidya.
9. Jyotisha Shastra—which includes Arithmetic, Algebra, Geometry, Geography, Geology and Astronomy—also practical training in these sciences.

In conclusion with this scheme Swami Dayananda mentions those books which should not be studied as they are written by atheists, because, once caught in them a student can never know the truth.

The Teacher and the Taught

The teacher and the pupils should observe the following rules given in Taittireya Upanishad (vii, 9) :

"Let them conduct themselves, properly, and study and teach; be truthful in word, deed and thought, and study and teach; be indifferent to joys or sorrow, worldly applause or censure, walk in the path of righteousness and study and teach the Vedas and the other true sciences; keep their senses under perfect control and study and teach ; restrain their minds from evil pursuits (such as the practice of injustice), and study and teach ; learn the properties of heat, light, electricity, and other natural forces, and study and teach ; perform Homa daily, and study and teach ; serve atithis (guests), and study and teach; fulfil their duties and obligations towards other men, and study and teach; protect their subjects and children, and study and teach ; preserve and perfect the reproductive element, and study and teach ; protect and educate their children and pupils, and study and teach." This very clearly shows the idealistic position how both the teacher and the taught partake in the common scheme of life. Besides, it also points out that the teacher's knowledge should be upto-date.

Both the teachers and their pupils should avoid all those things that act as hinderance in the way of acquisition of knowledge, e.g.:

(a) want of faith in Brahamacharya as the source of health, strength, intellect, courage, political power and wealth.

(b) instead of worshipping God, waste time in going about from place to place worshipping images, etc.

(c) absence of the worship of five true gods—father, mother, teacher, altruistic teachers of humanity and other great men.

The studies of true sciences and philosophies, the living of good and righteous lives, the practice of Yoga, and Communion with God alone can lead to eternal bliss.

Teachers should instruct their pupils as given in Taittireya Upanishad (vii, xi, 1-4), thus :

"My children, always speak the truth, lead a virtuous life, abstain from sexual indulgence, never be negligent in learning and teaching, devote yourself to sciences (physical and spiritual) till your knowledge is perfect, then procure for your preceptor anything that he needs, thereafter, go and get married. Never neglect your health or the cultivation of any skill or talent you may possess. Never be indifferent to the acquisition of wealth, power etc. Never neglect your studies.

"Never neglect to serve your father, mother, teacher and all preachers of the true religion (atithi). Love virtue and shun vice. Imbibe our virtues, not our faults and imperfects. Always keep the company of those Brahmans among us who are learned and imbued with piety: put your trust in them and them only. Be charitable." "If you are ever in doubt as to the truth of any practice of religion, or any doctrine, or mode of divine worship, follow the practice of those highly virtuous Brahmanas, whether yogis or not, who are free from prejudice, charitable in disposition, and well versed in philosophy and science (physical and spiritual), and extremely desirous of furthering the cause of righteousness. This is the advice. This is the commandment. This is the mandate of the Vedas. Ay, this is the law. Follow this advice. Obey this law."

It is clear that the teachers must be Idealists and men of knowledge and character. Dayananda advocates a close relationship between the teacher and the taught. He believes that most formative influence in the school should be the personality of the teacher—Guru. The students should be true and devoted to their teachers as well as to their studies. The role of a teacher is great, it is essentially leading the child from darkness to light and transforming him into a spiritual entity.

Views About Women Education

Swami Dayananda gives equal right to women and championed the cause of women's education. In this regards Dayananda cites a verse of the Atharvaveda : Just as boys acquire sound knowledge and culture by the practice of Brahamcharya and then marry girls of their own choice, who are young, well-educated, loving and of like temperament, so should a girl practice Brahamcharya, study the Veda, and other sciences and thereby perfect her knowledge, refine her character, give her hand to a man of her own choice, who is young, learned and loving.

Swami Dayananda has all praise for those parents who treat their children alike and provide opportunities for education to their sons and daughters. He asserted that girls should also practise Brahamcharya. He recommends for them Grammar, Dharma, Medical Science, Mathematics and Practical Arts. Since, the main sphere of duty for women is the home—its management, reproducing, bringing-up and instruction of their children, he prescribes different curriculum for them with special reference to home management so as to prove good wives and mothers. Thus, he was the champion of women's education and became the first Indian social reformer who vehemently pleaded for their education.

CONCLUSION

Swami Dayananda was mainly a social reformer. He was a Sanyasi, a Brahmachari, a Scholar and an Educationist. His mission was to revive the ancient Vedic Indian Wisdom and Spirit. In his quest to regenerate the society, he established the Arya Samaj and advocated certain principles of education which became the guidelines for various institutions.

It is true that Swami Dayananda did not give any technical system of education or a science of education. But it is also true that he saved the country at a critical juncture and fought for national solidarity and international understanding. His emphasis on moral values, purity of thoughts and deeds, character and righteousness of life, and above all his plea for democratic concept of education are some of the significant and remarkable contributions which have had a far reaching effect on Indian life and culture and the system of education.

14

Rabindranath Tagore (1861-1941)

Tagore is primarily a poet ; but his poetry is imbued with philosophy. The poet seeks beauty, the philosopher truth. Both the paths lead to the same Supreme Reality. Tagore's poetic rapture is 'soaked in his quest for the Beyond'. In his presidential address to the Indian Philosophical Congress **Tagore** said, "In India, philosophy ever sought alliance with poetry because its mission was to occupy the people's life and not merely the learned reclusion of scholarship. Instead of being logically intellectual, Tagore's philosophy is, a sight of the soul rather than a reasoned account of metaphysics ; an atmosphere rather than a system of philosophy'.

TAGORE'S GENERAL PHILOSOPHY

On the basis of Gitanjli, it is sometimes said that Tagore represents the teachings of Hinduism. But, neither the Hindu 'Karma' nor the Hindu doctrine of 'transmigration of soul' can be found in Tagore, although the idea of incarnation is met with in some of his poems. When asked whether his father had belief in transmigration of soul, he gave vent to his mind thus, "My father never believed in that fairy tale".

From the inheritance point of views, he is a Brahmo Samajist. His grand-father was the right hand man of Raja Ram Mohan Rai. His father kept the same torch burning. So after his father, Tagore was a member of the Adi Brahmo Samaj and thus he took his cue from Upanishads which formed the back-bone of his philosophy.

On deep study, we find that Tagore is out and out a Vedantist. He believes in One supreme being, the Braham. He believes that the various manifestations of nature all represent Him and the Braham pervades through all these forms. Among this empirical diversity there, is, thus an innate unity. This results, therefore, in there being a Spiritual Bond between man and man. Like a Vedantist he believes in "Aham Brahmosmi" or 'I am the Brahma'. Thus, according to Tagore, the true salvation comes when an individual feels the truth contained in the words, "Aham Brahmosmi". The Vadantistic philosophy also led him to have an implicit faith in the Brotherhood of Man and Fatherhood of God and in the need for universal religion.

Like Rousseau, Tagore is an "Individualist" and "Naturalist". He believes in the right and freedom of the individual to shape his life in his own way. But in the individual's development he ultimately wants the unity of mankind. He says that every individual is different from another and every one is unique. In every one of us the Creator manifests himself in a unique manner and every individual tries to realise the creator in his own way. In the creator and through him, we find unity not only among human beings but also between man and nature.

Tagore, a great lover of nature gives a very important place to Nature. This, he says, is the manifestation of the creator (Braham). Through its various forms, colours, and the rhythms the Braham reveals Himself through many ways. He reveals Himself more clearly through nature than through man. Tagore, therefore, wishes human beings to have a close communication with nature and with its purifying and vitalising influences. Just as a man realises his relationship with human beings, he should realise his relationship with nature.

'Experience of the Spiritual World, religion as the right centre of life's activities and the unity of thought and truth are the key-note of Tagore's philosophy. There should be a spiritual relationship between man and man. This knits human beings into communities. Tagore's individualism, therefore, is compatible with the growth of social units. He encourages the individual to reorganise the social groups on the basis of the individual's spiritual worth. By this he does not mean parochialism—intellectual, social, political and spiritual. The essential unity of the universe is evident to him. True, that he advocates internationalism, but not from the economic or political point of view. He realises and stresses the spiritual bondage of the universe. Having an explict faith in the fundamental unity of mankind, he preached human brotherhood.

Tagore, like most of the ancient sages and seers, believes, that man should live for the ultimate truth. He wants man to "have access to the life that goes beyond death and rises above all circumstances". His advice is "let us find our God, let us live for the ultimate truth which emancipates us from the bondage of the dust and gives us the wealth, not of things but of inner light, not of power but of love."

TAGORE'S EDUCATIONAL PHILOSOPHY

Tagores educational philosophy conforms to his general philosophy. He approaches education as he approaches life as a poet, from a comprehensive standpoint. "Education", he says, "...is a permanent part of the adventure of life... it is not like a painful hospital treatment for curing them (students) of the congenial malady of their ignorance, but is a function of the health, the natural expression of their mind's vitality". To him, the object of education is the freedom of mind through the path of freedom, though it has its risk and responsibility too. In his words "the best function of education is to enable us to realise that to live as a man is great requiring profound philosophy for its expression, and heroism in its conduct." "Most people", he says, "have forgotten that children are living-beings. They are more living than grown up people, who have built their shells of habit around them, while the children are always pliable". Therefore, he wants that children should not have mere schools for their lessons, but a world whose guiding spirit is personal love. "Love and action" he believes, "are the only media through which perfect knowledge can be obtained".

Tagore's educational philosophy is based on three cardinal principles namely (a) Freedom (6) Creative Self-expression (c) Active Communion with Nature and Man. For **Tagore**, "education has its only meaning and object in freedom ; freedom from ignorance about the laws of universe, and freedom from passion and prejudice in our communication with the human world." The genesis of the ideal of freedom lies in his own experience as a child and his experience of the prevailing system of education. About his early education he remarked, we had to sit like dead specimens of some museum, whilst lessons were pelted at us from without like hail-storms on flowers. He spoke of the existing school as being an "education factory, lifeless, colourless, dissociated from the context of the universe within the bare white walls scaring like eye balls of the dead". Our education has taken us away from nature and its vitalising and life-giving influences. It is dissociated from social contexts. An education,,divorced from the streams of life and confined within the four walls of the class-room becomes artificial and loses its value. The first and the foremost work, in his opinion is to bring the child's mind in contact with nature. Let the child imbibe and learn freely and spontaneously from the book of nature. Let him be happy and free. Education should be natural in content and quality. Through contact with nature the child will be introduced to the great world of reality spontaneously and joyfully.

Tagore does not want education to be shut off from the daily life of the people. However, the utilitarian aim of education is not ignored by him. According to him, educational institutions, in order to obtain their fulness of truth must have close association with economic life. The highest mission of education is to help us realize the inner principle of the unity of all knowledge and all the activities of our social and spiritual being. Society in its early stage, was held together by its economic co-operation, when all its members felt in-unison a natural interest their right to live." It was this idea of economic co-operation that formed the basis of Shantiniketan which was not only to be the centre of intellectual life of India, but the centre of her economic life also. "It co-operates with the villages around it, cultivates land, breeds cattle, spins cloth, presses oil from oil seeds. It is producing all the necessaries, devising the best means, using the best materials, and calling science to its aid. Its very existence tends to depend upon the success of its industrial activity carried out on the co-operative principles, which unites the teachers, students and villagers of the neighbourhood in a living and active bond of necessity.

Tagore's Views on Aims of Education

While considering the educational aims of Tagore, we should bear in mind that he was not an educationist in the strictly academic sense, and he never wrote any thesis on education, like Rousseau's Emile, or Spencer's Education. Nevertheless, in his countless writings, we find some direct and indirect utterances about the aims of education. I am presenting them here in a systematic form.

Physical Aims

Tagore was conscious of the importance of the education of the body. He attached so much importance to the healthy physical development of children that he strongly advocated their free, spontaneous movements and play in joyous, natural surroundings, even at the expense of studies, if necessary. "Even if they learnt nothing" he says, "they would have had ample time for play. Climbing trees, diving into ponds, plucking and tearing flowers, perpetrating thousand and one mischiefs on Mother Nature, they would have obtained the nourishment of the body, the happiness of the mind, and the satisfaction of the natural impulses of childhood."

Intellectual Aims

Tagore deplored the fact that the existing system of education encouraged slavery to books. Our mercenary education, inspired by narrow utilitarian motives of passing examinations and entering a job as quickly as possible and imparted through the medium of a difficult and alien language, led us to cram rules, definitions, facts, and ideas since early childhood without giving us either the time or the incentive to pause and think and assimilate what we had learnt. Thus, our intellect had never been exercised in a real sense, nor had our mind received any genuine intellectual food and nourishment. The natural consequence had been the starvation and stunting of our intellect on a nation-wide scale. We, thus, never succeeded in attaining the stature of intellectual maturity either as an individual or as a nation.

The power of acquiring ideas through independent efforts, of critically examining them, and of thoroughly assimilating them, was therefore. considered by Tagore the most important aim of intellectual education. He wrote, "Power of thinking and power of imagination are undoubtedly two very essential faculties for adult life. So. if one is to grow into real manhood, these two factors cannot be eliminated from life." Again, he wrote, "Even since childhood, instead of putting all the burden on the memory, the power of thinking and the power of imagination should also be given opportunities for free exercise".

"This ability of acquiring", writes **Dr. H. B. Mukherjee**, and assimilating ideas independently from books was considered by Tagore as only just a fraction of the intellectual equipment of an individual. He was far from advocating bookishness of any description; he indeed.

condemned it whenever the occasion arose. On the contrary, he always stressed the importance of the ability to learn directly from Nature and life. This is, in fact, a fundamental basis of his philosophy of Education in Nature." "There is education, "**Tagore** says, "in the mere effort of knowing a living person directly instead of through books. It not only gives some knowledge but develops the faculty of knowing to such an extent as is impossible in class lectures." Again, "Our intellect, emotions, or imagination, if divorced from reality, become feeble and distorted."

While developing the ability to learn directly from real life situations, a true intellectual education, in Tagore's opinion, must also aim at making the students familiar with and adjusted to the facts and conditions of real life and habitual environments. He asserted that unrealistic education was responsible for producing in our countrymen intellectual dishonesty, moral hypocrisy, and ignorance about their mother land. Hence, he argued that the first and foremost problem deserving our attention at the present moment is the problem of creating harmony between our education and our life.

Moral and Spiritual Aims

Tagore, as a moral teacher, has put forward a number of moral and spiritual values. One of these is the value of discipline, which is certainly a most fundamental element in the moral education of an individual. By the word, "discipline", Tagore does not mean either external order or blind obedience. Explaining its meaning in Siksa-Samasya, he said, "Real discipline means protection of raw, natural impulses from unhealthy excitement and growth in undesirable directions. To remain in this state of natural discipline, is happy for young children. It helps their full development."

"Inner discipline," writes Dr. H. B. Mukherjee, "of the self is at once the spirit and the fruit of all **Tapasya** and **Sadhna**. All worthy activities great or small succeed because of this spirit of austere devotion to the cause or the task. "Nothing great and Noble", he (**Tagore**) declared,. "can be achieved except through severe suffering and sacrifice." Time and again, he exhorted his countrymen, and specially the young people, to imbibe fully this spirit of Tapasya, of austere devotion, and to apply it to every sphere of national endeavour. He pointed out that Japan could rise to great heights in a very short time because of the power of her-people to devote themselves intensely to any work of importance. The West also attained ascendancy in the modern world through the same spiritual and moral force.

Another ideal of great value recommended by Tagore is the ideal of peace and tranquillity. "The essential spirit of the forest," he says, "is the santarasam, the spirit of peace and tranquillity, which is the consummation of all emotions, just as white is the consummation of all other colours. Attainment of this spirit of peace and tranquillity in one's character is an ultimate end of the process of self-discipline. This, in its turn, produces the spirit of humility which is a tremendous spiritual force and can be attained only by the strong."

In conformity with the ideal of self-discipline, Tagore advocates, a simple way of life achieved through the reduction of all unnecessary material equipment. "We should demonstrate the ideal", he said, "of reducing the unnecessary in life in every respect in our school..." Easy accessibility, simplicity, and naturalness—these comprise true civilization. The complexity of ponderous accountrements is sheer barbarity ; in fact, it is a rubbish-heap of sweating incompetence. That the dignity of man does not suffer through the want of some lifeless materials, but, on the contrary, it frequently becomes brighter with a natural glow—this truth will have to be learnt in schools since childhood, not through futile precept but through living examples. Getting rid of the luxury of materials, the child will acquire greater familiarity with the use of his hand and feet, the floor and the earth.

"Tagore laid stress," writes **Dr. Mukherjee**, "on another fundamental ideal which aims more at inner development than an outward expression. It is the attainment of an inner freedom, an inner power and enlightenment. This ideal of inner freedom may be expressed as the liberation of the self from all kinds of slavery. It aims at emancipation of the intellect from the domination of bookish knowledge." "The character of good education," according to **Tagore**, "is that it does not over power man ; it emancipates him."

Tagore's Views on Curriculum

Curriculum is the means to achieve the aims of education. Hence, Tagore's approach to curriculum was as wide and comprehensive as his aims of education. The main aim of education, according to him, was the development of complete manhood for the realization of a full life. Naturally enough, the curriculum envisaged by him partook of "that idea of fulness and referred to all aspects of human life, physical, intellectual, moral and spiritual from one point of view; individual, social, utilitarian, non-utilitarian, etc. from another.

This is the reason that Tagore advocated a fulness of experience for children so that they might acquire knowledge from multiple sources through the sub-conscious process. His chief complaint against the existing curriculum in the Indian schools of his time was that it concentrated exclusively on the mind, and was hopeless circumscribed by the narrow mercenary and utilitarian aims. Everybody was desirous, he said, somehow to get through an examination and secure a job. There was, thus, no incentive to any serious course of study of a comprehensive nature. The students had the bare minimum in view ; but the bare minimum, he pointed out never suffices for a healthy growth. Introducing a biological analogy in Siksar Herpher, Tagore significantly observed that, though a human being is only three cubits and a half in height, none can live and grow happily within a space only just as high. An ample space is necessary for free and healthy development. And this is as true in the intellectual sense as in the physical. Such ample space can be provided only through a full and wide curriculum that would ensure a fulness of experience to the growing children. "It was my desire," **Tagore** pointed out, "that I would establish in the Santiniketan asram a field for the pursuit of culture not merely the cultivation of knowledge within the narrow limits determined by the text-books prescribed in your schools but also all kinds of arts and crafts, dance, music and play, as well as all knowledge and skill necessary for rendering service to the villages."

Tagore's conception of the curriculum as fulness of experience show that he viewed curriculum "not in terms of certain subjects to be learnt but in terms of certain activities to be undertaken." As **Nunn** has written, "The school must be thought of primarily not as a place where certain knowledge is learnt, but as a place where the young are disciplined in certain forms of activity." We find, accordingly, writes Dr. Mukherjee, "that at the Santiniketan school, and later on at Visva-Bharati, not only did the teaching of the various familiar academic subjects like History, Science, Nature Study, Geography, Literature, etc., include a variety of relevant practical activities like drama, excursion, gardening, regional study, laboratory work, drawing, original composition, collection of museum and herbarium, etc., but a multitude of so-called 'extra-curricular' activities like games, social service, student self-government, etc. formed a regular feature of the normal working of the institution in order to bring into play all the essential faculties of the children. From this point of view, the curriculum introduced in Tagore's Institutions has been "activity curriculum" in a large measure.

Tagore's Views on Method

The most significant point in Tagore's philosophy of method was that the process of education should be full of life. He deprecated the mechanical and lifeless system of education. His main grievance against the schools of his time was that they were not centres of learning, but educational factories, turning out the same kind of stuff through their mechanical system of education. He developed an abhorrence to this system in his childhood when he was sent to a school. Since, that very time, he longed to save children from that ordeal. In this respect, his views were like those of the Naturalists, who stood against dead formation and sought to breathe into education the fresh air of light and life, placing it on the natural interests and impulses of the child.

Another point, which Tagore stressed was that education should be imparted on realistic lines. Just as the curriculum envisaged by him was to reflect the customs, traditions, social ideals, conditions and problems of everyday life of the pupil, so also the method was to be based on real life-situations, concrete facts of Nature, and social life. Thus, facts of Nature are to be studied through actual Natural phenomena and through the wild life in Nature, and facts of history, geography, and other social sciences are to be studied first hand from direct sources as far as possible.

Tagore's realistic approach was psychological. Expressing his views about it, he said. "Learning can become sound only when it proceeds from the near to the distant from the familiar to the unfamiliar. If our learning continue to be based mainly on what does not exist all around and what is not present before us, then such knowledge must be feeble. If we can fully and properly grasp what is familiar, only then can we apperceive what is unseen and unfamiliar."

Realistic approach to the learning process, as conceived by Tagore, 'presumed the idea that knowledge should be acquired through independent efforts and thinking. **Tagore** said, "In contact with the real objects that are present before the pupils their power of observation and reasoning will develop." Again, "There is education in the very effort to give up books and study men who are living and present. It not only leads to knowledge, but it develops the power of knowing to an extent which is never possible through class teaching." In his letter to Tanayendra Nath Ghose, dated the 10th of March, 1929, Tagore made a plea for a realistic education which is based on the study of life and society, and is independent of books. He wrote, "The students must be led to think. A variety of questioning and answering has to be conducted on what they have studied in books. Indeed, we should think that their education has been real if they venture to criticise the matter contained in the text books. Different problems of everyday life should be presented before them and discussion should be conducted on their solution. Note down many such problems in your note-book. Moreover, they visit Sriniketan, but they view it from outside and do not know what its essential problems are. They should be made aware of them and asked to offer solutions. What is the economic foundation of the village ; what does the co-operative principle mean ; why is it necessary for our country ; what drawbacks are there in the nature, habit, and custom of the rural population that they are dying through want of food and water and through diseases and afflictions?—We should see that they ponder over and discuss these problems—Remember, this education is much greater than class-teaching."

Another important principle in Tagore's educational method was the activity principle." This principle as conceived by Tagore has a much deeper meaning than that by which it is familiar to us. It is based on the philosophy of Tagore that body and mind are inseparable. He asserted that physical activity not only invigorates the body but also energises the mind. This is the reason that he advocated compulsory training in some craft for the students of his school. He also affirmed that such instances are found where skill in a physical activity has released the suppressed energies of the mind. "It is my firm conviction," he said, "that there is a close relation between physical and mental education, physical and mental movement. The rhythm of our life is disturbed if a proper harmony is not established between the two." It is on this ground that he regarded the mobile-school as "the ideal school." "Teaching while walking," he stated, "is the best method of teaching". It is so not only because walking facilitates learning many things through direct observation, but because it keeps our awakened mental faculties; constantly alert and receptive through contact with ever-varying scenes and objects and the rhythmic marching together of the inner and the outer... Such dynamic learning is entirely fruitful for living human being. The static education within the class-room, on the other hand, causes a divorce between the body and the mind, without initiative. In his document 'Movement in Education', he explains this idea very clearly. "To compel the mind to use only one portion of the body in the learning process." he states, "is not natural". In the process of taking in and of digesting our food, a whole symphony of life is being performed in which heart, eyes, tongue, and ears are playing their part. The same process should occur when you are taking your lessons or trying to swallow useful information. Life should be entire, a co-ordination of all the different faculties and functions." According to this principle, the children of Shantiniketan recite or think aloud, while walking. They carry their note-books with them to sketch or record "all the picturesque details of the life around them."

Even in class teaching Tagore applied the activity—principle to such an extent that many would feel surprised. He wrote, "I would allow all our boys and girls during class to jump up, even to climb into a tree, to run off and chase after a cat or dog, or to pick some fruit off a branch... I tried to keep in mind the need of the child to use the whole of its body in acquiring a vocabulary and in mastering a whole sentence. Most of our teachers used to get disgusted when they heard the children of my class laughing and shouting and clapping their hands." A boy would say to me, 'May I go for a run?' 'Yes, of course,' I would say, because I knew that by this means some tedium would be broken and that, when again he felt lively, it would be much easier for him to receive and to digest, It is while children feel dull, from the passivity of their minds and through being asked to be inert receptacles, without any activity of body, that they cease altogether to assimilate the non-living lesson." It is from the view-point of the physical activity theory that Tagore emphasised the importance of dancing and dramatic arts. He said to Elmhirst, "In the developing of your own school I advise you to make the practice of drama and of the histrionic arts compulsory for all children. We must make dramatic performance a regular subject of education. Children need the opportunity to give expression of their sentiments through perfect and graceful movements of the body. Never allow this capacity to use the whole body as a medium of expression, to die out."

MAIN FEATURE'S OF TAGORE'S EDUCATIONAL PHILOSOPHY

Tagore's educational philosophy is based on naturalism, humanism and internationalism—all saturated with spiritualism.

Tagore's Naturalism

Tagore finds a fundamental unity between man and nature. Therefore, he wants that 'the child's education must be organised in natural surroundings'. He believes that education given in natural surroundings develops intimacy with the world. Because of this intimacy the child develops of his own accord the power of communication with it. He says, "Children with the freshness of their senses come directly to the intimacy of this world. This is the first gift they have. They must accept it naked and simple and must never again lose their power of immediate communication with it." Tagore does not want that the natural senses of children should be debased in an urban atmosphere.

Like a true Naturalist, Tagore was very much influenced by Robinson Crusoe. He writes, "I still believe that it is the best book for boys that has ever been written. There was a longing in me when young to run away from my own self and be one with everything in Nature."

Tagore puts more faith in an individual than in any institution. He does not want that the child should be crushed into the heavy traditional methods of instruction. The individual child is more important to him than the books, method and the teacher. The chief teachers upon whom Tagore places his main reliance are the open spaces around the grooves, the tree, dawn, evening and moonlight, the winds and rainfall. Such teachers, he believes, nourish the child nature spontaneously. Nature inspires the human beings differently at different stages of human development. For the young child, Nature will become an unconscious symbol of super-personal growth and evolution, something that need not be questioned and which provides an ever-ready back-ground for its dreams and its play. For the adolescent, Nature will become an object of either scientific or lyrical curiosity. The adult will see in her the soil on which his country and his people grow, the cultural and economic back-ground of human existence. Nature to him, is the focus where the interests and aspirations of human beings meet. It is, therefore, essential not only to know Nature, but to live Nature. Man attains thereby the greater and deeper freedom. He will find fulfilment in the struggle from the dim dream lands of childhood towards the light of maturity.

School, according to Tagore, should be a place where the sunrise and sun-set and the silent glory of stars are not daily ignored ; where nature's festivities of flowers and fruits have their joyous recognition from men. It should be such a place where the young and the old, the teacher and the students sit at the same table to partake of their daily food and the food of their eternal life. Tagore says that we have come to this world to accept it, not merely to know it. The highest education is that which does not merely give information, but makes our life in harmony with all existence.

Tagore wants an equilibrium of the 'Natural' and 'Civilized' forces in man. The art of education, according to him, should consist in training the child to inhibit all those impulses that are anti-social. "For our perfection, we have to be vitally savage and mentally civilized ; we should have the gift to be natural with nature and human with human society." That is, why, he suggests that besides communion with nature, there should be communion of man with man. This would enable children to learn social behaviour and co-operation in educational activities.

Education, in the academic sense of mere acquisition of knowledge or information never appeared to the versatile genius of the poet. Education to be real, must be of the whole man, of his emotions and senses as much as of his intellect. A large part of man, believes Tagore, can never find its expression in the mere language of words. It must have many other languages—lines and colours, sounds and movements for the satisfaction of his aesthetic urge. The poet regards the language of sounds and movements to be the best means of self-expression. Side by side with this provision for creative self-expression, he stresses various forms of hard work. He says, "however great a scholar may be, if he has not educated his body, he has to live a life of dependence on others—in many ways he is an incomplete man. There is a close and inseparable connection between the faculties of mind and body. Each gains strength by co-operating with the other. If the education of the body does not proceed along with the education of the mind, the latter cannot gather strength." "Hard work, music and arts", he says, "are the spontaneous overflow of our deeper nature and spiritual significance".

Tagore's Humanism

To Tagore, '*man is the measure of everything*'. Throughout his life, he has been striving to make the people of the world conscious of this Supreme Truth. His conception of the universe is purely human. All values and virtues are to be realised through man. When our universe is in harmony with Man, the eternal, we know it as truth ; we feel it as beauty. This world is a human world—the scientific view of it is also that of the scientific man." Tagore thinks of a Universal Mind of Humanity. This Universal Mind transcends separate individual minds. Tagore regards God also as human. He says God is the Eternal Person manifested in all persons. He observes that "He is there where the tiller is tilling the hard ground and where the pathmaker is breaking stones." To Tagore, civilization should be evaluated in terms of what value it attaches to man and not in terms of how many scientific inventions it has produced. He says, "The decay and fall of a civilization is due to the causes which produce callousness of heart and lead to the cheapening of man's worth." It is this love for man that stimulated Tagore to turn to the education of children and he founded a school at Bolpur. Because of his humanism, he was a great lover of children and advises the teacher to be like children and not to think himself as their superior, but should regard himself as one of their elder brothers. While addressing a group of pupil-teachers, he advised them to cultivate the eternal spirit of child, if they desired to take up the task of training the children of Man. Tagore shuns all violence and force in the process of education.

Tagore's Internationalism

Tagore's Internationalism knows no bound. He is an ardent prophet of world unity. All through his strenous life, he has worked for a closer contact between the East and the West. He wants that the East should give its best to the West and in turn it should assimilate the best that the West has to offer. He felt grateful to both the East and the West and believed that the problem of the world could be solved only, if a judicious synthesis was attained between the contributions of the two for the benefit of man. He wanted to achieve this synthesis in his Visva Bharti which was accessible to all persons in the world irrespective of caste, colour, creed and sex.

Tagore's Universal Humanitarianism is the corner-stone of collaboration between East and West, says Lesny. He is the apostle of enlightened humanity and a strong champron of world unity.

Tagore's Idealism and Spiritualism

Tagore's educational philosophy is saturated with Spiritualism. He wants to achieve the essential unity of the universe through God. For Tagore the object of education is to give man the unity of truth.'

The sense of unity of truth may be given by emphasizing the inter-relationship between intellectual, physical and spiritual life. Tagore believes in a spiritual world which is the innermost truth of this world. The experience of the spiritual world must be gained by children by living in it and not by theological instructions. Tagore wants to make 'the purpose of education nothing short of the highest purpose of man, the fullest growth and freedom of soul'. He says, "it is India's mission to realize the truth of the human soul through it's union with the world-spirit. Tagore fought against the dominance of materialistic out-look of life and he was an Idealist to the core. But be believes that education should be related to the life-currents of the people for which it is meant. He says, "Our centre of culture should not only be centre of the intellectual life of India, but the centre of her economic life also." Here, Tagore shows a pragmatic approach to education.

TAGORE'S VISVA BHARATI

We have referred to Tagore's Visva Bharati at Shantiniketan. So, it is in the fitness of things to discuss here briefly the philosophy underlying this International University which was formally inaugurated on December 22, 1921, by the great scholar. Dr. Brajendranath.

A University, Tagore believes, should not be a mechanical organization for collecting and distributing knowledge. It should be a medium of enabling people to offer their wealth of mind to others. The conception of his Visva Bharati, is in accordance with his notion of Greater India where humanity will strive to reach a reconciliation of different races with different religions and civilizations. Tagore believes that this Greater India or New India will not belong to this race or that, this religion or that religion, but to humanity. Tagore's Visva Bharati is a symbol of his passionate faith in the Brotherhood of Nations. In 1934 while responding to Professor Gilbert Murray's invitation to help in bridging the gulf between various nations through international co-operation of thinkers in all countries, **Tagore** wrote, 'Willingly therefore, harness myself in my advanced age to the arduous responsibility of creating in our educational colony at Shantiniketan a spirit of geniune international collaboration based on a definite pursuit of knowledge, a pursuit carried on in an atmosphere of friendly community life, harmonized with Nature and offering freedom of individual self-expression." This is the ideal on which Tagore has based his Visva Bharati.

Purposes of Visva Bharati

Tagore had three main purposes in establishing the Visva Bharati. He has described them as follows :

1. To teach different cultures of the East, especially those that originated in India or found shelter within her shores.

2. To establish 'The Institute of Rural Reconstruction' in order to lay the foundation of a happy, and contented human life in the villages, and lastly.

3. To seek to establish a living relationship between the East and the West, to promote inter-cultural, and inter-racial amity and understanding, and fulfil the highest mission of the. present age—'the unification of mankind'.

Objectives of the Visva Bharati

The Memorandum of the Association of Visva Bharati lays down the objectives of Visva Bharati in the following words.

1. "To study the mind of man in its realization of different aspects of truth from diverse points of view.

2. To bring into more intimate relation with one another, through patient study and research the different cultures of the East on the basis of their underlying unity.

3. To approach the West from the standpoint of such a unity of the life and thought of Asia.

4. To seek to realize in common fellowship of study the meeting of the East and West, and thus ultimately to strengthen the fundamental conditions of world peace through the establishment of free communication of ideas between the two hemispheres.

5. And with such ideals in view to provide at Shantiniketan aforesaid centre of culture where research in the study of religion, literature, history, science and art of Hindu, Buddhist, Jain, Islamic, Sikh, Christian and other civilizations may be pursued along with the culture of the West, with that simplicity in externals which is necessary for true spiritual realization, in amity, good fellowships and co-operation between the thinkers and scholars of both Eastern and Western countries, free from all antagonism of race, nationality, creed or caste, and in the name of One Supreme Being Who is Shantam, Shivam, Advaitam."

Department of the Visva Bharati

The Visva Bharati has now been recognised as a full-fledged Central University by the Government of India by a special Act passed by the Indian Parliament. The following are the various constituent departments of the Visva Bharati :—

1. Vidya Bhawan (School of Research)
2. Siksha Bhawan (College)
3. Patha Bhawan (School)
4. Kala Bhawan (School of Music and Dancing)
5. Sri Niketan (Institute for Rural Reconstruction)
6. Shilpa Bhawan (School of Industries)
7. Vinaya Bhawan (Teacher's Training College)
8. China Bhawan (School of Sino-Indian Studies)
9. Hindi Bhawan
10. Islamic Research Section.

Atmosphere in Visva Bharati

Many of the classes at Visva Bharati are held in the open air. The development of individuality in all its aspects, is the aim of this unique institution. Every student is free for giving expression to his tastes and aptitudes. The curriculum is so broad as to provide far the various aptitudes of the students. The social side of the students is not ignored. The institution tries to keep itself in touch with the poor, unhappy and downtrodden masses of the neighbourhood. Thus, Tagore has tried to make the Visva Bharati a centre of Indian Renaissance. He has made it a venue for International Understanding. He also made it a place from where solid work may be done for social and economic reform of the nation. Above, all he made it a place where from India many give the message of humanity to the whole world. Tagore is physically no more now, but his personality still pervades the Visva Bharati.

CONCLUSION

In the words of Calcutta University Syndicate "Through him (Tagore) India has given her message to mankind and his unique achievements in the fields of literature. philosophy, education and art, have won imperishable fame for himself and have raised the status of India in the estimation of the world."

Tagore had a benevolent function to perform. His was the ideal that human personality should be developed in an atmosphere of freedom and fellowship, through impulses of life lived in nature and in close touch with varied creative activities of the human mind.. There (Shantiniketan) prevails the atmosphere of Nature's own beauty with her varied gifts of colour and dance, flowers and fruits. with the joy of her mornings and the peace of her starry nights.

The place of Visva Bharati in the educational system of India is great. While it is preserving and furthering the cultural heritage of India, it is combining it with the best from the West in art, science and literature. The ideal of developing the human personality in an atmosphere of freedom and fellowship through impulses of a life lived in nature and in close touch with varied creative activities of human mind have found a true expression in Visva Bharati.

Tagore loved humanity and the purest form of humanity—the child. To him he gave respect, love, freedom, sympathy and scope for initiative.

15

Mahatma Gandhi (1869-1948)

Gandhiji, the father of Indian Nation, the apostle of Truth and violence, stirred three hundred million people to revolt, shook the foundations of the mightiest imperial power with his unique weapon of Spiritual Force and wrested independence from its unwilling iron hand.

Of his many gifts to the nation, the experiment of new education is one of the greatest. New education aims to create a new type of Individual in our Society. The whole effort of education is to remake Individuals, to shape human beings in such a way that they can contribute to the well-being of Society. It seeks to prepare citizens for a new society by teaching young people to live together as a community on the basis of co-operation, love and truth.

GANDHIJI'S PHILOSOPHY

Gandiji's view on the nature of Reality is monistic, as can be seen from his writings "I believe", says he, "in the absolute/oneness of God and therefore also of humanity. What though, we have many bodies? We have one soul. The rays of the sun are many through refraction. But they have the same source." He again says, "I believe in education. I believe in the essential unity of man and for that matter of all that lives." **Gandhiji** further says in unequivocal terms. "I subscribe to the belief or the philosophy that all life in its essence is one, and that man are working consciously or unconsciously towards the realization of that identity. This belief requires a living faith in living God who is the ultimate arbiter of fate." For Gandhiji, God is the Reality behind the universe which is always in a state of flux. 'God alone is real, the world is an illusion. He alone persists in the midst of change. That God does not need any proof. It is an undefinable, mysterious power that pervades everything. "God is Life, Truth, Light. He is Love. He is supreme Good."

In Gandhiji's view, there is no other God than Truth?

Truth

What is truth? This is a difficult question, but Gandhiji's solves it for himself by saying that it is what the voice within us tells. Gandhiji would say, Truth is God rather than God is Truth; because the atheists in their passion far discovering truth do not hesitate to deny the very existence of God. The definition "Truth is God", give Gandhiji the greatest satisfaction. Though Gandhiji believes that Truth is God, but unlike ancient seers his concept of truth is not theology-ridden, rather it is a secular concept. Truth is eternal and absolute, but man can realize only a part of it. Man should adhere to truth firmly and should be ready even to die for that. But he should not impose his truth on any one else. It should not be presented in a bitter form, but at the same time it should not degenerate into hypocricy. It should be practised in all walks of life.

Non-Violence

If Truth is God, how to realise it? Gandhiji says that the only means for the realization of Truth is Ahimsa. Truth is God, is the ultimate goal of human life and Ahimsa is the means to this end. "Ahimsa and Truth", says **Gandhiji**, "are so interwined that it is practically impossible to disentangle and separate them. They are like two sides of a coin, or rather a smooth unstamped metallic disc. Who can say, which is the obverse, and which is the reverse? Nevertheless, Ahimsa is the means ; Truth is the end. Means to be means must always be within our reach and so Ahimsa is our supreme duty."

Non-violence is not, for Gandhiji, a negative attitude. It is positive and dynamic. As **Dr. Radhakrishnan** puts it, "It is not non-resistence or submission to evil. It is resistance to it through love. Satyagraha is the belief in the power of the spirit, the power of truth, the power of love by which we can overcome evil through self-suffering and self-sacrifice."

Summum Bonum of Life

Gandhiji firmly believes that the ultimate aim of man's life is the realization of God. Man is a part and parcel of the social structure through which alone he can realize this summum bonum or the highest goal of his life. Society or humanity is composed of human beings who are bound together by the bond of a universal. brotherhood, Man and Society can realize God who is Truth, only through Ahimsa, which implies love for all human beings, he should practise the ideal of service unto all. In such a society there is no domination of the strong over the weak and no exploitation in any form. The whole social structure is based upon moral principles of justice and benevolence.

GANDHIJI'S SOCIO-POLITICAL PHILOSOPHY

Gandhiji's socio-political philosophy consists in the evolution and establishment of an ideal society which is a stateless democracy in which social life has become so perfect that it is self-regulated and self-disciplined. "In such a state everyone is his own ruler. He rules himself in such a manner that he is never a hindrance to his neighbour. In the ideal state, therefore, there is no political power, because there is no state." Such an ideal democracy will be a federation of Satyagrahi village communities. In such a society every individual will be a believer in non-violence and will live a life of love, renunciation and social service. In such a non-violent society individual freedom will be reconciled with social restraint through. truth and non-violence.

GANDHIJI'S EDUCATIONAL PHILOSOPHY

With the object of realizing his ideal of Spiritual Society as a stepping-stone to the realization of God or Truth, Gandhi evolved an educational system as a dynamic side of his philosophy. There is a unity running through his concrete schemes and plans, making them a complete system of philosophy.

Gandhiji's Educational Philosophy and Basic Education

There is a tendency even among great educationists, to identify Gandhiji's Educational Philosophy with Basic Education or Wardha Scheme of Education. The Wardha Scheme of Education is, no doubt, an integral part of Gandhiji's educational philosophy, but it is a scheme or a programme of education not synonymous with Gandhiji's philosophy of education, which aims at bringing about a revolution in the hearts and minds of man all over the world. His thoughts on education well-cohere, into a complete educational philosophy, which is the coping-stone of his general philosophy. The Wardha Scheme is primarily concerned with the education of children between 7 and 14 years of age and that too, in India of British rule.

Gandhian Concept of Education

"By education", says **Gandhiji** "I mean an all-round drawing out of the best in child and man—body, mind and spirit. Literacy is not the end of education nor even the beginning. It is one of the means whereby man and woman can be educated. Literacy in itself is no education." The literary training in a school lays more emphasis on the tools and subject rather than on the personality of the educand which, according to Gandhiji, is the main concern of education. What does Gandhiji mean by drawing out the best?' This best is nothing else but the inner voice of Truth. Education which draws out the best or Truth consists in the development of the mind and body with a corresponding awakening of the soul. It is the function of education, therefore, to bring about a harmonious development of all the four aspects of the human personality, viz., body, heart, mind and spirit. "True Education", says Gandhiji, "is that which draws out and stimulates the spiritual, intellectual and physical faculties of the children."

Aims of Education

Gandhiji's aims of education are implied in the meaning of education, and they are correlative to his ideal of life. He has given two sets of aims—viz., the immediate and the ultimate.

Among the *immediate aims*, we may mention the 'bread and butter' aim, the cultural aim, the harmonious development of all powers, the moral or character development aim and the aim of 'liberating' the educand. The ultimate aim of Gandhiji is related to the ultimate goal of life—the *aim of self-realization*, the knowledge of Truth and God.

The Bread and Butter Aim. Gandhiji advocated bread and butter aim among other aims of education. It was in this context that he arrived at his theory 'of *self-supporting* education.' He remarks : "This education ought to be for them a kind of *insurance against unemployment*." Elaborating the same idea, he further says—"The child at the age of 14, that is, after finishing a seven year course, should be *discharged as an earning unit*. Even now the poor people's children automatically lend a helping hand to their parents—the feeling at the back of their minds being : what shall my parents eat and what shall they give me to eat, if I do not also work with them? That is an education itself. Even so the state takes charge of the child at seven and returns it to the family as an earning unit. You impart education and simultaneously cut at the root of unemployment." It may be remembered, however, that Gandhiji *never wants the child to be a mere bread-earner and to earn while he learns.*

The Cultural Aim. As against the bread-and-butter' aim. Of education, there is the cultural aim, according to which *knowledge is worth having apart from any material use that it has for its possessor.* Knowledge of this kind is the goal of liberal education. The advocates of the cultural aim of education tend to think that, because a person had been engaged in intellectual work, his mind is thereby, trained to behave better ever afterwards in all new situations. It should, however be borne in mind that *knowledge is not the same thing as culture.* "A man's culture is not be judged, "says **Dr. S. Radhakrishnan**, "by the amount of tabulated information which he has at his command, but by the, quality of mind he brings to bear on the facts of life."

Being practical to the core, Gandhiji would not enter into an academic discussion of culture. His conception of culture is typically *Gandhian, and he would not care* what others think of it. In his talk to the girls of *Kasturba Balikashram*, New Delhi, 22-4-1946, he said : "I attach far more importance to the cultural aspect of education than to the literary. Culture is the foundation, the primary thing which the girls ought to get from here. It should show itself in the smallest detail of your conduct and personal behaviour, how you sit, how you walk, how you dress, etc., so that anybody might be able to see at a glance that you are the products of this institution. Inner culture must be reflected in your speech, the way in which you treat visitors and guests, and behave towards one another and your teachers and elders." Thus, to Gandhiji cultural aim is an important aim of education. But in his view, culture is not the product of intellectual work, but the quality of the soul, permeating all aspects of human behaviour.

The Complete Development or Perfection of Nature Aim. The complete development or perfection of nature is another aim that Gandhiji advocates. According to this view, our various innate and acquired powers should be so trained as to bring about a harmonious development of all those powers. This aim accords well with Gandhiji's concept of education—"an all-round drawing out the best in the child and man—body, mind and spirit." The complete development implies, therefore, the education of 3 H's—hand, heart and head—rather than the education of 3 R's. The development of the mind and body must go hand in hand, with a corresponding awakening of the soul in order to save it (education) from being reduced to a mere lopsided affair, It is only a complete development that can give us a whole man.

In the light of this aim, we can easily see how the present education is a lopsided affair. It consists mainly in the training of the mind. The training of the soul as well as the heart is necessary because, it can lead to refinement of emotions and impulses ; it can awaken our deepest feelings of love, sympathy and fellowship—qualities that constitute Ahimsa.

The Moral Aim. The moral aim is also emphasized by Gandhiji in the sense of character formation or character development. Gandhiji attaches so much importance to character training that he was prepared to relegate to it a subordinate position or even sacrifice literary training, if the choice were to be made between the two. To the question, 'What is your goal in education when India obtains freedom?' he promptly replied :—"Character building. I would try to develop courage, strength, virtue, the ability to forget oneself in working towards great aims. This is more important than literacy. Academic learning is only a means to this great end." "The end of all knowledge", he further says, "should be the building up of character." Character development, for Gandhiji, implies the cultivation of such moral virtues as courage, strength of conviction, purity of personal life, righteousness, self-restraint and service of mankind. This character is to be built up in terms of non-violence and universal love. Gandhiji believes that such moral virtues, properly cultivated, will enable the individual to realise Truth.

Liberating the Educand Aim. Another subordinate aim of education, according to **Gandhiji**, is that it should liberate the individual leaner. Education should lead to political, economic, intellectual and spiritual freedom. To **Gandhiji**, 'spiritual freedom is more important than other freedoms.' Spiritual freedom alone can initiate an individual into the higher life of the spirit.

Self-realization Aim. The highest aim of education, according to Gandhiji, is realization of God or self-realization. All other aims are subordinate to this supreme aim of life and education. We have considered different aims of education as put forth by Gandhiji. With all these aims as the bases of educational activities, Gandhiji regards self-realization as the Summun Bonum of life and education. This is the ultimate goal after which human beings ought to strive. In his Autobiography, he clearly says : "Long before I undertook the education of the youngsters of the Tolstoy Farm, I had realized that the training of the spirit was a thing by itself. To develop the spirit is to build character, to enable one to work towards a knowledge of God and self-realization. And I held that this was an essential part of the training of the young, and that all training without the culture of the spirit was of no use, and might be even harmful." Gandhiji believes, "that those who defer preparation for this invaluable experience until the fourth stage of life i.e. Sannyasa, attain no self-realization, but old age amounting to a second and pitiable childhood, living as a burden on this earth." He regards the life of a brahmachari and that of a sannyasi as spiritually similar." In his letter to his son, Mani Lai, he writes ; "You have realised my ideal of education if you learn real virtues and saturate your life with them. Armed with these virtues, you will earn your living in any part of the world and will be on your way to the knowledge of God and self-realization." Gandhiji's ultimate aim of education, viz, self-realization includes and embraces all his immediate and subordinate aims.

Are Gandhiji's Aims, Individual or Social? We have dwelt at length on the immediate and ultimate aims of education as formulated by Gandhiji. It would, therefore, be in the fitness of things for us to consider whether his educational aim is social or individual or both. **Gandhiji** does not hesitate to state that "the individual is the one supreme consideration", and "I look upon an increase of the power of the state with the greatest fear, because, although while apparently doing good by minimizing exploitation, it does the greatest harm to mankind by destroying individuality which lies at the foot of all progress." Gandhiji has no doubt in his mind that individuality should be preserved and developed, if we are to achieve any progress, either material or spiritual. At the same time, Gandhiji believes in the good of the state whose service and interests should be the aim of its individual citizens. Service, he thinks, is an essential part of education.

Gandhiji thus, strikes a balance between the ideals of social service and individual development. He says, "I value individual freedom, but you must not forget that man is essentially a social being. He has risen to his present status by learning to adjust his individualism to the requirements of social progress. Unrestricted individualism is the law of the beast of the jungle. We have learnt to strike a balance between individual freedom and social restraint. Willing submission to social control and restraint for the sake of the well-being of the whole society enriches both the individual and the society of which the former is a member." Individual development and social progress are, thus, interdependent. At another place, he reiterates the same thoughts : "A nation cannot advance without the units, of which it is composed advancing, and conversely, no individual can advance without the nation of which it is a part also advancing." The individual can reach his highest development in and through a spiritual society. Acharya Kripalani, commenting on Gandhiji's synthetic view-point, says that the inter-relation can only be ignored at the peril of the individual and the society. Any over-emphasis on the one will be at the expense of the other. Such over-emphasis destroys the balance which a true and lasting civilization needs—sometimes the individual with his anarchic tendencies produces confusion in society. At other times, society so crushes the individual that his initiative and personality are lost and he becomes a mere automation, Humanity has been oscillating between the thesis of the individual and the anti-thesis of the society. But Gandhiji succeeded in achieving the proper synthesis between individual and society in his philosophy of life and education. The ideal of self-realization, the highest aim of education, combines both the development of individuality and social progress.

The Method and Procedures

How can such objectives be realized? Only a suitable method and a suitable curriculum can help in realizing these objectives. The system of education as it prevails, is too, literary and academic to fulfil these aims. It cannot train the whole man. Gandhiji believes that in order to train the whole man education should be craft-centred. A system of education in which a craft as the centre can lead to the highest development of the mind and the soul. The craft chosen should be manual and productive. It is to be taught scientifically and not mechanically. it is to be a starting point of other subjects as well; "a meeting point of both physical and social environment represented by such subjects as general science, social sciences and creative and expressional arts." When teaching the craft and through craft other subjects, stress should be laid on the principles of co-operative activity, planning, accuracy, initiative and individual responsibility in learning. Gandhiji attaches a spiritual significance to the craft-centred method. 'The notion of education through handicraft arose from the contemplation of Truth and Love permeating life's activities. True education should be easily accessible to all and should be of use to every villager in his daily life.

Craft-centred education lays emphasis on such important principles of teaching as provision of useful experiences and activity as well as correlation of subjects. All this helps to develop an all-round personality in which knowledge, action and feeling are evenly balanced. The craft-centred education will fulfil other objectives as well, such as 'the bread and butter aim.' There are influences in the craft-centred education which are favourable to virtuous dispositions even to a richness and fulness of culture. Its effect on character in general is very wholesome, irrespective of the fact whether the craft is going to be one's vocation for life or just an antidote to that lethargy, listlessness and weakness of all which is not consistent with and which is very, often generated by too much intellectual work, pure and simple. The craft is again in consonance with Gandhiji's ideal of non-violence. It will save people from exploitation, selfishness and usurpation-all expression of violence. The craft centred education will bring a new age from which class and communal hatred is eliminated and exploitation is eschewed, The craft will not only stimulate the creative urge of every individual, but also will develop co-operativeness and team work.

The craft chosen, as the medium should make education self-supporting. The child, after completing his course of education should be able to earn a living for himself; and education imparted in the Basic School should be self-supporting to an extent that the craft-product of the children should meet the expenses of teacher's salaries. This is in accordance with Gandhiji's emphasis on 'bread and butter aim' and his realistic approach to the problem of education.

The Craft in the school should be the craft of the locality as far as possible. Only then, some positive relationship between education and life could be satisfied. It is thus, a method which not only stresses the importance of student's activity, experimentation, discovery and discussion rather than passive reception and absorption of information, but one which establishes an intimate relationship of the school with life and reality.

The Curriculum and Content of Education

The curriculum and content of education, besides the method, is another means of realizing the objectives. Gandhiji suggests the following studies in the Basic Scheme in order to develop the whole man—his intellectual, physical and spiritual powers.

(a) A Basic craft in accordance with the local conditions.

(b) Mother-tongue.

(c) Arithmetic.

(d) Social Studies.

(e) General Science including nature study, botany, zoology, physiology, hygiene, chemistry and physical culture.

(f) Art Work.

(g) Music.

(h) Domestic Science for girls.

These subjects are to be taught through the craft as the centre of correlation.

Gandhiji's Concept of Discipline

Gandhiji thinks that the highest form of discipline comes through self-control and not by being free to follow stray impulses. "It is rather by denying himself such freedom that he becomes master in his own house, achieving the higher freedom to follow light that is in him unhampered by the chains of his lower nature." Gandhiji believes that real freedom comes through self-discipline—discipline that arises spontaneously from the inner springs of life rather than that which is imposed from without. Thus, he gave us the concept of "Voluntary discipline" which is a synthesis of freedom and external control. Such self-discipline arises from a life of restraint, fearlessness, usefulness and self-sacrifice—discipline through a practice of non-violent conduct. Gandhiji's craft centred education encourages conjoint and co-operative activities. And out of these, emerges a sort of social control or social discipline. That Gandhiji had in his mind the concept of social discipline is evident also from his emphasis on the ideals of citizenship through education.

Other Aspects of Gandhiji's Educational Philosophy

In this section we attempt to describe those aspects of his philosophy which constitute Secondary principles in the Basic Scheme. Craft-centredness and Self-sufficiency are the most fundamental principles that we have discussed briefly above. Now we refer to the ideal of citizenship which Gandhiji considers necessary for democracy. Education should enable each individual child to exercise his rights and duties of citizenship intelligently. It is in this context that the craft comes into prominence again. The craft-centred education will enable the citizen to repay society for all the rights conferred on him in the form of some productive service. The scheme aims at turning out useful productive citizens rather than drags and parasites whose attitudes towards work is unhealthy. It envisages the idea of a co-operative community in which the ideal of social service will dominate all the activities of children. It is through the various conjoint activities in the school and through a socially oriented curriculum that such social co-operative attitudes will be developed in the child.

Other aspects that need mention are free and compulsory education for 7 years and the emphasis on the mother tongue as the medium of instruction. Both these aspects need to be appreciated because they will help in realizing the goals of education as advocated by Gandhiji. While commenting on English as the medium of instruction, he says : "The foreign medium has caused a brain fag, put undue strain on the nerves of our children, made them crammers and imitators, unfitted them for original work and thought and disabled them by filtrating their learning to their family or the masses. The foreign medium has made our children practically foreigners in their own land." The Zakir Hussain Committee feels that the mother tongue "will introduce the child to the rich heritage of his people's ideas, emotions and aspirations and can therefore be made a valuable means of social education, whilst also instilling right, ethical and moral values."

Gandhiji thinks that only the right type of teachers can help us in achieving the objective of education. These teachers should possess knowledge, skill, enthusiasm, patriotism and special training. They should be inspired by social attitudes and be inbued with the ideals of Non-violence or Ahimsa.

Evalution of Gandhiji's Educational Philosophy

Gandhiji's Philosophy of Education is sound psychologically, sociologically and biologically. Gandhiji saw that the child can make intellectual progress only through activity which is purposive and productive. Working on a craft will involve planning, experimenting and reflection. It will accustom the child to look closely to attend to details to measure correctly, thus developing his observation. Manual work not only encourages intellectual development by associating muscular action with cerebral effort. "It also develops the child's imagination, for he must visualise in advance what he expects to make. It develops his reflection and encourages the co-ordination of the process by putting to work all the senses and organs. As children are to learn by doing, they will be able to satisfy many of their urges and achieve a balance, as it were, between the intellectual and practical phases of experience. Both body and mind will be educated in co-ordination. The child will thus, acquire not the super-ficial literacy, but the real literacy of the whole personality. The Basic Scheme which reflects Gandhiji's philosophy of education gives ample opportunities for self-expression. Ordinary education cannot foster the creative urge for self-expression, but the Basic Education, as outlined in the scheme, provides "an effective outlet for the creative urges innate in every human heart." The scheme satisfies some of the fundamental psychological needs of children-the need for affection and self-respect, the need for creativeness and activity and the need to develop a sense of security. Gandhiji expected the teacher to understand the child and love him, to make him happy and thus satisfy his need for affection. Manual work will satisfy his need for creativeness and will develop self-reliance and self-confidence leading to self-respect and security.

Pedagogically too, Gandhiji's educational theory is sound. The craft-centred education will give greater concreteness and reality to the knowledge acquired by children The principle of correlation will relate knowledge of life with other forms of knowledge. The very concept of 'education' and 'aims of education' show Gandhiji's breadth and depth of insight at the same time. According to Gandhiji, education is not mere literacy—it is an all-round development of the whole man.

Sociologically considered, Gandhiji's philosophy of education is as sound as considered psychologically. Education should fit a man for playing a useful role in the non-violent social order. He will cultivate the character appropriate to a social being. He will learn the art of discipline, self-government, breadth of vision, tolerance and good neighbourliness. And as, this social order is to be democratic every member of society has a right to free education. The introduction of the craft will bridge the gulf between manual and intellectual labour. It will remove the cleavage that exists in Indian society between the leisured and the labouring classes. It will cultivate a true sense of the dignity of labour and of human solidarity. This will make for better social unification. Mahatma Gandhi regards his plan as 'the spearhead of a silent social revolution fraught with the most far-reaching consequences." In the words of **Gandhiji**, "it (the plan) will provide a healthy and moral basis of relationship between the city and the village and thus go a long way towards eradicating some of the worst evils of the present social insecurity and poisoned relationship between the masses." Gandhiji wants the ideals of useful citizenship to be encouraged through education He regards the school as a co-operative community where students can learn lessons of love, truth, justice, co-operative endeavour, equality and brother-hood of man and social service. With these ideals in view, students will grow into citizens who will form a society known as the Sarvodya Samaj in which the aim is to attain a new humanism based on non-acquisitiveness, non-violence and truth.

Gandhiji's philosophy of education is biologically sound, in the sense that it lays emphasis on man's capacity "to go beyond the process of modifying the relations of his organism to fit the environment for promoting his best interests as well as, those of the society in which he lives." That man should be able to fit himself in a successful existence under the conditions of a complex and changing civilization, is what the biological aim in education demands—the demand of adjustment. And that was the implication of Gandhiji's belief that education should aim at developing the individuality of the whole man.

Dr. M S. Patel has beautifully summed up Gandhiji's philosophy of education from the three angles that we have referred to above.

Assuming that manual work or crafts is the core of his educational philosophy, it, "from the psychological point of view, balances the intellectual and practical elements of experience and may be made an instrument of educating the body and mind co-ordination. From the sociological point of view, it will conduce to a true sense of dignity of labour and of human solidarity, which would be an ethical and moral gain of incalculable significance. It will develop in the children the qualities of co-operation, brotherhood and service, which would make for a peaceful life in society, minimising all possible causes of friction.

Philosophic Tendencies in Gandhian Educational Philosophy. An interesting thing about Gandhiji's philosophy of education is that it combines the essentials of the three philosophical tendencies such as Naturalism, Idealism and Pragmatism. Of course, his philosophy is fundamentally Idealistic and Naturalism and Pragmatism are merely contributory to it.

This philosophy is naturalistic in as much as it considers the nature of the child how he learns and what his essential needs are. Like a biological naturalist, Gandhiji stresses the child's nature and its full development through education. This is borne out in such statements as "Children take in much more and with less labour through their ears than through their eyes." or that "Children should be educated in an atmosphere of freedom—freedom from super-imposed restrictions and interferences." Gandhiji, like the Naturalists, believes in the essential goodness of child nature, emphasises activity or learning by doing and shows aversion to artificiality and pedantry. He, like them, attempts to liberate education from the four walls of the school-room and wishes it to be given in a wider sphere of the natural surroundings of the child.

Gandhiji is an Idealist to the core. He has stressed the dignity of man, and the significance of the spiritual values in life like an Idealistic thinker. Other important aspects of Idealism are the ultimate aim of self-realization, the ideal of service unto humanity, preservation of moral values, the emphasis on religious education in the true sense of the word, and development of a harmonius personality. Like Froebel, Gandhiji believes that education should awaken the latent potentialities of the educand to fuller development. "Both of them discern in the divine plan, a symbolism which means that behind all activities there exist spiritual meanings and values."

While being a Naturalist and an Idealist, Gandhiji is also a Pragmatist. He believes that the absolute truth is to be realised through sustained experimentation. His autobiography entitled as "My experiments with Truth," shows that Gandhiji is a pragmatist. Education should equip the child with knowledge and skills necessary to deal effectively with the situations of real life. Again, there is a lot of similarity between the craft-centred activities and the learning activities as described by the pragmatists in the Project Method.

Gandhiji has tried to relate knowledge to the life of the people; the basic craft, like a project, is to be a socialised activity which makes for all type of social relationships, social participation, and vision of labour and willing responsibility to the community. Like the Pragmatists Gandhiji has emphasized the significance of correlation of the various subjects and social function of education or the school. In the words of **Dr. Patel**, "Gandhiji's philosophy of education is naturalistic in its setting, idealistic in its aim and pragmatic in its method and programme of work. All these tendencies are not separate in his philosophy. They fuse into a unity, giving rise to a theory of education which would suit the needs of the day and satisfy the loftiest aspiration of the human soul."

16

Education and Sociology

Education is a social process. It has a social function and above all, it originates in response to social needs and problems. The twofold relationship between education and society—education being both the product and the producer of the social environment—is quite evident. "The School", it has been rightly said, "is created by society to re-create society." Consequently, an adequate back-ground of sociological knowledge is indispensable for the proper understanding of the various educational problems.

Society is dynamic, it grows and changes. And as such, these social changes must not only be reflected in education, but they must affect, change or modify it. How the changing society affects education has been well brought out by Dewey in "The School and Society." Discussing the importance of society with reference to education, he says, "Whenever we have in mind the discussion of a new movement in education, it is especially necessary to take the broader social view. Otherwise changes in the school institution and tradition will be looked at as the arbitrary inventions of particular teachers ; at the worst, transitory fads, and at best, merely improvements in certain details. The modification going on in the method and curriculum of education is as much a product of the changed social situation, as much an effort to meet the needs of the new society that is forming, as are changes in modes of industry and commerce." It is only by connecting education with the general march of events that the school can lose its isolated character. Dewey has illustrated his view point by referring to the progress of science and how it has changed our religious ideas, our interests, our habits of living. All these have influenced the prevalent educational system, its methods and devices. The introduction of manual training, shop-work, household arts and other activities in the school is the direct result of these social changes. The school as such has "a chance to become the child's habitant, to be a miniature community, an embryonic society.

The study of history will reveal that in India, the educational system in ancient and medieval times was always actuated by the sociological thinking of the age. Not only was it determined by sociological factors, it modified and influenced education. During the British period, it was cut off from its roots. Recently, educational thinkers in India have begun to realize, in the words of **Prof. K. G. Saiyidain**, "that any theory or system of education which fails to take note of and respond to most emphatic forces of the contemporary environment, is futile and reactionary. It will never become thus an effective instrument of social reconstruction. ...Any attempt, therefore, to define the nature or scope and functions of education must constantly be referred back not only to its directive ideals and purposes (Philosophy of Education), but also the urgent dynamic forces which are re-shaping the pattern of society." Taking cognizance of this fact, Gandhiji, a great philosopher and sociological thinker of modern India, formulated the Basic Scheme of Education which is not only purposed to bring about a social change but is also the product of social factors of a growing democracy that have played a vital role in fashioning it.

THE MEANING AND DEFINITION OF EDUCATIONAL SOCIOLOGY

Having given a brief historical back-grouud to sociological thinking in education, we should turn our attention to the consideration of the meaning and scope of Educational Sociology.

Meaning of Definition of Educational Sociology

According to Brown, Educational Sociology is the study of the interaction of the individual and his cultural environment including other individuals, social groups and patterns of behaviour. Thus, social inter-action is the key-problem of Educational Sociology. The individual becomes a person as a product of this inter-action. Even Ottoway thinks that the sociology of education is speciality concerned with the influences of the social environment on the growing child. He remarks that Educational Sociology starts with the assumption that education is an activity which goes on in a society, and its aims and methods depend on the nature of the society in which it takes place. It is concerned with educational aims, methods, institutions administration and curricula in relation to the economic, political, religious, social and cultural forces of the society in which they function. In the education of the individual, it concerns the influence of social life and social relationships on the development of personality. Thus, according to Ottoway, the development of the child is to be thought of in relation to society and culture. It is not only that the individual cannot, in fact, grow up in isolation separated from his social group but that he becomes the kind of person he is, at any stage of development, by means of inter-action between himself and his social and physical environment..

Thus, Educational Sociology is the study of those phases of Sociology that are of significance for educative processes, especially the study of those which point to valuable programmes of learning and controls of learning process. Educational sociologists believe that the school problems of the greatest importance to the nation are not the problems of the school in any narrow, technical definition. They are the problems of society—they are problems of all social institutions. They are the problems of social direction, of individual motivation, of scientific knowledge and of effective group-action. Educational sociology analyses and evaluates the groups and institutions in which learning takes place and the social process involved in learning and teaching. It analyses and evaluates the social trends and ideologies which affect education. It helps us to understand how education can be a means of social control and social change. It throws light on human inter-action and relationships within the school, and relationships between the school and the community. It emphasises that learning is a social process. It is the modification of the organism in response to other organisms, and actuated by social motives and environments in the shape of culture, values, taboos and symbols. it is the total cultural milieu in which and through which the learning experience is acquired and organised.

Aims and Scope of Educational Sociology

A general view about the scope of Educational Sociology cannot be adequately formed without keeping in mind its aim. It aims at social control which means modification of individual's behaviour through inter-action with social environment particularly cultural. The achievement of better personality development by the promotion of social well-being and also by improving the social environment are some of the important aspects of the general aim of this science. According to "Harrington" its specific aims are as follows :

1. To bring out and explain the role, especially social, of the teacher and of the school as an Agency of Social Progress.

2. To analyse and study the social factors which influence an educational system at a given time and place particularly the democratic tendencies and the cultural, economic and social trends (movements) or changes in social life in general. It also aims at the assessment of their effect upon an educational system in general and upon the growth of personality in particular.

3. To socialise the curriculum i.e. to base it on and co-ordinate it with the demands, requirements or needs of the social environment. The realisation of these aims and several other allied problems like social inter-action, socialisation etc. which constitute the scope of the science as given below :

(i) The study of educational sociology is limited to those phases of sociology which are significant for the educative process and particularly for the growth of personality, the modification of behaviour and the acquiring of social control. As **Brown** says, "The social interaction of the individual and his cultural environment is the key-problem of educational sociology, which is primarily concerned with the influence of the social environment not only on the growing child but also the grown up individuals or the adults."

(ii) The study of the aims, methods and the curriculum of education as determined by the economic, political and cultural forces working in the environment of the educand—How far and in what way can the different agencies of education and social institutions be instrumental or effective for social control and conducive for social welfare.

(iii) The relation of education to various social trends or forces especially scientific and cultural—how culture is transmitted, preserved and revitalised through the formal and informal agencies of education like the family, the school, the community etc.

(iv) How socialisation takes place through different social processes like competition, co-operation, conflicts, accommodation and assimilation. The science is further interested in discovering the social institutions through which the individual gains his experience and develops social consciousness. Besides, the part played by some important psychological forces of social nature like imitation, suggestion, primitive sympathy and the gregarious instinct, is another problem that falls within the scope of the science.

As regards the scope of Educational Sociology, it includes the relation of education to various social forces, particularly culture, how culture is handed on through agencies like the school, the home, the religious organization, the play group etc., how socialisation takes place as a result of social inter-action which involves such processes as competition, conflict, co-operation, accommodation and assimilation. It also includes such topics as the place of the press, the radio, and the cinema as aids to social inter-action and communication, Education as a means of social change and social control are other themes of study for educational sociology. It deals with the impact of sociological thinking on the functions and aims of education, the curricula, school organisation and the methodology of teaching. The central theme remains to the social relationships of all types and how they affect the personality development of the learner.

The Main Problems of Educational Sociology

Educational Sociology has to take up the two-fold problems of social inter-action and socialisation of the individual. The former implies two processes whereby the social environments, particularly culture influences the individual's behaviour, and the individual modifies the social environment. It may be pointed out here that the modification of the individual's behaviour, social learning and the socialisation of the individual are. brought about more incidentally and informally through the cultural environment and the informal agencies than through schooling or formal teaching. The greatest educator, from the standpoint of Educational Sociology, is neither the teacher nor experience nor even experimentation, as pragmatists believe, but the social environment of the educand.

THE IMPACT OF EDUCATIONAL SOCIOLOGY ON EDUCATION

We have already discussed what Educational Sociology means and what its scope and problems are. We shall, now, try to understand the impact of Educational Sociology on education, on the principles of curriculum construction and its contents and on the method or methods of teaching.

Educational Sociology and Meaning of Education

Sociologically thinking, education is not the same thing as mere schooling, or the teaching or learning of a certain body of subject-matter. It is more than that. It is equivalent to the "development of character and personality by means of the social life of educational institutions". The social life consists of games, participation in dramatics and music and the visual arts, religious observances, debates and discussions, excursions and visits, i.e., all kinds of out-of-class activities. Again, sociologically considered, education is regarded as a process having psychological and sociological aspects. Of these two sides, the sociological aspect is relatively more important for the

Educational Sociologist who believes that true education comes through "the stimulation of the child's powers by the demands of the social situation in which he finds himself." One of the very important sociological factors is culture'. Education is a social process which may eliminate defects in a society and may perpetuate desirable institutions, and group activities. The Educational Sociologist attaches great importance to one aspect of education i.e. learning which, he holds, is the result of social inter-action and social motivation. It is a modification of the organism in response to other organisms. He regards education as a process of directed learning. This implies the necessity of providing children with purposeful experience so that they may become useful citizens through education.

The idea of directed learning is brought out by **Brown** when he says, "According to educational sociology, education is the consciously controlled process whereby changes in the behaviour are produced in the person and through the person within the group." To sum up, we can say with Ottoway that education when studied from the sociological point of view is a study of social relationships. "The sociology of. education focuses upon the social forces through which the individual gains experience."

Educational Sociology and Aims of Education

Educational Sociology as such does not provide the aims of education. This is, no doubt, the function of Educational Philosophy, yet sociological thinking in education has its impact on the objectives and the ends in education. Education should enable the individual, "to make his life for him better—both as an individual and as a member of his society, more generally acceptable, richer, more satisfying and significant to all concerned. Education should bring about a change not only in the amount of knowledge gained but in abilities to do, to think, to acquire habits, skills, interests and attitudes which characterise a person who is socially accepted, technically efficient, personally well-adjusted and socially responsible." The last sentence reflects the importance of the social aims in education or "socialisation" which, is supported by Educational Sociologists. As the thinking of educational sociologists is always in terms of the type of society that exists at a particular time, the aims of education according to him now in an age of democracy will be those that prepare an individual for democratic living. As such, worthy home membership, vocation and citizenship will demand our attention. Democracy, accompanied by rapid industrial changes, will also consider the proper use of leisure as an important end in education.

Educational Sociology and Functions of Education

Connected with the question 'What is Education?' is the question "What are the functions of Education?" We have already explained and examined some functions of education as such. Now we shall see how educational sociology views the question of functions. Payne thought that from the view-point of educational sociology, the functions of education were three in number, i.e. (a) assimilation of traditions, (b) development of new social patterns, and (c) creative and constructive role.

Education should help in transmitting the folk-ways, mores and other institutional patterns in social organization. The transmission will be facilitated through 'imitation' and 'inculcation' and with the help of such agencies as the school, the home, the religious organization and the play or occupational group. Even the radio, the television, the press and the cinema will perform the same function. "But education is not only to transmit the past cultural heritage, it is to help in the process of re-construction of our modes of living—i.e., it is to develop new social patterns in such areas as health, leisure, vocation and home-life. The reconstruction is imperative because of the scientific development and industrialization which are affecting the urban as well as the rural patterns of living, established for centuries. The creative function lies in providing for the development of open-mindedness to meet the changes which have already begun and which inevitably increase in our dynamic world. The ability to think creatively is essential for social progress.

Thus, from the sociological point of view, education can be regarded as a conservative force, a creative force and a critical force.

Educational Sociology and Curriculum

The function of Educational Sociology with regard to the curriculum is two-fold; first, that it should be selected with a view to accomplishing the social purpose of education and, second, that it should "be so organised and related to method and class-room practices that it may be an effective instrument of social control. When choosing subjects and activities, let the needs of society be borne in mind. As the needs of society are dynamic, the curriculum will also be dynamic and progressive. It should, therefore, be of a modifiable or flexible nature. It should reflect culture, customs and environment of the community.

Moreover, the Sociological Thinkers would like the curriculum to consist of the knowledge and skills that the child needs, not only for his life now as a child, but also for his future life as an adult. This view is shared by the Board of Education, London, and the Secondary Education Commission of 1952-53. The Board of Education says, "The curriculum should assist children to acquire or develop the habits, skills, interests and sentiments which they will need both for their own well-being and for that of the people among whom they will live". The following sociological principles can be noted regarding the subject-matter or curriculum. They are based on discussions held by Brown, Moor and Cole.

(i) The curriculum should reflect the basic cultural values of the society it serves, and at the same time should be an agent in the transmission of the highest values from generation to generation.

(ii) Curriculum planning should be based on the conditions, problems and needs of society, and on the real concerns, problems and interests of pupils.

(iii) It should provide educational programmes that give them whole-some participating roles in society. This participation is preparatory to responsible citizenship

(iv) The subject-matter of the school (curriculum) must be functional in its relation to adult living and, concurrently, be adapted to the level of development of the child.

(v) The school programme should treat with dignity all worthwhile vocations and services in community life.

(vi) The curriculum should increase the ability of students to define and solve problems that are meaningful and important, the ability to communicate, to participate in citizenship process and responsibilities, and to develop whole-some attitudes in human relations. It should encourage students to take responsibility for their actions and to take initiative and be creative in their outlook.

(vii) As the concept of world-society or world-brotherhood is gaining popularity due to rapid communication and other scientific inventions, the concept of education for international understanding is also gaining importance. Hence, the curriculum should prepare the child for the world society.

(viii) The curriculum should be flexible and changeable. It should change continually towards the more effective realization of socially determined objectives, which are also undergoing considerable change.

Bearing in mind these sociological principles, the curriculum must include subjects like Health, Physical Training, Social Studies, Languages, Mathematics. Elementary Science, Music and Art, the

Practical Arts, the Biological Sciences and a couple of Vocational Subjects at the Secondary School level.

Educational Sociology and Methods

The method refers to the procedures and principles which the teacher can and does adopt to establish relationship between the objectives and the curriculum. The teacher has to adopt some method or the other in order to realise the objectives with the help of suitable materials of instruction. The effectiveness of learning for social competency depends on the suitability of motives and procedures.

The Educational Sociologist according to Payne, judges the effectiveness of teaching method and technique in the light of three principles :

(i) The method of teaching is effective only in so far as the skills and knowledge acquired in the class-room are actually made use of by the individual in his adjustment to social situations.

(ii) The method of teaching must place primary emphasis on social behaviour outside the class-room.

(iii) The method of teaching must seek to utilize the social forces operative in the social life in order to develop capacity for social adjustment.

Further reflection on the question of teaching method will impress on us that sociologically considered, co-operative group patterns of learning which lay emphasis on group interaction, co-operative and democratic planning will always be preferable to others. The sociological thinking can not over-look the basic importance of sharing in teaching-learning process. And, because personality development is one of the main concerns of education, according to Sociological Thinkers, the method chosen should build and help in building personality which is emotionally stable and socially acceptable. The method again, should develop problem-solving and constructive thinking. The socialized techniques, the project and group methods, techniques of group dynamics fulfil most of these conditions. Hence, discussions seminars will replace the lecture or recitation method or the teacher's dictatorial pronoucement.

Some thinkers have criticised such socialized methods as, 'Soft Pedagogy'. If one deliberates over the situation dispassionately and calmly, he will realize that it actually means a programme of hard work in which each person reflects, plans and participates in bringing to pass a steadily improved process of learning and living—which is shared by all in associated living. It is such methods alone as will help us in realising the objectives that we have outlined above. Such methods will produce the genuine *'we feeling'*—"a feeling that he (student) belongs and has a part in an enterprize large than himself. They will stimulate a spirit of social interaction, a good anti-dote to selfishness. They will lead to an integration of the school tasks as much as to the integration of the learner's personality. They will develop the qualities of social leadership and emphasise the practice of social discipline, besides developing self-confidence in a social setting. These methods will accentuate the significance of purpose in learning and will impress on the students the real meaning of purpose. **Moor** and **Cole** point out : "...It is through group relationship (which are encouraged in socialised methods) that an individual becomes aware of what it means to work with a purpose... purpose lies within the individual, but its source, the stimulation for its growth, the nourishment, comes largely from without, and for these sources to be meaningful, the individual must be identified with the group—he must belong-to".

CONCLUSION

We have looked at the problem of relationship between Educational Sociology and Education from several angles, and from every angle, comes the demand for a sociological basis of education. What should be the aims of education? What should be the functions of education? What should be the curriculum and methods? Each and every educational problem is ultimately a sociological problem. The meanings, the aims and functions of education, the curriculum and methods of teaching are greatly influenced by social factors. Hence, the need for Sociological Foundations of Education.

17

Agencies of Education

Education, from the sociological point of view is a process of influencing the behaviour of the individual so as to bring him in line with his group. He is taught the behaviour patterns of his society and this goes to mould his personality. The process of the development of personality of the individual is thus the process of his education. The behaviour of the individual is influenced and shaped by a number of individuals and groups. A part of his behaviour he learns from his family, another part from his gang, another from his school. All these and other similar sources are described as "agencies of education."

The word 'agency' means operation or action of an agent. By 'agent', we mean a person or thing that acts or exerts power. Hence, agencies of education are those factors, sources, places or institutions which exercise an educational influence on the child.

KINDS OF AGENCIES

According to one description, agencies of education are divided into (i) active and (ii) passive, while according to another, they are divided into (i) formal and (ii) informal.

Active and Passive Agencies of Education

Active agencies are those which impart education through personal inter-action of the individuals. In case of active agencies, education is a two-way process. The educator and the educand are influencing each other, the learning situation becomes dynamic. For example, the family, the play group, the school, the church, the social clubs, the youth organizations of all types are active agencies, because all these involve personal interaction to some degree or the other. All these provide opportunities for social inter-action expressed in such forms as co-operation, conflict, competition, assimilation and accommodation. In the family, every member is influencing the behaviour of the other members or the family as whole just as the family as a whole is influencing every member. The school is influencing the individual patterns of behaviour although the individual, to a lesser degree, is modifying the patterns of the school. And if the individual happens to have leadership qualities, he makes an important impact on the school society in its various aspects.

On the other side, there are agencies in which the interaction is one-way process. The interaction that exists between parents, parents and children, between the teacher and students is two-way process, whereas the movies, the radio, the press "influence the behaviour of people, without being influenced themselves. The immediate two-way interaction is not possible in the case of such agencies as the movie, the radio, the television and the press. The picture goer may witness a picture and may feel satisfied or sad or happy. But the reactions, cannot, immediately, bring about or evoke any reactions in the actors, director or the story writer. The listener to the radio and the reader of newspapers, similarly, cannot, influence the radio artist, the singer, the writer or the editor or the correspondent, in that immediate person-to-person manner. In fact, passive agencies influence the individual but are not influenced in turn.

Formal and Informal Agencies of Education

There are some institutions and organisations which are set-up by the community more or less deliberately with the explicit object of imparting education to the individuals according to a consciously prepared plan. Such institutions and organisations are described as 'formal agencies' of education. Schools, churches, libraries, museums and art galleries, belong to this category. Influencing the behaviour and moulding the personality of the individuals is the only aim and function of these agencies. The time and place of such agencies are fixed. Their programmes are pre-planned. Their means and methods are clearly laid down. They have definite codes of discipline supervised by trained personnel.

There are other agencies, however, which exists primarily for certain other purposes, but they do exercise indirectly an important educative influence on the behaviour and character of the individuals. They diffuse and transmit culture and knowledge from one generation to another in an informal way. Such agencies are described as 'informal agencies' of education. Home, community, state, radio, press, play-groups, cliques, ganges and youth clubs belong to this category. They are brought into existence for some other purpose, but they exercise an important educative influence on the behaviour patterns of the individuals and contribute a great deal to the development of their personalities. They have no definite codes of discipline nor any formal rules and regulations. They do modify the behaviour of the child but the process of modification is indirect, informal and unconscious.

Differences between the Formal and Informal Agencies

The following are the points of difference between formal and informal agencies of education.

1. The specific and exclusive aim of formal agencies of education is to impart education. But the informal agencies of education do not impart education directly, though, indirectly, they exercise a great educative influence on the educand.

2. The formal agencies of education are pre-planned in aim, scope and programme. They follow a certain code of discipline and are kept under regular supervision. But, on the other hand, the informal agencies observe no formalities of rules, regulations and discipline.

3. The knowledge and culture is diffused and transmitted from one generation to another in an organized and formal manner through formal agencies. But such practice is not followed in informal agencies.

4. A lot of education is available without any effort and cost to the individual through informal agencies, which is not true in the case of formal agencies.

Merits and Demerits of Formal and Informal Agencies

The formal and informal agencies of education have both their merits and demerits. Formal education which is provided by formal agencies of education has its advantages as well as disadvantages. "Without formal education", says **Dewey**, "it is not possible to transmit all the resources and achievements of a complex society. It also opens a way to a kind of experience which would not be accessible to the young, if they were left to pick up their training in informal association with others, since books and the symbols of knowledge are mastered." But there are conspicuous dangers attendant upon formal education. "Formal education", say **Dewey**, "easily becomes remote and dead abstract and bookish., What accumulated knowledge exists in low grade societies is at least put into practice ; it is translated into character. But in an advanced culture much which has to be learned, is stored in symbols. It is far from translation into familiar acts and objects. There is the standing danger that the material of formal education will be merely subject-matter of the schools, isolated from the subject-matter of life experience. The permanent social interests are likely to be lost from view."

Dewey attaches greater significance to informal agencies of education. He calls them 'incidental', natural and important. The child is informally educated by living with others and the very process of living together educates. It enlarges and enlightens experience ; it stimulates and enriches imagination ; it creates responsibility for accuracy and vividness of statement and thought", points out Dewey, that unconscious influence of the informal agencies is very subtle and pervasive. They affect every fibre of character and mind. They incidentally help in the formation of habits, manners, tastes and attitudes. Informal agencies do not attempt to put a check on the child's freedom by making use of external pressure. It is in a natural interesting environment, that his behaviour is modified ; his habits and attitudes are moulded. So far informal education serves a very useful purpose, but because this education has no systematic planning, it sometimes results in confusion, and wastage of time and effort.

Proper Balance between Formal and Informal Agencies

Education both formal and informal is used by societies for preserving the values of the past and for proceeding on the path of progress. As societies become more complex in structure and resources, the need for formal teaching and learning increases. As formal teaching and training grow in extent, there is the danger of creating an undesirable split between the experience gained in more direct association and what is acquired in school, This danger was never greater than at the present time, on account of the rapid growth in the last few centuries of knowledge and technical modes of skill. "Hence one of the weightiest problems", observe **Dewey**, "with which the philosophy of education has to cope today is the method of keeping a proper balance between the informal and the formal, the incidental and intentional modes of education." This can be done by placing equal emphasis on the formal and informal agencies of education. Neither of the two should be given undue and greater emphasis at the cost of the other.

CONCLUSION

To conclude, we can say that all these agencies—active as well as passive, formal as well as informal, have their share in the social adjustment of the individuals, and the development of social control. In order to understand the sociological significance of education, we have to study the entire process of education, i.e., education provided by all these agencies collectively and variously. So in the next chapters we propose to discuss some of these important agencies of education in details.

18

The Home or The Family

The home or the family is an important informal but active agency of Education. It was the original social institution from which all other institutions developed. According to **Ballard**, "Originally, the family was the all-inclusive social institution. All human activity centred in the blood-bound,groups, hence, all human relationships were comprehended by it. It is only within comparatively recent times that the social order expanded beyond the control of the familial group." But in all human relationships is implied economic activity, play activity education, religious activity etc.

The family is important as an agency of education or socialisation, because it is the institution to which every individual is born. It is one of the most significant primary groups—the groups which are first in influencing the individual and in shaping his attitudes and behaviour patterns. Frank indicates the importance of the family by saying that it is the only institution which is an essential agency for child rearing, socialisation and for introducing the child to the culture of the society, thereby shaping the basic character-structure of our culture and forming the child's personality." Thus, the family, being a primary group provides intimate face-to-face association and interaction. It satisfies most of the needs of the child and provides emotional experience which may stimulate or retard the learning activity of children.

Again, the family has a virtual monopoly of the child's time and in serving his needs. If 'rapport' is of any significance for teaching-learning situations, the family provides the greatest possible opportunity for establishing this 'rapport' or sympathetic understanding because of 'bonds' of affection among various members and the possibility of suggestions being given and accepted.

THE FUNCTIONS OF A FAMILY

The basis of the family organization fundamentally is the instinct of sex—the mating urge. Biologically speaking, the purpose of the family structure is the procreation and perpatuation of the species. But this biological function of the family is not the only function performed by it. In fact, the family performs many more functions—social, economic and spiritual.

Ogburn assigns seven types of functions to the family. (i) Firstly, the family performs affectional function. The family is intended to provide an atmosphere of love for all its members (ii) Then comes its economic function. The family is required to produce goods and services needed by its members, (iii) The third function is educational. The family has to arrange to impart its mores and ways to its children. (iv) The fourth function is protective. The child being physically helpless and mentally immature has to be protected by the senior members of its family from all unfavourable influences. (v) The fifth function is recreational. One of the functions of the family is to provide means of play and enjoyment to its members. (vi) The next function is religions. The family is intended to initiate the child into its religious traditions, rituals and beliefs. (vii) The last function of the family is to give its members their family status. The family is to socialise the child by providing him with a social pattern of behaviour, and thus assigning him a status.

In the present, some of these functions have either dropped off or got modified in complexion as the result of industrialization, urbanization, increased facilities for travelling and advance of science. Educational and vocational functions were the main concern of the family in the past, but today in almost all the progressive countries of the world, their responsibility rests on the state or society. Nursery and kindergarten schools have taken over from the family, to a good extent, the job of bringing up and educating small children. Similary, specialised commercial or cultural agencies like the cinema, circus, radio and club have taken over from the family a very great part of the function of recreation. The growing materialistic outlook of people has made the family negligent of the religious function.

Since, the functions of the family have been constantly changing from the past to the present, a discussion of the role of primitive and modern family is essential.

THE ROLE OF PRIMITIVE FAMILY

In the primitive times the home was the only educational agency. Male children imitated their father and female children imitated their mother. The family has had varied educational functions in the past. These have changed with times, with changing technological advancements, economic conditions and social customs. The family in India, for example, was the centre of moral education. The oldest members of the family thought that it was their duty to acquaint the younger members with the family's moral code. The family imparted a certain type of religious teaching through religious ceremonies in which every member participated. If family determined the type of social relationships that its members could have outside. It determined the role and status of every member. The fixed roles and statuses resulted in rigid or fixed types of social interactions within the family or outside. The younger members were always to obey the elders in the family or outside. The family in India has been a centre of social activities, hence, it was an important agency for developing social behaviour and attitudes. Fellow-feeling and service to humanity were regarded as the highest aim of life, and the family life was more integrated and congenial. The joint family system was the only system which was popular with primitive societies under the joint family system. A host of members lived together in the same family in peace with an attitude of sacrifice, co-operativeness and mutual toleration. It was such altruism which contributed to the success of this system. So Indian culture has a high tradition of love, and service giving rise to a predominantly humanitarian outlook.

Thus, family was the cradle of all social virtues. Again, the family has been responsible for vocational education as well. Sons inherited and learned what their father 'professed'. Professions were passed on from fathers to sons. The family used to be self-sufficient even in its economic functions.

The Role of Modern Family

The family, now, has, different roles. It is in the process of disintegration. The big joint-families of the past are disappearing and in their place we have smaller families in which the contacts between various members are becoming less and less intimate everyday. It is no longer a centre for social activities or recreation. For this, people now go outside, to the pictures or theatres. The family code of morality is coming in conflict with the social code. Religion is an individual affairs now. Society is gradually losing control over the type or nature of religious education. And as vocations now-a-days are becoming highly specialised and varied, the family is inadequate in the sphere of preparing its members for vocations that were followed by the elders. This is more true of urban economy than of rural economy. Moreover vocations need a long and specialised preparation which the family cannot provide.

Even in India, with the growing impact of Western culture on our society, we have become more self-centred and less tolerant. The economic factors are, no doubt, responsible for such a change, but there are other forces which are equally responsible for this difference in outlook. As a result of all this, the Indian culture is under conquest, gradually giving way to the foreign influence in changed and continuously changing circumstances.

As days are passing, the number of broken homes, divorce and social cleavage are increasing even in our country. As a result, the development of the child cannot have its full scope. The spirit of tolerance and sacrifice is fast disappearing. Consequently, the functioning of a family is not smooth. With such family background a child enters into school and faces problems of adjustment. He cannot see things and conditions favourable for his social and intellectual growth. This is one of the main problems leading to the increase of backwardness, problem-behaviour and juvenile delinquency.

Educational functions which the primitive family used to perform, have been taken up gradually by the school in the modern times.

Although, with the growth of civilization, the school has taken over the educational function of the home, yet even now a good home does exert considerable influence in developing desirable and healthy ideals and attitudes which go a long way in modifying the behaviour of the young child. The home becomes the most effective educative agency, if education includes, as it does, the development of social attitudes and of correct ways of carrying on our relations with each other.

IMPORTANCE OF THE HOME

Although the organization of family has changed and some of its original activities have been transferred to other institutions. Nevertheless, it continues to be the basic social institution with important specialized functions to perform. It is still the only established agency for giving children nutritive and educative care during their early childhood. As a social institution, it is even now the organic starting point of children's education. The home environment is very largely responsible for modifying human behaviour in different directions. **Raymont** very rightly remarks. "Two children may attend the same school, may come under the influence of the same teachers and the same organisation, may pursue the same studies and perform the same exercises ; and yet may differ totally as regard their general knowledge, their interests, their speech, their bearing, and their moral tone, according to the homes they come from." Thus, the home leaves a permanent stamp on the child. He is, what his home makes him.

MEASURES TO MAKE HOME AN EFFECTIVE AGENCY OF EDUCATION

Home is a very important agency of education. But in order to be an affective educational agency, it must be run along right lines. It must be a well integrated, happy home. This implies harmonious relation between parents, absence of bickerings and dissention, affectionate and acceptant relationships between parents and the child and healthy, impartial sibling inter-relationship. But the home, in order to be an effective educational agency, must be run along right lines. Several measures can be suggested for making home an effective agency of education. Some of these have been discussed below :

Heredity Influence

A child's physical, mental, and emotional potentialities reflect the physical, mental and emotional characteristics of his parents. Through the accidents of birth, a young person inherits from his parents a greater or less degree of capacity to adjust to the demands of society. It is quite obvious that most of the Indian parents, illiterate as they are, cannot lay claim to the capacities and potentialities of educated parents. Hence, to make the home an effective agency, it is essential that immediate steps should be taken to drive out illiteracy from Indian homes. Parents should not only be given a reasonable amount of education, but they should also be trained in the functions of worthy home-membership. But this is not all. Some other type of training and education is also necessary. In the words of **Thomas** and **Lang**, Education for mating is necessary if biological inheritance is to be guarded and the child's right to be well born is preserved This includes information in regard to the laws of heredity, means of birth control, methods of checking the propagation of defectives, significance of love and engenics, and the importance of being discriminating in the formation of friendships with the opposite sex. Education for parenthood is essential, if the child's right to correct nutritive and educative care is to be guarded. This requires knowledge relative to child growth and development, health habits, language habits, child interests, and the formative importance of the child's earliest impressions of life and human sentiments. Education for married life is indispensable if the child's right to a good home environment is to be protected, and if the family dwelling-place is to afford the needed rest and security from the outside world and be the abiding centre of the affections. Home life should provide comfort, cheerfulness, comradeship, coziness, friendliness, and protection This demands knowledge concerning the care and management of domestic affairs, home-making activities, causes of family disruptions, aspects of sex life, and the importance of the cc-operative democratic ideal of home membership.

Physical Environmental Influence

Physical environmental influences of the average Indian home can in no case be called healthy. The situation of the home of a common man, its neighbourhood, its rooms, its furniture etc., present a poor spectacle. They are in no way conducive to the health and growth of children. As such, a change in the physical environment of Indian home is urgently needed. Only when the environment is purged of all its undesirable things, the children will get the right type of atmosphere for their mental and moral development.

Intellectual Environmental Influences

These influences are exercised by libraries, reading rooms and other agencies which foster the growth of the intellect. It is a naked truth that there is a very great dearth of libraries and reading rooms in our country. But how will they make home an effective agency of education? The reasons are not far to seek. To create the right type of intellectual environment in the home, it should have a suitable collection of books, pictorial magazines, illustrated weeklies, etc. so that the children may have an opportunity to see and read them. As the Indian families are too poor to buy them, it should be the function of the libraries and reading rooms to supply them to every home by rotation. Unless this step is taken by the government, the children will not get the right type of intellectual environmental influence in their homes.

Social Environmental Influences

In rural as well as urban areas the social environmental influences are generally very unhealthy. According to Crow and Crow, In rural areas the young child may be almost entirely dependent upon his family for his early education in human relationship. As a result, the influence upon him of home conditions and family attitudes is more potent than it is for the child whose home happens to be in an urban area. The city child usually has some opportunity to engage in activities with other children of his neighbourhood and to experience social relationships with adults in his community. But the rural as,well as the urban boy has to face a distinct disadvantage. While the rural child is more likely to develop basic behaviour patterns, the city child may be exposed to the unhealthful influences of playmates. To remedy these ills, it is necessary to have an environment that combines wholesome and neighbourhood influences. Only then children can be expected to have optimal educational advantages from.the social environment.

Aesthetic Environmental Influences

If you want the child to appreciate and create beautiful things, surround him with beautiful things. Beauty of form affects the mind. Hence, to produce the right type of effect on the child's mind, he should be surrounded by beautiful objects in his home.

CONCLUSION

To conclude, it may be said that home is still one of the most fundamental agencies for education in as much as it causes the development of attitudes and habits. It continues to be a source of giving and receiving affection, a source of giving security and belongingness to children—a feeling whose importance in learning and teaching cannot be overlooked. It still makes for highly educative interactions. It can provide cultural opportunities and can integrate the desirable influence of school and community by guiding the child's attitudes, habits and philosophy of life. This necessitates the presence of a harmonious relationship between school and home, between teachers and parents. Above all, the home should be an ideal home which must provide an atmosphere of freedom, confidence, fellowship and friendship. The home should be a place where its members are free to develop and express themselves as members of the home community.

19

The School

In the modern age when the society has been rapidly industrized, the science have grown tremendously, the data on history and social studies have grown rich, the school is considered as one of the most important agency of education. The knowledge has grown tremendously, and cultural needs have grown so much that it is almost impossible to provide education without the help of the school. Therefore, in the modern age of complex society, school is the most important formal as well as active agency of education.

ORIGIN OF THE SCHOOL

There was time when all education was given by informal agencies such as the church and the home. As social life was very simple, the family provided the child with all the activities and experiences, he needed for inter-personal and inter-social relationship of his group. Through the daily experiences of his life, the child became fully aware of the relationship that existed between him and his environment. Subsequently, religious places, like the temple, the mosque or church began to serve the purpose. Then, so long as occupations were centred round home or village, the family, the church and the local community performed the function of the school. The children learnt by imitating the work and the modes of living of their parents and neighbours.

But as society became more complex and civilisation advanced, various specialised agencies, the home or family and other informal agencies of education were found inadequate for the efficient transmission of cultural heritage to the future generations. It was thought necessary to have a new agency which could transmit the social and cultural heritage more efficiently, more deliberately and systematically. With the development of written language and the number system, the school was established in China, Egypt, Babylonia, India, Greece and Rome. The formal schooling in the beginning, "was confined chiefly to those areas of highest culture accumulation—written language, religion, philosophy and mathematics, and given only to the children of priestly and noble families. It was the informal agencies, however, which educated the general population. That all the children of all the people should be educated in schools, is a very recent development. It is an expression of democracy which has dominated thinking in a few countries. Even in these countries, the principle of sending every child to school is being practised rather slowly.

We have observed above that the school has become an important agency of education because of the increasing knowledge which every individual needs to acquire in order to live a full life—the knowledge about changes in the methods of production, distribution and exchange, the knowledge of the effects of the fast-increasing industrialisation, the knowledge of the human body, imparted by biological, medical and allied sciences, the knowledge of history, inter-national affairs, etc. A mere casual approach to this knowledge, as is assumed in receiving instruction from the home or the church, will not carry us very far. The school has became all the more important because of certain sociological changes too. The home, and the church are losing their hold on the people and have, thus, lost their original educational functions.

FUNCTIONS OF THE SCHOOL

The functions of the school have been variously interpreted, and in these differences lie the characteristic traits of schools of different nations and different times. We shall, however, confine our attention to the prevailing tendency of schools and discuss their functions in its light.

Two Broad Categories of Functions

The functions of the school can be conveniently divided into two broad categories—formal functions and informal functions.

Formal Functions. The following are the formal functions of the school :

1. To equip pupils with such useful knowledge which is not an end in itself but a means to an end. The end of knowledge is the

cultivation of a dynamic and adaptable mind that is always resourceful and enterprising in different situations and that is capable of creating values in an unknown future.

2. To develop in pupils the powers of thinking and judging so that they may be able to use their independent critical faculty to think, feel and act.

3. To preserve the cultural heritage of the past, to transmit it to the rising generation and to help it to make valuable additions to the existing heritage.

4. To develop the qualities of initiative and leadership in pupils so that they may efficiently perform their duties as good citizens in a democratic society.

5. To impart such training to pupils that they may be able to solve their bread and butter problem in an honourable way without being drags on society and others.

6. To impart training in character-building and spiritual freedom.

Informal Functions. The informal functions of the school can be summed up as follows :

1. To impart physical training to pupils by organizing games, sports, scouting, military training health campaigns, etc.

2. To impart social training to students by organizing social.activities like social service campaigns, social gatherings, etc.

3. To impart emotional training to boys and girls by organizing debates, dramatic clubs, art galleries, exhibitions, music concerts. dancing, painting, etc.

4. To provide an active environment to children for creative and recreational activities so that they may participate in the joys of creative self-expression and acquire actual life experiences.

Functions of School According to Thomson

Sir Godfrey Thomson has given the following list of the functions of the school :

Intellectual Training—By intellectual training, he means training in the sense of book-learning and abstract reasoning. This, according to him, is narrow function of the school, though an important, unique, and essential task.

Character Training—Character Training according to Thomson, is the most important function of the school. He says, "Character training, which in a simpler society was cared for by other agencies and by the general life of the community, must now, in our complex civilization, be looked after by the school."

Training Communal Life—Another function of the school is to provide training in communal life. **Thomson** writes, "School should be a place where natural communal life can be lived by the children, a life which will provide natural tasks to be performed, some individual and many in co-operation."

Training in National Pride and Patriotism—National pride and patriotism is a worthy sentiment. Without it a boy or girl can hardly rise to still higher ideals. Hence, the school must perform the function of giving training in national pride and patriotism. But one precaution is necessary. This sentiment must be developed in its purest form because there is "the obvious danger that pride in one's own country may pass over into contempt and enmity for another," as **Thomson** puts it.

Training in health and Sanitation—The school should perform the task of giving training in health and sanitation. This function can not be neglected by the school because our civilization has brought large numbers than ever before into cities, where people have to live under the influence of unnatural conditions of life.

Functions of School According to Brubacher

John S. Brubacher has assigned the following functions to the schools :—

Conservative Functions of the school. The school should conserve the existing social culture. This culture has been won at a great cost of time and suffering. Hence, it would be a great pity if any part of it were to be lost through failure to teach it to the oncoming generation. Moreover, as culture patterns are conserved through the school, it becomes especially important for the school to perform this conservative function, if other social institutions neglect to do so. **Brubacher** says, "Formerly, each institution like the family, church, and state tended to perpetuate its own mores. Latterly, however, these mores have become too complex for informal transmission, and these institutions have become too busy to attend to their educational duties adequately." Hence, the school must preserve the social patterns otherwise there is danger of their being lost through neglect.

Progressive Function of the School. Liberal and progressive thinkers believe that the school is not an institution to maintain things as they are but a means by which society can move ahead. They say that it is as,absurd to think that the school can preserve civilization from decaying as it is to think that the science of medicine can save a man from dying. Hence, the school must be the source of new ideas, of a social programme that is constantly changing. In other words, they think that the progressive function of the school should be to bring about major changes in the norms or frame of society.

Neutral Function of the School. It is not easy for society to be at one and the same time stable and progressive, free and secure. At the same time, it is possible that the community may look with anger at the school if it dislocates or tries to dislocate the peace and order of society by its teaching. Taking into consideration these two things, some neutralists say that the school must remain neutral or strictly aloof from politics. They say that the school should not be interested in useful knowledge or the practical clash of philosophic systems. They rather think that the school should stand high above the worldly affairs and should pursue eternal values and universal truths.

Other neutralists say that the school must be concerned with the affairs of men. It should exclude them from the curriculum only when they are so controversial that their discussion would divide the community. They claim that this is the only position to take in a pluristic culture, where the public school belongs to all the people. Still other neutralists say that controversial issues of economy and politics should find a place in the curriculum. The only safeguard that is necessary is that the school should maintain its neutrality. This can be done if the teacher impartially presents all sides of the issues taking care not to commit himself or the school to one side or another.

HOW TO MAKE SCHOOL AN EFFECTIVE AGENCY OF EDUCATION

The following measures can be adopted to make the school an effective agency of Education :

Co-operation with the Home

To become an effective agency of education, the school should working co-operation with the home. This, however, varies a great deal with the type of school. The boarding should almost replace the home when it is the place of residence for ten months of the year for some six or more years of life. Co-operation is needed most in the case of day schools.

In the day schools, the entire responsibility of educating the children cannot be placed on the school. The parents, too, should share it by co-operating with the school teachers. They can extend their co-operation to the teachers by telling them the family history, habits, interests, aptitude talents and weaknesses of the children. Equipped with such knowledge, teachers can handle the pupils effectively and give them the right type of guidance. Parents, in their turn, can profit by the observations of their children made by the teachers. In the absence of co-operation between teachers and parents, children may become victims of certain bad habits, physical defects, mental pervasions or moral lapses. To maintain a close contact between teachers and parents, the following steps can be taken :

Parents Association. Parents Association should be formed with the avowed object of bringing teachers and parents into closer contact. In the meetings of these associations parents should discuss the details of their childrens' education. Some of the meetings should be social in nature. Yet in others some eminent educationists should speak to the parents on new trends and methods in education. All such things will enlighten the parents and their co-operation with the teachers will become more valuable.

Celebration of Parent Days. Once a year, a day of the school programme should be set apart for inviting the parents of pupils, studying in the school, to the school. On this occasion, they should be taken round the school and shown what is actually going on therein. An exhibition of the work of pupils like calligraphy, models, maps, charts etc. may be displayed. Co-curricular activities such as debates, dramatics and sports may be organised. After this survey, the parents and the teachers should meet over a cup of tea when the headmaster should explain to the parents the difficulties and the problems, faced by the school. Problems of individual children may also be discussed with parents and their co-operation sought in the solution of those problems.

Visit to Pupils' Homes. Visit to pupils' homes by the teachers should be a permanent feature of every school. These visits will enable teachers to contact parents and discuss with them the problems concerning the children.

The false notions of prestige should not stand in the way of teachers visiting homes of the students. Through such visits, parents may be informed about the educational progress of their children in the class and their emotional development and general behaviour in and outside the class-room. Parents of problem and mentally handicapped children should be frequently contacted. Visits will help the school to know a lot about the physical and social conditions of children studying therein and thereby handle them in a psychological way. Thus, the great factors—the society and the home, influencing the life of the child, can be made to work together for bringing about the maximum possible development of the child.

Sending Progress Reports. There is yet, another important means of securing co-operation between school and home. It is that of sending reports on the work and progress of children to the parents concerned, on each occasion when an assessment is made. The cumulative record of each pupil, maintained in the school, should also be sent to parents for information and signatures, as the child is promoted from class to class. This will enable the parents to know in detail about the physical, academic, social and moral development of their children in school. Thus, the school will be able to supply those elements of training which the parents are not in a position to supply, for no fault of theirs. Basic schools, with all their community and social-service activities, play a very important role in bringing the school and the home closer together, in the task of children's education.

Inviting the Parents to School Functions. Moreover, the parents should be invited to school on various functions, organised by the school. These functions may include the Sports Day, the Prize-Distribution Day, the Parents Day, the Variety Show Programme and celebration of Independence Day, the Republic Day, the U.N.O. and the Human Rights Day. On such occasions, some of the educated parents or highly-placed old students of the school may be asked to preside or give talks as the case may be. Such occasions will encourage parents to associate themselves very closely with the work and ideals of the school.

Contact with Community Life

The school should be in close contact with community life, There is a general complaint that the school is isolated from life and does not give the students insight into the everyday world in which they are living. When they pass out of the school, they feel ill-adjusted and cannot take their place confidently and competently in the community. Unless the school is itself organized as a community and is in vital rapport with outside community life, this situation cannot be remedied. It is, therefore, necessary that the school should be a large community, but it should be a small community within a large community and there should be a constant interplay of healthy influences between it and the large community outside. The aim can be achieved by taking the following steps :

Participation in Social Service. Students should take an active part in various forms of social service for the good of the community and the school should not only inculcate the ideals and a desire for social service but also provide opportunities and the necessary material facilities. If the village or the town or the particular area of the city in which the school is located is unclean or happens to be infested with mosquitoes and flies carrying disease or is compelled to use water that is impure, it should be duty of the students to rouse the conscience of the local community to those evils and handicaps through effective forms of educative propaganda and also to do whatever they can to improve this state of affairs and win the enlightened co-operation of the public in this task.

Invitation to Members of the Community. Interested members of the community, engaged in various useful vocations and professions, should be invited to the school from time to time to talk about their particular work, to show its place and significance in the life of the community, to discuss its difficulties as well as its rewards. In this way, outside life will flow into the school and lower, if not knock down, the walls which at present isolate it from the currents of life operating outside.

Teaching of Social Subjects. The school should lay a particular emphasise on the teaching of social subjects. This will enable students to acquire some knowledge of the political, economic and social status of the community. This knowledge should be given a practical shape through group discussions in which prominent local persons should be invited to participate.

Centre of Adult Education. India is a country in which the number of illiterate adults is very large. Hence, every school should be a centre of adult education. This will have two-fold advantage. The problem of illiteracy will be solved to some extent and the adults of the neighbourhood will remain in contact with the school and its activities. They will begin to consider themselves part of the school. Thus, they will become interested in its progress.

Organization of Social Survey Clubs. According to K.G. Saiyidain, all schools should organize some sort of social survey clubs which should undertake to investigate into some of the crying needs and problems of the neighbouring community life e.g. the condition of roads, the drainage of the town or the village, the hygienic and sanitary conditions of the surrounding areas, the sources of epidemics, the supply of foodstuffs, the main industries and occupations of the locality. Each investigation should be undertaken by a small group of students who are interested in the problem and have made some study of the subject. They should work under the guidance of a teacher who should help them and suggest lines of attack. They should, at the end, draw up a report incorporating their suggestions which may, if necessary, be forwarded to the municipal committee through the Headmaster. The usefulness of such undertakings cannot be exaggerated. They will have a vitalizing influence on the child's school studies, because they will now have a motive and a purpose. At the same time they will have a reality and concreteness which they do not have at present.

Formation of Social Service Leagues. Social survey clubs will help us to know the defects in our environment, but simply knowing them will be of little avail. We will have to make our own little contribution to put them right. Hence, the formation of social service leagues in schools is essential. These leagues, Saiyidain says, should come forward whenever there is an occasion for their help at the times of flood or an epidemic or a festival or a procession or any other suitable opportunity demanding disciplined work. Their work can be profitably coordinated with the scout organization which is inspired by similar aims and ideals. These leagues can also take up work of helping the poor and needy students with in the school by providing books, scholarships and other suitable forms of assistance.

Throwing light on happy consequences resulting from an intimate contact between the school and the community life, **Dewey** observes, "We should make each one of our schools an embryonic community, active and with types of occupations that reflect the life of the larger society, and permeated through out with the spirit of art, history and science. When the school introduces and trains each child of society into membership with in such little community, saturating him with the spirit of service and providing him with the instruments of effective self-direction, we shall have the deepest and best guarantee of a larger society which is worthy lovely and harmonious."

State Patronage. Napoleon once said, "Public instruction should be the first object, of government." As such it can be said that the entire charge of education should be taken up by the State. The irony of situation that the State controls and finances schools established by it and extends a step-motherly treatment to schools set up by some enterprising persons or managing bodies. The, government can not shelve its responsibility of transforming the coaching schools into ideal centres of learning. Hence, it is imperative that the government should put into effect the following measures.

Establishment of Good Schools. A good school is one which contributes in the highest possible degree towards the realization of aims of education, as formulated by the Govt. It is a sad fact that very little efforts have been made by our Govt., in establishing such schools and in converting the existing ones into desired form.

Appointment of Qualified Teachers. The teacher is the most important factor in a school. Hence, it is necessary to attract to teaching profession young people more nearly at par with those who enter other professions. Teaching needs more men of a high calibre. Such men can be attracted to the teaching professions only when they are offered improved salaries and greater prestige in the eye of the public.

Liberal Financial Aid. Govt. should give liberal financial aid to schools for building, furniture, library, material aids, scientific apparatus, etc. Sadly enough, the Govt., puts forward the plea that substantial funds are not available to give the required aid to schools. This is simply a pretext not to come forward to help the cause of education because India has borrowed billions for industrial purpose, but not even a penny for education.

Reorganization of Colleges of Education. Existing colleges of Education do not send out the right type of teachers for certain obvious reasons. No camps, seminars, symposiums, study groups, extension lectures are organised by the Govt. making the presence of the lectures of Colleges of Education compulsory in them. Not only should the Govt., undertake these tasks but reorganise the colleges of Education in the light of the present educational trends and theories. Only then properly trained teachers will be available for schools.

Control and Supervision of Schools. Govt should tighten its control on the schools by increasing the number of school inspectors. They should be asked to inspect and supervise them regularly, solve their problems, and offer concrete suggestions for their improvement.

THE ORDINARY INDIAN SCHOOL

When so much has been written about the schools, it would not be out of place to give a pen-portrait of the schools of our country. In the words of **K. G. Saiyidain**, "The ordinary Indian School, as we know it today, has obviously failed to exploit most of what is worthy and valuable in the nature of youth. It has failed to tap the sources of their creative energies and to release them into fruitful channels. These schools are at best, places where formal training is provided in certain technical skills like reading, writing and drawing, or certain prescribed subjects of study like history, geography and science. At the worst, they are instruments for killing the spirit of joy, initiative and love of work in children." **Rabindra Nath Tagore**, who went to one such school vividly describes the education it gives, in these words, "Ours is an education of cage. We are being trained, like apes to imitate vulgar habits of a vulgar age. Detached completely from the main purpose of our life, we are being taught how to put up a mimic appearance."

Thus, we can say that an ordinary Indian school has failed to develop good habits among the students. It has failed to bring out the good latent in their nature. It has failed to direct their creative urges in the constructive channels. In Indian schools the knowledge of text books has only been given importance. Efforts have been directed chiefly towards this end that the minds of the individuals are stuffed with knowledge. Importance is excessively given to memory. The schools glorify the achievement of a degree or diploma and preach that there is no other end of education except to pass examination. The feelings of liberty, happiness, love towards work are emphasised as subsidiary goals. This situation is entirely different from that situation which is found in some advanced countries. There, the schools work ceaselessly towards the good of the society as well as the individual.

The organization of our schools is so defective that it has become very difficult that proper individual or social development can take place. Our schools can perform the functions required of them in a democracy only when the defects in their organization are removed.

20

The Community

Before we consider the community as the agency of education, it is essential that we understand its meaning and nature.

MEANING OF THE COMMUNITY

In ordinary conversation, we tend to refer to the community variously as our immediate neighbourbood, the group with whom we associate, the town in which we live the area by which we are surrounded, or the people by whom we are controlled or influenced. For our purposes, a more definite connotation of the term is needed.

Brownell defines a community in these words : "By a community I mean a small, diversified group of people, young and old, male and female, with different skills and abilities living together as kin neighbours. It is a face-to-face primary group, in which many of the major functions of life are carried on co-operatively with in the group itself. It is a small group where people know one another as whole persons not as, specialized fragments, and in which they have a sense of 'belonging.' This normal community has been the setting or matrix in which human activities have taken place since immemorial time. To it the human being is adapted ; he is, indeed, a community animal. When this community is dissolved, human life breaks down biologically, morally, even intellectually, and human education becomes futile."

The concept of a community has enlarged with the progress of civilization and the consequent increase of interdependence among the people of the world. The small, relatively independent rural community of the past gradually but surely is being superceded by a world community whose members are drawn together by an increasing similarity of ideals, interests, and interdependence, as well as by increasingly rapid means of communication and transportation.

We still refer rightly to the town or the city in which we live as our local community. At the same time as result of our inter-relations with the people who seem to be removed from us geographically, we are members of the state community. The community, then, may embrace less than a square mile in area or it may encompass the world, depending upon the extent to which its members are bound together by cultural, economic, or political ties.

IMPORTANCE OF THE COMMUNITY

The Community is as much responsible as the school or the home in modifying the behaviour of the individual in such a way that he may begin to participate actively in the activities of the group of which he is a member. We often hear that a child is what he is made by the elder members of the community. Truly speaking, community exercises a very deep influence on the growing personality of the child. As such, we can say that it influences his education from the very outset. Hence, if the right type of progress is desired in educating for life, we must regard the environment of the community as an essential part of the educational programme. When a child is born, he not only grows up and develops in the atmosphere of home, but there is an atmosphere of a wider whole—the community, which surrounds him and although unconsciously, yet most effectively moulds the habits, ideas and nature of the child. His culture, way of living and vocabulary, all are coloured and formed in a certain way exactly synonymous with the environment. The environment of the community makes an unfailing appeal to the general in-born tendency of imitation. It is but natural for the child to imitate the ways and manners of the people he sees around him. For example, if he lives and moves in the society of musicians, he will certainly be impressed with their artistic skill and perfection in music. Naturally enough, he will develop a taste for music and have a delicate ear for it. Children differ in their speech, attitudes and modes of behaviour, due to the difference in the pattern of the community of which he is a part. Hence, there is every justification in saying that community like family or the school should be considered as an important agency of education.

EDUCATIVE INFLUENCE OF THE COMMUNITY

The educative influence of the community is visible in many forms which have been discussed below.

Social Influence

The social influence of the community has a direct impact on an individual. The fact is that the community is the main source of man's civilization and his social progress. The child informly observes that the various members of the community join together to make their contribution to the advancement of their social organization and that if some of them do not do so, the community becomes static. From time to time, there are in the community, social, religious and cultural functions like fairs, festivals, social gatherings, religious rites etc. They offer the child an opportunity to participate in them and thus to acquire a first-hand knowledge of social life, social service and social sense. It is by living and working in the community that the child learns the true meaning of rights and freedom. He understands that rights involves duties and freedom implies restraint. It remains no secret to him that every member of the community is responsible for its good name and welfare. In short, we can say that community develops civic virtues in an individual and inculcates in him the spirit of service, sacrifice and co-operation.

Political Influence

The political influence of the community gives a shape and colour to the political ideas of an individual. While the people of the U.S. cherish and support democratic ideas and ideals, those of Russia foster communist principles and doctrines. The former are as antagonistic to the opinions of the latter as the latter are those to of the former. Speaking of another political influence, Crow and Crow write, "The political ideology of a community is reflected in the extent to which educational opportunities are offered to all its members and in the responsibility assumed by its political leaders for the educational progress of the citizens of the community.

Economic Influence

The economic influence of the Community is visible in trades and occupations. The child watches the grown-up members of his community engaged in different vocations. He naturally becomes interested in one of them and becomes curious not only to know more about it but also to learn it. It is not uncommon that he helps his parents or near relations in the work carried on by them, or he himself becomes an apprentice to a master craftsman. This is, true of the simple village community even to day to a very great extent. There the child either turns to agriculture or to some simple handicraft which meets the needs of the community. In case, an individual filled with new ideas, adopts a profession which is not permitted by his community, he is expelled by it, and is received back into it on the express condition of giving up that profession and accepting the penalty imposed upon him by it. This is a very common feature of Indian community even today. Thus, we can say that the community influences an individual in the way of life and in the choice of a profession, and thus enables him to become an independent member of the community.

Cultural Influence

Every community has a culture of its own—its traditions, customs, ideals, ways and manners. Every community tries to affix a permanent stamp on its members so that they may become attached and devoted to it. Consequently, it endeavours to make them fully familiar with its cultural heritage. Their belief or disbelief in the cultural traits of the community strengthens or weakens it. The child from the very beginning sees the grown-up persons preserving and respecting their culture and therefore, he in his turn, learns to do the same thing. We are quite familiar with the influence of the community on the language of the people. This is the reason that the children of one community differ from those of the other in speech, language and accent. You can note this distinction very easily among the children of rural and urban communities. Whenever there are social, cultural or religious functions, the child observes the various procedures and formalities. He tries to follow them and make them his own. Consequently, he develops a particular kind of sentiment for the culture and religion of the community. Hence, when a child comes to school for the first time, we find in him certain traits of language, religion, culture and morals.

Educational Influence

Though the social, political, economic, and cultural influences of the community possess a vital educational significance, yet the educational influence is no less important. Many communities set up and run their own educational institutions to train their children in a particular way of life, These schools have their own educational aims, objectives and practices according to which the children are trained for the service and welfare of the communities. Students studying in these schools generally belong to the same community and as such, they exhibit greater loyality to them and look upon them as their own. Orthodox communal schools, however, have a very pernicious influence. They make the children narrow-minded and infuse into them a narrow communal spirit. They, thus, create a wide gulf between the members of different communities, which look down upon each other. As such, communal schools are a curse to a country where they flourish. Their establishment, however, cannot be checked because they are considered necessary to impart the required, religious training to the children of a community. As there is no provision of religious education in government schools, many parents do not like to send their children there. Consequently, communal schools thrive. They find a very fertile soil in our country because of the presence of so many sects, faiths, castes, creeds, and religions.

Thus, we see that the educative influence of the community on the various aspects of a child's personality is very powerful. Only when this influence is of the right kind, our children will have the right kind of attitude. In this respect, **Nancy Catty** observes, "If all children were educated together until eleven ; if all educators, including teachers respected good work as good only, and refused to value it for such adventitious accessories as money or position ; if all of us who have work in which we find lasting interest felt so strongly that we owed a debt of gratitude to those of the community who take on the more monotonous tasks, that we were compelled to ensure them conditions of life at least as good as our own ; then, and then only, would the children growing up in our community have the right attitude towards all forms of work."

ROLE OF THE COMMUNITY IN EDUCATION

The community plays a very important role in education. This role is two-fold. In this respect, **Francis J. Brown** writes, "The role of the community in relation to education is two-fold, it inculcates in its children not only the folk ways but also attitudes and values, it sets the total pattern in which the school, as an institution, functions." We shall now enter into a detailed discussion of the aspects of this role, as given by Brown.

First Aspect of the Role

The first aspect of the role of the community is evident in the vocabulary of the child in his neatness and dress, and in many other exteremly important behaviour patterns which identify him with his community. Even more important are the attitudes and values which reflect his community environment. His attitude towards those who differ from him in race, religion, nationality or economic status ; his values in the utilization of free time ; his sense of his own role in relation to other children and to adults ; and evén his attitude towards the school are largely conditioned by his community. Jessie Bernard writes, "The community shares with the family, the task of socializing its members, and it continues in this role of socializer even after the family has ceased to function, long into adult-hood, indeed, its influence is felt as long as we are sensitive to what other people think.

Second Aspect of the Role

The second aspect of the role of the community is that is sets the climate in which the school functions. If the community is conservative, it will expect its school to avoid what it would consider to be "educational frills" and to instill discipline and respect for its elders. It may be niggardly in providing funds even for teachers' salaries. If the community is progressive and forward looking, it will encourage the school to experiment, to give its children the knowledge and understanding that they may have independence of judgement and to provide the educational setting for frank discussions of controversial issues. It will consider funds spent for education a sound investment in their children's and the nation's welfare.

RESPONSIBILITY OF THE COMMUNITY IN EDUCATION

A community has a very grave responsibility in matters of education. According to Crow and Crow, "A community cannot expect something for nothing. If it wishes its young people to serve their community well, it must provide whatever educational advantages are needed by the young people, individually and collectively, to prepare themselves for that service." Although, the Indian community has accepted its financial responsibility for the furthering of education, there is still much that can be and should be done for education by adopting the following methods :

Control of Education

Indian leaders are agreed that Indian schools should reflect democratic ideals in their objectives and practice. It is, therefore, necessary that the community, which finances its schools should direct that kind of education that shall be provided by the administrators and teachers of that schools. Hence, it is the responsibility of community leaders to determine what shall constitute the basic curriculum and the general organization of the school system.

Control of Schools

The influence of administrators and teachers upon the life and progress of a community is tremendous. Over a quarter of a century ago, it was stated by **Howerth** that, "the school is an instrument for modifying the character of society. Whether this modification is in the direction of social improvement, depends upon the ideas and ideals of those who handle the instrument."

On the basis of Howerth's view, we can say that it is not enough that community should finance education and maintain high standards of educational philosophy. It also must select as its school personnel those men and women who are well qualified to administer the practical details of school keeping in such a way that the ideals and the behaviour standards of the community may rise, through education ; to progressively greater heights.

Co-operation Between Citizens and School Leaders

Financing education and controlling schools alone will not do. To make them achieve their aim citizens and school leaders must cooperate. Emphasising this thing, **Crow** and **Crow** write, "All the citizens of the community, whether or not they are parents of school children should co-operate intelligently with the school leaders whom they have delegated specific educational responsibilities."

Provision of Informal Agencies of Education

An individual achieve, as much education outside the walls of a school building as in the regular class-rooms. Hence, it is the responsibility of the community to provide for its children whatever is financially possible in the way of out of school educational stimulation.

Museums, art galleries, libraries and music and drama centres are some of the educational media that should be made available to children. Educational programmes should be put into operation by community health centres and other departments and organizations. Moreover. books, periodicals, magazines and daily newspapers should be provided, because they wield a powerful influence over the attitudes and ideals of children who are stimulated by them. In fact, the power of the press is rivalled only by the power of the radio. Local newspapers reflect not only the educational level of the mass of the people who read them but also the ideals of community leaders.

INFLUENCE OF INDIAN COMMUNITY ON EDUCATION

In India, the influence of the community on education has been mainly indirect. We shall study this influence under the following heads :

Universal Demand For Education

"One of the striking features" write **Humayun Kabir**, "in the Indian science has been the almost universal demand for education." Some countries have considered it necessary to make attendence in schools obligatory. By and large, no such need has been felt in India. Here the problem has been one of providing enough schools for all who want to attend. This is the more remarkable. when we remember the prevailing poverty of the people.

Development of Primary and Pre-Primary Education

The influence of the community in the development of primary and pre-primary education has been tremendous. "Though elementary education is essentially a responsibility of the State, private enterprise has played an important role in its development. In certain provinces and in certain special fields, a major portion of the burden even for elementary education was borne by the community. Govt. is now taking up increasingly greater responsibility at this level, but the provision of pre-primary education and the initiation of new experiments or developments in this field still remains essentially the prerogative of non-official agencies."

Development of Secondary Education

The role of the community in the development of secondary education has been even greater. It would be no exaggeration to say that of all the middle and secondary schools functioning in the country, a large majority owe their origin to and are, even today, sustained by voluntary effort. The local authorities at various levels support a number of schools. The community has thus had a very decisive influence on the development of secondary education ; particularly on the development of local schools, so for as their establishment and multiplication are concerned.

Development of Higher Education

The Indian community has made very little contribution to higher education for two reasons. Firstly, during the British Rule, Indian universities were planned and set up by the government. Secondly, higher education, being abstract and general, hardly leaves any scope for the special needs of localities or communities which, therefore, very seldom take the initiative of establishing them.

CONCLUSION

Thus, we can conclude that the community is a potential educational force which the administrators and teachers must realise. They should not work in subordination to it, but should understand and work with it. Some disagreement may arise on certain points, but the same can be minimised or resolved through co-operation and sincere efforts at both the ends.

21

The State

State may be defined as an organized political community with the Government recognized by the people. There are two view-points regarding state. According to one "State is considered as a metaphysical entity over and above all the individuals which constitute it." According to the second view-point "State is an association of individuals, like any other grouping of individuals organized for the pursuit and conduct of an end common to all and resting upon the consent of its citizen. The first type of state is known as Totalitarian and the second type as Democratic.

DIFFERENCE BETWEEN TOTALITARIAN AND DEMOCRATIC STATES

There is much difference between a totalitarian and a democratic state. Their main differences are given below :

1. The totalitarian view-point is idealistic in nature. Such states are based on spiritual ideals. On the other hand, the democratic state is based on the fact of experiences. Thus, we can say that totalitarianism is based on an abstract idea while the democratic concept is concrete and practical.

2. In a totalitarian state the government exercises control through the creation of fear complex. The people are afraid of punishment and so remain under subjection of a tyrant. In democracy, on the other hand, the principles of justice and equality are the basic principles of the governance of the state.

3. In a totalitarian state. the individual is considered as a means and the state as end while in democracy the individual is considered as an end. The democratic slogan, 'Liberty, Equality and Fraternity' is replaced in a totalitarian state by the slogan, 'Duty, Discipline and Sacrifice.'

4. The totalitarian state is concerned, with its own good. It considers its own benefit, even at the cost of the individuals, as its main concern. The democratic state is however concerned with each one of its citizen's welfare. It seeks the all-round development of all of its people.

5. The concentration of power is the fundamental principle of totalitarianism, while the distribution of power is the main characteristic of democracy. In a democratic state the power remains in the hands of many who are the chosen representatives of the people but in a totalitarian state the power is concentrated only in the hands of a few or one man.

6. In a totalitarian state there is only one opinion and that opinion is of the authority. Thus, the authority's wish is law and its laws are subject to change with the shifts in authority's whims. In a democracy, on the other hand, there is individual freedom. The public is able to express its opinion without any fear or inhibition.

STATE AND EDUCATION

The State has begun to take interest in education very recently. In Europe as late as nineteenth century this principle of assigning the responsibility of the education of the citizens upon the state has become acceptable. In the ancient times, the state was giving financial assistance for the spread of education, yet it was not at all interfering with education. The modern state, however, takes full responsibility of the education of its citizens. It actively participates in planning, organization and expanding of education. But these functions are performed differently in two types of states—the totalitarian and the democratic.

Totalitarian State and Education

In such a state the individual freedom cannot be demanded in the form of individual right. It can be bestowed upon the individuals, if the state so wishes, for its own good. Therefore, in such state emphasis is laid on such values like harsh strict discipline, self-sacrifice, blind loyalty to the state etc. Education is considered as a monopoly of the state and a state-controlled strict, rigid and stereotyped system is maintained. The examples of such states are Germany of the Nazis and Italy of the the Fascists.

In the present times, the philosophy of education in a socialistic country (like communistic Russia and China) is considered akin to the philosophy of Education of a totalitarian state. it is thought that the leadership in the communist countries is of the same type as was existent in Fascist states. Therefore, in these countries, the state extols those very qualities which subjugate the will of the individual to the will of the State.

Democratic State and Education

In a democratic state also it is emphasized that one should be faithful to the state and obey its laws. It is considered that this obedience is not because the state is all-supreme but from the feeling that it is for serving the interests of the individual citizen. In a democratic country, all the institutions are not run by the Government. The other agencies are also given a right to establish their own institutions. The democratic state does not direct the children to read this or that to follow this method or that. It leaves ample scope for individual freedom.

STATE CONTROL OF EDUCATION

Is state control of education, desirable or not? In case, education is to be under the control of state, what should be the nature of this control? These questions have been engaging the attention of thinkers and politicians since long. There are two opinions regarding state control of education

Education Free from the Control of State

One opinion is that the state should not interfere in the education of its citizens. For example, Herbert Spencer considered that the national education should be given by private bodies. Similarly, **Raymont** says "The function of the state is to protect and promote not to absorb or take the place of the family and the individual." This is called the theory of Laissez-faire. The exponents of this view believe that education under the control of state cannot fulfil its aim of making free and all-round development of the personality of child. Therefore, the aims, curriculum and methods of teaching should be fixed up by family, religion and society.

Advantages. There are the following advantages of keeping education free from the control of the state :

1. The aim of education will not be narrow. We can have broader aims according to the needs of individual and society.

2. A great deal of co-operation of family, church and society may be obtained in order to set up the policy of education.

3. More attention may be paid to local needs.

4. Standard of education may be raised high, because of competition between different enterprises. This standard may fall down under state control.

5. Academic freedom may be maintained ; otherwise, educational institutions will merely follow the policies of state.

6. High class thinkers can blossom only in free environment. There is much possibility of the creation of great thinkers—philosophers, poets, artists, scientists and social reformers—in the absence of state control of education.

7. State may be checked by healthy criticism. The shortcomings of the state may be criticised. It is possible only when education is free from state control.

Difficulties. But the freedom of education from state control also creates some difficulties. Some of them are given below :

1. Educational institutions will have to face difficulty if state does not give subsidy. If state gives subsidy it is also entitled to control education.

2. Quarrels and struggles may take place in educational institutions on local basis.

3. Other institutions like family, church and society are for other aims They regard education as subsidiary and take very little interest in it. This makes degradation in education more possible than progress,

4. There is a lack of uniformity in the process as well as standards of education, because no one organization, other than state can manage all the educational institutions of the state.

5. The professional security of teachers may be at risk. A teacher may lose his service, if he does not satisfy selfish desires of the local persons.

6. Education cannot develop the feeling of benevolence for different social cultures in children. Every cultural group develops its own culture and children cannot cultivate sound attitude towards other cultures.

Complete Control of State on Education

The other opinion is in favour of complete control over education by the state. There should be a state-controlled system of education and all educational matters should be decided by the state.

Advantages. If the state has full control over education, there would be following advantages :

1. State makes educational institutions free from the worries of economic difficulties by giving subsidy.

2. There will be uniformity in the process and standard of education.

3. Feeling of security may be developed in teachers by control of state.

4. In the whole state a national policy of education may be fixed up so that national standard of education may be developed.

5. Education may be kept free from local quarrels and struggles.

6. State can preserve the culture of nation better than other organizations. State control over education will help preserving national culture.

Difficulties. If, on the one hand, there are some advantages of state control on education, there are some difficulties also on the other. Some of them are discussed below :

1. The aim of education may become narrow. State may declare its own policy as the policy of education.

2. Educational autonomy is destroyed and education becomes a powerful instrument in the hands of ruling party. The party in power may try to structure education according to its party policy. Indoctrination of party in power is a very great danger of the state control over education.

3. Local needs are shunned because the policy of education is fixed up by the centre.

4. Parents think that their duty ends after the birth of their children. In fact the management of the children's education is also their responsibility, but when there is state control, they think that state will make the management of education.

5. Teachers may have no say in curriculum construction although the function of making curriculum successful is theirs.

6. Control of state may create the feeling of security in teachers but they may live like a part of the machinery of administration. There is a lack of individual initiative in state services.

Compromise among two View-points

The views expressed above, represent extreme doctrines and have their own draw-backs. None of them can be accepted in toto. A compromise among them will have to be sought. State cannot escape its responsibility towards education. The control of state on education is essential for management and subsidy. But this control should be limited so that educational autonomy may not be destroyed. Education and state are not against each other. There should be co-operation between the two. Control of state on education should be only for guidance. The state is to supplement and not to supplant other institutions in the field of education. In this respect **Raymont** says, "We observe that education, like the other beneficial influences at work in a civilised community, may be conducted by all or any of three means; first, by voluntary effort with a view to profit ; secondly, by voluntary effort arising from philanthropic or religious motives ; thirdly, by the agency of the state.

STATE AS AN AGENCY OF EDUCATION

Whatever may be the view regarding state intervention in educational matters, one thing which we all realise is that education should be under the control of state to some extent. This is perhaps why we find the control of the state over education in one from or the other in almost all the countries of the world. This, if not necessary, is at least very desirable because the state within proper limits can perform functions which are beyond the means of any other agency of education. These educational functions of the state have been discussed below.

Training in Citizenship

An important function of the state now-a-days is to provide training in citizenship to individuals. This training has the following four aspects:

Economic Training. No nation can hope to progress without giving economic training to all types of citizens. Hence, it is essential that the state should provide facilities for scientific, agricultural, industrial and economic training. There should be a network of all kinds of institutions to which youth of the country can go for training.

Cultural Training. To preserve the cultural heritage, cultural training has necessarily to be provided. For this purpose, the state should set-up museums, art-galleries, cultural societies, dramatic clubs, entertainment halls, etc. At the same time, the state should liberally finance cultural, delegations, cultural tours, exchange of students, community centres, etc.

Social Training. The status of a nation is not determined by ideas alone, but social standards and social practices. A democratic country should establish minimum social standards for the healthy growth of the society and its members. This aim can be achieved if measurable standards of physical and mental health, of physical and mental development, and of freedom from economic anxiety are recognised, and proper training is imparted to the rising generation. Equally important is the opportunity for social contacts so that young boys and girls may inculcate the spirit of social service.

Political Training. To drive home into the minds of children the political ideology in which a nation believes, they have to be offered opportunities for political training. This training is also necessary to enable them to participate wisely and vigorously in the political matters of the country on growing up. For this purpose, it is essential that the state should arrange for free film-shows, radio-broadcasts, and political demonstrations.

Making Education Compulsory Upto a certain Stage

The state should provide the means of education and make education compulsory upto a certain stage and compel guardians to send their children to school so that they may go through the course. In many countries, education is free, universal and compulsory upto the primary stage and in some countries upto the secondary stage.

General Control and Direction of the School System

The State should assume the general control and direction of the school system.' The state should decide the courses of studies not alone, but with the advice of the teachers and the community. If the state alone does so, the result may be disastrous. In deciding the methods of teaching, the function of the state is still more limited. In selecting and using them, the teacher should have perfect freedom. What the state should do is to consult the best available opinion on the methods of teaching and then send the information about the improved methods to the schools. "State interference", says **Raymont**, "in the details of teaching is fraught with danger. The best guarantee of educational efficiency lies in requiring teachers to possess a sound education, in training them in the theory compatible with the duty of the authorities to deal with such cases of incompetence as may here and there arise."

Provision for Efficient Teachers

Providing efficient teachers to the school is the most important function of the state. Even if the educational authorities discharge their duties very thoroughly and efficiently, all is in vain unless teachers possessing knowledge, skill and sympathy are selected. To build schools, to fill them with students, to devise efficient means of supervision—all these are excellent things in themselves as machinery. But let us not forget that it is the teacher alone who supplies the driving power. **Raymont** very rightly remarks, "Educational salvation lies not in bricks and martar, nor in sumptuous equipment, nor in paper curricula, nor in elaborate machinery of whatever kind, but in the subtle influence of informed and cultured men and women upon the pupils committed to their care. A good teacher, in sympathy with his work, and doing it under reasonable liberal conditions of service, will achieve better things in a barn than a bad or dissatisfied one will achieve under the best of external circumstances."

The functions of the state with reference to education indicated above are absolutely essential and no state should dream of going ahead on the path of progress unless it performs them competently and liberally.

EDUCATIONAL FUNCTIONS OF STATE IN INDIA

We have so-far discussed the educational functions of the state in general. Now we propose to discuss these functions with reference to India. 'Education' is on the concurrent list. Therefore, the central and state governments both perform educational functions.

Educational Functions of Central Government

Below are given some of the Educational Functions of Central Government.

(a) To lay down general policies of Education to be carried out by the States.

(b) To give guidance to State Governments in carrying out those policies.

(c) To appoint Commissions to survey all India educational problems or to suggest changes in patterns of education etc.

(d) To maintain uniformity in educational standard in the country.

(e) To send delegations abroad and to invite scholars from abroad.

(f) To give financial assistance to State Governments and also to scholars from within and without the country.

(g) To start pilot projects and to do new experiments in the field of Education.

(h) To start institutions of all India importance.

(i) To recruit teachers for its own colleges and institutions.

(j) To answer questions in the Parliament.

Educational Functions of the State Governments

Below are given some of the Educational Functions of State Governments.

(a) To carry out the policy laid down by Central Ministry of Education.

(b) To lay down policy of education for the state in the light of general policy laid down by the central government.

(c) To open more and more institutions—Right from Primary to High.

(d) To give grants to the educational institutions.

(e) To distribute scholarships.

(f) To Maintain Uniformity of Standard in Education in various Districts.

(g) To gather statistics and also to pass them to Central Ministry of Education.

(h) To appoint committees to go into the problems of Education in the State.

(i) To recruit teachers for various educational institutions in the state.

(j) To encourage research.

(k) To answer questions in the Assembly.

CONCLUSION

To conclude, we can say that neither is the complete socialisation of education, nor is rigid 'Laissez-faire' satisfactory. In the best interest of an individual, the state, the home and the church should join hands. Let each supplement the other. There is a need for co-ordination. The state is to control education but at the same time is to give liberty to the family and denominational groups.

22

Other Agencies of Education

We have so far discussed some important agencies of education—the home or the family, the school, the community and the state. In this chapter we propose to discuss some other agencies of education, the church, the play groups, the youth organisation and movements, the press, the cinema, the radio and the television.

THE CHURCH

The Church is an informal, but active agency of education. It has always exerted a prominent influence in determining the personality of the individual, as well as in shaping the cultural pattern of society., The Church plays a three-fold role in the community. Firstly, it sustains the cultural pattern of the group. Secondly, it represents the highest aspirations of man and tries to translate them into visible behaviour. Thirdly, it tends to establish different groups within the total culture.

The Church is a very powerful agency for supporting the mores and values of the state and the community. In the modern times, the Church has begun to direct its attention all the more to the service and reform of the community in its ways of everyday life.

The Church is a means of relating the individual with the Supreme Being, embodying the highest aspirations of a community, and supplying spiritual sanctions to it. By doing so, it inspires man to live noble life, face his troubles with courage and remain calm in all circumstances. It provides a we-group in which every individual member finds a role and a status. It teaches him the common modes of prayer and methods of worship. The church originally dictated and enforced all values, moral and spiritual, economic and social, public and private.

The Church and Education

The Church has always imparted religious instruction and thereby influenced the conduct and behaviour of the people. To this extent it has always acted as an educational agency. Besides, much of the education during the early days was provided by religious bodies. During its early history, the Church always dominated the school curriculum. A good deal of the subject-matter of the public schools consisted of religious material. The text-books contained stories which concluded in severe punishments for evil-doers and rich rewards for the noble persons. Creation of spiritual values was regarded as the only function of education.

In the present times, the Church has become separated from the state and public education has come to be regarded as the responsibility of the state. So the importance of the Church as an educational agency has very much declined. Even the place of religious instruction in the school curriculum has come to be questioned.

Religion and the School

Religion creates spiritual values which is one of the aims of human life. Education is expected to train man for being able to create spiritual values. Naturally school is charged with this responsibility. It is, therefore, held that religious instructions and religious practices must form an important part of the school curriculum.

Opposed to this view is the view that the teaching of religion is the respomibility of the home and the Church ; the school has at best only to reinforce the home and the Church in discharging this important responsibility. Otherwise, the school should be altogether neutral towards religion and totally non-sectarian.

Some educationists hold that religion is not merely a faith to be believed but also a life to be lived, which involves group as well as individual behaviour. As such, the school which is responsible for the all-round preparation and training of the child cannot be totally absolved from responsibility for religious instruction.

The healthiest attitude in this regard, perhaps, is that the school must include in its scheme of studies the teaching of moral principles and the basic teachings of all religions, but it should keep itself aloof of the principles and practices in which different religions disagree. 'Narrow' religion had better be left alone ; only broad principles of theology may be taught as the principles underlying morality.

In the end we can say that Church, once an all important agency of education, is still a useful educational agency. The teaching of religious principles, and the basic principles of morality must form a part of the school curriculum.

PLAY GROUPS

Children organise themselves into groups for the sake of play. They organise cricket teams, foot-ball clubs, Kabaddi clubs, swimming associations, boy-scouts, girl-guide associations, etc. These organisations are known as 'play-groups'. The play groups are generally small in extent but, and perhaps for this very reason, they are most close-knit and strong. They are we-groups in the real sense of the term.

Play groups of young children exercise considerable influence on their personality development and thus on their education. They consist of children from two or more families who have assembled to play together. It is true that play groups of children are generally small and not well organised, yet they give equal chances to every member to assume leadership of the group. Hence, in these play groups, leadership shifts from one member to another. The activities of these play groups are highly imaginative. Play groups of teenagers "become more fully organised, leadership becomes better established, membership more selective and differentiated especially by sexes, activities more selective with one play group differentiated from another." In the case of play groups for younger children the activity itself is the basis for the organisation of the play group whereas in case of play groups of teenagers, the, group organisation is not determined by the activity. The Group in the words of **Brown**, "exists independently of a specific activity and selects the various activities in which it will engage."

Educational Values of Play-groups

Play Groups are highly educative. The following are the learning and educational values that emerge out of participation in such groups :

1. Children learn to co-operate with other children, as well as team play and the rules of the game. They learn to respect others' rights and privileges.

2. Play groups provide opportunities for both leadership and fellowship training.

3. Not only do the children learn to co-operate, they develop social attitudes, group values and the ability to go beyond one's ego-centric interests into concern for the group activity.

4. Play groups provide chances to all children from all socio-economic strata to play together and thus become conscious of the differences that exist in attitudes, values and behaviour in various groups of children.

5. Play groups are useful in learning the vocabulary of the group and in "providing the first experience of inter-group opposition"—the latter is possible because member of the group may compete for status and, through opposition within the group, discover their role, always seeking to improve it."

6. Play groups have all the advantages which play has for a child, development in the physical, emotional and mental areas.

7. The carefully supervised play groups may become therapeutic media for various types of abnormal or mal-adjusted children—aggressive, timid, hostile or withdrawn.

THE YOUTH ORGANISATIONS AND MOVEMENTS

Educational thinkers, all over the world, have given considerable attention to the problem of youth organisation movements as a factor in their education. The great concern over the nature and quality of such organisations can be ascribed to youth movements of Germany and Italy. England took this question seriously after World War II. The Government charged the Board of Education, towards the end of 1939, with a special responsibility for looking after the needs and interests of young people who had left school and started work." A Youth Advisory Council was appointed to advise the Minister of Education. Such a need was felt earlier in the U.S.A. where boy's clubs were established in some states as early as in 1860. Now there are more than 320 youth organisations in the same country including such organisations as the Red Cross Organisation, Boy Scouts of America. Young Men Christian Association, 4-H. Clubs, Girl Guides, Camp Fire, Girls, Pathfinders of America, American Youth Hostels, the Future Farmers and Young Farmers. Only recently, the Ministry of Education, Government of India have realised the importance of such organisations and have started a section in the Ministry under the name of Youth Welfare Section. This section organise every year Youth Festivals on an All-India basis. The various states in India are increasingly becoming alive to the need of organising these youth festivals and movements.

These organisations have been establised with the purpose of providing concrete activities in the form of games, gymnasium programmes, music, dramatics, handicrafts, vocational classes, specialised skills in agriculture and home-making. These concrete activities are expected to give satisfaction to the adolescent whose interests are increasing in number and who wants to find a meaning and purpose in life.

Principles of Organising Youth Organisations and Movements

In order that youth organisation and movements should perform their real educative functions adequately, there are certain criteria and principles. These are :

1. Youth movements should be non-political and secular. The exploitation of youth movements for political ends can do incalculable harm to the nation.

2. Youth movements should be national movements in the real sense of the word and should be based on the social and cultural ideologies of the nation.

3. The Government or the Civic groups should see that a large number of young people get opportunities for participation in the programmes of these organisations. The programmes should be flexible enough to allow for individual growth and initiative.

4. Youth Organisation should satisfy the psychological needs of the young people. Their programmes should provide opportunities for creative self-expression, should stimulate them to think for themselves, to learn to assume responsibility, new experiences and new adventures which satisfy their basic needs and thus enlist and maintain their interests.

If youth organisations have been adequately established and their work properly planned they will help the young participants to build up their character by offering a philosophy of life and socially worthy ideals. They can offer useful physical, social, aesthetic and cultural education by providing the corresponding activities. If properly organised, they can provide useful discussion on problems and occupational choice, health, nutrition, human behaviour, inter-personal relationship. racial understanding and tolerance, hobbies and other recreational pursuits and problems of adjustment.

THE PRESS

The press is a very important passive agency of education. By the 'press' we understand the agency that brings out books, newspapers, magazines and all other periodicals published and distributed in a country or community. As used in common language, the term 'Press' may simply stand for all these materials—the books, the newspapers, the journals etc., brought out by the printing press. It may be used as a collective name for all the printed and published materials. These publications are read by a large number of people. The tastes of the various classes of readers differ from one another. Accordingly, the spheres of influence of the different publications also differ. The reading habits of the members of a community are generally determined by the cultural patterns of their families and their community.

The school can go a long way in developing in them standards of value and appreciation which may help the children in the selection of their reading materials. The influence of the Press depends on the cultural background of the reader and this cultural pattern can and should be strengthened by the school.

The press exercises a great influence in shaping the attitudes, values and behaviour of its readers. The impressions they receive from the magazines, books and comics which they read go to mould their character and personalities in a significant manner, though they do not influence the adults as much as the youngsters.

The press influences the morals of the people as much as their intellectual concepts and views. This is why obsence and indecent material is generally banned and parents and teachers take a special care to direct the reading of the children along wholesome lines.

It cannot be denied that the press influences and determines very important patterns of social behaviour. Books and magazines appeal to people and influence their behaviour as much as their themes—sex, crime, love, courtship, etc., as by their attractive get-up, their pictures, cartoons etc. The educational sociologist is concerned with the study of the various ways in which the press exercises its influence.

THE CINEMA

The cinema is a very popular and powerful agency and an effective instrument for modifying human behaviour and disseminating cultural values and habits. Its popularity and effectiveness may be due to many reasons In this materialistic world, materialistic values are highly significant. The cinema stars, the directors, the story-writers and the music players are all known as people who are making a lot of wealth. Hence, these people are held in great social esteem. This makes for the effectiveness of suggestions that we get from them. Moreover, the cinema makes, an appeal to "our senses, to our imagination and arouses a variety of emotions and thus succeeds in developing and capturing the spontaneous interest of the audience." The appeal is made through word, sound, colour, through action and depiction of love, sorrow, anger, revenge and other basic human motives and emotions.

That the film has great educational possibilities can not be denied. The Film Enquiry Committee of 1951, with Sh. S K. Patil as its chairman, stresses the various directions in which the film can not only supplement the work of the teacher but achieve results which no amount of oral teaching can bring about, particularly in the presentation of a subject beyond the normal visual reach of the pupil, whether it is history, incidents connected with past periods, geography or biological processes that cannot be seen directly.

Various experimental studies made in the U.S.A, England and other countries show that movies modify the behaviour patterns of individuals and influence group standards of conduct. They succeed in doing so because they make the working of such processes as identification, imitation and 'stereotypes' possible. The process of 'opposition' operates in the sense that "it creates opposition between the standards of conduct portrayed on the screen and those of the real world of the child's home and community." Children and adolescents imetate the film stars. They play their mannerisms, dress, hair styles, attitudes and methods of speech. They bring new social habits into their everyday lives. The films have been found to arouse such unpleasant emotions as fear and joy felt in seeing the thrilling events. Some children can gather some factual knowledge of some value from the commercial films. A couple of research studies show that the cinema encourages anti-social conduct. There are very few films produced in India which have positive educational values. Of course, what we have said so far, is true more of commercial films than of educational films or children's films.

The educational films, in the form of 'features' and documentaries, have great possibilities. India is making rapid strides in this direction and some of its documentaries can be favourably compared with any in other countries. But it is necessary that even in commercial films motives other than mere 'money' and playing to the gallery should,operate in their planning and production. "If the cinema is not put to the right uses (for enhancement to tastes, for propagation of worthy human ideals, for courage, loyalty and other socially desirable values) it will almost certainly be put to the wrong ones."

THE RADIO

The radio has programmes for people of all ages. though no body takes a greater interest in its broadcasts than children. It is they who listen raptly to its thriller programmes, children's programmes, village programmes, film songs, radio plays and women's programmes, its adventure skits and love dramas, its comic shots and educational items. It is undoubted that the radio influences the behaviour of its listeners, especially its young listeners. They begin to identify themselves with the heroes or heroines of the dramatic broadcasts or even with their favourite news commentators. They sing their songs and imitate their behaviour, even adopt their views. The people who give programmes on radio-music, speeches, discussions, dramas—are people who enjoy a prestige and command a respect from their listeners. They appeal to the listeners emotions. Further, radio has a world-wide publicity. So its range of influence and its appeal is much wider than that of the press or the cinema. It is a much better agency for leisure-time social education.

The radio provides educational broadcasts too. These broadcasts can supplement the class-room work in three ways, (i) the school can adopt the radio programmes as a basis of discussion with students, (ii) it can utilise special broadcasts arranged occasionally by regional stations or by the centre and (iii) the school can provide programmes by students to be put up for the student community. These broadcasts include programmes by the students, programmes intended to form a basis of discussion with school children, and special educational programmes. The All India Radio has a daily school hour programme in which useful talks, dramas and discussions of literary, scientific, geographical and historical value are presented, these being specially planned and written by teachers and educationists. It is needed for a liberal for our children that talks on general topics concerning our daily life, inter-personal relationships, the impact of science on us etc. be transmitted. It is again necessary that the organisers of talks and news dissemination have a clear notions of the fact that the radio can either spread a more enlightened culture or stereotyped thinking and standardised ideas, that the radio, just as the press, can be used as an instrument of mere indoctrination. For a vital living democracy we need people who have not lost the power of free, honest and objective criticism. The radio and the press can play a significant role in achieving this.

THE TELEVISION

The television exhibits not only a programme—a speech or a song, but also the author of the programme—the speaker or the singer. Therefore, the television has a more effective appeal than the radio, especially for the young people. They enjoy the action as well as the sight of the actor.

Of late, television has become one of the major means of communication ; it has captivated the imagination of the younger people as no other means of communication has been able to do so far. Children love to spend maximum time they can afford before the television receivers. The growing popularity of television clearly indicates that its significance as a means of communication is bound to assume much greater proportions in the future.

The television programmes, like radio programmes, are subject to governmental regulation, so that they should, within limits reflect the needs and interests of the community, its education and culture. They are frequently integrated with regular school curriculum.

The television has great potentialities as an agency for influencing the cultural and economic life of the community. It can bring world personalities and events into the class-roorn and thereby enrich the school curriculum and enlarge the teacher's resources. It is thus a new promising tool for the achievement of educational objectives. It overcomes the shortcomings of the radio and augments the utility of the movie.

The television can prove specially effective for adult education and vocational training. But it is as yet only in its experimental stage, and it may take considerably long to play the role of a common and popular educational agency in the poor and scientifically backward countries like India.

CONCLUSION

In conclusion, we can say that in the past the home was the cradle of all social virtues. It was the only agency of education and socialisation of the child. It had many-fold functions. But in the modern complex society, there are so many agencies of education—formal and informal, active and passive which influence the personality of the individual and there must be a healthy co-ordination of school, home, community, state other such agencies to prepare healthy citizens and construct a new world where freedom, justice and peace prevail.

23

Education for Democracy

Freedom, it is universally admitted, is the very being of man. Human beings have always attached value to freedom. It has been always a motivating force in history. History is the story of the struggle of man for security from foreign invasion, and then freedom to govern themselves. Millions of Men and Women sacrified their lives in the struggle for freedom and thus gave us the boon of Democracy.

CONCEPT OF DEMOCRACY

Democracy is the voice of revolt raised by the human spirit against coercion and imposition. It arose as a rebellion against despotism. Democracy is opposed to arbitrary authority and the tyranny associated with it. It condemns exploitation of the weaker by the stronger individuals or groups. The concept of democracy, when interpreted in different ways, has taken different forms like, political democracy, economic democracy and social democracy.

Let us discuss each form of democracy separately.

Political Democracy

Generally, democracy is understood as a political institution. In "Government of the people, by the people, for the people", the remarks made by **Abraham Lincoln**, political democracy is implied. A democratic government is one which voluntarily gives sovereignty to the people. It is based on free and independent exercise of vote. Its three major institutions are (i) Elected Legislalure as the centre of political power and administrative control, (ii) A cabinet of elected ministers responsible to the legislature, and (iii) independent judiciary.

Economic Democracy

Economic democracy consists in a class-less society to which belong all the economic resources of a country. It is an organisation which holds absolute control of the wealth of the nation—means of production, modes of distribution and consumption.

Economic democracy does not permit glaring disparities between the earnings of different individuals or groups, or the exploitation of the poor by the rich. One of the most serious objections raised against political democracy is that it permits some individuals to hold and use means of production without any limit at the cost of the common man. Consequently, the common man is not in a position to fulfil his basic needs of food, shelter, clothing, medical aid and education. Unless every individual enjoys freedom from wants, he cannot be said to be really free. In fact, political democracy which provides freedom to exercise of vote and freedom of speech, but does not ensure freedom from wants is no democracy in the real sense of the world. It is held by some that the rise of communism and its growth in some countries is the result of the failure of democratic countries to ensure such economic freedom to the masses. Of course, to have freedom from wants at the cost of other types of freedom is like flying from the frying-pan into the fire.

Social Democracy

Social democracy consists in the absence of distinctions on the basis of caste, creed or colour. It provide scope for free social intercourse. It does not give special previleges to certain classes or deny equality of status to any individual or group. Social democracy is intimately related with religious democracy wherein, no invidious distinction is made between class and class or individual and individual on the basis of religion or rituals attached to it. Islam may be mentioned as a typical example of religious democracy, Sikhism is an other.

THE ESSENCE OF DEMOCRACY

Democracy is a way of living rather than a form of government, a rigid pattern or closed social system. Democratic living pre-supposes a democratic faith, that is faith in reason. Rational thinking and democratic living are inseparable, from a slightly different standpoint, the democratic faith is faith in freedom also. Freedom follows from reason automatically because rationality consists in freedom from passion and prejudice. To act freely is to act rationally and vice versa. The more rationally one acts, the more free he is. Of course, freedom does not in any way mean licence. Unregulated freedom is inconsistent with democratic living. Freedom consists in the rational control of animal drives and blind tendencies. The essence of freedom lies in self-control, which means freedom regulated by reason. In short, true or rational freedom, constitutes the essence of democratic living.

Democracy is the negation of all closed systems. The democratic society is a dynamic society. The democratic method is a peaceful method whereby change, if and when needed, is introduced gradually through persuasion. In fact, democracy is generally characterised as "exchange of ideas persuasion and enterprise of mutual education." In conclusion, it may be said that the democratic way of living consists in man's having faith in himself, in being free and self-reliant, in respect for truth, having courage of one's convictions and yet being ready to learnt from those who differ from us. Democracy believes in resorting to discussion rather than force, to bring our opponents round to our view-points.

RELATION OF EDUCATION AND DEMOCRACY

Our educational concepts, we know, have evolved under the impact of varied influences. What we think to-day about the aim, curriculum or the method of education is the product of history—certain broad movements, trends and currents of thoughts. The theory and practice of education is based on certain values, norms and principles accepted by a society. Among them democratic values and ideas occupy an important place. From this point of view, the student of the history of educational thought has not only to stress the part played by the Naturalistic,, Psychological or Sociological movements, but has also to assign proper place to the Democratic movement in education. This fact was particularly emphasised by John Dewey in his writings, like 'Democracy and Education' and 'School and Society'.

It is thus, evident that Education and Democracy are very intimately related. Such relationship can be explained in several ways.

Firstly, they have a common ground. Both Education and Democracy are concerned with the individual, with the modification of behaviour, and exaltation of his personality. Democracy and Education deal with a sublimated way of living. Secondly. they have a common function to perform. The integrated growth of the individual to the highest possible level, physical, intellectual and moral is their common aim. Both of them are stablisers of social order and instruments of social change. True education consists in the development of democratic habits and democracy cannot function properly without a sound educational system. Freedom is the common objective of both. In fact, it is the counter-part of education as wll as democracy. Democracy aims at freedom from want, disease and ignorance by providing equal opportunities to all. True education implies freedom of the mind from passions and prejudices. "Sa Vidya Ya Vimuktya", Education is that which liberates us.

Education is essential for the efficient functioning of a democratic society. A democratic social order is an organic whole consisting of inter-related and inter-dependent parts, that is its numerous individuals. In a connected whole, as in a democratic organisation, even a single weak link of the chain is likely to impair the efficiency of the whole. As **Dr. Radha Krishnan** says, "We cannot build rightly with bad material." Democracy without education is a mere myth, a form without matter. Education without democratic spirit or values is a body without the soul. Educational institutions wherein Education is democratised are the real nurseries of the leaders and followers of democracy.

Education and Democracy are related in their origin also. Not only this, their, progress is inter-dependent. The progress of democracy in U.S.A., U.K., France and other democratic countries during the past few decades is due mostly to universal primary and secondary education of the masses there. One of the causes of the progress of education in England was the triumph of democracy and the victory of the Labour Party after the Second World War. In India, the national movement and the attainment of the independence has been the chief cause of the extension and re-orientation of our educational system on democratic lines and in accordance with the needs of present day India. The progress in democracy during the last fifteen years has served as a strong impetus to the progress of education in many ways.

As **K. G. Saiyidain** says, the role of education in a truly democratic community is to develop the basic qualities of character on which depends the successful functioning of the democratic life, as for example, hatred for invidious class distinctions, respect for social justice, tolerance for difference of opinion, patriotism, love of work, co-operativeness and so on. Regarding the relation of education and democracy he writes, "An education that fails to inspire students with a burning passion for social justice, to break-down barriers of caste, creed and colour, to deepen their cultural understanding and sympathy and broaden their intellectual outlook to instill love for honest work and an attachment to national culture is unworthy of its high status and purpose."

MAIN FEATURES OF DEMOCRATIC EDUCATION

Before considering specific problems relating to different aspects of democratic education, we may briefly enumerate some of the important and general features of democratic education which are as follows :

1. Democratic education being based on freedom and being meant for social welfare is a recognised obligation of the State or Society. As democracy recognises the Sacredness of Personality or its inherent worth, it aims at providing equal opportunities to all individuals for growth. It makes special provision for exceptional, backward and handicapped children. Democratic education is universal. It is the education for the masses, education of all without distinction of caste, creed or colour. Under a democratic set-up, every Individual has a right to be educated. Adult Franchise requires a general enlightenment of the masses. Indian Constitution enjoins the government to provide free and compulsoty education for all children upto the age of fourteen. Adult education meant for the illiterate grown-ups is an essential part of democratic education.

2. Democratic education is broad-based. It is oppoed to the unnatural divorce of education from some of the allied Sciences with which it is vitally related. Such Sciences are Psychology, Biology and Sociology in addition to Philosophy. Psychology offers the raw material, Biology provides data and Sociology provides the environment for education. Philosophy guides and enlightens it by providing aim. The more democratised ducation is, the more broad-based it tends to become.

3. It is child-centred from the democratic point of view, the school exists for the child and not the child for the school. The primary factor in the educative process is neither the teacher nor the subject but the educand. The value or suitability of the method or curriculum of an educational system is judged with reference to the interests, needs and aptitudes of the child. In short, the child is the pivot round which the entire process of education revolves. In democratic education, child nature is considered as divine and not wicked as it is sometimes believed.

4. Democratic education is secular. It has already been said that it is not the privilege of a few but the right of all. The secular nature of democratic education consists in its being unconcerned with the faith or religion professed by an individual or a group. It rises above sectarianism, communalism or regional loyalties. It gives equal status to all citizens of the State without making any invidious distinction of colour, race or sex.

5. Democratic education is related to the social environment of the child. It is social in nature, it arises for the fulfilment of a social purpose or it has a social function to perform. Education and society are inseparably related. Democratic education is alive to the needs and problems of the community around it. The school is to function as a community on a small scale. In democratic education, there is no gulf between the life within the school and the wider life of the society outside it. The traditional school was divorced from life. It was not community-centred. It was, therefore, undemocratic. The community school advocated by Gandhiji in his scheme of Basic Education came into existence in India under the impact of the democratic spirit.

6. Democratic education is education for experience. Education in democracy is not considered as a pouring in process, nor is the learner a passive recipient of ready-made ideas of the teachers. Democratic education, on the contrary, is a truly bi-polar process. It is an intellectual enterprise. It aims at developing an experimental and problem-solvirg attitude of the child. The Heuristic method, Dalton Plan, Project method and the method of Correlation used in Basic Education are the outcome of such democratic attitude. Democratic education is not only preparation for life ; it is equated with life.

7. Democratic education stimulates creativity. It is not only an incentive for individualised instruction but also for developing the creative urge of the child. Creativity is a matter of an attitude of mind resulting from the habit of open-mindedness, suspension of judgement, dispassionate reflection and the courage of one's convictions. Democratic education is opposed to regimentation or indoctrination in education. The individual is not considered as just a link in a collective whole of mechanical nature. Individuals are as Fassism holds to think and act alike in a rigid manner under coercion, in accordance with an exterior end prescribed by some external authority to adopt and play whatever role is assigned to them in a rigid, sterile and completely crystallised society. They are not allowed to act freely.

8. Freedom being a counterpart of democracy is an essential feature of democratic education. Of course, freedom means not only absence of external restraint but also absence of passions, prejudices and whims. Freedom means rational freedom. It does not, in any way, mean licence.

9. For democratic education discipline is self-discipline. The school discipline is not an order imposed by a dictator, a teacher or some representative of the community to which the child belongs. To begin

with, discipline is in the form of social control. In course of time the child identifies himself with his society and its laws. He starts looking upon them as his own laws. Thus, external authority in democratic education is in course of time converted into internal authority of autonomy.

10. Democratic education is of a flexible nature. A democratic society is dynamic. Therefore, education in such a society should also be dynamic. Democracy has a liberal attitude towards change. It welcomes change if and when it is needed. This idea has been very aptly expressed by **Dr. Radhakrishnan** who says, "There are no changeless way of educating human nature a curriculum that had a vitality in Vedic Period may not remain unaltered in the twentieth century." Democratic Education serves as an instrument of social change. "The school", has been rightly characterised, as "an agency created by society for the purpose of re-creating society." In relation to society, democratic education has two-fold function to perform. It aims at establishing the social order and it also serves as an instrument of change. Democratic education effects proper synthesis between the function of conservation and transmission of culture on the one hand and that of its re-construction on the other.

APPLICATION OF DEMOCRATIC PRINCIPLES TO EDUCATION

After enumerating some of the general features of Democratic Education and specifying some basic beliefs of Democracy, we have now to consider as to what particular form is taken by important educational problems particularly those of educational aims, the curriculum, the method, the role of the teacher and discipline under the impact of the democratic spirit. In fact, democratic education pervades the entire atmosphere of the school in all its curricular and co-curricular activities. But the democratic spirit is manifested in a more distinct and visible form in the spheres of the curriculum and methodology.

The Aims of Education

In a general way, the aim of democratic education may be stated as the inculcation of democratic system of values by providing a democratic atmosphere in all aspects of school life—curricular or co-curricular activities. school management, pupil-teacher, teacher-parents and school-community relationship. Briefly speaking, democratic education aims at desirable social attitudes, worthy citizenship, patriotism and international understanding. Perhaps the best way of formulating the democratic aim is to say that its ultimate goal is the full and free development of the child into a well-balanced harmonious personality. It aims at providing equal opportunities and the widest possible scope for the integrated growth of the various talents, aptitudes or potentialities of the educand.

Democratic education aimes at the enrichment of the pupils life through providing a wide range of interests and useful outlets for acquiring mastery over facts, learning skills and developing habits of independent thinking, impartial or objective observation and dispassionate investigation To develop the full man or woman, democratic education aims at socialising the child, thereby transforming the individual into a person. Respect for individuality and exaltation of personality, figure prominently among the objectives of education. Democratic education has a predominantly social outlook. It serves as an instrument of social change and a great conservator of cultural heritage. Economic independence of every member of democratic society through vocational education is an essential part of the democratic aim. Democratic education goes beyond the school. It is a vital link between the school and the society. It aims at transforming the school into a community centre. The democratic school is, in fact, a community-based institution. Lastly, democratic education aims at assigning an important place to the supreme or the spiritual values of truth, beauty and goodness, Its aim is not purely material, its outlook is far from being extremely utilitarian.

In their report *"The Purpose of Education in American Democracy"* the Educational Policies Commission grouped its objectives under four headings :

1. The objectives of Self-realization (the person himself).

2. The objectives of Human Relationships (The relations of the educated person to others in the home and in the community).

3. The objectives of Economic efficiency (The educated consumer or producer).

4. The objectives of Civic Responsibility (the socio-civic responsibilities of the educated man).

1. The objective of Self-realization.

(a) Developing an inquiring mind.

(b) Mastering the tools of learning.

(c) Listening and observing skillfully.

(d) Using his leisure wisely.
(e) Protecting his health.
(f) Appreciating beauty.
(g) Considering life's purpose.

2. The Objectives of Human Relationships. (The educated as member of the family and community).
(a) Getting along with others.
(b) Placing human values first.
(c) Enjoying sincere friendships.
(d) Co-operating with others.
(e) Filling his place in the home.
(f) Preparing for his own family.
(g) Building a democratic home.

3. The objectives of Economic Efficiency (The educated producers or consumers).
(a) Taking pride in good workmanship.
(b) Appreciating the value of work.
(c) Selecting his occupations wisely.
(d) Succeeding at his work.
(e) Becoming a wise consumer.
(f) Learning to buy skillfully.
(g) Achieving economic security.

4. The objectives of Civic Responsibility. (The educated citizens).
(a) Considering human needs.
(b) Seeking reliable information.
(c) Tolerating other points of view.
(d) Safeguarding natural resources.
(e) Fulfilling civic duties.
(f) Serving democracy loyally.
(g) Seeking world good will.

(Recommendations of the Educational Policies Commission, 'U.S.A. 1937).

In brief the democratic ideals and the aims of education in India as envisaged in the Report of the Secondary Education Commission are as follows :

1. Development of ideas of citizenship.
2. Improvement of vocational efficiency.
3. Development of personality.
4. Education for leadership.

The Aims of Democratic Education with reference to the Special Conditions prevailing in India. Before specifying the aim of education suited to our needs, problems and aspirations, a brief reference to the various circumstances under which we live at present seems to be necessary. India is an infant and yet the largest democracy of the world. The economic resources of the country are to be developed. Giant steel plants like those of Bhilai or Rourkela and gigantic dams, big irrigation projects and mechanised farming of a scientific nature are some of our fore-most needs. The earning capacity of the common man and his standard of living are to be considerably raised. Men, money and material should be mobilised for collective and co-operative enterprises. Human planning is our foremost need. The nation is in need of men and women of real integrity. A house divided against itself and a heterogeneous society has to be integrated into a homogeneous nation. A campaign has to be launched against communalism, regionalism and linguism. Secular attitudes are to be developed. The average man has to be educated for the judicious exercise of vote. Political administrative authority is to be de-centralized. The village Panchayat and the Parliament have to be co-ordinated. Democracy has to be built from below. For the social re-construction of the Nation, a new orientation in our cultural outlook is needed. A compromise is to be effected between our obsession with the past and fascination for the future. "We must be critical and selective and use the past to illumine the future." Above all, the need for the development of an international outlook is very urgent, India has to play a significant role in harmonising conflicting world forces and hostile power blocs.

Significant light is thrown by **Dr. Radhakrishnan** on the nature of educational aim, suited to the social needs of free India. He writes, "Our educational systems must find their guiding principles in the aims of the social order for which it prepares, in the nature of the civilisation. it hopes to build. Unless we know whether we are tending we cannot decide what we should do and how we should do it, societies like men need a clear purpose to keep them stable in the world of bewildering change."

The aims formulated by University Education Commission in the light of the above circumstances are as follows :

1. To increase national wealth and enhance productive efficiency by developing the economic resources of the country through science, research and technology and well planned vocational education.

2. To develop social consciousness, a civic sense and to decondition anti-social attitudes.

3. To inculcate democratic values, qualities of leadership, secular,attitudes and to develop a wide outlook through education for democracy, citizenship, national integration and international understanding.

4. To develop qualities of character, tolerance, co-operativeness passion for social justice and independent thinking.

5. To stimulate cultural renaissance to conserve and transmit our rich cultural heritage and to re-vitalise it. To bring about a traditional synthesis between culture and civilsation.

6. To develop regional languages alongwith the national language and to ensure their judicious co-ordination.

As democratic education aims at providing opportunities for the integrated growth of the individual into a full man or woman, the curriculum in democratic education is rich in content and flexible in nature. **Dr. Radhakrishnan's** views in this context are enlightening. "The institutions of democracy must be flexible, capable of adaptation to the changing needs and conditions of men. We must make modifications whenever we feel that changes are necessary to realise more effectively the ends of individual development and social walfare.

Educational systems are built for a time and not for all times. There are no changeless ways of educating human nature. A curriculum which had vitality in the Vedic Period or the Renaissance cannot continue unaltered in the 20th century."

The Curriculum

The curriculum caters to all the basic needs and interests of the child. Curiosity about the physical environment structure or the body and mechanism of the mind, constructiveness and play, sociableness and other such basic urges of the child's mind should find proper expression in different areas of the curriculum. For providing simple understanding of his physical environment and subsequently, acquiring mastery over nature through scientific knowledge and technology, natural sciences like Physics, Chemistry. Biology are to be given a proper place. For the cultivation of reasoning power and consecutive thinking, teaching of Mathematics is required so that the learner may be made conversant with the quantitative study of special relations, numbers and geometrical forms to familiarise the child with his social environment and social changes and also to develop him into an intelligent citizen. Civics, History, Geography, Political Science, Economics have a special importance. To enable the educand to have an elementary knowledge about himself, his behaviour, human values and ideals, the curriculum should consist of the study of Arts, Culture, Ethics, Philosophy and Religion. To develop the child into a socially efficient and vocationally competent earning member of society, vocational technical education constitutes an integral part of the curriculum, at least the subjects taught should have, as far as possible, a vocational bias in addition to their cultural values. The curriculum of democratic education removes the apparent disparity between what is known as liberal and vocational education. As Educational Sociology guides us certain areas of the curriculum, as for example, the study of culture and comparative religion are needed for the development of healthy, social attitudes. As the child is primarily a doer, a builder or a creator rather than a thinker, provision should be made for the teaching of Arts and Crafts, so that the child can develop skills in different spheres of manual work of a productive and creative nature. The curriculum under a Democratic Educational system should provide ample scope for the expression of his creative urge.

In all respects, the curriculum should be child-centred. The major objective behind it, is unhampered and integrated growth of the child. It should also be capable of being adjusted to the requirements and psychological needs of the different developmental stages of the child. Above all, it should be of a thought stimulating nature and based on the well-known principle of learning by doing. It should be so devised that education does not degenerate into a bare pouring in-process, and ready-made ideas and conclusions are not imposed upon the learner. The social element in education should be properly emphasised. A curriculum that fails to socialise the child is unworthy of Democratic Education.

The curriculum should be constructed on the principle of integration. Integration consists in knitting together different aspects or inter-related elements of an organic whole under a unifying principle. The curriculum should be so devised that it may present what **Dr. Radha Krishnan** calls a "Coherent picture of the universe an integrated way of life." It is through an integrated curriculum that the education of the whole man or woman is possible. Piece-meal knowledge imparted in water-tight compartments is repugnant to Democratic Education. Integration implies the organisation of different intellectual disciplines in an inter-related manner round a central core. It also stands for the linking up of education with the needs and problems of the social environment of the learner. What **Adams** said, "A fragment of education addressing itself to fragment of a pupil about fragment of a subject" is not possible, at any rate, it is not approved in Democratic Education. The different features of a democratic type of curriculum are summed up by **Raymont** in the following words "The curriculum is the outer expression of the ideas and aspirations of the community, not of an individual. And the Community has a right to lay down in broad outlines which instruction should be followed in the school with due reference to the opinion of the professional elements as to what constitutes the mental food for the children. A wise educational authority, would, however, whilst, requiring conformity to a general plan of study would refrain from detailed prescription and would leave its, teachers for experiment and for the play of individuality."

The Method

Directly or indirectly educational procedures are determind by educational objectives. The problems of aim, curriculum and method are inter-related. When the aim of education undergoes a change, naturally the content needed for its realisation will have to be modified accordingly. And the method should also be in conformity with the educational aim and content. In a democratic educational system which is essentially child-centric, education must be activity-centred. Unless the self-activity of the learner is aroused and his independent thinking is stimulated, education cannot claim to be democratic. Education in democracy takes the form of an intellectual adventure of a bi-polar nature. It is neither the memorisation of dis-connected facts of knowledge nor a mechanical acquisition of certain quantum of information. No method can properly fit into a democratic educational system if it leads to passive acceptance of the teachers' ideas or beliefs.

Education takes the form of experience under democratic education. The principle of learning by doing, of imparting knowledge through activity is always to be kept in view while employing a particular method of teaching. The principle and practice of education through the medium or around the nucleus of a basic craft or productive work as embodied in the Wardha Scheme of Education will throw significant light on the nature of the method suited to Democratic Education.

The mass method of teaching involving a sort of mass drill in learning is undoubtedly undemocratic. The method of teaching should be adopted not only to individuals aptitudes and interests but also to the needs and difficulties of children at different mental levels. In a truly democratic method, individualised instruction has an important place. Such a method is based on the rccognition of an important psychological fact that each individual is unique or that no two individuals are exactly the same. The Montessori, the Heuristic or Project methods are some devices used by modern educational systems inspired by democratic values. Individualised instruction is one important aspect of child-centred-education. It is only through such methods that individual attention to the average, the backward, the mentally retarded, the gifted child can be facilitated and their difficulties solved. The method to be used should be based on active co-operation between the teacher and the taught and an explicit understanding or 'rapport' between them. The latter should be given the greatest possible latitude for the exercise of their minds and satisfaction of their curiosity. They should be encouraged to ask questions, express doubts, discuss and even criticise what is taught to them, without fear or mental reservation. Never should the teacher adopt a dogmatic attitude, while teaching something. The democratic method of teaching consists in receptivity to everything which is new and true everything that stimulate self-activity, ensures motivation and facilitates independent thinking and assimlation of the subject-matter taught.

Whatever form the method under a democratic system may take, it should be activity-centred and should make learning purposeful to the learner. Knowledge should be acquired incidentally through activity, preferably productive activity or project. The learner should be conscious of the goal, at least the immediate goal. The democratic method is flexible in nature. It is the anti-thesis of anything rigid or static. It has rightly been said that when in the educational enterprise, purpose is lost, in fact, all is lost. The matter presented to the student should be reduced to a logical whole. Different faces of knowledge should be inter-woven into a single unity. This can be done through integrating different related subjects round a central core which is a suitable craft in the case of Basic Education. What **Dewey** calls integrated learning as opposed to learning isolated bits of knowledge in water-tight compartments, is in accordance with the ideology of Democratic Education. The method of correlation employed by Basic Education is an example of an activity—centred method—a technique newly evolved in its present form in the Wardha Scheme of Education inspired by some basic democratic ideas.

The Teacher's Role

Our discussion of the application of democratic ideas to education will remain incomplete without considering briefly the status and the role of the teacher in a democratic educational system. The relation of teacher to pupil in a non-democratic set-up, particularly under totalitarianism is that of a dictator. Under the traditional system also, the teacher almost held the monopoly of the educative process. Education was unilateral in nature. It was teacher-ridden.

In a truly democratic system, the teacher's role is that of a sympathetic guide or a vigilant supervisor. He minimises active or unnecessary interference in the learning of the child. The teacher's role can be better understood in the context of the Naturalist-Idealist controversy. Naturalism considers the teacher as more or less superfluous. At best, he is regarded as a stage-setter or a background factor. Naturalism stands for 'auto-education' "education according to nature" or "education by natural consequences". Idealism, on the contrary, looks upon the teacher as a very important factor in the educative process. It over-emphasises his importance at the cost of the interests and rights of the child. In democratic education, both the extremes are avoided. It gives due consideration to the child's needs and interests, and assigns a proper status to the teacher who has to play a dynamic role. The democratic system of education being child-centred, the teacher has to know the child and has also to feel for the child. His insight into child's nature should be deep and scientific and his attitude affectionate.

The teacher should not only be conversant with democratic ideas and values, but should also possess the democratic spirit, so that he may serve to be a part of the environment from which the student, spontaneously or effortlessly, imbibes the democratic spirit. Through instruction, training and personal example the students develop into worthy citizens. Democracy, it may be remembered, is caught and not taught.

The teacher should not feel satisfied by enforcing an officially prescribed curricula and syllabi for different subjects in a rigid manner. In making neccssary changes and adjustments in accordance with the aptitudes and mental levels of the child and the demands of his social environment. He has a free hand in the internal mangagement of class work and the organisation of the school activities. He has to establish a link between the school and community. In the planning of instructional and co-curricular activities, he seeks the co-operation of the students in a spirit of comradeship. Above all, he acts as a guardian of national culture. He is also to assist the nation in pursuing her basic policies and implementing developmental projects.

The Concept of Discipline

"That man is free who is conscious of himself as the author of the law which he obeys" says **T.H. Green**. The democratic view of discipline has been aptly summed up in the above remarks by T. H. Green. It has already been explained that freedom is the counterpart of discipline. The essence of discipline lies in freedom regulated by reason. In a slightly different language, discipline consists in the control by the rational-self of the non-rational or the animal nature of man. From this point of view, true discipline is self-discipline.

In the light of what has been said above, it is evident that discipline in democratic education does not consist in an external order created by some external authority. Nor does it consist in certain commands issued by the teacher in the capacity of a dictator. It is only when children live, learn and acquire experience by self-activity in an atmosphere of freedom, that there can be true discipline in the school. Under coercion and fear of punishment, an artificial atmosphere of orderliness and decorum can, no doubt, be created. External social control may lead to discipline but it is not discipline in itself. Unless external pressure is replaced by the willing acceptance of the code of conduct or the social or political laws enforced by society, truly speaking the educand cannot be said to be disciplined. For being disciplined, an individual must identify himself with the political laws or religious commandments. He should feel that these laws are not external. They are his own laws because he is a member of the society which has made them. Thus, gradually the child learns to replace authority by autonomy.

To ensure the transition from external to internal authority, from coercion to freedom, the school should provide an atmosphere conducive for it. The curriculum, the method and the teacher's role should be such as can stimulate the self-activity and creativeness of the child without imposing unnecessary checks on him. The school as a part of the social environment and particularly the teacher as a representative of community and the guardian of its culture should convert the school which under the traditional system has for long been a slaughter house of the child's initiative and freedom into a veritable centre and training ground for providing free, law-abiding and truly disciplined person. Optimum conditions and adequate avenues should be provided by the school for experiments in self-discipline. Institutions like the student's council, discipline boards, sanitation boards or organisations like Boy scouts, Girl guides.

Mock Parliaments, Self-Government in school can prove helpful for training the young learner in voluntary self-discipline which is a good synthesis of freedom and external control.

Cordial pupil-teacher relationship, selection of good student-leaders entrusting some responsibilities to them suited to their mental level, the home-school and the school-community co-ordination and in general a judicious co-ordination of the formal and informal agencies of education, can prove helpful for ensuring the right kind of discipline consistant with the fundamental principles of democracy.

In conclusion, guidance about the concept of discipline may be sought from the Board of Education Pronouncement. Discipline is the means whereby children are trained in orderliness, good conduct and the habit of getting the best out of themselves ...the crucial test of its soundness is whether it represents a real sense on the part of the children of the rightness of the behaviour that is expected of them. It cannot be considered good unless it is founded upon worthy ideas of conduct that are becoming or have become, embedded in the children's characters.

24

Education for National and Emotional Integration

India, that is Bharat, a subcontinent comprising of the union of states, is a federation with a unitary bias. It is inhabited by people of many religions, castes and creeds and federating many states with different languages, regions and economic interest. It presents a remarkable variety of people with different ways of thinking, acting and feeling. In spite of this diversity, there is a general 'feeling of Indianness' which transcends all these distinctions and makes its inhabitants one Indian people. There is a sense of belongingness to, an identification with this India ; a sense of pride in, and affection for it. This gives a unity to the people which is the distinctive quality of nationhood.

India the biggest democratic country of the world, is surrounded by theocratic, totalitarian and war monger countries. These are great menance to her security and integrity. But the external danger is not so great as the internal danger of disruption of national unity and the apathy of people towards national questions. The country has a large number of diversities which are raising their head again as the undercurrent of unity is being weakened and is being forced to go dormant by the various forces which in short can only be described as anti-national. These forces which have always got the upper hand throughout the Indian history and had brought her downfall and numerous humiliations are again trying to repeat the history.

Can we repeate history being repeated? Can we stop the country from disintegration? Can be bring a sense of unity among the people of our country? Answer to all these questions is in affirmative. We can create among all the citizens of this country a spirit of patriotism, a love to one's own people and a realization that their destiny lies with the other people of this land. This can be achieved through sound system of education right from Nursery to the University. An education which can bring the over-all unity in diversity is required to be given to each and every citizen of the country.

Let us examine this position more thoroughly.

THE DISRUPTIVE TENDECIES

India is a nation in infancy. But there are some factors that are working at present against India's growing into a mature nation. Many fissiparous activities and disuptive tendencies have been set operating in the country. They spring from differences in religion, caste or language and concern territorial or sectional interests. The so-called grievances are given political colour and are made a cloak of politician's ambitious designs in other fields, particularly politics, employment and other personal advantages. They have whipped up disturbances, destruction and national property and sometimes even broken down the social and administrative machinery. Democracy itself has been used as a dividing force to realise the ambition of the political parties by exaggerating minor differences into major points of conflict. These undermine the unity and dignity of the nation and hamper national integration. These should be eliminated as early as possible so that India marches as a United Nation on the path of progress and prosperity. We will briefly examine these tendencies.

Casteism

It is an anachronism and curse of the Hindu society. By sheer accident of birth, people enjoyed certain rights and privileges and dominated other group of people. This dominance of higher castes is tending to pass to numerically larger castes and the process of transfer is far from being smooth and peaceful. The political parties exploit appeal to caste loyalties in local and national elections. The individual failure and frustration are translated into caste terms and the result is the increase in tension and bitterness between the differeat sections of society.

Communalism

Communalism divides people professing different religions. These differences were played upon by the alien government in pursuance of the policy of 'divide and rule' and resulted in the partition of the country. People even today have their kith and kin across the national borders and this may develop divided national allegiance. We are a little too much obsessed by the grievances of the minority communities and have granted them constitutional privileges. They have no doubt a right to ask for the redress of their grievances, but any attempt at exclusiveness and isolation is likely to be misunderstood and harm those who seek them. It is but natural for various communities to wish their own religious groups well; but it is undesirable to seek advantages for one's own community at the cost of others.

Regionalism

It is the result of a wide-spread desire for economic development and for formation of distinct states of people speaking a single language. In the economic sphere it has led to inter-state squabbles in the distribution of money and privileges by the centre; and in the other sphere, it has developed a controversy on the union language.

Another type of regionalism has been based on a quaint idea of race and history by Dravida Kazhagam and its off-shoot Dravida Munnetra Kazhagam. They have built up an elaborate theory that the Aryans of the North are imperialists, that they wish to bring South India under their domination, that Sanskrit and Hindi are the instruments of domination, and that the South Indian Brahman is the representative of Aryan exploitation. Hence, an anti-North, anti-Hindi and anti-Brahman movement has been built up which has no following beyond Tamilnadu. Their real grievances should be redressed and the people should be weaned away from this dangerous distruptive ideology.

Different Political Parties

In the country there are different, political parties, Out of these some work for national unity, but there are many which are always ready to bring national disruption. There are some parties which took to the interests of only particular regions or religion. There are some other parties which get inspirations from some foreign powers, such parties can never bring national unity.

Corruption and Favouritism

It seems very difficult for any one who does not have any push or pull to get a job. Favouritism is eating the nerves of the nation. If the people know that merit is no consideration for promotion they will not care for merit but try to indulge in those activities which may benefit them, but may be anti-national.

With favouritism we may put corruption. Corr ... social evil, a crime against individual and the society. Y... rather encouraged. The apathy of the people and thei...

things done by hook or crook are the reason for its tolerance. This attitude in a nation breeds fifth columnists, traitors, and those who can sell the nation for their selfish ends. In this country at present there seems to be no dearth of such people. They are being tolerated and sometimes patronised as we are accustomed to tolerate corruption.

Linguism

This has recently leapt into prominence and caused much dissension and destruction. The people are divided on the choice of a common link language for the country. The fear, real or fancied, that of a language does not receive prominence, those speaking it will be denied opportunities of employment and political influence, has been mixed up with some other minor matters and worked up to create tension and bitterness.

Youth Frustration

The latest is that the youth of the Nation are in fury and indisciplined so that they show scant respect for law, teachers and leaders. This is because education has expanded enormously in recent times and employment opportunities have not kept pace with this expansion. This leads to frustration and anger which are taken advantage of by the anti-social and anti-national elements. There is unrest and indiscipline, lack of values and loss of moorings among the students. This is partly due to the absence of idealism which could inspire them to something higher and nobler. Mahatma Gandhi has amply demonstrated in recent times how idealism can inspire our people to nobler and higher deeds.

These factors are undermining the Nation's unity. But there is nothing to despair of in the face of these difficulties. The forces unifying India represented by the culture, history and germinating values are stronger. To them have been added new factors of economic growth, industrialisation, mobility of people and modernization of agriculture. All these will help to build a strong united Indian nation, soften regional and social inequalities and calm down the people. Differences in opinion among the people is a sign of dynamic society and need not be unduly emphasised. The multi-lingual countries like Switzerland, Canada, Russia and Indonesia could settle their differences and develop strong nationality. India shall also solve her problems and emerge a stronger nation out of the present conflicts, and controversies.

NATIONAL AND EMOTIONAL INTEGRATION

In order to overcome these fissiparous tendencies, lest they should trench themselves, education for National and Emotional Integration was proposed a few years ago. Let us understand the term 'National and Emotional Integration' before we discuss education for them.

National Integration

It is 'the will to live together', 'a sense of belongingness', a 'feeling of oneness', 'a feeling of Indianness' which is the essence of the nation.

National integration is a psychological and educational process involving the development of a feeling of unity, solidarity and cohesion in the hearts of the people, a sense of common citizenship and a feeling of loyalty to the nation.

Emotional Integration

Many of these disruptive tendencies often start with an individual. Some self-interested individual gives birth to an idea which he harbours till a feeling set grows. He then weaves a web of public involvement round it and passes it on to the others, many of whom catch it and soon the mischief is on its legs. It should be nipped in the bud before it attracts the crowd. It is in this context that we think of emotional integration. The individual must thread his diverse feelings and emotions into a total harmonious feeling. Emotional Integration in the case of an individual will then mean a completely satisfied personality whose urges, aspirations and emotions are sufficiently sublimated and directed towards healthy fruitful channels and who should have been sufficiently trained in the creed of temperance and toleration.

Besides having a reference to an individual, the term has been used from a social point of view in the context of national integration which is a much wider term. Emotional Integration is only an integral component of it. In this context it refers to "a strong feeling of harmony and oneness that inspires people in spheres of its thought and activity and helps it to sink and ignore all types of differences. It seeks to develop a mental outlook which will prompt and inspire every person to place loyalty to the country above group loyalties and the welfare of the nation above narrow sectarian interests, They must feel emotionally drawn together on all vital national problems. It is indicated as a belief in a common destiny which expresses itself in feeling, thought and behaviour, particularly in times of stress and danger. The problem of emotional integration is not the problem of welding but the problem of synthesis and the problem of organised consciousness to certain common ideals and values.

The individual must, therefore, be educated to exercise a severe psychological discipline whereby he learns to surrender his narrow loyalties, when required, for the achievement of national objectives.

He should build up a hierarchy of values and learn to put proper priority on them. He shouid develop right type of attitudes and emotions and attach them to right kind of activities. This emotional integration in individuals will definitely mean greater integration in the society and the nation.

Briefly speaking, by means of Emotional Integration we want to bring some changes in the behaviour of individual. Undoubtedly, India is nation. It is also necessary to regard the whole nation as one. We should have emotional experiences accordingly. National Integration is the aim of Emotional Integration. Therefore, often no difference is made between National Integration and Emotional Integration. National integration is related to the development of nationalism therefore, we shall discuss it in the next chapter. In this chapter we are confining our discussion to emotional integration. As the students of psychology and philosophy we have to understand that construction of the nation is based upon the emotional world of the people. If we develop the emotion of love, sympathy, anger etc. on the basis of language, region, and community, our nation would also be broken into fragments on the basis of caste, language etc. There is no contradiction between individual and society. If proper redirection and sublimation of the individual's emotions are made, he would certainly love his Nation and then only the progress of the nation and society is possible.

Negative meaning of Emotional Integration is to hate digruptive elements and save the nation from disunity. Its positive meaning is to make attempts to unite the nation and to love the whole nation as one's own.

Stages of Emotional Integration

There are four stages of integration. At the first stage people start living with each other. At this stage the habit of living in group and association and nation instead of living lonely is developed. At the second stage people living with each other start understanding each other. At the third stage people start taking interest in each other's activities, functions and customs. At this stage, hatred towards other's traditions is given up and people live peacefully. At the fourth stage people living together start regarding other's traditions, customs and standard as their own and are influenced by them. This fourth stage is the stage of Emotional Integration. At this stage individual starts loving the whole Nation regarding it as his own.

EDUCATION FOR INTEGRATION

Education provides the most important means of bringing about National and Emotional Integration. The problem of integration or national unity essentially involves the attitudes of groups or large sections of the community, and education in its broadest sense has been recognised as a powerful instrument for influencing or modifying these attitudes.

John Dewey said, "what nutrition and reproduction are to the physiological life, education is to social life. Society organizes education and sets up educational institutions to disseminate among its members those knowledges, skills, beliefs, faiths, hopes, attitudes and dispositions that are basic to the preservation of life of the society ; and without ensuring respect for them by the coming generation it cannot ensure its existence. Therefore, for its very existence education must preserve society.

Objectives of Education for National and Emotional Integration

The following should be the objectives of education for national and emotional integration.

1. To train emotions and develop an emotionally integrated personality.
2. To inculcate the spirit of sacrifice and tolerance.
3. To create a feeling that the country and its resources belong to the citizen who thereby acquires certain rights and privileges along with corresponding duties and responsibilities.
4. To give to the pupil an intimate knowledge of the different aspects of the country, including the events which led to freedom.
5. To encourage such studies and activities as lead to greater understanding between communities and states.
6. To develop the habit of friendly co-operation with others, even with those who are critical.
7. To inculcate a sense of public duty and responsibility to the nation.
8. To develop tolerance, endurance and breadth of out-look.

THE EDUCATIONAL PROGRAMME

We may now discuss in some detail the various programmes and activities that will be conducive to developing National and Emotional Integration at different stages of education.

Elementary Stage

The elementary school is the first social environment of the child outside his home. Besides developing his physical and mental capacities, the social sense should be instilled. He should learn to live in harmony with other children, show politeness and consideration for the equals and respect and regard for the elders. Working with small groups of classmates, he should learn lessons of sociability, consciousness and sense of responsibility. The 'we feeling' should develop in them.

Working under-own-direction, activities should be organized where the children are put on the way to finding out and pursuing their objectives. The stage for it should be set by the teacher who should carefully observe them at work, so that they develop the qualities of initiative and resourcefulness and not the habit of shirking responsibility and skin-saving attitude.

The child is incessantly active and opportunities should be provided to him to learn by doing about his environment physical as well as human. His make-belief can be utilized to identify himself with some great person, some benefactor of the nation, some famous man with noble qualities and deeds. He plays their role in dramatic performances, speaks their language, and acts in their way. Thus, he should get a vision of their greatness through play.

The pupil should get ample opportunities of good impression and creative expression. They learn many things from example and the teacher should set a high standard of behaviour. The norms of life in various spheres of juvenile activity should be set and encouragement be given to attain them. The pupil should express orally or in writing about everyday happenings, things he sees and people he meets. He may write notes, diaries, short stories and engage himself in painting, clay-modelling and craft-work. In all these activities the veracity in expression and the attempt to put his true self in them should be insisted upon.

Secondary Stage. The children at the secondary stage are grown up. A majority of them are in adolescence which is a period of great stress and strain. They arc very inquisitive and highly emotional. Strange emotions surge up and sweep their intellect. This is the time when the training of emotions can be emphasized. The pupils should be trained to restrain their emotions, develop a feeling set for higner values and conditioned responses for day to day behaviour.

The pupils can be inspired to collect folk-tales, biographies of national heroes and display material of different regions. They may study about other states in the library and discuss it in the class-room. They may form clubs and societies where exchange of ideas and letters with pupils of different regions can be arranged. Languages centres may encourage study of other regional languages. Inter-state tours may be arranged to foster better relations between pupils of different regions and develop understanding, tolerance and adaptability.

Suggesting a 'curricular approach' to emotional integration, it has been proposed that a "special area of study" should be prescribed to help understanding the creeds, faiths and aspirations of the people. The reading material should present a picture of cohesiveness and co-operation, minimizing the social, religious and regional differences.

The Three-Language Formula should be accepted and the study of one regional language besides the mother-tongue should be insisted upon.

The text-books of history, geography and civics should be rewritten to emphasise the integrational points of view. The teaching of history of India should enable pupils to appreciate the contributions of various groups of people towards the development of the composite culture of India, its glorious saga, and the co-operation of all people in building up the nation.

The books of geography should impress on the minds of pupils the territorial unity of the country, its rich resources and varied human life and the inter-dependence of various communities. It should emphasise that the basic needs of the people are the same everywhere and explain how man has adjusted to his environment in different regions.

The teaching of civics should inculcate in the pupils the qualities of a citizen of the Democratic Republic, faith in the fundamental principles of our Constitution, respect for law, duties and obligations and the method of mutual discussion and give and take in the solution of differences and grievances.

Economics should emphasise corporate living, inter-dependence of states for the essential commodities and the socio-economic life of the people.

The teaching of science should develop in the pupils the habit of scientific truthfulness which bases conclusions on observations and objective reasoning.

University Stage

The universities are seats of higher learning and their role in developing and strengthening national integration is very significant. They should provide proper leadership and foster necessary climate for emotional integration. They should maintain high standards not only in teaching and research but also in judicious admissions, and just appointments of staff. They should help to overcome the social and economic disabilities of students. Their guidance bureaus should assist students in proper placement on leaving the university.

The universities should arrange extra-mural lectures on subjects of social and political importance and place impartial and academic point of view before the country on burning topics of the day. Inter-regional seminars and conferences should be organised to discuss common problems. The distinguished professors should establish closer contacts by visits to other universities. The students should participate in social service programmes and inter-state work camps be organised. Adequate provision should be made for training in leisure time activities of the students.

The universities may start a department of modern indian languages where regional languages may be studied and standard books in various languages may be translated. The medium of instruction should be the mother-tongue but the means to acquire access to world literature and knowledge should be provided.

K.G. Saiyidain has pointed to an important problem that our universities face today. It is that "students are being sent out at present without that balanced outlook and general cultural equipment which is the hall-mark of a properly educated person." The universities must work for bringing about intellectual synthesis in the students. The "vision of greatness" which the child sees in the early years of his schooling, must come true to him at this stage. The intellectual freedom and integrity which are the core of learning must be achieved by our students in the universities.

Other Programmes for National an Emotional Integration

The following curricular programmes are suggested for promoting National and Emotional Integration.

Curricular

(i) The text-book in languages should be prepared on all India basis incorporating selections from all that is best in the literature of regional languages.

(ii) The supplementary reading material should be prepared giving biographies of state leaders who have been known for their national outlook and great men of letters, arts, architecture, sciences, who have contributed to the greatness of the nation.

(iii) The best books in one regional language should be translated in all languages of India. Anthologies of poems, short stories, one act plays, essays, etc., from literature of different languages should be published. Thus, a continuous flow of inter-lingual literature.should be ensured.

(iv) Simple guide books to learn the regional languages should be prepared in every language. Multi-lingual dictionaries should be made available.

(v) A special paper dealing with India's diverse cultural heritage, her plans for economic development and the background of her freedom struggle may be introduced at some appropriate stage of education. It may not affect the examination results of the students,' but special prizes should be given and a mention made in the diploma or degree for commendable performance in this paper.

Co-curricular

Following co-curricular activities can be arranged for promoting National and Emotional Integration.

(i) The children in schools should be taught to sing National Anthem in chorus and respect the National Flag when hoisted. They should learn to behave in a disciplined way wherever these National Emblems are displayed.

(ii) On special occasions the 'Pledge of Loyalty' to India as suggested by the National Integration Conference of 1961 should be taken.

(iii) The National days should be celebrated with due enthusiasm and the participation of all students teachers, as well as the members of the community should be secured.

(iv) The educational and travel documentaries depicting various aspects of Indian life, its flora and fauna, its monuments and development projects, should be shown to the students.

(v) The poster and pictures giving vivid descriptions of Indian life in various parts of the country should be displayed in the institutions.

(vi) The cultural programmes, folk dances and songs and historical dramas showing unity in diversity should be organized.

(vii) The activities like Junior Red Cross, Scouts Clubs and Girls Guide should be started in as many institutions as possible.

(viii) The games and sports meet should be organized on inter-state and all-India basis where large number of students should participate.

(ix) An all-India Council should organize youth activities in order to bring together the youth in one part of the country with those in the other regions.

(x) The All-India Radio should broadcast programmes stressing the unity of the country.

(xi) The denominational institutions and hostels that lay stress on communal and sectarian interests should be abolished.

All these activities and many more which can be thought out and planned by the teacher will help in bringing the people together. The teacher occupies the pivotal position and he can in his day-to-day teaching find innumerable occasions when he can tilt the discussion in favour of it without resorting to any formalized teaching The teacher has a great responsibility in this respect and he shall rise to the occasion to do his duty to the nation. The older members of the society should realise their responsibility of keeping the social atmosphere clean and conducive to the development of such integration among the younger generation. The political leaders will do well to withdraw their hands from the temples of learning.

Once an atmosphere of hope, expectancy and optimism is created, the fears and suspicions which are at the root of the disruptive tendencies will have little scope for mischief. A dream of new India in which all languages, all religions, all communities, in a word, all interests and aptitudes will find ample scope for expression and fulfillment will become real.

CONCLUSION

National integration is vital for India's survival. It is the cry of the moment. The country must mobilise all its resources to evolve a concrete national programme involving every significant section of our society in purposeful action to combat in every town and every village and street the dark forces which seek to disintegrate the very fabric of our social, political and economic existence. In the words of **Mrs. Indira Gandhi**, 'We must find a way of harmonising the basic decency, the basic commonsense of the average citizen in order to over-come these forces which threaten the future of the children". She further says : "The question (of national integration) is serious enough to be studied calmly... It needs a deep conviction that this is the most urgent question of the day and also burning passion to summon all strength and will to surmount it by fighting all that leads to injustice, inequality, discrimination and citizenship. Let us not degrade the very name of Indian citizenship." Let us live up to the ideals and values for which India had stood through the ages. Let us join hands and heads and hearts to build India of our dreams.

25

Education for Socialistic, Pattern of Society

On 15th August, 1947 Indian people won the first phase of their struggle by attaining independence from the foreign masters and immediately after that entered into the next phase. The next phase as enuciated by the great leaders of the people was dirceted towards the establishment of a Socialistic Pattern of Society. The biggest party of the country to which the reigns of the government were handed over by the British and which subsequently in general elections won the largest number of seats, both in Central Parliament and state legislatures, the congress embarked on a programme of rebuilding a society which may truly be socialistic in pattern and outlook. Mahatma Gandhi dreamed of such a society in the form of Sarvodaya. The Sarvodaya ideal envisaged a society in which the good of all through all and through mass awakening and equalisation of opportunities was ensured.

It is true that to achieve the objective of Sarvodaya or Socialistic Pattern of Society is not an easy thing. This requires much serious efforts and great sacrifices. In the efforts to gain the socialistic pattern the help of education would be greatly contributive for success. Half the battle for socialistic pattern can easily be won if education is commissioned to the task of creating this type of pattern. The other half may be won by a number of other measures like social legislation, social reforms and provision of facilities for employment of all kinds to all the people. How education can help for a better social order and for winning half the battle for the socialistic pattern need some more elaboration. But before we do that let us first try to understand the nature of the Socialistic Pattern of Society.

THE NATURE OF THE SOCIALISTIC PATTERN OF SOCIETY

To understand the Socialistic Pattern of Society let us first of all concentrate towards the Resolution to this effect at the Avadi Session of the Indian National Congress. It reads :

"In order to realize the object of the Congress as laid down.in Article I of the Congress Constitution and to further the objectives stated in the Preamble and Directive Principles of State Policy of the Constitution of India, planning should take place with a view to the establishment of a Socialistic Pattern of Society, where the principal means of prcduction are under social ownership or control, production is progressively speeded up and there is equitable distribution of the national wealth." The three essential conditions underlying the Socialistic Pattern of Society can be gathered from the above resolution :

(i) the principal means of production be under social ownership or control.

(ii) production is progressively speeded up.

(iii) there is equitable distribution of the national wealth.

The above principles are in true spirit of Article 39 of the Constitution which requires the State to direct its policy towards ensuring for all the citizens men and women equally—"the right to an adequate means of livelihood and that the ownership and control of the material resources of the community are so distributed a best to subserve the common good."

It is very difficult to define Socialistic Pattern of Society. A variety of Socialism and Socialistic Ideals are current in the present-day world today. Hence to specially point out that this is the definition, nature and complexion of the Socialistic Pattern is just to enter into a controversy of a very serious nature. Since, this book is not intended to be a Treatise on Socialism, we will be content here to point out the nature and complexion of Socialistic Pattern of Society as is widely understocd in this country and as is enunciated by the leaders in the government and the framers and initiators of the Avadi Resolution of the Congress and the expositors of the Socialism at the Bhubneshwar Session of the Congress.

The nature and complexion of the Socialistic Pattern of Society to be established in India is determined by her ideals of Democracy and Sarvodaya. The democratic ideal of equality and justice are considered to be fully compatible with the ideals of Socialism and so the protagonists of Socialism in this country assert that this country will be able to rid her people from the bondages of economic and Social slavery if the Political Democracy is to lead to the Economic Democracy.

The democratic way of life emphasises that in the society there should not only be Political Democracy but Economic Democracy as well. The Economic Democracy ensures that each individual is free to realize his aspirations of his own economic well-being. The Socialistic Pattern of Society thus in its nature is essentially democratic. Jag Pravesh considers that "the Socialistic Society represents the highest phase of democracy." He gives the "reason that while democracy remains content with the equalisation of rights and duties, a socialistic society aims at creating an identity between rights, and duties." In his opinion, this is the reason "why in a truly Socialistic Society, democracy reaches the supreme stage of Ethical Democracy."

OBJECTIVE OF THE SOCIALISTIC PATTERN OF SOCIETY

The objectives of the Socialistic Pattern of Society are broad-based, enveloping justice and equality on all social pedestals. In the words of Jag Pravesh, "The broad objectives of the Socialistic Pattern of Society are political equality, religious equality, economic equality and at the individual levels to create new human beings by full growth of human personality." According to *Shriman Narayan*, "The basic objective of a Socialistic Pattern of Society would be the establishment of social and economic order based on equality of opportunity and on the social, economic and political justice."

The above objectives are fairly comprehensive as they include both the individual refinement and social upliftment of Indian masses.

ESSENTIALS OF A SOCIALISTIC PATTERN OF SOCIETY

For the success of a Socialistic Structure of Society, it is necessary to fulfil the following conditions :

(i) There is equality of opportunity in all spheres—social, political or economic.

(ii) There are tremendous job opportunities by recognising every individual's right to work.

(iii) There is effective state control over the principal means of production and other community resources.

(iv) There will be economic equality and no concentration of wealth in the hands of a few.

(v) Peace, non-violence, peaceful co-existence and other democratic methods shall become the watch-words of that society.

(vi) There, shall be a bold decentralization of economic and political power. The village panchayats shall form the nucleus of political, social and economic life.

(vii) There will be systematic attempts to eradicate poverty to produce more wealth in the country rapidly.

(viii) Small scale industries and cottage industries shall receive incentive and thus flourish to enhance national income..

Thus, we may conclude that a Socialistic Pattern of Society will be a society which will be decentralised. Its economic order will not be based on large scale industries, gigantic projects and too much centralised control over means of production and distribution. The control over means of production and distribution will be there but it will be exercised by decentralised power starting from village panchayat at the village level.

In short, the "Socialistic Society of India will be wedded to peaceful methods, democratic procedures and ideals of non-violence."

EDUCATION FOR A SOCIALISTIC PATTERN OF SOCIETY

Education is a great force of social regeneration and social revitalisation. The role of education in achieving the ideals of a Socialistic Pattern of Society cannot be under-estimated. As such, education must be geared to the following principles :

(i) full employment and right to work.

(ii) maximum production of the national wealth.

(iii) maximum national self-sufficiency.

(iv) the social and economic justice.

(v) the use of peaceful, non-violent and democratic methods.

(vi) the decentralisation of economic and political power through the establishment of village panchayats and industrial co-operatives.

With these principles in view, education can help in transforming the society and in improving the lot of one and all, high and low. These principles should be properly and fully incorporated in the system of education that plans to create a generation based on the principles of Socialism, Justice and Equality. For this purpose there is a need of re-evaluating and re-defining aims of education, curriculum and methods of teaching.

The Aims of Education

The aims of education should be re-evaluated and re-defined in the light of the above principles. The recommendations of Secondary and Indian Education Commissions should be implemented. Democratic living, vocational efficiency, training for leadership, increasing national productivity, promoting social and national consciousness, accelerating the process of modernisation and cultivation of social, moral and spiritual values are a few aims to be achieved through education. Education as a whole gives us zest and energy to work and social service. It should cultivate a deep love for the nation and a faith in the establishment of a Socialistic Pattern of Society.

(i) Linking education with the social and national services.

(ii) Gearing education to productivity, practice and utility.

(iii) Reshaping and re-designing the curriculum.

(iv) Introducing socialised and group-techniques of teaching.

(v) Giving practical shape to the Constitutional Directives of Education.

Education should inculcate among the higher caste' people a realization of their duty towards the low and the down-trodden. It should also free him from religious dogma and should encourage him to strive for social reforms. In the end, we can say that Socialism is a way of life based on certain cultural, ethical and spiritual values. It seeks to create a social order founded on individual freedom, equality of opportunity and fellowship of men. A good system of education will provide to the nation honest, cultured, self-sacrificing and duty-bound citizens who will be real assets to the nation. This will ultimately bring a cultural reformation, a strong national character and economic prosperity.

The Curriculum

In order to realise the above aims, the curriculum shall have to be reshaped on democratic lines. The Secondary Education Commission (1953) gave a liberal curriculum to achieve democratic ideals. Much of what is being done in our schools and colleges today is not in true spirit of the suggestions made in this regard from time to time. Now the need is to give our students training in improved crafts in addition to training in liberal arts. The emphasis should be on the vocationalisation of education. The following items are suggested to be included in the broad pattern of socialistic curriculum :

1. Study of social forces and social values as a part of social studies.
2. Study of science and technology, including apprenticeship training in various industries.
3. Study of socialistic trends in other socialistic countries.
4. Study of techniques of planning and their actual working in other socialistic countries,
5. Variety of crafts like agriculture, wood-work, poultry, piggery, etc.
6. Special study of the political, economic and social history of advanced countries.
7. Training in small scale and cottage industries.

The Methods of Teaching

Dynamic methods of teaching like the Project Method, Problem Solving etc. shall be employed to put the socialistic curriulum into practice. Besides, emphasis should be laid on inculcating healthy social and moral values through training in co-operative living. Other activities which may become an integral part of dynamic teaching can be :

1. Work in workshops and farms attached to the school ;
2. Visits to factories during vacation ;
3. Social and economic surveys ;
4. Village cottage and small scale industries should be started unded the guidance of the school squads ;
5. Educational tours ;
6. Adult education activities ;
7. Occasional lectures by eminent personalities ;
8. Study of current affairs ; etc.

CONCLUSION

In order to bring the discussion to an end, let us remember the words of **Sri Jaya Parkash Narayan**, "Socialism is way of life based on certain cultural, ethical, and spiritual values. It seeks to create a social order founded on individual freedom, equality of opportunity and fellowship of men." This "way of life" cannot be brought about by legislation or force or coercian. It has to grow silently in the hearts of our people and the greatest binding force that can quicken it is the force of education. Therefore, it can be said that the classless society will ultimately emerge from the class room itself.

26

Education for International Understanding

Education for 'International Understanding' is acquiring a growing emphasis day by day. It is a burning topic popular with socialogists, politicians, religious leaders and educationists. It appers that the new idea in the near future will pervade almost the entire curriculum of the school. A special emphasis is being laid on its importance both at the primary and secondary stages. However, about a quarter of a century back education for International Understanding had practically no place in the text-books or co-curricular activities of the school. We, thus, find an important change in the outlook of the educator as well as the administrator relating to the place of education for International Understanding on our scheme of education. This radical change in our educational outlook is not accidental. It is, on the contrary, an inevitable result of a number of causes.

WHY INTERNATIONAL UNDERSTANDING

Some of these causes are given below :

1. The horrors of two world wars made humanity conscious of the threat to human peace and prosperity. In fact, the leaders of different countries feel convinced that another world conflagration, if it takes place, would not only destory civilization and culture, but would almost wipe out humanity from the face of the globe. The painful recollections of the fate of Nagasaki and Hiroshima are still vivid in the memory of the present generation.

2. Progress of science has minimized distance. It has almost annihilated space and time. Geographical barriers and cultural disparities are disappearing at a tremendous speed. The whole world has been converted into a single social order. Science, as has been rightly said, has given us knowledge, power and possession, but it fails to give us insight into spiritual values. As **Dr. Radhakrishnan** remarks, "It has given us power, but not goodness ; civilization, but not culture." There is, thus a huge disparity between man's control over nature and his control over his mind. In the absence of International Understanding the scene is likely to prove fatal for national security as well as international peace.

3. The nations of the world actuated by motives of utility, exploitation and cut-throat competition are divided in different powerblocs. An atmosphere of world tension and constant threat to peace prevails every-where. Under such conditions the salvation of humanity lies in mutual good-will and cordiality.

4. The social consciousness of man has been gradually widened. The primitive man considered himself as related to a small clan or tribe. Consequently, his moral horizon was extremely limited. Through socialization, membership of a tribe took the forrm of the membership of a small community. In course of time, the individual became the citizen of geographical and political unit called the state and finally he developed a cosmopolitan outlook. In other words, modern internationalism can be traced back to the primitive social life, lived in small group, under most primitive conditions. Thus, through a process of social evolution and growth of civilization, the narrow concept of citizenship and nationalism has been converted into a still wider concept of humanitarianism and internationalism.

5. It has also been felt that in certain cases, the human gregariousness has taken a morbid shape. The we-feeling associated with the in groups has sometimes led to certain extreme forms. False Nationalism, for example, engenders isolationistic tendencies and cutthroat competitive attitude. Ethnocerticism with its slogans, 'my country right or wrong' morbid patriotism, known as chavenism, dictatorships, like Hitlerism or Fascism may be mentioned as some of the perverted forms of the social evolution mentioned above. Internationalism and more particularly, education for this purpose, constitute the only ray of hope, under such threatening conditions and atmosphere of fear and suspicion.

Closer international contacts have given rise to the feeling of inner-dependence among the nations, What happens to-day, in Jordan or Vietnam, on the Indo-Pakistan border, or in the Rann of Kutch, has far reaching repurcussions affecting the destiny of the world. The peoples of the world feel convinced that they would sink or swim together. As **K.G Saiyidain** writes "Peace and war have both become one and indivisible. They are literally 'global'and we are in actual fact living in what Wendell Wilkie has called 'One world'. "A war starts in Europe and three million people die of famine in Bengal and millions more find themselves uprooted from their homelands".

INDIA'S SPECIAL NEED AND ROLE

Evidently, International Understanding needs a new ideology based on respect for freedom and regard for personality. The ideas of freedom and tolerance are firmly rooted in Indian thought and culture.

In fact, our history is a long story of the assimilation of foreign cultures and tolerance for the out-groups. The conviction that growth in mutual understanding arises from the recognition that "the different cultures arise as dialects of the one language of spirit", is an essential feature of Indian culture. Education for International Understanding is based on the philosophy of love and universal brother-hood, some of the basic principles of Indian ethics. Consequently, internationalism suits Indian genius more than in the ethos of any other nation. Our international outlook is the product of our lofty ideals of Ahimsa and glorious traditions of service to humanity.

Consistent with our philosophical background, ethical ideals and cultural heritage, education for International Understanding is as important as National Integration, and even more. Living, as we do, in a world of material values, considerations of philosophical insight, cultural values and ethical ideals may not appeal to, or may not be given precedence by the present generation which thinks generally in terms of utility, profit, economic reconstruction and expansionism. Even from the point of view of expediency, International Understanding is one of the foremost needs of the nation passing through one of the most critical junctures in her history. Unless hostile world-forces and un-compromising ideologies are brought together and a mutual understanding is developed, the future of humanity is very dark indeed.

Security and integrity of the nation, naturally come first. Consequently, the freedom won after a long period of hard struggle and tremendous sacrifice has to be preserved through goodwill and friendly relations with other countries. The resources of the country are to be developed through science and technology. For undertaking big projects like Rourkela or Bhillai, we need foreign help in the form of technical know-how, capital and experts in different fields of study. For the execution of gigantic developmental projects and implementation of the Five Year Plans, it is essential that our men, money and material are utilised for building up a strong democracy and a prosperous welfare state. The teeming millions, mostly rural population, underfed, poorly housed and steeped in ignorance, have to be educated and trained in democratic living and constitutional procedures. Our interests, attention and energies should be focussed upon national construction or re-construction.

India has to play the vital role of balancing conflicting ideologies of the power blocs, nations with imperialistic designs and condemning aggression whenever or wherever it occurs through her creed of Panch Sheel and also to resist force, if needed, for the fulfilment of this noble task. India, facing a many-fold challenge—social economic, cultural, political and of foreign aggression, can ill afford to see her marvellous achievements in national reconstruction demolished and her peace-loving population devoured the monster of another world war.

India's firm faith in the United Nations Organisation and its ideals of peace and international co-operation was unequivocally affirmed as early as 1946 when **Jawahar Lal Nehru** declared. "In the sphere of foreign affairs, India will follow an independent policy keeping away from the power politics of groups aligned one against the other... Towards the United Nations, India's attitude is that of whole hearted co-operation and unreserved adherence in both spirit and letter, to the charter governing it".

Almost invariably in all situations of tension, conflicts and critical moments when international peace was threatened, India has vindicated her faith in the principles and policies of the United Nations Organization most unhesitatingly. India displayed initiative in acceeding to the partial test ban treaty signed in Moscow in August 1963. Today, when dark clouds are hovering over the international horizon, the United Nations Organization is for India and the rest of the world, one great hope of peace and cordial co-existence. At no time was this firm faith vindicated in greater measure than when the world organisation faced critical moments in its task of peace-keeping almost from its birth. At all such times, India unhesitatingly gave her support to United Nations. In 1953, she played no small part in securing the cessation of fighting in Korea the re-patriation of prisoners of both sides and generally bringing about a settlement. Indian troops form the largest contingent of the United Nations Emergency Force in Gaza and have helped to prevent a conflagration there... The part played by

Indian Army officers and men in the United Nations operations in the Congo, is well known.

Consequently, it is in the fitness of things that India is the chief venue for the implementation of the Associated Schools Projects started by the Education Department of UNESCO. P.N. Kirpal, Education Secretary and Secretary General Indian National Commission for Co-operation with UNESCO said, "Half the global project, the Associated Schools Projects or even more than half is now being operated in India". Such in brief is our contribution to the cause of world peacc.

THE RELATION OF NATIONALISM AND INTERNATIONALISM

It is sometimes believed that loyalty to the nation is contradictary to loyalty to the world. As a matter of fact, nationalism or the sentiment of patriotism attached to it is not incompatible with international good-will and peace. As International outlook is only an extension or the natural development of the social urge in man, the conflict between Nationalism and Internationalism is only apparent and not real. The conflict, if any is based upon our ignorance of what Nationalism means. True Nationalism leads to Internationalism, and International Understanding is a means for understanding Patriotism in its proper perspective.

Of course morbid nationalism is an exception to what has been said above. It is fatal for world peace. It is fatal for national welfare also. **Dr. David Blickenstaff** rightly remarks, India obviously, like other countries, speaks with many-voices Many of these voices are centrifugal : they are the voices of sectional interests they are the voices of dis-agreement, they are the voices of regionalism; all of these voices tend to tear apart the unity of Indian fabric. There is one area in which India speaks with one voice and that is when India speaks as a member of the International Community". In concrete terms, it means that when Indian leaders discuss problems relating to Sino-Indian or Indo-Pakistan border or that of Vietnam, they are as much inspired by love for India as by respect for the rights and interests of other nations. Nationalism and Internationalism, if rightly understood always go together, and are inter-dependent.

DIFFERENT APPROACHES TO INTERNATIONAL UNDERSTANDING

International Understanding through education is the latest phase of the numerous attempts made from time to time for the promotion of World peace. Such approaches have varied in nature under varied conditions. All of them, however, aim at a common objective of establishing a single-world-order. Briefly speaking, they are as follows:—

The Political Approach

This approach is of a militant nature. Attempts were made at different stages of World History to estahlish a single state through invasions and conquests as was done by Alexander, Napoleon, Changez Khan and some others. Religious conversion by force was another device used for this purpose. Actuated by religious frenzy, wars were fought and crusades or Jehads were led in the name of God and for the establishment of a so-called Kingdom of God on earth and Universal Brotherhood of Man.

Policy of Maintaining Balance of Power

The policy of maintaining balance of power was pursued by several monarchs. In modern times, the establishment of the League of Nations after the First World War was a step in the same direction. The emergence of power-blocs and political organisations based upon appeal to force or military action like NATO and SEATO may be mentioned as some suitable examples.

Hitler tried the metl od of extermination of the Jewish race for converting the whole world into one kingdom under the control of the German Nation.

The Economic Approach

This approach is no less prominent in building up of a classless society on an equitable basis, of equal distribution of wealth and means of production. It has been tried to establish peace through the creation of a homogeneous economic structure. This approach has found favour with U. S. S. R. and the People's Republic of China. It is an attempt at converting the whole world into a vast society, suddenly through drastic change and revolutionary methods based upon violence under the dictatorships of proletariat.

The Latest Approach

The in-adequacy and ultimate failure of all the attempts mentioned above made to release world tension led finally to a new approach based upon mediation, negotiation and exchange of ideas. International peace, it has recently been realised, is inconceivable without mutual understanding. Such understanding depends upon education oriented for this purpose. As **President Eisenhower** once remarked, "Security can not be achieved by arms alone, no matter how destructive the weapons or how large their accumulation." The most objective and realistic view about the inefficacy of the various approaches to the solution of this problem made in the past is evident from the following evaluation made by UNESCO; "...a peace based exclusively upon the political and economic arrangements of Governments would not be a place which could secure the unanimous, lasting and sincere support of the people of the world, and it must therefore, be founded, if it is, not to fail, upon the intellectual and moral solidarity of mankind."

The United Nations approach to fostering International Understanding is psychological in nature. It is a matter of common observation that ignorance based on lack of contacts is very often the cause of social prejudices. Such racial prejudices lead to fear, distrust and feeling of insecurity, which have caused terrible wars between different peoples. Mis-understanding in simple words, is very often at the root of international jealousies and conflicts. Consequently, if psychological help is to be availed of mis-understanding is to be converted into faith and pugnacity into love." Since, war begin in the minds of men, it is in the minds of men that the defences of peace must be constructed..." The psychological nature of the new approach, as evident from this off-quoted extract from the significant preamble indicating the sound analysis made by UNESCO of the intricate problem of international conflicts. And the remedy suggested is as scientific as the diagnosis made of this fatal malady with which humanity is affected.

The educational approach to the problem of International Understanding has not only a psychological but also a Socioligical basis. Aggressive designs and tendencies for exploitation and expansionism leading to social conflicts are the products not so much of inherited biological or psychological urges, as to the social conditions that engender prejudices in the minds of one group against another. Such prejudices in course of time develop into enduring attitudes of hate and jealousy on the part of the members of the in-groups for the persons belonging to an out-group. It is evident, therefore, that nations should understand the minds and win the hearts of one another. They should develop favourable social attitudes towards the out-groups, if world peace is to be ensured.

Its seems worthwhile to write a few words about the meaning and importance of attitudes. As educational sociologists point out the special role of educational agencies, both formal and informal, consists in developing social attitudes in the young learner, favourable for International Understanding and for eradicating or de-conditioning those, that are likely to be impediments to the establishment of world peace.

An attitude is an acquired pre-disposition of a permanent nature, of love, hatred, or indifference towards certain objects, individuals or groups. They are the sources of different types of behaviour under varyings situations. Behaviour is the expression of attitudes under specific conditions and attitude is the relatively permanent basis for the individuals behaviour in a given situation or in relation to a particular individual or group. Attitudes being the product of social interaction, their study is an important problem for Educational Sociologist. Such attitudes determine and influence cultural values and patterns and are also the product of cultural norms. "Attitudes vary from the extreme of strong attraction expressed in the emotion of love to that of repulsion and hate."

Attitudes are acquired unconsciously through mimesis, imitation, suggestion and primitive sympathy. Customs, conventions, traditions and taboos play an important part in their development. Besides, they are formed consciously through planned and formal agencies of education. Missionary work, propaganda and indoctrination. It has to be remembered that when attitudes are transformed into a deep rooted mental structure, when they get hardened, they become sources of the manifestations of prejudices which prove to be a serious obstacle for communal harmony, National Integration and International Understanding. Consequently, they have a special significance for education for International Understanding.

EDUCATION FOR INTERNATIONAL UNDERSTANDING

Then, what can education do for International Understanding? Let it be made clear at the very outset that education cannot take up any responsibility other than that of educating a child for a good civilized living. It has been almost a fashion in India to burden education with the responsibility of all sorts of programmes for social, political and economic reforms. We have been asked to educate for campaigns like "Grow More Food" "Stop Drinking", "Eradicate Illiteracy and Untouchability", "Fight the Epidemic and Dacoity Menace" and lately "Plan the Family". This has been done because of the easily available crowd that throngs the schools and colleges and the satisfaction that the sponsors of such programmes derive from the meaningless shouting of slogans by the unwary children. We should stoutly refuse to undertake any such responsibility.

Education cannot take in any corpus of subject-matter for any such programmes and much less treat International Understanding as a branch of study. At best some information which forms part of the school subjects and naturally springs from their presentations can be given to the pupils. It is not possible to provide education of International Understanding in schools but education for International Understanding can be given along with the usual school work ; and this is quite a different thing. It will be the end product of a full and balanced education and not a separate element in the educational programme. It will consist of developing some skills, certain interests. and some few attitudes which are fundamental to all good education.

The skills that can be developed in pupils are the ability to read and understand about United Nations and ability to analyse new situations by using relevant sources of information. Social skills may develop ability to discuss problems un-emotionally and objectively and ability to contact strangers tactfully, impressively and confidently. Interests may grow out of emphasis on our interdependence and making correct choices when faced with alternatives ; and curiosity may be aroused about other cultures and peoples. Attitudes may be in the form of amiability, co-operation, freedom from prejudices, sensitivity to human aspect of problems and acceptance of differences in ideas and interests as inevitable. The aim of all this should be the modification of behaviour patterns of children in schools which is consistent with the general purpose of education.

Principles of International Understanding

Before discussing some more aspects of education for International Understanding, it will evidently be worth while to understand the groundwork or the foundation on which it rests. For doing so, some basic principles underlying this concept should be briefly mentioned. They are as follows :

International understanding pre-supposes breadth of view

The social horizon of every student should not remain restricted to a limited social-group. The realisation that our nation is one among so many other nations of the world and the consequent respect for their rights and interests is the first principle that serves as a basic for education for International Understanding.

Objective and Independent Thinking

Unless individuals or nations are wise enough to distinguish truth from false propaganda, the possibility of any International Understanding will be very remote. This principle consists in adopting a sort of impartial attitude and judging things on merit in the light of facts. Unless a nation is judicious enough to differentiate between truth and propaganda and is strong enough to resist indoctrination or dangerous ideologies, world peace will ever remain in danger. Hence, education for International Understanding should aim at developing the requisite ideas and attitudes in the child.

The Inter-Dependence of Nations

Education for International Understanding should be planned and imparted with the motive of bringing home to the educand that no nation is self-sufficient in the matter of the fulfilment of its needs, raw materials, as well as furnished goods and that every nation has made its own contribution to building up of civilisation and establishing cultural norms.

Education for International Understanding depends upon the development of right to concept of patriotism or nationalism. Unless patriotism is interpreted as consistent with internationalism, the foundation for world peace can not be stable.

Fear and prejudices should be eliminated from the minds of the students through proper orientation or the curriculum and the textbooks. Due emphasis should be laid on the democratic values or mutual regard, tolerance and co-operation.

The Objectives of Education for International Understanding

An important obligation of the school in relation to education for International Understanding is to construct or reconstruct the curriculum of primary as well as secondary education with a view to,achieving this goal. However, mere reshuffling or recasting the syllabus or the re-orientation of text-books may not suffice our purpose. It can be done aimlessly or in a haphazard manner, unless some well definded objectives are in view. The objectives of education for International Understanding may be briefly mentioned as follow :

1. The students should be familiarised with the Geography, History, Culture, Scientific development and the daily life of people living in different parts of the world. The curriculum should be properly adjusted to the realisation of this goal.

2. The inter-dependence of and mutual co-operation among nations should be brought home to the students. Another objective to be achieved by education for International Understanding is the emphasis on the contribution of different nation to human welfare.

3. Education for International Understanding should acquaint students incidentally with the basic similarity underlying superficial differences in the modes of thinking and living of different nations.

The students should feel convinced that human nature is the same all over the world. The motives of fear and anger, envy and jealousy, love and hate are universal. The interests are alike and basic problems are common in almost all cases. People are people everywhere.

4. Perhaps one of the most important objectives is to develop attitudes favourable for internationalism and to de-condition anti-international attitudes.

Let us now go to the school and consider what activities can legitimately be carried on there to help education for International Understanding and co-operation. There are mainly two types of school programmes, namely (i) class-room teaching often designated as curricular programme, and (ii) out-of-doors activities sometimes called co-curricular programme. We will briefly examine the possibility of developing International Understanding through teaehirg of some subjects and through organizing of various co-curricular activities.

Curricular Programmes

The subjects that easily lend themselves to teaching of International Understanding are history, geography, civics and literature. They can help to make us realize our place in relation to space and time, rights and duties, and develop attitudes of tolerance and sympathy towards other countries and races.

History should be taught as 'story of man' on earth studying man in his relations with man—social, political, economic and moral. It should provide a world setting for teaching national history which may be more broad-based. As soon as the events and movements go out of the national scene teaching may be oriented towards International Understanding. Sometimes history is taught with the attitude of "my country, right or wrong" exalting it above all others, exaggerating its achievements and white-washing its defects. The historical traditions are often imbued with myths of national origion, of national excellence and national greatness. This is a wrong view of patriotism. True patriotism is critical of evils and misdeeds wherever found, motherland not excepted, and appreciative of all that is good in the history of man whether in the mother country or foreign land.

Geography studies man in his environments all over the world. It can arouse sympathy for men struggling with difficult geographical conditions, develop a sense of interdependence and solidarity of mankind. It destroys prejudice which springs from ignorance, and points to the fact that areas politically distinct may often be linked by the necessities of life. It should bring home to the pupils that the standards of life cannot be maintained unless there is a rational pooling of resources and that problems of health, hunger and habitant cannot be solved unless they are tackled at international level. Geography should develop imagination to transform printed descriptions, figures and maps of countries into warm living concrete pictures of men inhabiting this great planet.

Civics and social studies tell about the rights and duties of a citizen and the relationships of the individual with society and nation. Its teaching should cross the narrow boundaries of the city or the country and extend beyond to the world and mankind.

National sciences like geology, botany and zoology deal with lot of data valuable for study of world problems concerned with health, nutrition, agriculture, epidemic, pests and forestry. Biology and physiology can contribute towards racial studies. The achievements of great scientists who have benefited mankind can be used for better understanding among peoples. A singular contribution that the sciences give is the training in accuracy, integrity, exactness in observation, objectivity in education and insistence on proof.

Language and literature can portray to us the basic emotions, urges and beliefs of man ; they highlight the mores of life, the cultural and social conditions of the people in a given historical and cultural milieu. The biographies of great persons who have served humanity through their thoughts, deeds and artistic creations may be taught to create better understanding among peoples. It is through literature and language that the pupils come in contact with the mighty minds and lofty thoughts of those who interpreted the spirit of man in its innumerable permutations and combinations.

The teaching of these subjects can emphasize habits of clear thinking, logical reasoning, weighing evidence and arriving at independent and balanced judgement. The press, the platform, the radio, the television, the cinema and the theatre all these sometimes try to exploit a person by confusing thinking and meddling with truth ; our teaching should enable the pupils to seek truth and stick to it in spite of all loud and tendentious talks.

Music and art provide occasions to develop International Understanding. Their appeal is universal and transcends all barriers. Music has a language that is international which touches the heart. Radio or recorded music of various countries can leave a deep impression on young minds. With small children who can not easily express themselves in writing we can use drawing, painting and handwork for expression and bring children nearer by organising art competitions like that of Shanker's Weekly. The best paintings may be used to popularize the great artistic achivement of the world.

It should be noted that U.N.O. and its agencies are producing lot of literature which will be useful and some which may be dull reading for the pupils. Some may not be conducive to development of any behaviour patterns and attitudes. Therefore, judicious selection for the students from this mass of information becomes very necessary.

Co-curricular Activities

The out-of-class activities have the advantage of ensuring voluntary participation of pupils, providing natural atmosphere for action and motivating the pupils. The school assemblies, clubs and societies, excursions, exhibitions, exchange schemes, games and sports are shared by other schools and groups of community and cultivate interests and co-operation which leads to better understanding.

The school may celebrate annual days of international importance. 'United Nations Day', 'Human Rights Day', 'World Health Day' and other important dates may be used to call assemblies in which the work of international co-operation may be explained. Lectures by foreigners in the neighbouring universities and embassies may be organized. The visit of a person from another country may be the occasion to invite him for a talk to the students about his country.

The mock assemblies of various organizations may be arranged when pupils may act as representatives of different countries to put up their point of view on some burning problem of the day. International relations centre or pen-friendship societies may discuss current events or questions raised in the letters.

Dramatic presentations and pageants of folk-lore, literature or drama of other countries may, besides giving an understanding to the pupils may pass on their impressions to a wider public who come to seek the entertainment. Funds raised through sale of tickets or handwork may be contributed to the Red Cross or UNICEF. Subscriptions may also be raised to provide aid to the refugees, to the flood-striken, to the poor children and for construction of school buildings.

Bulletin boards may display news cuttings and pictures of other countries which may have some international significance. Essay competitions and elocution contents may be held on some important topic or on the work of the United Nations Organisation.

The Red Cross, Boy Scout, Girl Guide movements inspired by the ideal of 'Service to All' can develop proper attitudes and correct feeling sets in the pupils in pursuance of our goal. The Red Cross activities aim at improvement of health, prevention of diseases and mitigating the suffering throughout the world and can help to develop feelings of humanity, neutrality, impartiality and universality. The Boy Scout and Girl Guide movernent is international in spirit for "a scout is a friend to all and brother to every other scout, no matter to what country, class or creed the other may belong." Its ideals of self-help, comradeship and service provide immense possibilities for developing feelings of brotherhood and world-mindedness. These are dynamic activities psychologically and educationally sound for training in International Understanding and co-operation.

It is not ordinarily possible for a school to finance travel to foreign lands. But the governments of some countries invite students and exchange-programmes are arranged by UNESCO which help in strengthening the bonds between peoples.

The United Nations and its specialized agencies produce and circulate useful teaching material. The schools can obtain the book-lets, illustrated posters, photo-prints and film-strips from the U. N. Information Centres which have been established in the member states. The UNESCO periodicals like the courier which is an illustrated monthly containing world news about art, science and education can be subscribed to by the school. Various countries also publish illustrated book-lets and periodicals giving information about the people and their activities and these can be obtained from the embassies or legations in the country.

Associated Schools Project

The UNESCO started the Associated Schools Project in 1953 and India joined it a year later. There are 204 secondary schools and 78 training institutions in 43 countries under this project. Of these, 13 institutions from India—ten secondary schools and three teacher training institutions—are participating in this scheme. The three major fields of study in these schools are lives of people in distant countries, human rights, and work of theUnited Nations and its specialized agencies. The schools are free to adopt the form of experiments best adapted to their situation. UNESCO on request provides expertise and some documentation. The school evaluates the work and sends report to the national supervisor of the project. The aim of the project is to promote general development of education for International Understanding and co-operation and to provide substantial information on the effectiveness of different approaches, methods and materials used in various Associated Schools in developing attitudes favourable to International Understanding and co-operation. The project is in an experimental stage and evaluation of its effectiveness in school is the main concern of sponsors. The assessment of the project so far made is hopeful of extending the scheme in other states.

The expert committees called by the UNESCO to spell out education for International Understanding and co-operation have formulated eight ideals of this education. The first ideal seeks so educate mankind for the world community, the second to inculcate the duty of co-operating in international organisations, the third to lay stress on the necessity of these organizations and the fourth ideal demands the effective support of the people in their programmes. The remaining ideals pertain to emphasizing interdependence, unity in diversity, responsibility for peace, and development of healthy social attitudes. The first four ideals deal with the education of the organizations and may perhaps be more suitable for adults. The latter four may be suitable for school population. As we have said earlier any formal teaching about international organisations cannot possibly be mixed up with the formal education of the child. Of course certain skills and attitudes can be developed which might usher in good international relations.

The role of the Teacher

The teacher occupies the pivotal position in education and if the education for International Understanding is to make any headway and advance, he must form the spear-head. There are many opportunities in class-room teaching which an intelligent teacher can utilize to foster attitudes and behaviour patterns in pupils favourable for International Understanding and co-operation. It is upto him to tilt the discussion on a subject in favour of International Understanding, without making any conscious effort to introduce the subject-matter in some direct formalized manner to the pupils. He should consider it a part of his duty to develop such traits and qualities in his pupils whenever and wherever an occasion arises. In case he fails to do it he must know that, if the world peace is disturbed, there must come a time when there will be no one left to educate. Therefore, the urgent need of the present time is to prepare boys and girls, men and women to take an active part in developing International Understanding and co-operation and creating a world society.

CONCLUSION

Education for International Understanding is yet in a nebulous stage. It does not only lack means and method but is also limted in its extent. No doubt Associated Schools Project has been started but it is only experimental and tentative and its effectiveness has to be evaluated before it can be extended to make any impact on the people at large. The contents in school curriculum as they are today emphasize national and local interests and neglect study of human relations. The traditional methods of character building are not applicable to developing desired, attitudes, interests and habits. New methods of teaching have to be discovered. The training of teachers has to be given a different orientation for this type of education. They should know how to develop desirable personality traits in the pupils, how to create school atmosphere favourable to their development and how and where to get subject-matter from social sciences and human relations which may be amalgamated with the contents of common school subjects. The evaluation of the work requires new tools. Vigorous research is, therefore, necessary in four fields of education for International Understanding :—

(i) **Selection of pupils**—Which age-levels of children are most suitable for various aspects of this programme ;

(ii) **Preparation of teachers**—What kind of training or briefing should the teachers receive for this work ;

(iii) **Content of the programme**—What subject-matter should be given, what skills and interests should be developed; and

(iv) **Method of instruction**—Which methods will develop the right personality traits ?

Constant evaluation of the programme and the improvement particularly at this initial stage of educational understanding need little emphasis.

Having said all this, one must sound a word of caution. All constructive and creative programmes for school children require a basic framework of understanding, peace and concord among the society at large built up by the thinking and action of its adult population. Those adults who are charged with the destinies of mankind—its politicians, scientists, industrialists and economists—have to be eternally aware of their role in the education of the younger generation that would succeed them in future. Given such awareness, the education for International Understanding as it may be pursued in our schools, would become realistic and effective.

27

The Curriculum

We have already discussed the aims and objectives of education. Now we have to discuss the problem, how these aims are to be realised. In other words "what" forms of knowledge and experiences are to be given to children at school to prepare them for effective living. This brings us to the problem of curriculum.

MEANING AND DEFINITION OF CURRICULUM

Etymologically the term 'curriculum' is derived from the Latin word 'urrere' which means 'run'. Thus, curriculum means "a course to be run for reaching a certain goal or destination. In this sense, education is imagined as a race, with its aims as the goals and curriculum as the course, leading to that goal.

Curriculum is not a race but a chase

But such a concept of the curriculum fits in extremely well with the traditional view of education—education being conceived as training in such skills as reading, writing, arithmetic and in acquiring mastery over certain areas of knowledge. As the trainer trains the horse to reach the target by leading him through the course, so does the teacher train the pupils to realise the educational objectives by leading them through the curriculum prescribed for the purpose. It provides the necessary practice and indicates the necessary reading which would help the pupils in gaining the desired knowledge.

But in recent times, the tendency is to view education as a dynamic process. It has to deal with living organisms, each one of whom is different from the others. It concerns itself with the growth and development of the pupils, which instead of resembling any set pattern, are unique individually. So no mechanical conception of the curriculum can serve the purpose of true education. The viewing of the curriculum as a "chase" instead of a "race" removes a good many misunderstandings. In case of a race, the goal is fixed with exactitude and the course through which the goal is to be reached is also outlined with precision. In the case of a chase, however, the goal is fixed only in a general manner ; it does not remain fixed, but varies from time to time in the course of the pursuit. The course, therefore, cannot be decided with precision, it has to vary with the variation in the nature of the goal.

The latest trend in this respect, therefore, is to regard the curriculum as flexible rather than rigid. It may differ from school to school and even in the same school and in the same grade from individual to individual. The content of education can be outlined only in a general way allowing enough scope for variation within the general frame-work. For example, knowledge of the environment may be decided upon as an item in the curriculum, but its scope will differ from school to school. Not only this, even the activities through which knowledge is expected to be gained, may also differ in accordance with the resources of different schools and the characteristics of the pupils, they have on roll.

It is clear from the above discussion that some confusion exists as to the precise meaning of the term 'curriculum'. According to the old conception, curriculum represents the accumulation of knowledge and skills organised into systems, not from the point of view of the needs of the pupil, but from that of the specialist who enjoys knowing a particular field of knowledge and skills for their own sake. The new view is that the curriculum is a set of experiences, or the activities in which one engages, or a series of life situations one faces. In the light of the new view, we can say that curriculum is more than the text-books, more than the subject-matter, and also more than a course of study. It is the total situation or group of situations available to the teacher and the school administrator through which to make hehaviour changes in the endless stream of children and youth who pass through the doors of the school.

To present a clear picture of curriculum, some definitions of curriculum are given below :

1. The curriculum may be defined as the totality of subject-matter, activities, and experiences which constitutes a pupils' school life. A course of study in the material, usually in pamphlet form,

which sets forth for the teacher such items as the objectives and content of a given subject, and the activities and books to be used to accomplish desired results.

2. "The curriculum according to **Crow** and **Crow** "includes all the learner's experience in or outside school that are included in a programme which has been desired to help him develop mentally, physically, emotionally. socially, spiritually, and morally. These experiences include that subject-matter gained through direct experience and that which is secured vicariously through the utilization of text books and other learning aids. Curricular offerings thus include the content and the materials of instruction, techniques of procedure, and personal influences."

3. Curriculum does not mean only the academic subjects traditionally taught in the school, but it also includes the totality of expriences that a pupil receives through the manifold activities that go in the school—in the class-room, library, laboratory, workshop, play-grounds and in the numerous informal contacts between teachers and pupils. In this case, the whole life of the school becomes the curriculum which can touch the life of the students at all points and help in the evolution of balanced personality.

DIFFERENT TYPES OF CURRICULUM

The following are the different types of curriculum :

1. Traditional or Subject-Centred curriculum.
2. Activity curriculum.
3. Experience curriculum.
4. Integrated curriculum.

Traditional or Subject-Centred curriculum

Ever since education has aimed at equiping the child with the adult standards, the principle of 'equipment' supplemented with the psychological conception of 'transfer of training' has led to the philosophy of traditional curriculum, that is, conceiving the curriculum in terms of subjects, each one of which is given pre-determined place and allotted a fixed amount of time. The exact and precise extent and scope of each subject which is to be studied in a particular class or in a particular session is carefully and strictly defined. The job is strictly entrusted to and carried out by adults in terms of adult values. Emphasis is laid on learning and acquiring of habits and skills which might not be of any utility to the child in the period of life. He is actually living or passing through, but is supposed to be useful in adult life, for which he is being prepared.

In traditional curriculum, irrespective of considerations of the needs and interests and the psychology of the child, which stresses that, the human knowledge is divided in compartment for the convenience of mastering it. It is properly analysed and classified. The labels attached to such parts of human experience become subjects. The classification is based upon two considerations (1) Nature of the contents and (2) the methods of the teaching. The division is highly logical and pieces of human knowledge are put together in it. There is no place for the view point of the child. The contents are those fixed by the adults for the perpetuation of their standards and values. The method of teaching, more often than not, is rote learning. Neither do contents immediately interest the child nor can methods make learning easy.

Human knowledge is conveniently divisible into three broad fields:

(1) Natural sciences including (a) the Physical sciences pertaining to phenomena of the universe, such as Physics, Chemistry, Geology and Astronomy and (b) Biological sciences, such as Zoology and Botany.

(2) The Social sciences, which relate to the origin, organization and development of human society, especially to man in association with other men. Such as History, Geography, Civics, Economics, Politics, Sociology etc.

(3) Humanities which, pertain to that branch of knowledge which humanises man. They relate to art, literature and human thought, ideals and feelings. Philosophy, Literature, Fine Arts, Painting, Drawing, Drama, Music, etc. come under this head. This education restricts itself to the use of words and symbols. It does not present to the child the actualities of life. He is not kept busy in solving some present problem or doing some activity for the achievement of an immediate goal. The criterion being "education for preparation" for future, which is often uncertain, does not leave chances for the child's present. With many defeats inherent in such a conviction in the highly dynamic modern society in which nobody can fore-tell what is to happen in the near future in which values are changing and disappearing so fast, the traditional curriculum is nothing but a body of factual information and those essential skills and techniques which man has discovered to pass on to the new generations through the school by the process of explanation and repetition.

The traditional philosophy, thus, regards education as static, something which takes place in the school room during a fixed number of periods everyday. Education accordingly is synonymous with school going. It starts when the child reaches the school, and continues as long as he is there, and ends when the child has left it.

Such an education provides ease in the methods of teaching to the teacher. He is not to worry about the techniques of imparting different kinds of knowledge in different ways. The prescribed book, which limits his course, is required to be learnt by heart by the children. The children are to devour these bitter pills, though with strain and no interest. But knowing the lore, initiative, discrimination, originally, resourcefulness and creative thinking, they settle themselves with ease in the pages of the books.

But logical order in place of psychological consideration of the dynamics of the child mind, domination of books, faulty methods of teaching and prescription of adult standards have done a great harm to true education of the children. The curriculum is narrowly, conceived. It prepares the child for the uncertain future at the cost of his present problems. It takes into consideration his literary interests only.

The un-natural division of knowledge into subjects has landed us on such a ground that we see dissection everywhere. There is no end to that. And as traditional curriculum does not admit knowledge except literacy, a long list of co-curricular and extra curricular activities is being added to that. The importance of these activities is being increasingly realised but is not given proper place. And this shows narrowness of the traditional curriculum.

This curriculum is abstract. The child's present needs are neglected for the past human-experience with which the child is to be saddled for being prepared for adult life. The child's activity has no place, studies become sheer verabalism and are cut off from the life of the child. It does not provide concrete experience to the child which is the fundamental basis of learning.

The method of learning in parts is also psychologically wrong and has led to memorization through drill or recitation of the unrelated information. For teaching different subjects different teachers are employed. This minimises the possibilities of co-ordination of studies. It has increased the burden on the mind of the children for the disconnected mass of information lacking inherent relationship. It is not an easy task for making knowledge a useful means to solve problems of life.

Such curriculum has a specific and fixed programme. The books give a uniform text and a fixed quantitative standard of attainment as the goal. The individual differences are totally ignored and no scope is left for individual attention and development of individual skills, interests and aptitudes. At best, the studies are carried on for a hypothetical average child who does not exist at all. To worsen the situation, the curriculum is framed by politicians or administrators for the utter neglect of those who are concerned with learning and teaching students and teachers. All this has led to uniformity and rigidity and unrealistic nature of the methods of education.

Since, education is wrongly considered as synonymous with schooling, the informal agencies of education have no significant place for educative purposes. The effects of home, society, club play-ground and many passive agencies which are powerful media of imparting education to the child are totally neglected. It is paradoxical that the learning is aimed at the preservation and betterment of social standards, yet the society is considered as passive and ineffective for learning. Thus, education is supposed to end with the school and is not conceived as a life-long process.

In India, it has done greater harm by stressing foreign language, not merely as a subject of study, but as the very medium of instruction. But slowly we are realizing its defects and new schemes are being put to practice. The Basic and Higher Secondary schemes lay stress upon activities and interests of the child besides the cultural heritage of the people.

To sum up, we can say that traditional curriculum is conceived in terms of subjects. It is rigid and static and is constructed by adults after their own image. It stresses repetition and memorization. It neglects the importance of other informal agencies of education, and above all, it is not an expression of our cultural and spiritual heritage. Thus, the traditional curriculum is 'narrowly conceived', 'unpsychologicaly' planned and ineffectively executed". It leads only to intellectual development at the cost of physical, social, moral, emotional, aesthetic and spiritual development. In other words, it is inadequate, un-satisfactory, un-inspiring and un-scientific.

Activity Curriculum

It is a pity that even at present, educational system in India lays undue emphasis on verbal information. It is universally admitted that whatever has to be learnt, must be learnt by doing. Activity is the cardinal principle of child behaviour. The child is active by nature. He desires to deal with things, to make, to construct, to destroy, to plan, to observe and to enjoy. The formal information regarding things has little values for him. He may cram, but does not understand the matter memorised by him. Education is not mere craming. To be really educated one has to assimilate the matter so that it may affect his dispositions, modify his behaviour and his way of life.

The educationists and psychologists have realized the need of the child for activity and that is why Montessori Method, Dalton Plan, Kindergarten and Project Method have been used in the teaching of the child. The Naturalists have supported the activity principle. **Ross** says, "extreme naturalism concentrates in school on the present experience, activities and interests of the child himself, it is these and these alone that may legitimately determine, what he is to do in school. Let him have his own proper experience, unhampered and unhindered by adult-interference, direction or even coaxing." A pragmatist also believes in unfettered activities of the child. "Since, activity is the essential characteristic of childhood, the child must be active, the experience he undergoes in the school must be firmly based on his natural activities and interests." The framers of Wardha Scheme also took note of activity in framing Basic curriculum. They say, "We have attempted to draft an activity curriculum which implies that our schools must be places of work, experimentation and discovery, not of passive absorption of information imparted at second hand."

For **Dewey** activity curriculum is a "continuing stream of child activities, unbroken by systematic subjects and springing from the interests and personally felt needs of the child." Now we have to see what these activities could be? Shall we have only those activities which we now a days characterise as extra-curricular or co-curricular in the syllabus, or shall we exclude them and give place to literary activities only or shall we have both? Banchara Branford has given a three-fold diversion of human activities as there are three centres of activity the head, hand and heart of man a trinity in unity, Accordingly, there are three instruments of culture, science, arts and crafts, and language including music and literature of all kinds. Also man's objects of interests are three—nature, crafts and folk. Hence, to keep all the centres of activity engaged, to satisfy human interests and to make use of the instruments of culture, we can introduce in the school (a) nature-crafts, study of external nature, (b) Hindi-craft or study of arts and crafts and (c) language or folk-craft or study of language in its various forms.

Nunn divides activities in two groups :

(1) The activities that safeguard the conditions and maintain the standard of individual and social life : such as the care of health and bodily grace, manners, social organization, morals and religion.

(2) The typical creative activities that constitute, so to speak, the solid tissue of civilization, will comprise (i) literature including at least the best literature of the motherland and (ii) some forms of art including

music the most universal of arts. (iii) handicrafts, taught with emphasis either on its aesthetic aspects as in the weaving, carving, lettering or on its constructional aspect as in carpentry and needle work. (iv) science including mathematics, the science of number, space and time, History and Geography should appear in it, in a double guise.

Definitely Nunn's second type of activities do not comprise simple activities, they become pure subjects of study and include the racial experience in them as **Nunn's** notion of schools is not merely activity-centred but for him "a nation's schools... are an organ of its life, whose special function is to consolidate its spiritual strength, to maintain its historic continuity, to secure its past achievements to guarantee its value." But since his activities fall in line with Branford's division of activities, which make up for past experience for making a good activity curriculum. However by leaving that, the curriculum remains defective.

There are simple activities of kindergarten for very young children. If we narrowly conceive activity-curriculum, we will have the activities related with (i) exercises for physical development (ii) exercises of daily life, (iii) Dramatic and constructive plays and various other occupations for muscular, sensory and intellectual development. (iv) story telling, observation of nature and discussions arising from handling of things and looking at pictures, (v) rhythmic work and singing and work of reading, writing and number through various play-activities and projects which engage the child's attention.

These are good amount of activities, but activities for a particular age, that is, childhood. It is difficult to prescribe activities like this for every stage. The only cardinal principle for them is the child's interest whatever interests children which varies from stage to stage and from society to society, must be included in the activities of the school. That is why, crossing the limit of naturalist, who lay store by the present needs and interests of the child to circumscribe his activities. Dewey, as a true pragmatist, includes those activities also which prepare him for his future life. Definitely the child has interest in his future. Thus, **Dewey** according to natural interests of the child, prescribes activities relating to "the interest in conversation, or communication in enquiry or finding out things in making things or construction and in artistic expression." The 3 R's are to be added to facilitate learning and to serve as tools and not to be ends in themselves.

Thus, the provision for the activity dealing with realities of child's nature and his life facilitates the framing of the activity curriculum.

The activity curriculum is (1) to furnish the child a sufficiently large amount of personal activities in occupations, expressions, conservation, construction, and experimentation so that his individuality—moral and intellectual, shall not be swamped by a disproportionate amount of the experience of others to which books introduce him and (2) so to conduct this more direct experience as to make the child feel the need of resorting to and command of traditional social tools furnish him with motives and make his recourse to them intelligent, in addition to his powers instead of a servile dependency." And this is possible only when every activity is well thought of before undertaking it and is purposeful. The needs and interests of the child become the medium of the capitalized experience of human race and make activity curriculum cut across the subject barriers and give integrated knowledge. Therefore, instead of subjects, the activity curriculum suggests activities to be performed in the school, the nouns of subjects to be converted into verbs of activities. It must not merely remain a play. "The play should", in the words of **Sir Percy Nunn**, "lead continuously from the irresponsible frolic of childhood to the disciplined labours of mankind."

Mere activity curriculum, if taken in a narrower sense, is defective. We cannot ignore the past experience for mere likes and dislikes of individual children. They can be allowed to play and engage in some activity of their choice till certain age only. After that the social heritage must surely he made to carry. After all the individual is not merely an individual. He is a part of social group, an important humanizing agency. That agency is not to be neglected if individuals are to benefit from it and therefore, its experience and heritage must also supplement activities to make curriculum a complete one.

Experience Curriculum

The curriculum that gives rich and varied experiences of knowledge, skills, attitudes and appreciation, is called ",experience curriculum." "Whatever forces may govern human life, if they are to be recognised by man, must betray themselves in human experience."

According to **William James** "The only function that one experience can perform is to lead to another experience, and the only fulfilment we can speak of is' the reaching of a certain experienced end." Thus, experience being both process and end of learning, we cannot ignore it in the curriculum or in the framing of curriculum. The exponents of Wardha Scheme took this into due consideration and pointed out, "We have attempted to organise the subject-matter into significant and comprehensive units of experience which will, when mastered enable the child to understand his environment better and react to it more intelligently because they throw significant light on the problems and conditions of the life around him."

Experience requires direct dealing with the things which results in the modification of the behaviour of the learner to modify the thing or situation and also to make it serviceable in changed circumstances. But the things and situations to be experienced must have utility for the child. But those things only can be of use which invoke needs and interests of the child or are drawn from his social life. Hence, the basis of experience curriculum, must be the needs and interests of the child in his environments.

Experience is neither merely a knowledge affair, nor a physical thing infected throughout by subjectivity. Nor a thing of the past nor committed to particularism, only. It suggests experiments with the present to gain control of the environment for future good. It takes the whole situation and all knowledge in an integrated form, into consideration. The mental organism puts together relevant pieces of knowledge obtained from past experiences to refer to in future and to draw inferences. As experience, modifies the behaviour of the learner, which leads to the modification of the environment, itself, which provided the experience, future good becomes its watch-word and' experiments with social and physical environment its means.

Hence, let experience be direct, or dealing with the present or modifying the past, it is reflective and takes into consideration the comulative experience of the past. It cannot ignore the environment with which the experience is held and which is the creation of past generations. Experience is a process of reflective adjustment of life to changing environment.

Idealism concentrates not so much on the present experience of the individual as on the experience of the human race as a whole. It considers the rounded whole of human knowledge and experience and seeks to epitomize it in the school to bring it to the child. "It stands on the position that the purpose of the school is to reflect the civilization itself, the main purpose, therefore, of courses of studies is to epitomize and organize in respective fashion at least, the capitalised experience of the race of which the child is a member."

But experience is at last two-fold, being concerned with (a) physical environment and (b) fellowmen. Hence, we can divide the curriculum broadly in (a) the sciences and (b) the humanities, each one of which can be sub-divided in many courses of studies.

According to psychological analysis we can divide the experience into (a) conation, or the active striving experience (b) cognition, or knowing experience and (c) affection or feeling experience.

Accordingly, the studies must represent (a) what man does and strives to do, (b) what man knows and (c) how man feels. Under (a) we can include the major crafts of mankind, specially those which subserve the fundamental needs of food, shelter and clothing (b) must be the representation of man's major modes of thinking, so language, literature, science, mathematics, history and geography, the traditional intellectual studies may be included, (c) man's main modes of feeling and their expression in arts, music and poetry may be included.

Experience, curriculum is centred in learning. It emphasises. promoting the all-round growth of the learner. Its subject-matter is : contents of experience curriculum. Psychologically, human experience is divided into three major parts, namely (1) conation or doing and striving experience (2) cognition or knowing experience and (3) affection or feeling experience. Accordingly, the following contents are included in experience curriculum.

Human activity	*Human experience*	*Human environment*	*Contents or subjects of study.*
Hand	Conation	Aesthetic	Arts, craft and music.
Head	Cognition	Literary	Languages and literature.
Heart	Affection	Spiritual	Humanities, Religion, Morality, and Philosophy.

There should, however, be no hard and fast lines of demarcation. There should rather be complete integration of experiences and contents under the co-operative control of teachers, pupils, parents and others, concerned with the education of children.

Experience and Traditional Curriculum Differentiated

As it has already been discussed, the traditional curriculum laying its stress on subject-matter, is meant to serve the needs of the adult life. On the other hand, experience curriculum as a series of purposeful experiences, growing out of pupil's interest and moving towards an ever-more adequate understanding of an intelligent participation in the surrounding culture and group life. Thus, it is clear that these are two extreme types of curriculum.

Hopkins has made an attempt to analyse these two extreme types of curriculum and bring out the salient point of difference between them. His characterization of the type is indeed very useful and profitable. It is, in fact, a masterly analysis of the philosophies, and therefore, we take the liberty of producing it rather extensively. The differences as stated by him are as follows :

Subject Curriculum	*Experience Curriculum*
1. Cenetred in subjects.	1. Centred in learners.
2. Emphasis upon teaching subject-matter.	2. Emphasis upon promoting the all-round growth of the learners.
3. Subject matter selected and organized before the teaching situation.	3. Subject matter selected and organised co-operatively by all learners during the learning situation.
4. Controlled by the teacher or some one representing authority external to the learning situation.	4. Controlled and directed co-operatively by learners i.e. pupils, teachers, parents, supervisors, principals and others related to the learning situations.
5. Emphasis upon teaching facts, imparting information, acquiring knowledge for its own sake or for possible future use.	5. Emphasis upon meaning which will function immediately in improving living.
6. Emphasis upon improving method of teaching subject-matter of specific subjects.	6. Emphasis upon understanding and improving through process of learning.
7. Emphasis upon teaching specific habits and skills as separate and isolated aspects of learning.	7. Emphasis upon building habits and skills as integrated parts of larger experiences.
8. Emphasis upon uniformity of exposure to learning situation and in so far as possible uniformity of results.	8. Emphasis upon variability in exposures to learning situation and variability in results expected and achieved.
9. Education as conforming to the patterns set by the curriculum and its various associated instruments.	9. Education as aiding each child build creative individuality.
10. Education considered as schooling.	10. Education considered as a continuous, intelligent process of growth.

Integrated Curriculum

Since, quite recently we are hearing of the term 'integrated curriculum', let us try to find out what integrated curriculum is? Explaining the meaning of and defining integrated curriculum, Stella **V. Henderson** writes, "A curriculum in which barriers between subjects are broken down is often called an integrated curriculum." Such a curriculum provides experiences which are supposed to facilitate the psychological process of integration and in connection with which' children will learn the subject-matter suitable for understanding or reconstructing their experience. Such an experience curriculum abolishes the old compartmentalization and the categories of subjects as such, introducing subjects only as they pertain to the centres of child interest.

As a better human being will never emerge from a mere juggling with subjects but only from a whole experience, an attempt is made to provide whole experience through an integrated curriculum. Knowledge is treated as one unified whole and its division into a number of unrelated and at times mutually exclusive subjects is not favoured.

We can follow various approaches for integration of curriculum :

1. Individual subjects may make the starting point for a partial or total integration of the curriculum.

2. The idea of citizenship has sometimes been put forward as a principle of correlation. Subjects are justified and linked together by the contribution which they make, like the pieces in the jigsaw puzzle, to the picture of a community of free and responsible citizens.

3. The principles of logical thought have been used as common elements in many subjects, and though they are unable to group subjects together, they may at least associate them in a common purpose.

4. We may abandon separate 'subjects' as the skelton of the curriculum altogether and think rather in terms of 'areas of activity.' These areas must be representative of all the great avenues of activity and experience down which the mind and spirit, of man make their approach to life. They are as follows :

(i) The area of physical activity, in which a child must learn to understand, to control and to use his body ;

(ii) The area of social activity, in which an awareness of the community is fostered, the art of expression and of social inter-course are mastered, and an active responsibility for the common good experienced ;

(iii) The area of imaginative activity, in which the spirit goes off on its own into the romantic and illuminating worlds of literature and of art, and makes strange discoveries there ;

(iv) The area of creative activity, in which the cravings of a skill-hungry animal are satisfied ; and the bards are busy with pen or pencil or brush or tool ;

(v) The area of spiritual activity and of the study and practice of religion.

In all these approaches at integration of curriculum, there are certain significant points :

(a) All these are areas of activity and not of receptivity.

(b) In each area the whole human-being is active, and not any, part or faculty of him.

(c) There are five subjects to work into the curriculum and to be placed in the time table. If we can confine ourselves to six, some of the problems of over crowded curriculum will solve themselves and dis-integration will be at least integrated by the reduction in the number.

The purpose of integrated curriculum is to cater to the integrated personality. If a boy is at work in the school workshop, he should be so taught that, in Rousseau phrase, he becomes a philosopher while thinking himself an artisan. If the child is engaged on vocational training, he must develop the human considerations which give to the reaction its meaning in society. If the child is busy on a more cultural subject, he must give it a focal point in some specific contribution which the individual understanding his material and using his tools, as the technician does, is preparing himself to make to the community.

Why Elective Subjects? Inspite of the advantages of an integrated curriculum, it is being felt that personality curriculum cannot be totally ignored. A need is being felt for giving privileged position to some subjects because of their utility and other subjects to be elective. Thus, curriculum is being arranged in a manner that both concentration and distribution is provided. There are prescribed groups of studies with the scope of elective sub-groups within. These are in the form of curriculum consisting of prescribed studies, but the content and activities are to vary to suit the individuals.

PRINCIPLES OF CONSTRUCTING MODERN CURRICULUM

The modern trend in education is diversion from traditional bookish knowledge which is ready-made distasteful mixture prepared in most cases, by politicians and administrators, neglecting the child for whom it is meant, for the purpose of attainment of certain standards and values. Now we aim at fuller development of the child, body, mind and spirit. We wish to develop his capabilities, potentialities aptitudes tastes and interests which are different in children from different walks of life and from different parentage. We wish to draw out of each individual what is the best in him. The regimentation of the students in one type of produce, through the introduction of prescribed courses has to give place to realization of individual differences and development accordingly. Now the call is to make curriculum life-centric.

Education is to be for life and through living. This means that the present life of the child is to be fully developed and through that the child is to be prepared for adult life also. The medium of development is to be living experience of the child with his social and physical environment and not the dead and chilly words of the books. For this, we will have to draw certain principles on which the curriculum is to be drawn. They are as follows :

The Principle of Child Centredness

The traditional conception of subject-centred education must give place to child centred education. Latin is for the child not the child for Latin. His aptitudes, interests, capability and needs determine what he is to learn and to what extent. It is the child who is to be taught and without understanding him no efforts on educating him can bear fruit. He cannot be developed by providing knowledge which is foreign to his needs. His immediate needs—physical, mental, emotional, spiritual and social, must be made the basis for imparting knowledge Education... regards the child as an individual growing by his own activities, living in his environment and preparing himself for adult life not by imitating the adult but living as fully as possible in the environment of childhood. This opens the matter to question. How to provide environments to students from different walks of life in the school, particularly in democracies where differences are little recognised. The only way to do so is to provide ample opportunities for activities according to the tastes of individuals in the school and to make curriculum as broad-based as possible, The activities must be made the centres round which the knowledge of the subjects must revolve in variation according to the needs and interests of the child, as is done in Basic Education.

The Principle of Activity

This is an another principle, underlying curriculum construction. The child is to be provided with activities for the purpose of learning. The child is active by nature. He wants to make or construct things by himself, to satisfy his instinct of constructiveness and that of self-assertion, That is why, learning by doing is considered as the best method of educating the child. The child's growth, through continuous process of activity, resulting training of hand, eye, and other organs of the body, and mind is facilitated. Hence, in order to stimulate growth at a particular stage of development, activities must be introduced in the curriculum appropriate to the particular stage.

But the activity is not to be introduced for its own sake, only to become frivolous play. It must Lead continuously from the irresponsible frolic of childhood to the disciplined labours of manhood. To make education really life-centric, the activity must be purposeful and productive as in Basic Education. **John Dewey** both, for practical and philosophical considerations, wants to "utilize various forms of occupations typifying social calling." For "their intellectual and moral content", the school is to be a miniature social group for active experience. Since, "play-ground, shops, workrooms, and laboratories, not only direct the natural, active tendencies of youth but they involve inter-course, communication and co-operation."

The Principle of Integration

The library, class-room, laboratory, workshop, play ground and the numerous informal contacts between the teacher and the taught, and the community and the child are all educative and help to evolve all-round personality of the child. But they specifically and specially influence the body, mind and heart of the child. This specific work will definitely create lopsidedness in the personality as a whole. Therefore, taking curriculum in the terms of totality of experiences, we must aim at its integration to remove this defect. This will bring out integrated personality and at the same time remove false distinction between curricular and co-curriculur activities, and the life of the child will become the true medium of education.

The Principle of Community Centredness

But the child is not to live the life by himself. He is essentially a social being. His capabilities, interests and needs find development in the society and for the society. We cannot neglect his social side merely for the sake of individuality. He is conscious of social rights and liabilities. Without that, social life would be impossible and man will become a beast. Education for life cannot neglect this aspect of the child. He is to be prepared for the present social living and the future adult social leadership.

The Principle of Forward Looking

The community centredness leads to the principle of preparation for the future life. We look forward to act in adult-hood, in future. The foundation for the future of the child has to be laid down. But in the fast changing scientific age, it is difficult to predict what part is to be played in society, the child must be prepared for the dubious future, otherwise the equipment cannot he ensured. From the child's point of view, of course, we can rest upon the principle of continuity. If life is well-lived at one particular stage, that lays strong foundation for the next stage. Hence, the development of the present possibilities in succession, is the best method for preparation for the future. If the child has faced squarely the present problems he can surely face them in future. The future emerges out of the present and is in continuation with it

"What a child learns in the present must help him to adjust himself to conditions of living in this world and must further give him a foundation of knowledge, feeling and willing, which will enable those conditions when they need changing," says **W. M. Ryburn**. The spokesman of the Board of Education, London, said, "Our attitude towards the curriculum has been influenced by a desire to assist children to acquire or develop the habits, skills, interests and sentiments which they will need both for their own living and for that of the people among whom they will live."

The Principle of Conservation

The preparation for adult life in the community takes us to the principle of conservation of traditions, folk-ways, mores, experiences and the heritage of the past. Adulthood stands for the values of the society as does childhood for play. If the child is to be prepared for that life, the heritage, traditions and social values must find place in the curriculum of the school. The society carries the educational enterprise only for its own preservation. Also for the development of the individuality, the child has to have experiences with the conditions in the community, which are already fixed for him. For that also the community's heritage becomes part of the child's education. All round education is meant to fit our generation to take up the burden of the previous one and to keep up the life of the community without breach of disaster. The burden of social life is continuous and if at any stage our generation gets completely out of touch with the efforts of its predecessors or in any way gets ashamed of itself or its culture it is lost. "It is in fact being increasingly recognised that the various subjects of the curriculum represent certain forms of skill and certain branches of knowledge, which have proved to be of importance to the experience of the race, and which have to be taught to each succeeding generation.

From this point of view this is the function of the school to preserve and transmit the tradition, knowledge and standards of conduct on which our civilization depends."

But every past experience cannot be carried on. There are dogmas, superstitions, prejudices and unscientific attitudes. Much becomes' obsolete in the context of changed circumstances. Therefore, selective attitude must be blended with the conservative. What does not serve our purpose in the present, must be shattered or modified and the new added. But this must be done cautiously.

The Principle of Creativeness

This addition too and modification of the past heritage brings us to the principle of creativeness. New values emerge in new circumstances and old values begin to leave their hold. In order to prepare the child for life, he must be equipped for ready adjustment to the changing conditions and to evolve new values. This can be done by allowing the child to exercise his creative and constructive powers at present to make him an intelligent creator and modifier of environments and values which he can use in later life to 'create new things in future according to the needs of the time.

The Principle of Individual Needs and Interests

The traditional curriculum does not enable the child to be actively free and a worthy member of the society. It does not take into consideration his individual needs and interests. It neglects the child totally which is the main centre of education. Now the circumstances and the conditions have changed. Consequently the new educational system, also has taken a new form. The shift has gone now from subject or teacher to the child in the method and practice of teaching. It is the child for whom education is planned and the child does not exists for the education. The educative process takes into consideration, the age the interests and the needs of the child. If we do not know the nature of the child and his needs, framing the curriculum is as futile as to prescribe medicine for the patient whose disease a doctor does not know. Thus, the subjects of curriculum must be selected in the light of the knowledge of child nature. If we wish a child to live fully at any stage, we must pay attention to what interests him at that stage. What special attitudes he is likely to have, what is likely to appeal to him, what advantages he will take of the dominant instinctive tendencies of the stage. "Education ...regards the child as an individual growing by his own environment and preparing himself for adult life, not by imitating the adults but by living as fully as possible in the environment of childhood," said **F. Smith** and **A. Harrison**.

Recent developments in Educational Psychology have made it clear that learning is essentially a need-centred process and a goal seeking activity. It is a cycle process which begins with the stimulation of need in the learner and ends with its satisfaction. In the words of **Professor H. R. Hamley**, "it is a persistent and continuous process which takes many forms in response to many needs."

These important contributions in respect of the changed concept of learning and better understanding of children have gone a long way in changing, rather revolutionising our concept of the curriculum. Instead of starting with the cultural heritage to be put across the children, so as to be mastered by them or preparing them for a future life, we start with the children as we find them, discover their needs, and try to meet them in the best possible manner. These needs are not mental or intellectual needs only, but include physical, social and spiritual needs also. The physical needs mainly mean a mastery over the movements of the body mechanism. This is essential if a child has to find his own way in this world. The social needs of children originate from their gregarious tendencies which are the very foundation of their social life and of their personal relationship with their fellow beings. The physical and social needs do not exhaust the entire store of a child's needs. He has a craving for a particular kind of inner satisfaction which leads to the creation of spiritual needs and they have also to be satisfied. The mental needs lead the child to understand the world around.

As needs and interests go together, we have to take interests also into consideration. **Dewey** gives four-fold analysis of natural interests of the child. "The interest in conversation or communication, in enquiry or finding out things, in making things or construction and in artistic expression." These are the natural resources, un-invested capital upon the exercise of which depends the active growth of the child.

The above needs and interests are personal to every child and their. degree of intensity is also different in different cases and at different times. Moreover the learning capacity of each individual is also peculiar to himself and not uniform with others. It follows from these two principles that a curriculum intended to serve the needs of a community must be very elastic and flexible. It has to vary from locality to locality, from school to school, from teacher to teacher and even from individual to individual. If it is rigid, mechanical or super-imposed from above in the form of detailed out lines, it will meet with failure and defeat its own purpose. It has to be elastic so that changes and variations may be made in it, keeping in view the needs of 'the individual at present and at different stages of his development and the requirements of the environment in which he is placed. Hence, it is not only desirable but should also be possible to have only a general frame work of learning. leaving enough scope thereby, for changes or variations considered necessary to suit individual needs, requirements and circumstances.

This has, all the more been made necessary by the in-coming of democracy. In democracy generally the education is made free and compulsory by law, as is the case of India. The students are drawn from different walks of life. They have different ways of living, environments, cultural norms, tastes, ideals, aptitudes, capacities, and needs. Democracy does not provide different status to different persons in social life. All have to learn together, to reduce distinctions and to have lessons in co-operation. Under such circumstances to provide fuller development of the individual personalities and to realize their differences the only way seems to lie in flexibility and broad-basedness of the curriculum.

Viewed thus, the concept or the curriculum becomes very broad and fluid. Spontaneity becomes its watch-word and any sort of predetermination, fixity or rigidity is disapproved, disliked and discarded. Besides, it emphasises attitudes more than acquirement of knowledge or skill and even that in spirit of freedom combined with maximum of self-direction and self-determination.

It has been suggested above that the curriculum should be child-centred and that it must be based on the present needs, requirements and circumstances of the child. This is the first and' most important 'principle of curriculum construction. But it is not enough by itself. The curriculum in addition to its being psychologised, has to be socialised. This is so because in thinking and in planning for children, we must keep two facts in mind. Of these two facts, the first is that each child is an individual and must be treated as such. Secondly, he will always have to live with other individuals, and therefore, it is just desirable that, as far as possible, his needs and desires must harmonise with the needs and desires of those amongst whom he has to live.

To sum up the curriculum must have individual relevance. When education was considered identical with the imposition of knowledge upon the child, the question of individual relevance did not arise. The child was regarded as a passive agent in education. He was to be prepared for his future life and moulded and disciplined as the teacher thought fit. The curriculum could, thus, be settled in advance, for the pupils and the arrangement of the curriculum was, therefore, logical rather than psychological. The area of knowledge to be acquired and the logical step's to be taken for the purpose were fixed in advance without any reference to the pupils. But Educational psychology has proved that teaching may not necessarily result in learning, because learning cannot be successful without interest, spontaneity and free initiative on the part of the learner. Hence, the curriculum must be child-centred. It should be based on the present needs of the child. In fact, every activity undertaken in the school should suit the age, intellectual ability and the level of attainment of the pupils. "Psychological curriculum" is the maxim to be constantly kept in view. Moreover, it should be meaningful to the pupils, and as far as possible, should be voluntarily selected by them., Every activity in it must have connection with one or more felt needs of the pupils.

CRITICAL SURVEY OF EXISTING CURRICULA IN INDIAN SCHOOLS

A critical survey of the existing curricula in Indian schools, however, reveals many short-comings which may be summarised as below.

1. The 3 R's are still over-emphasised; in fact in rural areas excepting a few villages, primary school instruction is limited to these and the real aims with which these are to be taught, are entirely ignored. The life outside the school has little or nothing to do with the teaching in the school. The child cannot make any practical use of what he has learnt, nor can he apply it in his daily life; he lives in two different spheres, the dull atmosphere of the school, and the world of freedom outside it.

2. The curricula attaches too much importance to the subject to be taught, and does not take into consideration the child who is to learn. His needs, his health, his social and civic training are entirely ignored, and the emphasis is not upon the present use of the knowledge and skills learnt at school but upon some use which may be made of them in the distant future. Moreover, too much stress is laid upon

knowledge rather than on thinking and doing. Merely acquiring knowledge does not mean learning ; the children remember facts, but they do not gain ideas, acquire attitudes, or form high ideals which should be the result of successful learning.

3. The curriculum scarcely makes any provision for the teaching of these subjects, or the inclusion of these activities which will develop initiative, self reliance and mental alertness in the pupils. Everything is done for the child, and he gets no chance to think, act or choose for himself.

4. Besides, rigidity and uniformity characterise the curricula of Indian schools, leaving little scope for variety and experimentation in their working. The special qualifications of teachers and the widely varying abilities of children are entirely ignored.

5. Examinations dominate the curriculum at every stage, hence children have to memorise facts ; they merely load their memory and are deprived of the joy of learning.

6. The curriculum, in many cases, takes very little account of local and community needs. Local efforts and needs are not considered, and scarcely any use is made of the Indian heritage of songs, poems, drama, folk-lore, and other things.

7. The school curriculum is heavy and over-loaded. A student in the high or higher secondary school has normally to study three languages, social studies, general science, craft and physical education besides the elective subjects. The multiplicity of subjects, which was criticised in the report of the Secondary Education Commission Report has not been reduced in spite of the revision of the curriculum.

8. Our curriculum makers have usually suffered from the besetting sin of the 'specialist' who tries to put as much of his favourite subject-matter as possible into the curriculum and the text books. They are more concerned with the logical and scientific demands of the subject than the needs, the psychology and the interests of the learners. Often Committees of Courses which meet for the re-organization of the syllabus, end up by introducing additional subject-matter, unrelated to students' life and interests, instead of carefully.

CONCLUSION

Our schools need continuous programme of curriculum improvement to meet the problems posed by our complex culture and the ever-changing world. According to the Secondary Education

Commission's Report, "A curriculum cannot be regarded as fixed for all times—it should be a matter of constant experimentation with a view to revising it from time to time, according to changing needs. The bounds of human knowledge are constantly expanding and, therefore, it is essential to go on examining and evaluating the contents of the curriculum, adding to it significant new items and weeding out from it whatever has ceased to have direct significance for the pupil and his immediate and future life."

Every nation is deeply concerned with relating its curricula to present day needs as the dogmas of the quite past are inadequate to the stormy present. The realisation of this led UNESCO to call on the International Advisory Committee on the School Curricula (1956-60) to investigate the problem. In India, Secondary Education Commission strongly recommended the establishment of Bureaus and Boards for curricula research.

The greatest need in the direction of curriculum improvement is that the research scholars in this field of curriculum development should also work with the teachers who has the responsibility of translating their findings into a school curriculum. Unless this is done, the process of teaching will continue to be in a state of aimlessness.

28

The Teaching-Learning Process

We have already discussed that educative process has been regarded by Adams as bi-polar in nature inasmuch as it involves the interplay of the educator and the educand. The personality of the educator acts on that of the educand in order to modify the latter's development. Therefore, from the point of view of the child the educative process is an act of learning and from that of the teacher, it is a process of teaching. Hence, educative process may be called teaching-learning process. Informally this process starts right from the very birth of the child, as he comes in contact with certain informal agencies of education like the home, the society, the church etc. Formally, it consists of educating or teaching on the one hand, and learning on the other,. In fact, teaching and learning are inseparable, they go side by side. The teacher is to teach and the child is to learn. But the child is not a passive recipient of what the teacher proposes to give him; rather he is an active share holder in the teaching-learning process.

THE CONCEPT OF TEACHING-LEARNING PROCESS

The concept of teaching-learning process has undergone a revolutionary change during recent years. The modern concept is best understood in the light of the traditional concept. A comparision of the two will help to make the concept of the "teaching-learning process" more vivid and clear.

The traditional concept

In the past the whole stress was on teaching and no consideration was given to learning. Teaching-learning process was confined to teaching process only. The teacher was considered to be the sovereign as far as the teaching-learning process was concerned. He was a dictator who could dictate practically everything in the sphere of education. The children were considered more or less alike and, therefore, the teacher expected similar reactions from everybody. He expected that everybody should learn at the same speed with the same method, and the pupils who could not compete well with their class-fellows were punished, without going into the causes of their backwardness.

Teaching was, therefore, mostly one-way process. It laid the whole stress on teaching even at the cost of learning.

The modern concept

The modern view is an outcome of the emancipation of the child. It is based upon researches in the field of educational psychology, which have brought into limelight the cardinal fact of individual differences. It is now an admitted fact that no two individuals are perfectly alike. Every human being is a novel experiment in the hands of nature.

The child's mind is no longer considered to be like a clean slate on which anything can be written. The child, on the other hand, is considered to be full of potentialities, craving for expression and development. Prominent educationists like Froebel and Montessori are of the view that everything is already contained in the child in the form of innumerable potentialities and capacities, and the function of the educator or the teacher is to help them grow and develop.

The foundational principle of the modern concept is the principle of child-centredness.

The concept of child-centredness implies that child occupies the central place in the educational process. The traditional concept of education emphasised the importance of teachers, whereas the modern concept of education gives the pride-place to the child. This shift of emphasis is mostly due to the researches in educational psychology. As the child is full of potentialities, the teacher is obliged to use such methods of teaching as will help in the development of those potentialities. Not only this, as every child differs in his innate capacities, the teacher must adopt his methods of teaching to suit the individual differences of children. This means that a teacher cannot employ a particular method of teaching without taking into consideration the needs and requirements of the children. Moreover, all the progressive educationists Rousseau, Froebel, Montessori, etc. have been advocating freedom for the child and psychologising the entire educational process, which means basing the teaching process on the capacities and requirements of the children.

Above all, it is a simple fact that it is the child who is to be educated, and the teacher and all the other agencies of education are really means to educate the child ; the central place, in the educational process, should naturally go to the child.

But, it must be mentioned here that it is in a special sense that we say that child is the centre of educational process. That in no way minimises the importance of the teacher. In a way, the teacher's responsibility has rather increased, his functions have become varied and complex. He must study the child psychologically, which means assessing and measuring the innate capacities of the children, a gigantic task in itself. Then, the teacher has to use his ingenuity to adopt his method of tèaching to suit the individual differences. The teacher, in fact, is indispensable; instead of transmitting knowledge only, his function now is to develop the entire personality of the child.

The teaching-learning process can be better understood, if we analyse first the process of teaching and learning separately, and then integrate them to have a complete picture of the same.

THE NATURE OF TEACHING

Teaching is more than standing before a class and applying a few specific techniques. Teaching is not merely presenting text-book information and then testing students ability to repeat it : there is no magic formula for transforming knowledge from the teacher's mind to the pupil's. Teaching is not a mechanical process. it is an intricate exacting, challenging job.

Almost all other professionals who deal with children, can afford some amount of specialization : much of the physician's attention is given to the diseased child : the psychiatrist is concerned largely with the disordered personality. The teacher must pay attention to the entire complex organism. He is concerned with the development of the child, intellectually, socially, spiritually, and to some degree physically.

Main Characteristics of Teaching Process

Below are given some of the main characteristics of teaching process:

1. **Teaching is a triangular process.** The modern concept of the nature of teaching is that it is a triangular or tripolar process. The three focal points of this process are the teacher, the child and the subject-matter. There is a close relationship among the three ; in fact, teaching is the uniting force.

Teaching is the process by which the teacher brings the child and subject-matter together. These three are closely associated. To bring about this effective relationship, the teacher must understand his pupils on one hand and have a thorough knowledge of his subject on the other.

2. **Teaching is giving information.** There are so many things which the child does not know or cannot know. It is, therefore, essential to provide some useful knowledge to the child, keeping in view his needs and capacities, and in a systematic and interesting way.

3. **Teaching is causing to learn.** We cannot force the child to learn. He will learn only, when he is willing to learn. So the teacher is to make the child a willing learner. He is to help the child to learn for himself.

4. **Teaching is stimulating learning.** The child will not automatically become a willing learner. The teacher must think of ways and means of stimulating and encouraging learning on the part of children. He should create conditions in which they feel the need to learn.

5. **Teaching is giving guidance.** The child must be guided to do the right things in the right manner and at the right time. He should be able to make correct responses to the various stimuli in his environment.

6. **Teaching is helping the child to make effective adjustments to his environments.** This will enable him to lead a successful social life.

7. **Teaching is helping the child to develop emotional stability.** Right actions spring from right feelings. The child should feel a sense of security which is possible in atmosphere of love and freedom. The teacher should have encouraging and sympathetic attitude towards his pupils.

Teaching, in short, is a process of imparting knowledge, motivating and guiding the pupils to learn through their own activities, training their emotions and developing their powers and capacities so that they are able to make effective adjustments to their environment and are better prepared for successful social participation.

THE NATURE OF LEARNING

From the layman's point of view, learning is the acquisition of knowledge. But this, conception is rather too narrow. Actually, it is the new 'experience' that causes learning. Every time an individual gains some new experience, he learns something. The process of learning is explained like this. An individual reacts to a particular situation. As a result of his reaction, he gains some new experience. This experience causes modification or change in his behaviour. He remember the situation and its impression is left behind in the mind in the form of engrams. Learning may be thought of as the progressive change in behaviour which is associated, on the one hand, with successive presentations of a situation and on the other, with repeated efforts of the individual to react to it effectively.

MAIN CHARACTERISTICS OF LEARNING

Yoakam and **Simpson** give the following characteristics of learning:

1. **Learning is growth.** Learning leaves behind impressions which are synthesised with the mental structure and these engrams enrich the personality and effect growth.

2. **Learning is adjustment.** Learning causes acquisition of new experiences which help the individual to make better adjustment with life or new situations.

3. **Learning is organised experience.** Learning is not only acquisition of new experience, but also synthesis of the previous experience with the new. The experiences are organised in a synthetic whole to form a complex mental structure.

4. **Learning is purposeful.** As learning is purposeful in the sense that given a particular situation, every individual will gain new experiences from the same situation in accordance with his own interests.

5. **Learning is intelligent and creative.** In animals, learning is instinctive ; but in human beings all new experiences leave meaningful impressions which guide future behaviour.

6. **Learning is active.** Learning presupposes activity rather than passivity, on the part of the learner. The learner applies his mind, reacts actively to a situation, remembers the new experiences and utilises the same in future situation. This is definitely an active behaviour.

7. **Learning is both individual and social.** Man is a social animal and therefore he learns mostly in the society. Most of the experiences he gains are through the mutual interaction of the individual and the society.

8. **Learning is the product of environment.** All learning takes place in particular physical and social environment. The environment provides the stage for all types of actions. It stimulates and causes reaction. It presents variety of situations leading to variety in learning.

9. **Learning effects the conduct of the learner.** Learning means acquisition of new experience in the form of engrams in the mental structure. When new engrams are synthesised in the mental structure and the process takes place continuously, the whole conduct of the learner is modified. Learning and experience change the

behaviour pattern of the individual. For example, after touching something hot and feeling the burn, the child's behaviour will be rather different from what it was before the experience.

Learning, in short, is the pivotal problem in education. The learner must be actively involved in the process of learning. Learning is growth, adjustment, and is purposeful. It cannot be enforced.

CONCLUSION

After discussing the nature of teaching and learning processes, it is not difficult to understand the nature of teaching-learning process. There can be no teaching without causing learning and there can be no learning with teaching. Therefore, teaching and learning processes taken separately have no meaning. These processes are inseparable. The educative process may be called teaching process, when it is taken from the point of view of teacher. The same process may be called learning process, when it is taken from the point of view of pupil.

In reality, educative process is teaching-learning process. The teacher teaches and the individual learns; both the process go side by side. Teaching is the complement of learning process.

Teaching-learning process is tri-polar. It establishes intimate relationship between the teacher and the pupil in the context of environment. In fact, it is sharing of educative experience by both the teacher and the taught.

29

Basic Principles and Maxims of Teaching

Planning before partaking is an essential element of good teaching. Since, the teacher is to deal-with children, therefore it is the teacher who has to come down to the level of the children to have intellectual coincidence with them to raise them up. He may at sometimes be childlike though not childish in the least. The teacher is to see that teaching is only effective when the pupils take interest in it and are active participants in its practice and process. As the teacher is to facilitate the learning process, it is to be. borne in mind that good teaching is a sort of providing guidance to the students through demonstration, suggestion and discussion. Teaching is to consist of a few modes of personal inter-communication between teacher and pupil. The broad principles of good teaching can be briefly summarised as follows:

Principle of Learning by Doing or Active Participation

W. M. Ryburn gives the first and the most important place to the principle of activity because it is in conformity with the child's nature. He says, "One of the most important facts about children, which we have to remember throughout our teaching work is that children are naturally active. What we call our instinctive tendencies, are ways in which this general urge to activity express itself. The chief characteristic of the life of children is activity, mental and physical. Thus, our first general principle of teaching method is the principle of activity."

Learning is a psychological process and consequently, it lays a stress on the importance of unrestrained activity on the part of learners. The traditional method of pouring packets of information into the unwilling minds of young children has been severely criticised. Putting them in their seats during the years of their growth and educating them in a static way arrests their progress and development. Mere passive listening hardly helps them to understand things. Hence, the necessity of activity on the part of children has been realised. The more the activity of the children, the more efficient is the teaching-learning process. When they are actively engaged in doing a thing, they attend closely to it, and close attention helps understanding to a very great extent. Physically active children are always mentally alert and hence, they learn better. Mere verbal explanation of a certain new game may not be effective, but if actually played out, it enables pupils to understand it thoroughly well. A certain episode in history will be appreciated well if it is acted out. Geography will be learnt better by drawing maps, geometry by cutting figures and arranging them, civics through self-government in the school, etc. Learning by doing enforces whole-hearted attention, creates interest, and facilitiates understanding.

A misconception about the principle of activity is that it is more suitable at lower stages. Experiments carried out in the field of learning prove that even at the higher stages the adoption of this principle leads to improved efficiency. Truly speaking learning becomes effective only when it is acquired through some activity and is applied to some activity after it has been acquired. Heuristic Method, Project Method, Assignment Method, Basic Method and Dalton Plan are some of the methods where the principle of learning by doing is adopted at later stages. Co-curricular activities, which are an essential part of child's education and provide the means of the cultivation of desirable patterns of behaviour and attitudes, make a very effective use of this principle.

Writing in support of this principle, Ryburn says, "The ultimate aim of our work is that the child may learn to live and to do. And he learns by doing. Knowledge only becomes his, as he uses it as real part of his life and experience. Hence, this principle of activity on the part of the pupil is of the first importance in all teaching. This does not mean that the pupil will be active in every lesson, though he should be so in most, but it means that every lesson of every kind must lead to activity. if it does not involve activity itself."

Hence, in teaching children, we should always keep before ourselves the above mentioned principle. "What has to be done", observes **J.A. Comenius**, "must be learned by practice. Artisans do not detail their apprentices with theories but set them to do practical work at an early stage ; thus they learn to forge by forgoing, to carve by carving, to paint by painting, and to dance by dancing. In schools, therefore, let the students learn to write by writing, to talk by talking, to sing by singing, and to reason by reasoning. In this way, schools will become workshops humming with work, and students whose efforts prove successful will experience the truth of the proverb. We give form to ourselves and to our materials at the same time."

Principle of Motivation and Creating learning Situations

Teaching is a tripolar process. It involves the interaction of the teacher, the taught, and the subject-matter. In order to achieve the aim of this process, co-operation of the teacher and the taught is of utmost importance. It has been rightly said that we can take the horse to water, but we cannot make it drink. In the same way, the teacher cannot make the child learn ; he can only help him in learning. The concept of teaching-learning process has undergone a revolutionary change. It is no more regarded as a process of teaching. In place of teaching, emphasis is now given to the learning by the child. For carrying out this process efficiently, it is very essential that the child should co-operate. His interest in the lesson shows whether he is offering his co-operation in the process or not. Thus, the function of the teacher is to create learning situations for his students and to make them understand in them. Once children become interested in any lesson or subject; the process of learning-teaching goes on unobstructed. The process of creating interest in any learning situation is called motivation. If children are properly motivated for a lesson or topic, half of the battle of teaching is won by the teacher. In the absence of motivation, all the efforts of the teacher to teach are wasted.

The question which now arises is: How should the children be motivated? For this, the teacher should rely on the innate tendencies of children. They are inquistive to know about their surroundings. They have a very strong instinct of curiosity, which can be fruitfully exploited by a resourceful teacher. He should present before his students the subject-matter in the form of a problem, which they may believe to be their own and feel interested in finding out its solution. Children's curiosity can be aroused in so many ways. Students can be taken to places of historical interests viz., the Taj, Fatehpur Sikri, Sikandra, etc. On seeing them, the students would naturally become curious to know about the historical events related to these places. Similarly visits to factories and art galleries can serve as motivation to science and art lesson respectively.

Tough subjects can be presented to children in the form of play and they can be motivated by introducing the spirit of healthy competition and rivalry among them. This device can go a long way in removing the boredom and drudgery of spelling and vocabulary lessons.

Direct and immediate application of the knowledge or skill acquired by children can serve as motivation. For example the counting concept of coins and simple arithmetic can be very conveniently applied in purchasing things. Children will be more attentive and interested in these lessons if they are aware of the use to which their knowledge is put.

There is a very close relationship between activity and motivation. In this respect, **Ryburn** observes, "We have seen the importance of the principle of activity in teaching. It is natural for children to be active in one way or another. Human beings all have a strong urge to activity, at any rate, when they are young. As long as we give our pupils the chance to be active, physically and mentally, if they are normal and in good health, they will be interested. The general urge to activity show itself along different lines or channels which we call instinctive tendencies. Successful motivation depends on the successful use of these natural powers and tendencies to action. When these are in action and a purpose is being followed out, much of what would otherwise be drudgery, is cheerfully undertaken."

For example, we encourage our pupils to ask question and to explore and to find out things for themselves. We find that when they are doing so, they are interested. The reason is that we have given opportunity for the instinctive tendency to be curious to function. We use competition either among groups or by matching individual pupils against their own records. Again, we find keen interest. We find pupils taking increased interest in their work when they are praised or when they find themselves excelling others. The reason is that the instinctive tendency to the self-assertive is being given opportunity to function. We find children interested in doing things in groups, in working together, because we are using the herd instinct. We encourage pupils to make things, to draw their own pictures, to write their own stories, to compose their own poems, to run their own magazines, and find many of them intensely interested in their work as a result. The instinctive tendency to create has been given an opportunity to be active.

Thus, we find that whenever we can use the various powers and urges to activity, we solve the problem of motivation. The most successful methods are those which give scope to the urge to activity."

Principle of Linking with Actual Life

According to John Dewey, education and life are two different names for same phenomenon. In simple societies, this relation is quite apparent and education is mostly of the informal type. But when societies advance and become complex, and educational institutions, like school are set up, we sometimes become obvious of the intimate relation or interdependence of life and education. John Dewey advocated that the existing gulf between the life in society and the life in school should be bridged over. By ignoring life, we disregard one of the most important sources of Motivation. **Gandhiji** firmly believed that the instruction imparted in a school should be correlated with the crafts of the area where it is situated. Later on, this principle was extended and today it is maintained that correlation with physical and social environments should form the guiding principle of education. In other words, learning should be linked with life.

"Now life," says **Ryburn**, "is a continuous experience. Everything we do is linked up with what has gone before and with what comes afterwards. The child's experience begins long before he comes to school, and goes on out of school in other spheres of life while he is at school. He is already being active mentally and physically. When we wish him to have a new experience therefore, it is impossible to think or to act as if we had before us an empty box into which we could pack information without any relation to any other information which the child may have. All information which is really assimilated has been taken up through activity. The activity is continually going on. If we wish our new information to become a real part of the child's life, we have to get it linked up with the child's activity. This means that we have to link it with his past experience."

Viewed from the above stand point, science should first deal with those principles which are applicable to every-day life. Arithmetic should deal with those calculations which are likely to be needed in life. The teaching of geography should begin with local geography. Civics lessons can be based on the rights and duties of the Village Panchayat or Municipal Board. Post-office, Bank, and Hospital can form the basis of lessons on different topics.

Principle of Interest

An important principle of teaching is to rouse the interest of the child. If we link our teaching to the active life of the child, we automatically succeed in rousing his interest. The child feels interested in those things which further his instinctive activities. For example, a child is interested in finding out things due to the working of his instinct of pugnacity. He is also interested in those things which will help him to conquer difficulties in the way of achieving a purpose. This is also due to that working of the instinct of pugnacity. Thus by linking our work to purposes and activities we rouse interest. This interest will be reinforced as we go along, if the activity principle is observed also.

Principle of a Definite Aim

It is very necessary that the teacher should have a definite aim of every lesson. Many teachers develop the habit of teaching a lesson without paying any attention either to general or particular aim that they have before them. The students remain in dark about it. In the words of **Ryburn**, "It will clarify our teaching, and make it much more definite, and therefore, much more interesting and effective, if we make clear to ourselves the aim of the lesson. It is necessary for us to be definite about the aim of the lesson, as our aim will depend our detailed procedure as we go along. If our aim depend our detailed procedure as we go along. If our aim is to teach appreciation of a poem we will conduct the lesson in a very different way from that in which we will conduct it if our aim is to touch skill in reading poetry. Then too, the children should know the aim of the lesson. It is a great help to know what we are trying to do, and adds greatly to our interest in what is going on. Children feel the same way about this as we do. They like to have something definite before them."

Principle of Selection

The principle of selection of the subject-matter is a most important one. If a teacher possesses the ability to select well, he can achieve a good deal of success in his work. Man since his coming on earth, has accumulated a vast knowledge about this intricate universe. It will be unwise on the part of a teacher to expect that all the heritage of man can be transferred to all children. He will have to make a wise selection as to what he should teach to children of a particular class keeping in view the individual capacities for learning. For example, a teacher of history cannot teach everything about Akbar in a lesson on Akbar. Nor can a teacher of English teach all the grammatical rules in one period. It will be necessary for both of them to select what they judge is needed for the students of their classes.

Principle of Planning

After selection comes the principle of planning. Efficient teaching can be possible through planning only. A teacher should be able to visualise the problems with which he may be confronted at the time of teaching and he should well prepare himself for them before hand, otherwise he will find himself in a very ugly situation. Keeping in view the problems and the material available as aid during the lesson, he should arrange his, subject-matter in a definite way in which he wants to present it to the class. But he should not forget the fact that the lesson-plan should be his servant, not his master. Any plan of any lesson can be modified by him during the course of the lesson according to the demand of the situations. Hence, his planning should be flexible and elastic.

Principle of Recognizing Individual Differences

It has been established by psychological investigations that all children are not alike in aptitude, intelligence, temperament and inclination. While teaching, a teacher should keep in view the individual differences in capacity for learning. He should never expect that all the students will achieve the same standard. He should not get irritated and annoyed with those children who learn things slowly. He should extend a sympathetic behaviour to abnormal children. He should not grudge to give guidance for further reading to those children who are above the average. In a word, he should recognize individual differences and treat the children accordingly.

Principle of Creation and Recreation

Teaching is based on spontaneous activities of children and therefore, leads to joy and fulfilment of purpose. It has no extraneous motive. This work is its own award. Really, educative activities are both creative as well as recreative. Besides helping in restoring spent energy, they manifest themselves in the creative activities of pupils."

Principle of Democrative Dealing

"In the age of democracy, the principle of democratic dealing should permeate every aspect of the educational system. Teaching is no exception to this principle. Teacher's attitude in the class should not be dictatorial which may result in crushing the personality of his pupils. The teacher should allow his pupils to express freely their doubts and ask questions. Good teaching liberates the mind and enables the pupils to stand on their own legs so that they may be able to continue their education even after leaving the school. Opportunities of free expression stimulate thinking among the pupils and through this they satisfy their instinct of assertion and gain feelings of security."

Principle of Flexibility and Elasticity

Teaching to be good must be planned before hand. But it should not become rigid and stereotyped. It should be flexible and elastic enough to make room for changes as the situation demands. The teacher should be resourceful, imaginative and original. The teaching should be adopted to the circumstances which necessitate departure from the original plan.

MAXIMS OF TEACHING

The principles discussed so far and some other methods of teaching are to facilitate the teacher's work. A successful teacher always make use of the methodical procedure based on the well known maxims of teaching. The maxims of teaching are not methods but they are of much help to the teacher No method can work successfully if these maxims are not kept in mind and made use of.

Some of these maxims have been discussed below :

Proceed From the Known to the Unknown

When we say that in teaching we should proceed from the known to the unknown, we simply mean that we must link up our teaching with the life and experience of our students. We should never think that we can teach a lesson in a vacuum as it were. We should start teaching with something that the children already know. When they come to the school, they are not clean slates. They have a definite store of previous knowledge, although it may be vague. It will assume a clear and definite form as the lesson proceeds. "New knowledge expands," write **Ryburn**, "and fills out the old. But from the point of view of interest and integration of knowledge, our starting point must be with something known. This maxim stands for what we seek to do in every lesson, namely, to form a link between old and new."

A teacher can exploit the previous knowledge of the children to build up a new lesson. It is always a good policy to link up a new lesson with the previous knowledge because it gives continuity to the curriculum. Previous knowledge can be utilized for the purpose of motivation. It has been found to be of great help in affecting economy in educational effort. Hence, a new lesson should always begin with the knowledge already known to the pupils. For example, a history lesson on Shah Jahn should start from his monument of love, The Taj; a geography lesson on cotton industry with the clothes the children wear ; an arithmetic lesson on profit and loss with buying and selling.

Proceed From the Easy to the More Difficult

Subject-matter to be taught to the pupils should be so graded that they may achieve success in the first lesson. This is possible only when easy lessons precede the difficult ones. If difficult lessons are taught in the beginning, children develop a complex for the subject.

They begin to feel convinced that the subject is difficult and beyond their capacity. Consequently they do not show any inclination for its study.

While assessing whether a subject or a particular topic is easy or difficult, we should take into account the psychological make-up of the child. Sometimes what seems easy to us from a logical point of view, may not be easy from the view point of a child's psychological make-up. We think that similar words like 'pen', 'hen', 'men' are easy to remember. But actually speaking, children learn those words more easily which are quite different from one another, viz ; 'table',,chair', stool'. "Thus in determining what is easy," write **Ryburn**, "We have to take into account the psychological make up of the child, and not close our eyes to everything save the logical. What seems easy, logically to us, may not be really easy for the child. We should always use the psychological in preference to the logical method of approach".

Proceed from the Simple to the Complex

A lesson should always begin with simple things within the reach of the pupils. Based on simple things, the teaching of complex things becomes easy. "For example, in the teaching of history, simple stories regarding the lives of heroes like Shivaji, which are easily understood by pupils should be told. From these stories evolve, in the next lesson, the complex things, like battles, treaties, policies etc. In the teaching of grammar, take simple examples of sentences from practical life and then arrive at rules, etc. afterwards. For instance, while teaching adjectives, take simple sentences with one objective in each and show its qualities of qualifying the noun. Show how very word—an adjective—tells something about the noun. Then take adjectives of different types and study them."

Here, a word of caution seems necessary. We should think a—'Simple' from the point of view of the child. It is possible that what appears easy to us, may not be so for him. We think that in the teaching of English it is easy to give drill in tenses, but in actual practice, we find the case to be just the reverse of it. Study of tenses becomes easy to children only when they have studied for two or three years. They find it easy to start learning by reading sentences and then coming to words and letters.

Proceed from the Concrete to the Abstract

Conception of children are always in terms of concrete objects. They find it very difficult to make concepts of objects from verbal descriptions. It is not possible for them to think in abstract terms. Hence, it is not only desirable but also necessary that their imagination is aided by concrete objects. A number of facts should be discussed and studied in a concrete way before the formulation of any abstraction or definition.

"Let us take an example from grammar. When 'objectives' are to be taught, the teacher should not give them straight way the definition of the 'adjective' which they find difficult to follow. The best way, therefore, is to give a number of sentences in which nouns shall be qualified by adjectives. After having underlined the nouns, say, in red and adjectives in green in those sentences, the teacher should draw the attention of pupils to the relation between nouns and adjectives. When a number of examples are studied in this way, children should be led to formulate a sort of definition of an adjective. The teacher, should, however, help them, to give a decent form. A definition thus framed by pupils themselves is fairly well understood.

Another example may be taken from Mathematics. In deriving a certain formula, the teacher should take a number of illustrations and ask pupils to study them carefully. The product of two expressions, for example, (a – b) and (a + b) should be actually worked out and the teacher should help pupils to understand the nature of the first and the second terms and the relation between them. The formula would then be thoroughly grasped and comprehended. From the concrete illustrations taken at the initial stage, pupils have come to form an abstract notion regarding the product.

Proceed From the Whole to the Part

There is common misconception that parts of a situation can be very easily understood by students. It has been proved by Gestalt Psychologists that our ideas about objects are not fragmentary. We always make an effort to understand the situation as a whole. In the earlier stages, many new details of a situation are noticed by us, but as we become more familiar with the situation, our concept assumes a more vivid form. It is because more details of the situation make its pattern complete. Hence, the study of language should not start with words and their grammatical forms, but with sentences expressing some ideas. Sentences should be analysed into words and the arrangement of words in sentences should be studied. Another point worth noting about this maxim is that 'whole' should be interpreted in the terms of the understanding of the child. It will be wrong to suppose that pupils can understand earth as a whole in the form of globe. Their concept of the whole is confined to physical environment, which should be further analysed into soil, climate, altitude, latitude etc. While teaching metals in science, they should first be taken as a group. Only after that each metal should be discussed separately.

Proceed from the Indefinite to the Definite

In the beginning, the knowledge of the child is vague and indefinite. The teacher has to make this indefinite knowledge the starting point of the child's education. By slow degrees, he gives it a definite form. For example, in the beginning a child's concept of a cow, a dog, or a horse is indefinite. This is so because he has no knowledge of the parts in detail. The teacher makes the mental picture of these animals formed by the child's indefinite notion of a plant, the teacher gives it a definite form by explaining the functions of its different parts.

Proceed from the Particular to the General

Particular instances are simple and concrete, 'while generalizations are complex and abstract. Hence, the teacher should invariably begin with known particular facts and arrive at generalizations with the help of the pupils. He should not make use of particular instances when he finds that the pupils can apply the general statement to clarify other particular facts. In algebra, a formula should be derived from particular cases, and then it should be applied to solve more questions. In order to ensure better understanding inductive and deductive methods should be applied in turns.

Proceed from Psychological to Logical

"Logical order is rational, but children are not able to understand logic or arguments. Subject-matter should be presented in such a way that pupils may understand it easily. This is possible only when subject-matter is arranged in accordance with the mental development of the pupil. Our approach should be based on child's tendencies, interests and reactions. For Example, while teaching arithmetic, simple arithmetical operations should come after students have mastered counting up to five or ten. In drawing, children should be asked to draw animals first and later emphasis may be laid on the details of form and proportion. Algebra should come after a good deal of arithmetic has been covered. In teaching languages sentences should come before words and words before letters. The whole lesson should proceed along psychological lines i.e. first creating interest in the lesson and then presenting the facts."

Follow Nature of the Child

"It is very essential to secure the co-operation of the child to achieve maximum efficiency in learning-teaching process. We can secure that co-operation if we understand the fundamental urges of the child. If activity in the class-room is such that the child's instincts are satisfied, the teacher need not worry about the outcome of his efforts.

Whenever, the child is not interested in any activity, the efforts to teach him go waste. There may be two possible reasons for this lack of interest. Either the child is not mature enough to grasp whatever is being taught or he is not in a respective mood at the given moment. So, the teacher should arrange the curriculum according to the mental development of the child and the subject-matter should be presented in such a form that the urges of the child may find expression in the learning process. Whatever the child does not want to learn, is not worth teaching.

Proceed Inductively

"It means proceeding from particular to general and from example to formula. There are two ways of teaching any principle of generalization. First, the students may be expected to accept the principle or theory without demanding any proof. Later the proof may be given by the teacher which also the students may memorize. Second procedure is to give examples in the beginning. The students may be asked to think about them so as to the first one because students are mentally active throughout the process and, therefore, learning is more efficient. Thus, in a language instead of giving the kinds of adjectives it is better to get examples from the students and then asking them to classify the objectives. The classification given by the students may be improved by the teacher. He should fill in the gaps. In a geometry lesson proof should come before the proposition or in a science lesson experiments should precede the statement of the law."

30

Teaching Devices

As discussed in the preceding pages, good teaching is causing, facilitating and promoting learning. In order to achieve this purpose, the teacher like other craftsmen has to use certain tricks, commonly styled as 'devices of teaching'. These devices are the external modes or forms which teaching may take from time to time. According to John Mander there are five main reason which might justify the use of these teaching expedients. They are :

(a) To teach something more thoroughly so that the children may retain the subject-matter taught.

(b) To teach something more quickly. This will result in 'covering more ground' in a given time, and thus give a better chance of "getting through the syllabus".

(c) As a means of creating or sustaining interests.

(d) As a means of integrating a number of separate pieces, of work already learned by other means.

(e) As a means of bringing with the experience and understand of children something which is new to them. This often includes the presentation to children, in simplified form of matters which are appreciated fully only by adults.

Thus, a proper use of these tricks of trade makes learning quicker and interesting. Some of the important devices have been discussed in this chapter.

NARRATION

Narration is one of the most important methods of communicating knowledge. In subjects like history, literature and descriptive geography, narration can be used as one of the most effective devices.

Narration is a kind of speech in which the teacher delivers a lecture on an incident or a context. Description produces verbal picture of a person, place or object whereas narration is an attempt to produce a verbal picture of an incident, event or happening. Narration is also an important device of teaching. The teacher has to produce the narration on an incident for many times. Narration is used mainly as a story. When the teacher produces an incident in the form of a story, he takes the help of the technique of a narration.

Narration is an art which every teacher should learn as he has often to narrate or tell a story, give accounts of events or to sketch and recount some happening. To be a good narrator, a teacher should know the skilful use of language and speech. He should be able to use appropriate language which should clearly depict situations and happenings. The chief form of narration is story telling. Children's love for stories is proverbial. It will give the teacher rich dividends, if he were a good story-teller.

The greater defect of this method is that the student remain sitting as a passive hearer and the teacher takes the place of an anecdote reader or a preacher. In this situation the atmosphere of the class becomes dry unless special care is taken. Therefore, it is the duty of the teacher to make his narration attractive. Some main techniques of making the narration attractive are given below :

1. Narration should be according to the mental age of students.
2. The language and the style of narration should be easy and interesting.
3. The narration should not be very long. Long narration should be divided into many meaningful units and produced at different times but not on different days.
4. Narration should suite the audience. If it is a story it should be adapted to the audience, although the historical facts should never be distorted.
5. While narrating a story, proper intension, gestures are very necessary. It should be told vividly in a natural tone and in a pleasant manner. It should never be read from a book, magazine or news paper.
6. Narration should be made interesting by the use of handy illustrations such as metaphors and similis relating the verbal experiences with which children are familiar. These illustrations add to the effectiveness of the narration.
7. Pictures maps, diagrams sketches and models may be used whenever needed in the course of narration.
8. The teacher should himself be interested in the narration. It is said that interest is infectious. When the teacher himself is

interested, the pupils will also be interested. For this it is essential that the teacher understands the purpose of narration. The purpose can be either enjoyment or development of imagination, taste etc. The teacher must see that the narration achieves the purpose.

EXPOSITION

Exposition is another important device of teaching. It means opening, exhibiting, displaying, disclosing ; it just means making clear the new information. The purpose of exposition is to enable the pupil to grasp the sense or meanings of the subject-matter presented to them in an intelligible manner.

Exposition is the presentation of the subject on the basis of previous knowledge of students and discussion on it. This technique includes the presentation of the subject and discussion on it. Clear and detailed presentation of new knowledge is the aim of exposition. Exposition does not include interpretation or criticism. In description, a verbal picture of an object, a person or place is presented but that is not the aim of exposition. In it the subject is to be presented without any clarification. Narration is related to incidents. Exposition is related to ideas whereas description to an object or a person. Therefore, the use of exposition is made mainly in language lessons.

The following points need special attention while using exposition:

1. The matter to be expounded must itself be a unity. A lesson to be good must be on some definite point. The teacher should arrange the matter so as to leave a single, clear impression on the minds of the class.

2. A lesson should be divided into natural units and every unit should be separately exposed.

3. Exposition should be evaluated through suitable comprehensive questions.

4. Proper use of black-board should be made at the time of exposition. Other audio-visual aids may also be used according to need. The help of oral and visual illustrations should be taken.

5. Opportunities of repetition are also necessary for the benefit of dull children.

6. Exposition should be relevant. Irrelevant ideas should not be exposed.

7. Students should also be given opportunities to put questions in course of exposition.

8. Exposition should not be too long. Keeping the interests of students exposition should be brief but complete in itself.

It is necessary that the teacher should have a clear enunciation and the trick of putting things plainly. If the teacher has these qualities, be will win the whole attention of children faster than his fellow teacher slower or less distinct in speech.

DESCRIPTION

Description is an important technique of teaching. Description is the introduction of an object, place or person in words or signs or both. In it verbal picture of an object is produced. Through description the teacher provides the knowledge of the qualities of an object. This knowledge is provided in such a way that appropriate picture of the size, structure and colour of the object may be painted in the mind of the students. Therefore, description is the portrayal in words of a person, object, thing or event. The purpose is to give a definite mental picture of the same to the pupils. Every teacher should be clever in the art of description. Some people naturally make animating descriptions, but the power of description can be developed by exercise. The art of description can not be hereditary. Man develops this art in the environment through suitable education.

While describing, the teacher should take the following precautions.

1. The teacher should have a clear and strong visual image of the object, place or person to be described.
2. Description should be brief. Long description may be boring.
3. The language of description should not be out of the comprehension of children.
4. Mere word-pictures are not enough. As far as possible description should be illustrated with the help of models, diagrams, pictures etc.
5. Handy illustrations such as metaphors and similis help to verify description.
6. There should be a sequence in description. Un-organized description becomes meaningless.
7. In description the teacher should proceed from easy to difficult, whole to parts and familiar to unfamiliar.
8. At the time of description the teachers should have perfect self-confidence. if there is lack of self-confidence in the teacher, he will not be able to produce a lively and impressive description.

EXPLANATION

Explanation is also a very important device of teaching. Explanation forms a kind of bridge between telling and revealing knowledge to the learners, and it involves a number of other techniques as well as narration and description. Throughout the process, the teacher must keep in close touch with the minds of his pupils, suggesting lines of thought, questioning them, answering their questions, setting them on practical work, examining the results obtained, discussing significant problems etc.

Explanation differs from exposition in that exposition as such aims merely at placing facts clearly before the learner, while explanation aims at showing facts in their proper relation to other facts in a system. In pure expôsition, significant relations may be taken for granted ; in explanation they must be made explicit.

The following points should borne in mind while using this device.

1. There should be a logical sequence in explanation. The teacher should be clear and straight-forward and not beating about the bush.

2. Language used to explain things must be very simple and suitable to the comprehension of the children. Voice and manner should also add to the effectiveness of explanation.

3. Various types of illustrations or audio-visual aids should be used to make explanation effective and interesting.

4. During explanation, the children should be encouraged to ask questions to clear their doubts if any.

5. Proper stress should be laid on the essential points. It is better if those are noted on the black-board. Difficult material should be elucidated through sketches. drawings and pictures,-etc., as the case may be.

6. The aim must be kept in view. Explanation should not be for its own sake. The students must feel its necessity.

7. Explanation should come at the proper time. No time should elaps between when it is due and when it is tendered. Psychological law of association must be strictly adhered to.

ILLUSTRATIONS

To illustrate a thing means to explain it, to make it intelligible and to throw light upon it. Illustrations means such things—models, pictures, charts etc., which help in the explanation of difficult ideas and processes by throwing light upon them. They make an appeal to the senses and the imagination of the learners, make the idea clear and enable the children to grasp correct knowledge. They overcome and clear up difficulties. They help in simplifying matter and giving vividness to explanations. They stimulate interest and excite curiosity in learning. They introduce variety in the lesson and secure better attention. Illustrations are good antidote to the disease, of verbalism. Easy and familiar things help in explaining difficult and complex ideas.

Illustrations lessen the intellectual tensions, lighten the knowledge-load and effect economy by proper associations.

Types of illustrations

Illustrations are of various types. They can be divided into two main categories.

(a) Non-verbal, natural, objective or concrete illustrations.

(b) Verbal illustration.

Under the category of non-verbal illustrations we have :

1. **Real Objects.** Display of original objects is an important illustration to explain anything. Geographical subjects can be easily taught by taking the students to rivers, mountains, forests etc. Good knowledge of historical buildings may be given by showing those to them.

2. **Pictures.** It is difficult to get original objects in every subject. Moreover the real object sometimes cannot be brought in the class whereas pictures can be brought to the class-room.

3. **Diagrams.** When pictures are not available the teacher can draw the diagrams of teaching material on the black-board.

4. **Maps.** Geography and History are taught with the help of maps. Besides general printed maps the teacher may prepare the outlines of maps on the role up black-board and show the production, population etc. by a piece of chalk.

5. **Posters and Charts.** Posters and charts may also be made to explain the subject-matter.

6. **Models.** The model of the real object is very attractive. By showing the statues of clay and other objects, we can give a knowledge of great personalities and historical places easily.

7. **Graph.** Graph is also used in teaching of Mathematics, Science, Economics, History and Geography. In it the subject is graphed with curve lines and different kinds of pillars.

8. **Sketches.** There would be no need of depending on other sources if the teacher can produce a sketch of original object on the black-board.

Under the category of verbal illustrations we have :

Analogies, comparisons, similis, word-pictures, etc.

The relative importance of these two types of illustrations depend upon :

(a) The nature of the subject.

(b) The level of the pupils' development.

Lower the classes, the more profitable will be concrete illustrations. As the child grows and his intellectual level rises, we can use pictures, diagrams, sketches and graphs etc. Verbal illustrations such as analogies, and similis etc. should be, used with children at the higher stage.

Proper use of Illustrations

It should be remembered that illustrations are a means and not an end in themselves. They are good servants but bad masters. Their proper use helps in learning proper teaching but their misuse or over use is likely to spoil the lesson in hand. Therefore, they need to be used with care and caution. The following points will be useful in the proper use of illustrations.

1. Illustrations should be simple and comprehensible. They should be easily understood without any need for comments and explanations.

2. Illustrations should be accurate and exact. Exaggeration, unnecessary elaborations, or wrongly depicting the material invites commentary and criticism and sometimes has the adverse effect.

3. Highly finished illustrations are not always the best ones. An over-elaborate picture, model, or diagram is more likely to obscure than illustrate. Simple illustrations prove to be more effective. Illustrations should be so simple that those can be worked out readily in the presence of the class. The teacher should acquire efficiency in sketching and free-hand drawing on the black-board.

4. Too many illustrations should not be used in a single lesson. Only few but best should be made use of to illustrate a lesson. Too many illustrations spoil their value many a time.

5. Illustrations should be properly handled and exhibited so that every child is able to see it clearly and easily. They should be kept before the students for a sufficiently long time so that they could observe them fully.

6. It is not a good practice to lay out a number of illustrations on the table before the class, just in the beginning of the lesson. Pupils become more interested in the illustrations than in the lesson itself. The relevant illustrations should be shown at the proper time during course of lesson.

Caution. The teacher must dispel the notion that a lesson cannot be successfully delivered unless it is properly illustrated. There is a fallacy. It is not the use but the right use of illustrative material that determines the success of a lesson.

Wisely selected, timely presented and intelligently used, they are unparalleled asset. Clumsily handled, they may spoil the whole show and prove to be the worst liability. Therefore, the teacher must be cautious and careful while using illustrative material.

QUESTIONING

Questioning is one of the most effective device of teaching. It plays a very important part in teaching, learning and testing. It has been well said that the question is the key to all educative activity A good teacher, therefore, must be a good questioner. According to Raymont a good questioner may not be a good teacher but there is no doubt that bad questioner cannot be a good teacher. Therefore, the acquisition of a good style of questioning may be laid down as one of the essential ambition of a young teacher. **Rudyard Kipling** has well said :

> "I keep six honest serving men ;
> They taught me all I know.
> Their names are What and Why and When
> And How and Where and Who."

Questioning, in fact, is one of the most effective tricks of trade for a teacher.

Purposes of Questioning

Questioning encourage and stimulate the mental activity of the pupils. Inattentive pupils are made attentive. The purposes of questioning may be many. These are generally asked :

1. To test the previous knowledge of the pupils on the matter to be presented, i.e., to find out what they already know.
2. To stimulate interest and effort, to keep them alert and attentive.
3. To assert whether they are understanding the knowledge presented or not and following the steps of the lesson or not.
4. To guide, direct and encourage thought and thus to stimulate mental activity.
5. To recapitulate the learnt matter and to fix it securely and clearly in the minds of the pupils

Thus, the purpose of questioning may be to direct the learning process. **Prof. Frank A. Butler** emphasises the following purposes of questioning :

1. To change view-points.
2. To bring out cause and effect relationships.
3. To develop new ideas.
4. To promote understanding.
5. To apply information.
6. To stimulate thinking.
7. To develop appreciation.

8. To discover the status of group or individual learning.
9. To create mind set.
10. To test objectives taught.

Thus questioning stimulate pupils to think and is a test of what they have assimilated questioning reveal to the teacher the range and breadth of pupils' knowledge and remove the inconsitencies in thinking.

Questions may reveal to the teacher the short-comings of the pupils in poor reading, careless interpretations, defective vocabulary, inability to locate information, and lack of organised and clear ideas etc. Hence, they are a good fact finders concerning the pupils' mental processes. Questions reveal interests and organise the material learnt.

Classification of Questions

Question may be classified in a number of ways according to the purpose they serve, the stages of the lessons where they are put and according to the particular form or structure. However a general and broad classification may be as follows :

1. Natural Questions
2. Formal Questions

Natural questions come automatically in teaching. The teacher has not to make efforts to put these questions. Natural questions are those where the questioner does not know the information about which he asks and make a query. He wants to elicite some information. Children spontaneous questions are of this type. On the other side questions are formal, when the questioner already knows about the information asked for. Class-room questions asked by teachers belong to this type category. Teachers often put formal questions to the students to stimulate some type of response, though the students questions may of a natural type.

Formal question may be further classified as under :

(a) Testing questions.

(b) Developing or teaching questions.

Testing questions may further be sub-divided as :

(i) Preliminary questions.

(ii) Recapitulatory questions.

Preliminary or Introductory Questions. These questions are generally asked at the beginning of a lesson. An attempt is made to test pupils' previous knowledge, as to what he knows regarding the particular topic. The teacher wants to prepare the pupils for the reception of new knowledge. He tries to know what the pupil knows and leads him to know what he does not know already. Introductory questions should be very few in number and must be asked briskly.

Preliminary questions must focus the attention of the pupils on the topic in hand.

Developing or Teaching Questions. These questions are asked by the teacher in the course of a lesson. These questions help the teacher introduce the new principles, elicit the information and impart new knowledge with the help of developing questions, the teacher develops a particular line of thought, leads the pupils to discover facts for themselves and enables the pupils to formulate new generalization. The knowledge is built up step by step.

Such type of questions must be asked with great care. Each question should be a step forward in the development of the lesson and the questions should be connected with each other in such a way that one question grows out of the other preceding that. Vague and irrelevant questions should be avoided. The teacher should know how much to elicit and how much to tell. The pupils should be encouraged to ask questions and develop their own knowledge. When the teacher is narrating a story, he should not ask questions in between. It is advisable that he asks questions either at the end or he may narrate again and then put the questions to the class to find if the narration has been rightly understood.

Recapitulatory Questions. These questions are asked at the end of each section in a lesson as well as at the end of a lesson. Such questions are asked to make the teacher sure that knowledge has been properly learnt and grasped. Revision and repetition also help in fixing the knowledge learnt in the minds of the students. These questions deepen the impression already made.

The recapitulatory questions should not merely test the factual knowledge, these may test the application of the principles or facts learnt. Comparison and appreciation type of questions can prove more useful. Recapitulatory questions should be differently worded from the questions at the sectional revision stage.

Technique of Good Questioning

All types of questions are not of the same value. Art of questioning is to be learnt with great care. This device defeats its purpose if the questions are wrongly worded, defectively put and carelessly attended to. The characteristics of a good question are its clarity, simplicity, challenging nature, specificity and definiteness.

A good teacher should bear in mind the following points :

1. The language of the questions should be simple. The vocabulary should be suited to the ability of the pupils and the subject. The questions should not be ambiguous, vague and lengthy. These should

be easily understood, relevant to the topic or theme and should be definite. What do you see outside the class-room? Or do you agree with the statement that Rajputs could not establish a strong Central Government, because they were loyal only to their leader and not the country? Such questions are not worthy of a good teacher to ask.

2. Questions should be neither too easy nor too difficult. These should be framed in such manner that no guess work is possible. Questions of the type which can be answered in Yes or No should not be put. Questions must demand reasonable thinking from the students. These should be thought-provoking and not merely leading to mechanical elimination. Was the first battle of Panipat fought in 1926? or Do you know that India got freedom in 1947 ? or Was Chanakya a king, minister or an ordinary man ? Such questions encourage no mental activity and are not of a desirable type.

3. Questions should not be suggestive, leading or of elliptical nature. In such questions the child gets a key to the answer from the question itself. Answers to them should not be so obvious as require no serious thinking. The teacher who after having made a terrific explosion of Oxygen and Hydrogen asked the pupils if they had heard anything, is an extreme example. Suggestive, leading, elliptical questions encourage inattention of the part of the students. Do you know that Akbar was a great king ? or Mahatma Gandhi was better known for his character than his political genius, was he not ? are leading questions. Such questions : Who was Lord Clive ? What did he do? When did he do it ? Why ? What were the results ? should be avoided ? Double questions as who was Kabir and why was he famous ? is a poor specimen of a good question. Elliptical questions consists of making an incomplete statement and asking the pupils to complete it e.g. when Babur reached Panipat, he was opposed by, such type of questions encourage the child to depend on rote memory.

4. Questions should be well distributed over the whole class. These should not be confined to a few bright students or the front benchers. This a bad practice to ask from the bright pupils at the expense of others, or to call on those only who raise their hands of calling exclusively on the dull ones. Questions should never be asked in a certain rotation. Pupils should never know before hand, who is to answer the question. The teacher should put the questions to the class as a whole and then ask some one to answer it. It is not a good practice to make a particular pupil stand up and then to put him a question or when the students are required to answer the questions turn by turn proceeding alphabetically or row by row.

5. There should be no repetition of the questions and these should be asked in a business-like way. Echo question should be discouraged. Maharaja Ranjit Singh died in 1839. When did Maharaja Ranjit Singh die? is a case in point.

6. Questions should be properly graded. They should be varied in form and difficulty. Proper sequence must be maintained. Sufficient number of questions should be asked in order to stimulate children to activity. But it should not be a barrage of questions requiring only one-word answers.

7. Leaving aside the case of quick drill work, when questions are quickly followed by answers. The students must be given some, time to think out the answers. To run through a series of questions, without paying proper attention to the answers, does no good.

8. Inattentive children and back-benchers must be properly attended to. The teacher should not accept the first correct answer and pass on. At least two pupils must give the correct answer. It is mere wastage of time to put questions to those who have not shown their hands to answer them. But it is a good practice to put the same question to such categories of dull students after the question has been correctly answered by a bright student. These show-movers are not to be ignored and neglected.

9. Whenever preparation is required, do it before you put questions to the class. It is not a good practice to change the structure of the question or rephrase it after you have once put it to the class. It may discourage response and hinder the mental activity of the students. The question should be put in the very first instance in the best form. The form and content of the question should be previewed. Faulty questioning on the part of the teacher is due to impatience, unfamiliarity with the subject or to confused thinking.

10. Questions which are above the books of the students need not be asked. If the class as a whole cannot answer a particular question, then either the language of the question is defective or the question is irrelevant and complicated. Better avoid such questions. The teacher is not to show off his knowledge or the fluency of asking questions. Two questions in one should never be asked e.g. How did Ashoka embrace Buddhism and what steps did he take to spread it? The questions should be audible to the class and well voiced.

11. Good questions should always conform to the immediate objectives. Questions which have no relation to the objectives lead the children astray resulting in a good deal of loss of time and effort.

Questions should not be of a purely routine character. These must fix the limits of the task expected from the learner.

12. Questions should always be asked in a pleasant manner. The teacher should not create nervous tension in the pupils and hinder their thinking. A volley of questions disconcert the pupils.

Questioning is a great art which every teacher should learn and cultivate not only in himself but also in the pupils who should be encouraged to ask questions and they may take an active part in the revision questions at least.

Outcomes of Questioning

The teacher must bear in mind that for effectiveness of his questioning technique the following outcomes must have been achieved.

1. Difficulties in knowledge and thinking should have been removed.
2. A distinct reorganisation of ideas of the pupils should have occured.
3. Need for more knowledge or more thinking should have been felt.
4. New curiosities must have been awakened and new interests established or discovered.
5. Essential points and significant conclusions must have been brought home to the pupils.
6. Encouragement to the pupils to ask questions should have been provided.
7. The pupils' participation in the discussion must have been ascertained.
8. Pupils' reactions to the subject-matter must have been gained and their attitude improved.
9. The study habits and abilities of the pupils must have become known.
10. Definite impressions about the pupils' progress must have been formed.

ANSWERING

Questions are asked to know what the pupils know. How much the pupils know will be reflected in their answers. Lot of tact, insight and effort is required for dealing with the pupils answers. Complete development of answers requires effort, and the effort put forth will depend upon the standards upheld by the teacher. Pupils do just what is expected of them.

The pupils' answers can be classified into five types :

1. All correct answers.
2. All wrong answers.
3. Partially correct and partially wrong.
4. Correct but incomplete.
5. Wrong, but intelligent.
6. Mischievous.

Let us see how to handle the different types of answers.

All correct answers should be accepted. They should be welcomed and appreciated. Such answers are worth repeating. Stereotyped pharases like "Very good", "Quite right" in reply to every answer is to be avoided. All wrong answers should be rejected but without ridicule. A wrong answer should merely draw the comment "Wrong" and the teacher should proceed asking that very question. Wrong answers are better corrected by getting the right answers from other pupils. And the pupil who gave an all wrong answer should be asked to repeat the correct answer, when it has been given by some other pupil. An incorrect answer should never be repeated.

In the partially correct and partially wrong answer. The teacher should accept the correct part, reject the wrong part, ask a supplementary question to get the wrong righted.

In a correct but incomplete answer accept the correct part and ask a contributory question to get the incomplete part completed.

The inadequacy of the answer should be exposed but with kindliness not with irony or ill humour.

Wrong but intelligent answer can be due to various factors, e.g., the language of the question was difficult, or the subject-matter was tough. Very sympathetic handling is required because the pupil is sincere. The only problem is he has not been able to follow the question. An honest answer should never be snubbed for such action. It may discourage the very attitude of mind a teacher wishes to promote.

A pupil giving mischievous answers should be cautioned.

Guide Lines for Dealing with Answers

The following points must be thoughtfully considered when the teacher is to deal with answers :

1. Collective answering should be discouraged. Simultaneous answering except in quick revision or drill work may not enable the teacher to find out those students who have not picked up the material.

2. Incomplete answers are not to be passed over. Answers which are partly correct are very common. The teacher is often impatient to make the necessary correction or completion himself. It is wise to give

opportunity to the pupil to correct or complete himself, or take the help of other pupils to do the needful.

3. Answers should always be accepted in complete sentences. Complete expression is what we aim at from the children. Never accept single word incomplete answers. Pupils should be trained to give well-rounded answers to question.

4. Wrong answers should be tactfully, dealt with. As far as possible the class-room atmosphere must follow a natural every day conversation. The teacher should avoid making sarcastic remarks or ridiculing the pupils. The teacher may try to find the cause of the mistake. The question may not have been well understood. Repeat or explain the question, or break it into more simple questions. The mistake must be explained to the class, and the pupil should be led to correct himself or with the help of his class-fellows.

5. The teacher should not point to the answers written either on the black-board or in the exercise books. Pupils should be discouraged to answer merely from reading the book.

6. Answers are to be concise, relevant exact and accurate in wording and content. There should be no beating about the bush when the pupil stands up to answer. The answers must be audible to the class.

7. The teacher should lose no opportunity to commend and appreciate good answers. It costs nothing but gains much. Pupils feel recognition and are encouraged to be up and doing. Good answers may be repeated for emphasis, but echo repetition is to be avoided.

8. Pupils should be given sufficient time to think of the answer, but not so much that the more brilliant pupils may become impatient.

9. The teacher should make all efforts to get answers from as many pupils as possible, but in his such efforts he should not consistently ignore the front rows at the cost of back rows. Pupils who know the answer and are eager to give it, should not remain unasked.

10. The pupils should be trained to answer not only the questions asked by the teacher but also to answer questions asked by their class-mates. It is always better to shift the responsibility to the pupils as far as possible. The teacher should not be the quite and final authority either to correct the answers of the pupils or to give answers to their natural questions.

11. If there is anything in the answer which can be conveniently salvaged, the teacher may do it. But the teacher retort. "It is dead wrong" be benumbs the pupils. Better use such expressions as, "This idea can be used in another topic. It may be partly the cause, but we

may use better reasons. Your ideas is correct but not applicable here etc.". The teacher should clearly bear in mind that encouragement motivates and discouragement represses.

The teacher should exact himself. Carelessness and thoughtlessness is to be checked on the point of the pupils. Half hearted acceptance of answers on the point of a lethargic teachers may do incalculable harm. The teacher is to be sympathetic and kind, but not to the verge of losing control over the class. Reproof administered sometimes in a kindly way bring good dividends.

ASSIGNMENTS

Assignments helps to give direction for learning. It aims at providing some work to do. An assignment may be revision of the lesson learnt or a sort of preparation for the lessons to be learnt. It may be the memorising of a small paragraph, solution of a few mathematical sums, making a chart a model or writing a detailed account of some historical events, etc.

Assignment is supplement to class-room teaching. It provides the teacher with 'an opportunity to direct learning activity and giving habits of extra study. But the teacher must bear in mind that the assignments are very carefully prepared. Elaborate hints, references to study and books to be consulted, must be suggested. Mere dictation of questions is not assignment. The teacher has to do a lot in order to prepare these assignments. Assignments should be well-graded and should not be lengthy ones. These may be daily or weekly assignments. Weekly assignments are far better than either daily or monthly ones. The teacher should not feel contented merely by giving the assignments, he should check the work done. Teaching, according to Dalton Plan, is wholly based on assignment system.

Importance of Assignment

The assignment as a technique of successful teaching has received some attention from the writers, though its importance, until very recent times, has not been fully realised. The significance of assignment is based on the fact that the desire to learn is more important than are methods of teaching. It is pupil's attitude towards learning that matters and not the well-organised courses of instruction. These reasons specify the educational importance of assignment. Teachers all over have started realising that pupils' interest in learning has to be directed and this can best be done with the help of assignment. The assignment gives them that guidance (in their activities) in an expert way, prevents failure, provides for the arousal of interest, and makes success reasonably sure. Independent study is not possible without good assignments. That is why the teachers are coming to realize that time and thought spent on planning and making the assignment are likely to affect profoundly the study habits of children and to result in economy in both learning and teaching. If good assignments are made, children can and will study independently with success; but if poor assignments are made children will fail to profit by the time spent in independent or supervised study.

Purpose of Assignment

The assignment being centrally important in the technique of teaching, may be said to fulfil the following chief purposes :

1. It gives the teacher opportunity to give direction to the learner's activity.

2. It provides the stimulus to which the subsequent activity is the response.

3. It is the determining factor in directing the development of effective habits of study.

In short, the assignment motivates study, clears up misunderstanding and develops insight.

Characteristics of a Good Assignment

The chief characteristics of a good assignment are :

1. A good assignment relates new unit to previous knowledge to give the impression of continuity of learning.

2. It is definite in outlining the work to be done.

3. It is clear and well-defined to the extent of reducing to minimum the loss of pupils' energies in meaningless or fruitless activity.

4. A good assignment clearly indicates the sources of reference to be used during the act of learning.

5. It is interesting and stimulates interest.

6. It guides learning by anticipating difficulties that are likely to arise during the execution of the work in hand. It also suggests ways and means to overcome them.

7. It provides for differences in the ability and interests of the learners.

8. In a good assignment the essential points are emphasised and attention is drawn to them.

9. A good assignment is not just like one-way traffic. It is co-operative and develops with the joint efforts of both the pupils and the teacher. That way it emphasises the '*we*' spirit.

10. It stimulates thought and develops insight and understanding for carrying out work.

11. The assignment should be concise but sufficiently detailed to enable each pupil to understand the task assigned.

12. Motivation is a definite function of a good assignment. For that reason, it should arouse an interest in the advance work.

13. By making use of the element of suspense, assignment can be made more attractive and more useful than otherwise.

14. "The assignment should be motivated chiefly by the hope of worthwhile achievements, rather than scholastic reward or the fear of punishment."

15. The assignment should be adjusted to the time and opportunity of the class.

Making the Assignments

It is generally believed, and for good reasons, that assignment should be prepared in written form. But it is more useful if the task to be done is discussed by the teacher in the class orally in order to pin-point the essential features of the work. It is also desirable that the teacher should indicate the relevant portions to be studied to guard the pupils against wasting their time in irrelevant and unnecessary engagements.

"In making the assignment, the teacher must avoid acting like a commander-in-charge of troops. He must rather regard the assignment period as a time for co-operative thinking and for suggestion." This means there should be "*we*" feeling rather than "I" feeling. The teacher should give the impression that he is helping the pupils, whereas, the pupils should be made to indulge in maximum individual independent work.

Time-factor. When to make the assignment is a widely debated issue. In fact, it is not a matter of hard and fast rule. The only thing for consideration is that the assignment should not be made in a hurried moment. From practical point of view, assignment may be made just in the beginning of the lesson or it may be made at the close of the period. In the former case, the chief advantage is that the assignment will attract better attention and will be made less hurriedly. In the latter case, the chief advantage is that the assignment will enable the teacher to adopt the assignment to the progress that was made during the period. In making the assignment at the outset of the period of work, the teacher cannot be sure that it will be completed as planned.

Steps in Assignment Making. To ensure success in assignment making, it suggested to keep in mind the following steps of procedure in which the assignment should generally proceed :

1. Reference to a previous experience.
2. Discussion.
3. Proposal of a new activity.
4. Discussion leading to acceptance of the activity.
5. Explanations and clearing up of difficulties.
6. Outlining the materials to be used.
7. Distributing the tasks to be done.
8. Overseeing the beginning of the work, if possible.

The assignment should be recorded either on the black-board or in children's exercise books or in the form of cyclostyled or typed sheets. This way it is likely, to be forgotten and the child may use the material as a guide in study.

The length of the assignment varies with the age and maturity of the children. The following division, though tentative, may be quite convenient :

Primary Grades : Fifteen to twenty minutes duration.

Middle Grades : Thirty minutes to an hour and a half duration.

High or Higher Secondary Grades : About two hours duration.

Assignment Materials. Assignment materials, the chief among which are the text-books, special reference books, maps, charts, pictures, guide sheets, work books, etc. involve special skill in their handling. Teacher's familiarity with such materials and his skill in their use will create interest in the task in hand and will help both the teacher and the pupils in successful completion of the assignment. The choice of printed as well as audio-visual materials should be made strictly according to the needs of the children. This will promote independent study and it "goes a long way towards creating interest, defining work to be done, preventing failure and ensuring progress.

Evaluation of the Assignment

It is good policy for the teacher to evaluate the success of the assignment. Though it is a difficult task to do so in the absence of some experimental procedure, yet a resourceful teacher can make the evaluation by using a good check-list, which he may prepare of his own, based on the criteria laid down above or he may use the check-lists prepared by some writer of repute. Such check-lists have been given by Carr and Wagge in The lesson Assignment, by Yoakam in 'The Improvement of the Assignment' and by 'Bossing in Teaching in

Secondary Schools'. In evaluating the assignment, maximum accuracy with the minimum of detail should be the ideal.

HOME-WORK

Home-work is a kind of independent work which pupils' are expected to do at home, away from the atmosphere of the class and in the midst of home surroundings, to supplement instruction received at school. The child is expected to carry out this work with the assistance of the class-room instruction or sometimes with the help of his parents, elders or private tutors. As a practical teaching device, home-work is a step towards self-education, to steal a phrase from **Adams**. "It is a means of enabling the child to use his own resources and work unsupervised."

Controversy over allotment of home-work

Contrasting views regarding allotment of home-work have come down from teachers, educators and parents. Those who opine unfavourably say that no home-work should be given to the pupils. **Bray** denounces it by saying : "Under normal conditions a reasonable day's work for a child has been done at the close of the afternoon and home-work as it is generally organised does more harm than good." It often seems to parents that home-work is bound to become a cause of friction between home and school in the sense that "the school makes unreasonable demands on the child's powers and time, and is guilty of carelessness in organising such work". They feel that home-work snatches away the easy moments of the child and begets worry, fatigue and distaste and hence, is bound to become a source of weakness.

There are others who believe that home-work is necessary to supplement the five or six hours work at school. They agree that "home-work affords a valuable opportunity for the pupil to develop the power of independent and unaided work," and thus gain confidence that he knows what he is taught. Even certain parents especially mothers, also feel that some amount of home-work is fundamentally necessary to enable the child to engage himself in useful activity at home. Otherwise, he is necessarily to become a 'devil's workshop' in the spare moments when he is even free from home responsibilities. Home-work spread over the prescribed syllabus is an efficient means of fixing up the subject-matter taught in the class. In fact, home-work "properly understood, skillfully planned, intelligently assigned, and sympathetically checked, is indispensable."

Dispassionate View. A dispassionate examination of the two-fold controversy would lead us to understand that it is not the home-work that is objectionable, but its nature and amount that stands critical examination. Home-work has to be given if success in teaching and learning is our aim. The true objection may be directed against unproportionate, unintelligent and unsympathetic assigning and checking of the same. It is not in one subject that the child is expected to do the home-work, he has to satisfy the demands of all the courses of study.' Over-burdening the child is simply sinful. The whole charm of concentrated study loses its significance and the child being away from the playground, is likely to develop school mania. Thus, home-work should be carefully manipulated.

Home-work, no doubt, is important. For many reasons it is desirable to assign. It leads to "the formation of independent effort and self-study, the acceleration of the advance of pupils in their work, and the opportunity of securing more effective co-operation on the part of the parents in the education of their children."

Suggested Conditions for Assigning Home work

1. Home-work should be devoted to topic covered in the class or to practice in activities already understood.

2. Home-work should form an integral part of the course of study which is being followed at school. Apart from academic work, it may involve informal activities like hobbies connected with various school subjects.

3. Home-work should bring into play, to some extent, individual likes and dislikes. It should satisfy the needs of the particular age-group of children for whom it is meant. For this reason, home-work should also be graded, its nature and amount be determined according to the individual's interests, capabilities and conveniences.

4. Home-work should be so assigned as not to give the impression of punishment. The pupils should feel that it is meant for their self-improvement.

5. There is no harm if the parents help their wards in successfully completing the home-work. But as far as the work lies within the ability of the pupil, it ought to be done without the help of parents or friends

6. Home-work should be definite, and limited in scope and should be adjusted to the time at the disposal of the pupils. Preferably it should not exceed half-an-hour for lower class children, one hour for pupils of about thirteen years age, and two hours for boys and girls of above thirteen years.

7. Home-work should not be hastily assigned and carelessly planned. Asking the pupils to learn the meanings of a few words or to

"read the next paragraph" or to "solve a few arithmetic sums" or to "read from their books whatever you have learnt today in the class," etc. does not speak of certain forethought given to the problem of home-work.

8. Mere assigning of the Home-work is not all that is desirable. It should be sympathetically checked and encouragingly,corrected. In the absence of regular checking, the pupils are likely to cheat their parents as well as teachers, thus defeating the very purpose and utility of the task.

9. **Prof. Cole** is of the opinion that "since the parent knows better than the teacher whether the work is too much or too little for the pupil, the parent ought to be consulted from time to time about home-lessons, and a half-done lesson ought to be accepted when the exercise book bears a parent's initials."

10. The teacher should not be very rigid in getting the children do the whole of the allotted work. The slow learner should be given the advantage of some reduction in the amount of work ; for more intelligent and very quick workers, he should invite the performance of additional voluntary tasks. The pupils who do extra work should be commended in the class to encourage the rest of the pupils 'to improve their habits of independent work.

11. Peculiar home conditions which are likely to interrupt the work of some students should be discussed with them. They should be advised to arrange their work at a time least likely to be interrupted by domestic duties, or by visitors, or by the affairs of the other members of the family.

12. Home-work should also encourage library readings. Library facilities should be made available to the students for the maximum possible time.

Suggested Type of Home-Work

The current trends in educational practice provide numerous opportunities through home-work which can be best utilised for the development of not only academic side of the pupils but also various hobbies according to the tastes and interests of the pupils. So, instead of becoming a means of spending some dull and dreary hours on the printed pages of the texts, home-work can be rendered an affective tool for developing many-sided personality of the pupil. A few types of home-work are suggested below.

1. Academic type, such as assigning some exercises in school subjects like mathematics, languages, social studies, science, etc. These

exercises are based on the principles, rules, and generalisations learnt in the class. These exercises are mostly meant for giving practice in the work or subject-matter already done in the class.

2. Cultural and practical type, involving the use of hobbies and other activities in which the pupils are likely to take interest. This type of home-work is meant to break the monotony and boredom of the academic engagements of the pupils. Making models, charts, maps and a few drawings, collecting pictures and preparing scrapbooks, planning out some play and asking the interested students to learn their assigned role, memorising certain lines in respect of debates and declamations, are some such exercises.

3. Advance preparation for the new lesson, can be very helpful both to the teacher and to the pupils. The teacher should guide the pupils through well-prepared assignments for the advance work. It should not be taxing. In language the pupils may be required to find out difficult words, phrases and sentence-patterns; they may just go through the new lesson in History or Geography or even Science, and so on.

CONCLUSION

In conclusion, it may be remarked that home-work remains an indispensable device provided its nature is properly understood by the teacher and it is intelligently planned and sympathetically checked.

31

Procedures of Teaching

The main task of teaching is to enable the pupil to learn in such a way that all the potentialities of his mind are engaged actively in the task. It is well known that the good teaching consists of a training the pupil to think independently as far as possible. To do this all successfully, the teacher has to make use of different devices of teaching. Besides that he has to seek help of various external aids to make his performance worth the name. Not only this but the teacher has always to keep the various accepted and established principles of teaching in mind. As we know every lesson has one or more aims and whatever the aim is the teacher has to consider some factors which determine the success of a lesson. These considerations can be laid down for the convienience of understanding them fully.

(a) The purpose behind the lesson.

(b) The subject-matter, its preparation by the teacher.

(c) The suitable presentation of the subject-matter to the class.

(d) The assessment of what has been taught and actually learnt.

(e) The art of making the students to put self effort in learning more with the help of what has been taught to them.

The teacher has to carefully plan and prepare his lesson because it is the lesson through which he has to teach children. He has to prepare his lesson by way of putting down the entire material in the form of a lesson-note for the days work in a particular subject. Such a note fully indicates the various steps which the teacher is going to follow in the teaching. Lesson notes are nothing but a careful plan of what the teacher is going to do during the period. Or it can be said that a teacher outlines all that he wants to achieve. About the body of the plan it is very necessary to mention in it the class which is going to be taught, approximate or average age, the level of their previous knowledge on which the teacher has to build the new knowledge, the duration and length of the lesson. In it, the teacher has also to mention the aids and apparatus which he is going to use in the lesson. A mention about the subject and topic has to be made in the plan. The procedure to be followed for teaching the lesson has also to be mentioned in the lesson note and the devices which are planned for the work. It has been educationally and psychologically found that all lessons can be divided into three main categories. It is needless to add here that each lesson involves one of the three aspects of consciousness cognition, conation and affection.

Whatever the lesson may be, it is well nigh possible to separate these aspects and all the three aspects can be present in any single lesson. This division depends on the nature of the subject-matter and the type of activity that is essential for the acquisition of knowledge. To make it clear we must understand that for learning history, geography, science or nature study the main aim is the aquisition of knowledge, in learning how to write, to draw or to knit and stitch we aim at the acquisition of some skill and while listening to music, songs, poetry, enjoying movies and dramas the chief aim is appreciation of the quality of art and beauty. For example, if a student is learning music he can not avoid learning a little bit about the theory of music and the students' feeling towards music will be a natural outcome.

In one lesson the students can be made to change from one activity to another and obviously the method of teaching will have to be changed accordingly. It all depends on the alertness of the teacher.

In the past, the information or the knowledge aspect was emphasized and little attention was paid to development of skills or the faculty of appreciation. That approach led to a lopisded development of the pupils. The other aspects of personality development were ignored. But advancement in the field of Educational Psychology has brought to light the defects and shortcomings of that one-sided approach. Recent approach to education is to make it more and more comprehensive, taking within its perview not only the knowledge aspect but also the other aspects of personality development. The aim, now-a-days, is to develop the personality of the child in an integrated and harmonious manner. All the three aspects—cognitive, conative and affective—of the personality are to be developed harmoniously. Only then can we have a well-balanced and harmonious development of personality.

LESSON CLASSIFICATION

These three types of lessons can be termed as (a) the knowledge lesson, (b) the skill lesson, and (c) the appreciation lesson.

The learning of Languages, History, Civics, Geography etc. constitutes the knowledge lesson. The learning of specific skills such as spinning, wood work, painting, tailoring etc. constitutes the skill lesson. And learning to appreciate beauty in art, and poetry, and to enjoy music constitutes the appreciation lesson.

Each type of the above mentioned lessons emphasizes at least one aspect of the personality i e., cognitive, conative or affective, although the other two are not wholly eliminated or neglected. Personality is one whole. Mind is a unity. These cannot be divided into water-tight compartments. One aspect cannot be completely isolated from the other two. All the three aspects are present in every activity. Take, for instance, the learning of History. When the bare facts of History are learnt, it is acquisition of knowledge; when the children draw maps, locate places, sort out references, they are acquiring skill; and when they are being charged emotionally at the time of studying the history of their country, emotional development is involved. Similarly with poetry, art, or craft. If the three aspects of mental life are not closely connected in any one activity or experience, the result will be defective. Knowledge divorced from doing and interest will be barren and waste. It will be forgotten soon. Skills acquired apart from understanding will only be mechanical and are likely to fail. Feeling separated from action and thinking will degenerate into sentimentalism. Hence, three types of lessons cannot be completely separated from one another.

THE KNOWLEDGE LESSON

Here we are concerned with the imparting of knowledge to the students, but it cannot be done in a haphazard way. It has to be done in a definite manner, following a particular procedure. It is to be imparted in a way so as to facilitate effective learning on the part the pupils. Educational psychologists and pedagogists have attempted to formulate some general procedure for the conduct of the lesson. Herbart and his followers evolved the famous Herbartian Steps based on the analysis of the learning process.

Herbartian Steps

Herbart himself propounded that teaching method should proceed in four steps but these were latter elaborated by later Harbartians into five as given below :

1. Preparation (or Introduction or Motivation).
2. Presentation.
3. Comparison or Association.
4. Generalization.
5. Application.

We shall now discuss these five steps separately.

1. **Preparation.** Harbart thought that it was necessary for a pupil to be prepared to receive new knowledge. Just as the field is prepared to sow the seeds, the child's mind is also to be prepared to receive the new knowledge. In order to make some new piece of knowledge acceptable to pupils, the teacher should link the new knowledge with the old. The old knowledge or the previous experience of a child acts as a sort of host to the new knowledge. The child can be prepared in a variety of ways. The teacher may ask questions relevant to the lesson, he may initiate a discussion on the subject, he may tell a story and so on. Such a preparatory step involves testing of the previous knowledge of the children and the announcement of the aim by the teacher. Besides arousing the interest of the children and preparing them to receive new knowledge, it helps the teacher to know where the pupils stand, what they already know ? Herbart called this 'apperceptive mass'.

Such a preparatory step is also psychologically sound. It motivates the pupil. That is why, sometimes, this step is termed as motivation or introduction. It introduces the pupil to the new knowledge or experience that is to follow. It makes him mentally alert and active. It assures active participation of the pupils in development of the lesson.

At this stage nothing new should be told to the pupils. As it is an introductory step, it should be brief, brisk and straight-forward leading to the lesson in hand.

2. **Presentation.** After the teacher has introduced the lesson and has announced the aim clearly, he proceeds to present the new knowledge which marks the actual commencement of the lesson. It is assumed that the teacher has selected the subject-matter according to the needs, abilities and mental level of the pupils and that it has been arranged in a logical sequence. For successful teaching, the teacher has to make sure that the children are actively co-operating in the

development of the lesson. They do not sit as passive listeners but regard the new knowledge as a mental challenge. It should provoke their faculty of thinking. All their thought processes should be brought into action.

In order to secure the maximum possible active co-operation of the pupils, the teacher skilfully and resourcefully organises his material. He elicits as much from them as possible, and provokes them to recall relevant ideas, concepts, and facts. He may ask developing questions in order to present the new matter or unit. He may use audio-visual aids and other teaching devices to make his lesson effective. Certain factors are to be borne in mind while presenting the new knowledge to the pupils. There are :

(a) **Systematic Exposition.** The subject-matter of the lesson must be systematically presented to the pupils. The teacher should take up various parts of the lesson one by one in such a way that each part leads to the next part and so on. This will give continuity to the subject-matter presented and prevent confusion which is caused in case of haphazard teaching.

(b) **Clear Understanding.** The teacher is not to pass on mechanically from one part of the lesson to the next. He is also to see that the portions of the lesson taught become clear to the students. He should proceed with the next part only if the previous parts are clearly understood by them.

(c) **Correlation and Integration.** The teacher is to teach the lesson as a whole and not in isolated parts. Definite link must be maintained between the various parts. These should be well-integrated so that the lesson appears as one whole.

(d) **Principle of Revision and Fixation.** The cautious and careful teacher shall always revise the unit in hand before proceeding to the next unit. He should assure himself that the pupils have grasped the unit and the new piece of knowledge is fixed in their mind. The different units should not be hurried through.

3. **Comparison or Association.** Then the facts or ideas presented should be compared or associated with one another. Whenever a new set of ideas or facts is presented to the pupils, they may be asked to compare and contrast these new ideas or facts with the ideas or facts they have already learnt. Such a step would help in establishing associations and in enhancing the process of assimilation. The act of comparing and contrasting sharpens the mental faculties of children. This act involves higher mental processes than mere

memorizing and recollecting. Knowledge is like a tree that grows. Children grow in their knowledge not by memorizing isolated facts, which are soon forgotten, but by establishing associations between ideas. A new experience becomes a part of the child if it is associated with some relevant previous experience.

Hence, comparison between facts or ideas is most important particularly in an inductive lesson e.g. a formula in Algebra, grammar work, framing of principles in Science, bringing out similarities between two events in History and so on. The pupils observe the new facts or ideas and compare them with already obtained results. Thus, the blending of the new with the old results is broadening the horizons of knowledge. It helps in establishing meaningful relationships between facts or ideas.

However, it may be pointed out that comparison or association does not mark a separate step in itself. It is a part of the presentation step. Comparison or association of ideas, concepts, examples, facts etc. goes on side by side with the presentation of the new matter.

4. **Generalization.** When mind has comprehended a new piece of knowledge and compared it with the old, the next step involves arriving at a general idea underlying various ideas and formulating some laws or principles, specially in an inductive lesson. In this way, the pupils may arrive at a formula in mathematics, or discover a rule in science or state a definition in grammar. The pupils observe and compare ideas or facts and locate points of agreement between them, thus finding out the common element. Of course, the generalizations arrived at by the pupils would be incomplete and wrongly stated. It becomes the job of the teacher to help them draw out generalizations from the relevant data completely and state them in a correct manner.

This step is important in as much as it develops the independent thinking of the pupils. The teacher should not hint at the generalization but ask the pupils to discover it themselves. It is only then that it becomes a permanent part of their knowledge. They will take it as their own discovery and shall have the satisfaction of achieving something. They will clearly understand the general rule, formula or principle so evolved. It will constitute a real learning situation.

5. **Application.** According to **Raymont**, "The mere acquisition of rules, precepts, principles, definitions and laws makes directly for pedantary rather than for healthy mental development." Knowledge which cannot be applied is useless and dead. Inert ideas are of no utility. It is very necessary that when a rule, formula or principle has

been evolved, it should be tested and verified by applying it to new situations. The inductive process employed for arriving at generalisation should be followed by deductive applications, otherwise it would be incomplete. Knowledge acquired is of little value if it is not used in the discovery of further facts and their application to new situations. In this way the new knowledge will be fixed in the minds of the children.

6. **Recapitulation.** In fact, recapitulation of the lesson, section or unit-wise, goes on side by side with the development of the lesson. Recapitulation consists in revision and repetition of the knowledge acquired. It may be resorted to either at convenient units of the lessons or at the end of the lesson. Sometimes, both the procedures are adopted. Pupils are required to reproduce what they have learnt during the lesson. All the points in the lesson may not be revised but only the main points. Sometimes in doing so, original expression is also sought for but recapitulation mainly consists in reproducing important points in different units.

Recapitulation is not entirely the same thing as application. Application consist in applying the new knowledge acquired to new and novel, problem or situations. It is the testing and verifying of the rule, 'formula or principle' evolved. On the other hand, recapitulation consist only in revising and reproducing what has already been learnt. In recapitulation the emphasis is on memory and attention testing, while in application the emphasis is on higher mental processes. Application of knowledge is more valuable than mere recapitulation, although it is important, too.

In fact, sectional or unit-wise revision is the best means of assuring that the lesson is progressing satisfactorily. A particular unit might have to be gone over again if the unit-wise recapitulation does not bring satisfactory response. Recapitulatory questions, should be stimulating and well framed. Poorly framed questions would not reveal the strengths and weakness of the lessons. Special attention need be paid to the weaker students to ensure that they are understanding the lessons.

Critical Appraisal of Herbartian Steps

The Herbartian scheme is a significant landmark in the field of teaching. The formal steps indicate the importance of an orderly procedure of teaching. A lesson to be effective must be planned and presented according to the working of the child's mind.

The scheme is based on an analysis of the learning process. It shows clearly that the precepts lead to the formation of concepts. That is to say, formation of ideas in the mind is based on the study of systematically arranged particular facts. This is in accordance with the maxim 'proceed from particular to general or proceed from percepts to concepts.' The ideas of generalisation are firmly fixed in mind when these are applied. Knowledge is useless unless it is put to any use.

The step 'preparation' necessitates that the child's mind should be prepared and his interest be aroused before giving him a new piece of knowledge. The new knowledge should grow out of the apperceptive background of the child. His previous knowledge or past experience, also known as 'apperceptive mass' is always to be the starting point for the teacher. This is according to the maxim 'proceed from the known to the unknown.'

The Herbartian Steps are meant for a unit or a topic of learning which may be spread over a number of periods. In this case, these steps or stages apply to the whole series of lessons on that topic or unit. All the steps may not be present in one time-table lesson period. The teacher is warned not to think of the pupil's activities in terms of time-table lesson periods. He should think of these in terms of the learning-process.

Though Herbartian scheme has effected the modern teaching procedures to a great extent, yet it is not foolproof. It suffers from the following defects :

1. These steps are suitable only for knowledge lesson, not for skill or appreciation lesson, demonstration of the skill by the teacher and practice by the pupils are needed. The steps comparison and generalisation are needless. In appreciation lesson, the aim is to acquire neither any knowledge nor skill. The steps comparison, generalisation application, etc. are not needed. So, we see that the steps suit only the teaching of academic subjects.

2. All the steps are not suitable even in all knowledge lessons. For instance, in an informative lesson on intensive reading, the steps comparison and generalisation are superfluous. In the same way, nothing can be generalised in history. Generalisation is possible only in inductive type of lessons.

3. The scheme is teacher-dominated. The teacher decides what the pupils are to do and what they are to conclude. They are not to choose but to accept. There is no scope for pupils' initiative and participation.

4. The Herbartian pattern of teaching is rigid and stereotyped. The teacher tries to put every lesson into the steel framework of this

plan, with the result that the teaching becomes dull, monotonous and lifeless.

5. There may not be effective motivation in the Herbartian scheme as no motive is provided for learning. In the first step, we stimulate the 'apperceptive masses' of the pupil and make them fill gaps in their knowledge, but this may not motivate them. All the students do not receive knowledge for its own sake. The majority will acquire knowledge only when it is required to fulfil their immediate needs. So in the absence of any effective motive, the pupil may not become willing worker.

6. The step 'association or comparison' is regarded as a separate step in this scheme, but it should be a part of the previous step, that is, 'presentation'. The process of association goes on all along with the 'progress of the lesson. It will seem artificial and involve much repetition if the teacher starts comparing or associating facts after the presentation is over.'

7. The term 'presentation' is also criticised on the ground that it indicates inactivity on the part of the students. They are not to be passive recipients of knowledge. Active pupil participation should be taught during teaching. In fact, the lesson should better name this step as 'development'. The lesson is not to be presented but developed in the class.

8. The term 'preparation' is also' regarded as vague by some critics. It is not clear whether this indicates the preparation of the pupils or the teacher or of both. It may simply stand for the work, the teacher does in planning his lesson and collecting the requisite material.

The criticism against the Herbartian Scheme is justifiable in so far as it makes the procedure of teaching rigid and stereotyped, otherwise its importance in guiding the teacher activity, can hardly be minimised. It points out an orderly procedure of teaching based on sound psychological considerations. The teacher is advised not to stick too much to these steps. These steps are suggestive rather than perscriptive. He is to seek guidance from these steps rather than become their slave. He should be resourceful enough to mould his teaching according to various situations, circumstances, needs of the pupils etc.

Alternative Scheme

In an attempt to remove some of the defects in the Herbartian Scheme, **A. H. T. Glover** in his book 'New Teaching for a New Age' recommends an alternative scheme based on the modern concept of the educative process. The steps of the scheme are as under :

(i) Questions.

(ii) Discussion.

(iii) Investigation.

(iv) Pupil activity (Expression).

(i) The lesson is introduced through skilful questioning. The teacher puts some specific questions to create some learning situations and stimulate pupils activity. The pupils are also encouraged to ask questions

(ii) Questioning is followed by discussion. The preliminary questioning may lead to some differences of opinion, which have to be discussed. The class may be divided into small groups and the teacher may guide the discussion. Irrelevant discussion should be checked. The pupils should be given full freedom to, express their opinions and make observations. In the end, the teacher may sort out main points of discussion and, sum up. Discussion will bring forth the points to be investigated in the next step.

(iii) Discussion is followed by investigation. Again, all should take part in this process and the class may be divided into groups. The different groups may be given different points for investigation. Any information required is supplied by the teacher. The teacher is to guide the process of investigation lest the student should go astray. The written work will proceed side by side.

(iv) Expression is the last step. It may take the form of oral, written. visual or concrete activities by the pupils. Glover classifies the activities under four main heads—passive, active, artistic or creative organizational.

The difference between passive and active activities is largely of emphasis. In passive activities the emphasis is on absorption of experience e.g., observation, visual, listening, etc. although it is not strictly passive because the mind is active all the time. Active activities include handwork, craftwork, drawing, agriculture etc. Artitistic activities constitute music, dancing and creative art work, etc. It also includes games and physical education. Organisational activities are those which require organisation into groups.

Glover's alternative scheme in place of Herbartian Steps can systematically be shown as below :

Explanatory or Initial Questions

↓

Group Discussion

↓

Topic Selection

↓

Investigation

↓

Expression (written, oral, practical)

↓

Practical Activities

↓

↓	↓	↓	↓
Passive	Active	Artistic	Organisational.

Glover's scheme ensures active participation of the pupils in the teaching-learning process. Here they are active discoverers of knowledge as against the Herbartian scheme where they are more recipients of knowledge. However, his scheme is not fool-proof. It also has its limitations. It may not prove useful for small children as it is very difficult for them to take part in active questioning and discussion because of their limited knowledge. It cannot work under restrictions of time-table and curriculum. The logical sequence of lessons will also be difficult to maintain. But the spirit of the scheme viz., active pupil participation cannot be ignored in any good scheme of teaching.

THE SKILL LESSON

To learn various skills is a human need, Psychology has confirmed the claim that the use of the muscles is not only good for the body, it clearly is also good for the mind. "No impression without expression" clearly speaks of the value of skill. Rousseau wrote long time back, "If I have made my meaning clear, you ought to realise how bodily exercise and manual work unconsciously arouse thought and reflection in my pupil. He must work like a peasant and think like a philosopher if he is not to be as idle as a savage." L.P. Jacks has so well put it. "The human body is naturally skill hungry and until that hunger is satisfied, it will be ill at ease, craving for something it has not got and seeking its satisfaction in external excitements which exhaust its vitality and diminish its capacity for joy. Short of skill, the perfect health even of body, is impossible." No wonder great importance is attached to skill Lessons.

The arts of reading, writing, counting, speaking and singing, the representational art of drawing, painting and modelling, and crafts like wood-work, metal-work, cookery and needle-work, while they contain intellectual elements and involve knowledge, are first and foremost affairs of skill. Not only that we are not only to be concerned with the teaching of the techniques of the skill but also with its creative aspects.

Method of Teaching Skill

A skill may be taught by any one of the following techniques :

(i) Demonstration.

(ii) Verbal Instruction.

Demonstration. In a skill lesson, the teacher has to demonstrate the use of new tools or appliances and the performance of new processes. The demonstrations should be thorough and neat in execution. The teacher's own demonstration table should be orderly arranged as the pupils follow good examples. Throughout the demonstration the teacher should emphasise how to use the tools and appliances relying on his actions rather than on his statement to drive home his point.

For the simple uniform skills the teacher may demonstrate the best way and insist on a faithful imitation ; in the fine arts he must be more tolerant of variations. In these differences lie the seeds of originality which lifts imitation above slavish copying. The teacher is justified in checking and repressing variations where they lead to inefficiency—but those which seem to express intelligent reflection and ingenious experiment should not be condemned. Not all teachers are perfect exponents of the art they teach.

All the significant points in the skill should be stressed during demonstration.

Verbal Instruction. Although verbal instructions are no substitute for demonstrations, yet it is a useful teaching method if the teacher has the clear mental imagery to describe the movements in details and the learner has sufficient experience to grasp them. The teacher may describe the process with the help of technical terms, illustrations and sketching of diagrams.

Steps for the Skill Lesson

Just as there are various steps in teaching a "Knowledge Lesson", similarly there are steps in teaching a "Skill Lesson". The following are the broad steps that can be followed while teaching a "Skill Lesson."

1. Preparation (including the announcement of aim).
2. Presentation.
3. Statement of rules.
4. Practice.
5. Correction practice.
6. Application.

1. **Preparation.** This step may also be called motivation or introduction. The teacher can prepare the students for any activity in a number of ways. He can exhibit the model of some work already done. This may instill in the minds of the students a desire to make a similar model themselves. Some oral explanation about the work will enhance the motivation. The main purpose in this step is to create interest. There is no need to ask questions as asked in a "Knowledge Lesson". Simply taking the students to the craft-room or placing them in a situation where they feel the need to learn the particular skill, is enough to arouse their inner urge to learn the activity. Soon after, the teacher should announce the aim of the lesson.

2. **Presentation.** It is here that the teacher presents the new form of skill that is to be acquired. It involves (a) demonstration by the teacher, (b) observation and imitation by the students. (c) verbal explanation by the teacher, and (d) blackboard diagrams etc. First the teacher practically demonstrates the skill whether it is drawing and, painting, spinning, gardening or any other activity. The students carefully observe and then imitate the teacher. Demonstration and verbal explanation both are necessary. Neither alone is sufficient. The teacher should demonstrate the skill and explain each and every step side by side. The students will wrongly imitate the teacher unless he explains each step. The teacher can break up the activity in different parts, as it were, deal with each part exclusively and thoroughly and then combine the whole thing. Without demonstration and verbal explanation, students will not acquire the correct method.

3. **Statement of Rules or Formulation of Rules.** More often than not, the students would wrongly imitate the teacher and would not understand the basic principles involved in the activity. Hence, the need for the 'Statement of Rules'. The rules can either be stated by the teacher or can be formulated jointly by the teacher and the students. It all depends upon the type of activity, the situation, and the age of students. But there is no doubt that joint formulation of the rules by the teacher and the students is decidedly a better method. This leads to clearer understanding by the students.

Statement of rules is necessary to economise time. It will also help in eliminating wrong habits of acquiring a skill and will result in quicker proficiency. There should, however, be no rigidity about the rules and true art should not be bound down by rules, as **Raymont** rightly said, "There is a sense in which rules are the death of true Art". Rules are, therefore, only temporary expedients especially useful in the initial stages of skill learning. Once the students master the technique of performing the skill as suggested by the teacher, let them modify its procedure and make improvements on their previous performance in their own ways. This would mean greater motivation, efficiency and creativity on the part of the pupils.

4. **Practice.** After demonstration and verbal explanation, the students should be asked to practise the skill. It takes a longer time. "Practice makes a man perfect." Repetition is the key to success in acquiring any skill. The teacher is to supervise the students and guide their practice. Individual attention has to be paid by the teacher.

5. **Correction Practice.** This is an important step. While the students are practising the skill, the teacher is to attend to each individual student and point out his mistakes. He should check the wrong movements and should show the right method of performing the activity. He may again demonstrate the activity or state the rules, as the situation demands. It is very essential that errors should be pointed out, eliminated and corrected otherwise wrong habits are acquired and they become fixed. As correction by the teacher goes on, further practice continues. Thus, the cycle of 'Practice-Correction-Practice' goes on until mastery is achieved.

6. **Application.** The acquisition of a certain skill is useless if it is not applied or put to use. The acquired skill can be put to a variety of uses—immediate and remote. For example, if the students have learnt how to draw a particular design, they should be asked to draw similar other designs.

Suggestions for the Success of Skill Lesson

In order to achieve success in any 'skill' lesson, the teacher should bear in mind the following considerations :

(i) The pupils should be adequately motivated 'for a skill. They must feel the need to learn it. For this, the skill should be linked to their immediate needs and interests.

(ii) The skill to be learnt should be according to the standard of the pupils. It should not be too difficult to discourage them. It should be such as can be learnt through reasonable amount of effort by the average child.

(iii) It should not consume too long time otherwise fatigue sets in. For small children especially, the practical activity should be of short duration.

(iv) The teacher should show patience with children. They are slow in learning any new skill. He should encourage and sympathise with children.

(v) The activity should provide a useful channel for self-expression. It should be creative so that each child can get the satisfaction of achieving something.

THE APPRECIATION LESSON

The appreciation lesson aims at aesthetic development in the pupils. It is to provide them with emotional experience and develop emotional stability in them. They are to be enabled to enjoy and appreciate beauty in its various forms. If the students fail to appreciate beauty, fail to discover grace in performance, fail to enjoy the knowledge or skill acquired, the purpose of education would be defeated. A person may be a great scholar, a great artist, he is not a balanced personality if his emotions are not well trained. The main objective of an appreciation lesson is to train and develop the emotional life of the students, the affective aspect of personality. Many great men are a failure in this world because they are emotionally ill-balanced. Training of emotions is probably more important than acquisition of knowledge and skill.

The development of taste and training of emotions is an important aspect of child development. Taste constitutes training of the faculty for discerning and enjoying beauty in music literature, any work of art, etc. It is an expression of feeling rather than of thinking, although thinking is not altogether absent. Children appreciate music, rhythm, coloured objects, and flowers which are all expressions of beauty. Hence, the development of this aspect of personality cannot be ignored.

The teacher should provide the necessary environment for the success of an appreciation lesson. He should be fully prepared for the lesson and be motivated himself. Whatever he selects for presentation, it should be according to the ability level of the students. It should be within their comprehension ; otherwise all effect would be lost. The teacher's own enthusiasm and expression will also be an important factor for the success of the lesson.

Steps for the Appreciation Lesson

Aesthetic appreciation is caught rather than taught. Still, it is rather anomalous to suggest formal steps for the teaching of appreciation because it concerns the inner urge. Yet there are certain steps which would be helpful to the teacher in conducting an appreciation lesson. These are :

(1) Preparation.
(2) Presentation
(3) Contemplation
(4) Expression
(5) Critical appreciation

1. **Preparation.** The students should first be motivated. This can be done by the teacher by creating a suitable atmosphere. There must be silence and all kinds of distractions should be eliminated. There should be no likelihood of any disturbance. The teacher is to induce suitable mood in the pupils for the lesson. Their curiosity and emotions are to be aroused and stimulated so that they begin to expect something beautiful or enjoyable. The teacher should select suitable content of the lesson. In doing so, he must bear in his mind age and mental level, knowledge, interest, needs etc. Of the pupils. The teacher should announce the aim of the lesson, after he is sure that the physical conditions are congenial and the proper atmosphere has been created for the conduct of the lesson.

2. **Presentation.** When all is set, the teacher should present the subject-matter. Various kinds of devices may be used by the teacher to arouse the imagination of the pupils. He may recite a poem in a melodious and rhythmic manner. He may show a picture or sing a song to play upon an instrument and bring out a tune and so on. The subject-matter should not be broken into parts as that would mar the very essence of appreciation. It has been rightly said, "Much of the world's finest literature has been spoilt for individuals by the teacher's over analytic treatment. The teacher who dissects a poem word by word, who paraphrases the contents; underlines the assonance, be labours the rhythm or hammers at rhythming scheme, gives knowledge at the expense of appreciation." And the teacher who himself enjoys, and appreciates, can alone create the suitable atmosphere.

3. **Contemplation.** Presentation is followed by contemplation by the students. The teacher gives some time to them to think, feel and contemplate about the poem taught or a piece of art presented or a song or a tune composed. The contemplation step is a brief one.

4. **Expression.** The students are then allowed to express their ideas, opinions and sentiments about the matter presented. They should be trained to express their likes and dislikes freely and frankly. They should tell frankly what they have enjoyed or liked and to what extent, but they should not pretend to have an appreciation which they do not really have. The expression of sentiments leads them to select a particular idea, a particular part liked by them the most. For younger children, generally, the lesson ends here, but this step may lead to critical appreciation in higher classes.

5. **Critical Appreciation.** At higher levels, the students would be required to appreciate critically the poem or the work of art. They would discuss the parts of the poem they liked best. They would place themselves in the position of the poet and replay his moods and sentiments. They will express the impression the poem left on them, the feelings experienced by them. They may discuss the technique employed by the poet, painter, musician, etc. to produce the desired effects. They may consider the use of similes, metaphors, tools. etc, therein. It may be repeated here that this step is suited to only mentally mature students.

6. **Practice and Creation.** Here the children may re-read the poem rhythmically and melodiously. In case of music, they may sing the song, individually or in chorus. This will help in fixing the joyful experience in their minds.

The pupils, especially the older ones, may be asked to create similar pieces of beauty themselves. They may write a poem or a play, paint a picture, make a scenery, etc. However crude their effort, it is of great educative value. They learn more about the techniques involved and therefore, are in a better position to appreciate the work of others.

These are only broad guide-lines and main points which need to be kept in mind while delivering an appreciation lesson. There cannot be any rigidity. The whole plan should be flexible and the crux of the problem is simply the creation of an appropriate atmosphere and environment.

CONCLUSION

The three types of lessons have been discussed not that the three aims—to impart knowledge, to impart skill and to enable the pupils to appreciate—are to be achieved exclusive of each others. To know, to feel and to do are the ultimates of living ; they are indissolubly bound together. Any analysis of method is so far formal and artificial, and the teacher together with his pupils must achieve the synthesis which reunites the components in experience. The teacher is greater than the method he uses, and the child is greater than the teacher, for the teacher is to serve the child, and to help him to achieve his freedom. This aim transcends all, for the purpose of education is to enable the child to live a richer life by the development of his natural powers within the framework of society. No formal steps of teaching and no particular lable of method will suffice for all the situations that emerge in the school, since life will not conform to the limitations they would impose. The teacher may learn from them, and develop his own power of self-criticism with their aid but he, too, is both artist and craftsman claiming the freedom of the expert to fashion the material in ways that he discovers best suited to the nature and to the development of his pupils knowledge divorced from doing and interest is barren. indeed nothing more than waste mental lumber that the healthy child drops as quickly as possible into unconsciousness. Skill acquired apart from understanding is obviously mechanical and likely to fail at an emergency when it is most needed ; and feeling divorced from action and unchecked by thought can easily degenerate into sentimentalism or hysteria. Consequently, to plan the knowledge lesson and leave it unconnected with a child's interest and with no thought as to the use he can make of it is to court failure, to try to give a child the power of doing any simple thing quickly and mechanically—even for instance, saying tables-without making the mechanical—process the outcome of understanding—takes longer and is a less durable possession than if practice is intelligent ; in the same way feeling that cannot spend itself in action or grow through knowledge at the best fails to develop.

32

Lesson Planning

School is a formal agency of education. The class-room is a formal place where teachers and pupils meet—the former for teaching and the latter for learning. Meetings between teachers and pupils should be occasions for learning, thinking and understanding. To achieve maximum advantages, it becomes imperative that educational activities be best planned and best conducted. The teacher should create learning situations and organize them in such a way that the child is motivated to know to think and to do.

WHAT IS A LESSON PLAN ?

"A lesson plan", in the words of **Laster B. Sands**, "is actually a plan of action. It, therefore, includes the working philosophy of the teacher, her knowledge of philosophy, her comprehension of the objectives of education, her knowledge of the material to be taught, and her ability to utilize effective methods."

A lesson plan points out what has already been done, in what direction the pupils should next be guided and helped and what work is to be taken up immediately. "It is the teacher's mental and emotional visualization of the class-room experience as she plans it to occur." "It is in any ways the core, the heart of effective teaching".

A lesson plan should tell very simply the story, the way the teacher intends, rightly or wrongly, to employ children for a given period. What she and they are going to do. This written "story" should show both sincerity and a plan—a flexible and informal plan.

The "story" of the intended lesson should however, not look like a story. In one sense, the teacher is playing a role—possibly, the chief role—in a performance (with no play-acting, of course!) The plan, therefore, should look more like a programme. There should be bold headings and lesser headings indicating ; the different things that are to go on at different times, who are to do those things teacher or children or both, what instruments are to be used, and a certain amount, not every word, of what is to be said.

Thus, a lesson plan points out what has already been done, in what direction the pupils should next be guided and helped, and the immediate work to be taken up. It begins with goals of instruction and ends with a well-conceived means of arriving at those goals.

WHY LESSON PLANNING

Careful planning is the foundation of all good teaching from the first day of student teaching to the last day of the month of the retirement year. The nature of the lesson-plan may change as the years go by, but planning should never stop.

Lesson-planning performs some specific functions as described below :

1. It forces consideration of goals and objectives, the selection of subject-matter, the selection of procedure, the planning of activities and the preparation of tests of progress.

2. It keeps the teacher on the track, ensures steady progress and a definite outcome of teaching and learning procedures.

3. It is essential to effective teaching. It requires the teacher to look ahead and plan a series of such activities as will progressively modify children's attitudes, habits, information and abilities in desirable directions.

4. It prevents waste. It helps the teachers to be systematic and orderly. It encourages good organisation of subject-matter and activities. It prevents haphazard teaching. It goes a long way towards eliminating disorder and other ills of thoughtless teaching.

5. It helps the teacher to delimit the field in which she is teaching. It gives her an immediate impetus to realize the aims and objectives set, and initiates her on her educational adventure.

6. It encourages proper consideration of the learning process and the choice of appropriate learning procedures. The teacher gains confidence. She employs the best technique to judge the outcome of instructions.

7. It serves as a check on un-planned curriculum. It provides a sensible frame-work to help the work, directing along the lines of the syllabus at a suitable rate. The hierarchy of lessons becomes well-knit, inter-connected. Continuity is assured in the educative process. Needless repetition is avoided.

8. It gives the teacher greater confidence and, therefore, greater freedom in teaching. It can ensure that the teacher does not "dry up" or forget a vital point. It can remind him of the telling phrase, the apt quotation or the effective simile or illustration at the moment in the lesson. The teacher can enter the class-room without anxiety, ready to embark with confidence upon a job she understands and prepared to carry it to a work-man-like.

If hit or miss techniques are to be avoided in education the task of education must be taken earnestly. It certainly entails hard work. "Yet it is potentially the most rewarding sort of professional work that a teacher can do, because in this planning, the teacher has the opportunity to use every bit of his skill, intelligence, ability and personality... in short, every opportunity to become a really fine teacher. Regardless of how long he has served the profession, no teacher should enter a class-room without a lesson-plan developed for that specific class. A teacher may teach a subject such as social studies for 25 years, but each year calls for new planning. Every subject takes a new meaning each year from (a) the new group of pupils to be served by it and (b) the constantly changing social setting which the school and all its work constitute partially.

DIFFERENT TYPES OF PLANS

The teacher has to arrange the knowledge for the purpose of teaching and this necessitates planning. There had been different approaches to lesson planning but generally two main approaches have been considered of some significance. The older view recommends daily planning and requires the plan to be rigidly followed. The whole knowledge is to be divided into small fragments or in watertight compartments. Each subject is divided into topics and sub-topics thus isolating the very link of the subject-matter. These lessons are apt to become dry and mechanical. Students differences are not considered and individual difficulties not removed. The main stress is laid on imparting knowledge based on the subject-matter. There is no unity or continuity in the subject as the knowledge is presented into pieces and segments. The latest thinking in this field does not favour old type of planning and they recommend a new type, a new procedure of handling teaching work.

The followers of the new technique are for 'whole' experience. This school of thought does not like routine or mechanical way of presenting the subject-matter. They want to develop sound habits, abilities and attitudes, capacities and experiences. Teaching must centre around the needs and interests of the students. The knowledge has to be presented to them in an integrated manner. Preference is not given for isolated daily lessons but for the total programme in the subject. Subject matter is not considered as important as the students and as such the whole emphasis is laid on the interest and ability of the students.

It is now psychologically clear that a human being as a whole of not in fractions, or as an entire organism to the whole, not to the parts. This proves the necessity of emphasising the importance of unitary concepts of learning. Atomistic concept of learning has now been condemned and there seems to be growing acceptance of the 'Grestalt Theory of Learning'. It has to be borne in mind that every phase of the operational procedure has to be viewed as a relational part of the total learning situation in almost all the subjects. Advocates of the unitary learning strongly feel that this type of learning helps in the attainment of a staill, concept, understanding and appreciation of the knowledge.

Obviously this approach is based on the assumption that its aim at thorough understanding of the whole knowledge of the situation and its proper application to other situations of the similar nature. In case the learner is not able to apply the learnt experience in the allied situations he has just a fragment knowledge. Unitary learning guarantees successful application and integration of all knowledge. In a nutshell it brings together the various parts into one whole. It may not be wrongly concluded that every thing should be taught together in one course or combined into one lesson. Subjects have to be taught separately but these lessons have to be taught in such a way, so as to ensure integration of whole knowledge in student's mind. Coherence of ideas gained after studying different subjects is essential. If the ideas have been interlocked there will be fuller and better understanding by the students. This is usually known as a unit of technique of planning the educational effort.

We find various types of lesson plans for the sake of convenience and fruitful discussion.

The Short Daily Plan

Many authorities especially the heads of schools require the staff members to keep ready made plan books with them. These books are generally approved by the authorities for uniform. shape and design' one for each subject and for each day of the week to be done in each subject and for each day of the week, generally a week in advance. To, encourage systematic planning and for raising the tone of teaching some authorities believe it to be a necessary administrative device.

The work of the class will not suffer even if the teacher has to be replaced by another teacher for a day or two on account of any kind of absentisism from the school. It serves as a record of work to be done. Many teachers resent to this sort of preparation of an outline for the work. They are under this impression that no lesson planning is required as soon as they become full-fledged teachers. This is quite a wrong attitude. They think themselves to be able to teach without prior planning of the lesson. The most serious type of teachers who are dedicated to their work know that planning is very necessary and they have plans ready even if they find no demand for them. The ready-made plan book gives a systematic planning of the work thus facilitating the teaching assignment. Good teachers usually make more comprehensive plans to achieve better results.

The Longer Daily Plans

Many school teachers plan for important lessons and these plans are in no way less than those usually written in training institutions during their training period. These plans cover important aspects such as :

(i) aims of the lesson.

(ii) material required for the lesson.

(iii) procedure to be adopted.

(iv) procedure of assessment.

Sometime plans are written in a very simple form. The whole page is divided into two parts. On one side the subject-matter is written and on the other the method of teaching including some questions. Teachers get valuable training in self-discipline from writing such plans on different subjects because the writer of the plans will seldom teach in a haphazard manner. Practically it is not very much desirable to write such big plans as no teacher can always depend on the plans. To gain speed and accuracy it is very essential for the teacher to draw some plans on different subjects and he can, this way reduce the length of the plan by and by as after sometimes he will master over the systematic procedure.

The Unit Plan

Unit Plan is very essential for a clear and easy apprehension of each fact by the student, comparison of facts, classification of facts and lastly the application of the knowledge learned so far. As we know learning is an active process involving emphasis on students' behaviour, learning activities have to be meaningful and inter-related to achieve the required results. So in a way experience learning is regarded as the heart of the unit plan idea. In unit plan the most important factors are its objectives, the subject-matter and the activities to be followed during the lesson. It also appears that unit plan is different from old system of organising daily lesson plans rigidly and to suit to the gap of the class period. The individual grows gradually and as such the lesson and knowledge must proceed ahead systematically. In a continuous integrated and unified manner the child easily learns and the unit plan is the most successful technique of teaching.

Educationists who belong to the recent part accepted the idea of integrated knowledge. They also emphasise learning by doing. Project Method, Problem Method are the result of this ideology. The Unit Plan method must be provided with some purposeful activity without which the plan has no value. As the term unit implies wholeness so it has to include in it many things. All the activities centre around, common interest, objective and a significant relationship. In case there is a series of units the whole scheme is known as Semester or half-yearly plan. Such a plan can be made by a single teacher or by groups of teachers. The main advantage of the Unit Plan is that it represents a careful planning of unified activity for the pupils.

A hasty daily plan is done away with the Unit Plan. All the schools which experiment with this form of plan are of the view that such a good plan improves the teaching and learning process. As a matter of fact these units represent record of work rather than plans. These plans are more suggestive and are worked over in almost the same way many times. There are some well known types of unit plans which are practised in progressive school.

Subject Units. Subject units lay more stress on the subject and also the learning of it. A topic is usually selected and presented to the class in an integrated manner. The subject is the main concern in this type of unit. But this is presented in an integrated way rather than in an isolated fashion.

Experience Unit. In such units the centre of experience is the interest and all activities are geared to attains and develop the interest of the learner as the learner may not be interested in all the activities. The child must derive sufficient experience out of the activity and that should in no case ignore the interest of the learner. Perpetuation of interest of the learner is the basic need of the experience unit.

Resource Units. For a definite time and for a particular class and for a select number of students such units are of great value, but not always. A resource unit is prepared by a group of teachers and for its functioning the help of the library and specialists is very essential. The child here, is required to trace knowledge for himself from the sources made available to him.

Dynamic Units. In this type of units more emphasis is laid on the learner rather than on the subject-matter. A dynamic unit has a chain of planned activities for the development of skills, habits, knowledge and provision for adopting to the various life situations. In an integrated and coordinated manner the child learns to meet life situations. It is based on dynamic, functioning and creative learning.

THE TERM SYLLABUS

The term syllabus or term outline for the work of a single subject has been gaining popularity as a means of obtaining systematic progress in the study of a particular subject. From a simple logical outline of the subject to a series of carefully prepared lessons with the procedure indicated, so that a teacher is never at a loss as to what to do next. In short, this is the form of the term plan. It is always better to proceed by such an outline than making use of the book or attempting the assignment in a hotch potch manner. It is clear that when a plan is ready for teaching and for indicating the subject limit, it is of great use to the teacher. It usually leads to a high grade teaching. The preparation of such outlines naturally takes sometimes. Many teachers do not understand the importance of such outlines and they want to avoid it for not shouldering a big and added responsibility. Some other teachers carry with them some such outlines from their period of training which they carry for their use in actual teaching. If this plan is carried out in letter and spirit it may not necessarily suit to changing conditions. These plans have to be modified here and there to ensure more success and effectiveness.

The present needs of children and their interest have to be accounted for to make the teaching-learning situation easier and acceptable to children of different classes and varied interest and age groups.

The Plan for Both

By the term 'Plan for Both' means a plan for the teacher and the taught. We must plan lessons for the convenience of both the teacher and the taught. It gives a detailed outline of study of all the activities of a unit in such a manner that it serves as a plan for both the teacher and the taught. Such a plan is a printed guide worked out by an experienced teacher for the guidance of the students in study. It is also used as a plan for teaching as well as for learning. It also constitutes the only needed material apart from books, text and reference for carrying out a profitable learning exercises. Such study guides contain the same major divisions as the unit plan. In a printed form these plans are put into the hands of the pupils for use in the study period. When used wisely such guides are often productive of good teaching and learning. The only danger in their use is the failure to regard them as suggestive rather than compulsory and to modify them to meet the needs of particular individuals and groups. These plans have to be used widely and objectively otherwise their failure is evident.

Printed exercises for daily units are also prepared by the teacher as he or she proceeds in teaching. These exercises or duplicate exercises are sufficient for a daily lesson or for longer period and are used profitably by many teachers in conducting the work in many of the school subjects. It is a common practice for the teacher to prepare and duplicate them himself. Children seem to enjoy such exercises. The exercises lead to systematic learning and teaching. More or less these exercises resemble practice exercises commonly fond in good text book. The pupil can learn certain things independently even at his own place and after school hours.

Commercial Books and Notes

Work books or commercial books are generally those which are organised to furnish enough teaching material for a year or six months. These are going to gain popularity and will take the place of lesson plans. These books are available for the subject of reading, language, history and geography. These books contain detailed exercises, outlines which are printed by publishers for use by the students and teachers and also furnish material to accompany the text-books. There is one major objection that these books cause many teachers to stop planning and thinking about teaching and hence they cease to grow in the profession. These books are valuable only, if properly used and help teachers to do teaching work systematically. These books must be used as aids to teaching rather than as text books to be seriously followed both the teacher and the students.

Some teachers are in the habit of writing hasty notes. This lapse on the part of a teacher to excausable in the initial stages but not when the teacher has grown up in the profession. It is also understandable when the teacher has to deal with many subjects or plan units. Hasty notes are better than no note or plan at all. The teacher must not enter the class-room without some plan in his mind otherwise, he will be just wasting the time of his students while teaching the subject in a hotch potch manner.

THE PRE-REQUISITES TO LESSON-PLANNING

There are certain pre-requisites which must be kept in view before writing Lesson Plans. Some of these are given below :

1. The teacher must have mastery over the subject-matter he is going to present. He should sort out the major points in the lesson and have a clear perception of the activities that are to be pursued in the class-room.

2. He should not only have mastery over subject-matter but should have a thorough grounding in the principles and techniques of teaching. He should be clear in his mind about the various tools and techniques in his armour that he would employ. That is to say, he should be well-conversant with the 'what' and why' of teaching.

3. He should have a sound knowledge of child psychology and possess knowledge about the children he is to teach. He should keep in mind the various principles of learning while thinking about the selection of various kinds of activities. He should possess the ability to create learning situations appropriate to the age and ability level of students. He must also keep in mind the feasibility of conducting the learning activities successfully. He should do well to think of individual differences in children and catering to the needs and interests of each individual child.

4. The teacher should be clear in his mind about the aims and objectives of education, which he wants to realize by going over a particular lesson. He should further not lose sight of the bigger aims of education. It will give the teacher width. and breadth of outlook that are essential for professional advancement.

5. The teacher must know thoroughly the previous knowledge or experience of the pupils about the topic he is to teach. The new topic is to grow out of the apperceptive back-ground of the pupils.

ESSENTIALS OF A GOOD LESSON PLAN

It is rather difficult to specify the essentials of a lesson-plan. An outline that best serves one teacher may not serve another at all. A safe statement to make is, "The plan which best serves the individual teacher is for him, at least, the best plan to use." In fact, successful teaching depends mainly upon two. factors : a careful but flexible plan, and a teacher so secure in the plan that he feels free to change it as the developing lesson and the needs of the children require. The plan is to be used as a guide rather than as a rule of the thumb to be obeyed blindly. The teacher should have the courage to depart from it when the needs of his pupils demand.

Below are given some of the essentials of a Good Lesson Plan:

1. Lesson plan should preferably be written. That assures the teacher that he has gone over the lesson from every angle. After considerable experience a teacher need not actually write his lesson notes because he is experienced enough to make mental notes of the lesson. Mental planning becomes almost a "second nature" with him.

2. In a good lesson plan, the objectives of the lesson, both general and specific, should be clearly and concisely stated in unambiguous terms. It helps to clarify the activities which are to be directed to achieve those objectives. It will help in evaluation too.

3. The lesson plan should be related to the past knowledge of the students, that is, their previous lessons. It should not stand in isolation from the knowledge the pupil already possess. Some working link should be established.

4. The subject-matter should be carefully selected and well organised under significant points stage by stage. It should be progressively correlated with what has gone before and with what is to follow.

5. A good lesson plan should clearly indicate the type and nature of activities that are to be introduced in the class-room. It should clearly mention the learning situations along with the corresponding subject-matter.

6. A good lesson plan will clearly state the tools and techniques to be used by the teacher in presenting and developing the lesson. It should clearly indicate the method of presentation the questions to be

asked, the illustrations to be used, other aids e.g., maps, charts, diagrams, films and TV. etc.

7. The lesson-plan should indicate the blackboard work to be done by the teacher as well as the assignments to be given to the students.

8. It should mention the evaluation procedure, preferably some concrete evaluation exercises. The exercises may be recapitulatory questions, problems demanding application of knowledge, etc.

9. The selected reference books, magazines etc., should also be indicated in the plan. However, the material referred to must be easily available to the students.

10. The lesson plan should clearly indicate the age of pupils, and time allotted. It should preferably be divided into sections or units to facilitate the presentation and evaluation procedure.

11. And at the end of the lesson plan, there should be some space for criticism where the teacher himself or some of his colleagues can write down the good as well as weak points of the lesson.

All the above points are the essentials of a good lesson plan.

ESSENTIALS OF A WELL-DELIBERED LESSON

Here are some suggestions for a lesson to produce a good effect:

1. The contents of the lesson should be well-selected, planned and remembered. The teacher should bear in mind the children's level, their interests and needs, aims of teaching and the time at his disposal.

2. The teacher must be clear about the general as well as specific aims of the lesson. He should always keep these in mind while teaching. This will give a definite direction to his teaching.

3. The teacher must have complete mastery of the subject-matter. He should gather appropriate facts for the development of the general theme and refer to the appropriate and adequate source material to substantiate the running thread of the lesson.

4. Arrangement of the illustrative material should be made before hand. The teacher should keep the apparatus, aids etc. ready for use. He should also be clear as to when, where and how these aids are to be used. He should also see that there is proper place in the class-room for displaying these aids.

5. On entering the class-room, the teacher should see that the physical conditions of the room are satisfactory. The windows and ventilators should be open. The black-board should be clean. The students should be properly seated.

6. The relevant previous knowledge and experiences of the pupil's should be made use of while introducing the new lesson. The introductory step should be brief, to the point and straight forward leading to the heart of the new lesson, This step should not take more than six or seven minutes in a period of 40 minutes.

7. The teacher should not forget the announcement of aim when beginning to start the lesson. It should be written on the black-board also.

8. The contents of the lesson should be systematically presented. The different parts of the lesson should be so arranged that each part leads to the next and so on. The various parts of the lesson should be well integrated.

9. Wherever possible, the lesson should be correlated with various topics, subjects, crafts and life-situations. This will make it more meaningful to the pupils.

10. The adequate pupil-participation should be sought during the development of the lesson. The pupils are not simply to listen to the teacher passively. Let them put and answer questions, solve problem, perform experiments, give opinions and suggestions.

11. The teacher must not forget to give individual attention to the pupils. He is to see that all the students take part in the development of the lesson. Individual doubts and difficulties should be removed.

12. The question to be put by the teacher must be brief, clear and properly worded. He should observe the general precautions while putting questions. The back-benchers and the students sitting in the remote corners of the class should be especially kept alert and active by the use of questions.

13. The answers of the pupils should also be properly dealt with. The collective answer should be discouraged. The mistakes in an answer should be corrected by the pupils themselves.

14. There should be no rigidity and monotony in teaching. The teacher must modify his teaching according to the class-room situations, even if he is to depart from his original lesson plan. He must never ignore the correct responses, suggestions etc. Of the pupils. They should never get the impression that he is not prepared to tackle anything new that has crept into the lesson.

15. The teacher's movements while teaching should be timely and appropriate. He should avoid such movements as rolling a piece of chalk in the hands, playing with duster, leaning over the chair, a table etc. He should also not stand at one place like a statue.

16. Attitude of the teacher towards his pupils should be encouraging and sympathetic. He should encourage the pupils to ask questions, give suggestions and opinions, and express their doubts and difficulties freely without any hesitation. He should avoid ridiculing them in the class.

17. The teacher should attend to the work habits of the pupils also. Faulty postures and habits of reading, writing, standing, etc. should be checked. Habits of neat, clean and systematic work should be insisted upon.

18. The teacher should not forget to do sectional recapitulation if the lesson is divided into sections. At the end of the lesson, final recapitulation should be done.

19. The formulation of generalisations, if any, should be done with the help of the pupils. The teacher should not give ready-made generalisations.

20. There should be proper division of time to be devoted to the various parts of the lesson, otherwise the teacher may spend too much time on certain parts and rush through the remaining parts.

CRITICAL OBSERVATION OF LESSONS

In the light of the above practical hints for teaching, we hereby give the following lesson-observation guide for the critical observation of the lessons :

Lesson Plan

1. Was the lesson plan well-prepared ?
2. Was it free from all types of mistakes ?
3. Was it followed rigidly ?
4. Was there any departure from the plan ? If so, to what effect ?
5. Was the subject-matter suitable and adequate ?
6. Was it divided into suitable units ?

Objectives

1. Were the general and specific objectives clear to the teacher?
2. How far has the teacher been successful in achieving these objectives ?

Introduction and Motivation

1. Was the lesson associated with the previous knowledge or experiences of the pupils ?
2. Was the introduction relevant ?

3. How far did it prove effective ?
4. Were the students motivated ?
5. Did it lead straight forward to the lesson ?

Announcement of Aim

1. Was it announced at the proper time ?
2. Was it announced in a natural way ?
3. Was the language used clear and simple ?
4. Was it also written on the black-board ?

Presentation

1. Was the subject-matter presented in a systematic way?
2. What was the participation of the pupils in the development of the lesson ?
3. Did the teacher make effective use of black-board ?
4. How were the other aids and devices used ?
5. Was the method of teaching appropriate ?
6. Did it evoke satisfactory response from the students ?
7. Can improvement in the method of teaching be made ?
8. What was the type of questions put and in what way ?
9. Did the teacher encourage students to ask questions ?
10. Did he try to clarify their doubts ?
11. Did he pay individual attention to the various pupils ?
12. What was the type of language used by the teacher ?
13. Did the teacher correlate the lesson with life, crafts or other subjects ?
14. Did the pupils seem to understand what was being taught ?
15. Was the teacher careful about the pupils' comprehension of the subject-matter ?
16. Were the pupils led to think for themselves ?
17. How did he deal with the responses extent did the teacher impress the students ?
19. Did the teacher check the work of the pupils ?
20. Did he help the Pupils to make generalisations themselves?

Application or Recapitulation

1. Was the application or recapitulation done at the time ?
2. Whether was it done with the help of the pupils or by the teacher alone ?

Home Work

1. What type of home-work was given to the pupils ?
2. Was it based on the lesson just taught ?

3. Whether or not was it according to the standard of the pupils?
4. Was it free from overloading and repetition ?

About the Teacher

1. What was the effect of the teacher's general appearance?
2. Was he making appropriate movements and gestures ?
3. Was he teaching with confidence ?
4. Did he face the students for most of the time ?
5. What was his attitude towards the students ?
6. How far did the teacher exercise control over the language ?
7. Whether or not was his voice audible to all the students?
8. Was he fully prepared for the lesson ?
9. Was he teaching enthusiastically ?
10. Was he resourceful ? Did he show his originality anywhere?

Miscellaneous

1. Was the lesson finished in time ?
2. Was the class control and management effective ?
3. Was the interest of the students maintained throughout the lesson ?
4. Did they feel relieved at the end of the period ?
5. What was the overall effect of the lesson on the class ?

33

Micro Teaching

We have explained above a number of requisites for art and skill of teaching. Various devices of teaching were explained as well as steps in planning and delivering a lesson. All this knowledge helps a teacher trainee in a College of Education, who has to prepare himself for effective teaching in the class-room after he leaves the College of Education and enters the regular profession.

The pupil-teacher in the College of Education is given a lot of training in student teaching through :

(a) demonstration lessons by the staff members of the College of Education.

(b) discussion lessons delivered by the pupil-teachers, supervised by the staff supervisors and observed by other pupil-teachers.

(c) short-term and long-term class-room teaching in practising schools.

Attempt is made in imparting training to the pupil-teachers in :

(a) organisation of the curriculum, and specification of general and special objectives of each lesson in terms of behavioural traits and learning experience.

(b) organisation of various audio-visual aids.

(c) getting training in communication skill in the actual class-room situation.

Supervisors in the colleges of education, observe the lessons and write their comments on the lesson-note-book. Suppose they write few sentences like :

(a) Black-board writing is poor.

(b) Class control needs considerable improvement.

(c) The teacher failed to elicit right answers.

(d) There was one-way traffic etc.

The staff supervisor of the College of Education feels satisfied, but it hardly makes any improvement on the work of the teacher. The pupil-teacher himself does not understand the exact mistake he has committed, or the exact skill he is teaching. What is actually required is :

(a) defining and identifying all the various skills in teaching,

(b) imparting training to the pupil-teacher in every skill,

(c) giving opportunity to the pupil-teacher to improve, through what is called 'feed back'.

Now a question arises, can actual teaching skill in the class-room be decomposed into minor specific skill ? Can the entire process of teaching in a particular period be analysed into component parts or steps ?

As for the second question, a lot of work has already been done. Long ago Herbert devised five steps of teaching a class-room lesson. Bloom made specific contribution in defining the various objectives of a lesson in terms of 'knowledge, understanding, application, skill and attitude, and further into various learning experiences and behavioural patterns. He suggested three main steps of (i) objective formation, (ii) presentation and (iii) evaluation.

Methodologists proposed a number of instructional methods like:

(i) Heuristic Method, (ii) Discussion Method, (iii) Lecture Method, (iv) Demonstration Method, (v) Laboratory Method, (vi) Inductive Method, (vii) Deductive Method, (viii) Analytic Method, (ix) Synthetic method etc. A number of instructional processes have been suggested, as part of the teaching skill, viz. (i) art of questioning, (ii) answering, (iii) drill and review, (iv) testing and (v) class-room management.

Even though, so much of guidance is available to the pupil-teacher, but in actual practice, all the above knowledge of methodology and class-room management does not give him enough training in all the necessary skills. It is here that the supervisor, and the pupil-teacher fail.

Robert Glaser made improvement on Herbert's plan, by suggesting 4 major steps like (i) framing instructional objectives, (ii) entering behaviour (interest, aptitude etc.), (iii) following instructional procedure and (iv) performance assessment. Psychologists explained levels of teaching, namely, (i) memory level, (ii) understanding level and (iii) reflection. They further decomposed the three levels as :

Level of Teaching	*Factors*
A. Memory	1. Registration 2. Retention 3. Recognition 4. Recall
B. Understanding	5. Relationship 6. Generalisation 7. Insight
C. Reflection	8. Reasoning 9. Deep insight 10. Problem solving

All the above 10 factors are actually involved in class-room teaching. But this does not exhaust all the skills needed in a teacher.

Basic Skills in Teaching

In order to help the pupil-teacher and the supervisor, a lot of guidance is provided during the last two decades on the subject of the Teaching Tasks or the Basic Skill in Teaching.

Neel Flanders made an analysis of the Interaction between the teacher and the taught, and defined 10 categories of the total interaction. In the process of interaction between the teacher and the taught in the actual class-room situation, **Neel Flanders** made a double division into (i) Teacher talk and (ii) Pupil talk. Teacher talk also may be either direct or indirect. Besides, there may be a situation, where both are silent.

The following table explains all the ten categories included in the teacher-pupil interaction.

CATEGORIES GIVEN BY FLANDERS

Major Categories		*Categories*
A. Teacher Talk	Indirect Talk	1. Accepting feeling of pupils 2. Praising and encouraging the pupils 3. Accepting ideas of pupils 4. Asking questions
	Direct Talk	5. Lecturing 6. Giving Direction 7. Criticising or justifying authority
B. Pupil Talk		8. Responding to teacher 9. Initiatory talk
C. Other Events		10. Silence on confusion

Neel Flanders' Technique of Interaction Analysis is more or less an observation technique, which can be used by the supervisor while he supervises the pupil teacher's teaching. By a detailed process explained by Flanders, the supervisor can find out :

(i) whether the teacher, is more direct or more indirect in presenting the material,

(ii) whether he is able to motivate the pupil,

(iii) whether he asks relevant questions etc.

After the observation the supervisor explains facts, and provides feed-back to the pupil-teacher for further improvement at the time of second lesson.

Classification of teaching skills with the purpose of modification of teacher behaviour have been made by many more experts.

Categories of some other Experts

Some experts have given the following broad categories :

1. Motivational skills, including encouraging pupils, set-induction, displaying warmth.

2. Presentation and communication skills including explaining, using aids, clarifying ideas, giving examples, lecturing, drilling etc.

3. Questioning skills, including using different types of questioning, using probing questions etc.

4. Skills of small group instruction, including individualising instruction, counselling, developing indirect thinking etc.

5. Developing pupil thinking, including fostering inquiry, self-direction, problem-solving and critical thinking etc.

6. Evaluative skills, including assessment, diagnosis of difficulties, providing remedial measures etc.

7. Class-room management and discipline.

Categories of CASE

The Centre for Advanced Studies in Education (CASE), Baroda (India) has finalised a complete list of 21 skills.

The following are the major skills finalised by CASE :

A. Planning Skills

1. Skill of writing instructional objectives.

B. Presentation Skills

2. Skill of introducing a lesson. .
3. Skill of fluency in questioning.
4. Skill of probing questioning.

5. Skill of explaining.

6. Skill of illustrating with examples.

7. Skill of stimulus variation (making encouraging remarks, using gestures and saying 'look carefully', 'listen carefully.' etc., for sustaining the attention).

8. Skill of silence and non-verbal cues (like smile, facial expression etc.).

9. Skill of reinforcement (or encouraging the pupils to participate).

10. Skill of increasing pupil participation.

11. Skill of using black-board.

3. Closure, Evaluation and Managerial Skills

12. Skill of achieving closure.

13. Skill of recognising attending behaviour.

14. Skill of evaluating.

15. Skill of maintaining discipline.

METHODS OF IMPARTING BASIC SKILLS

The most common methods of imparting basic skills are :

(i) supervisor or the staff member of the College of Education (say teacher-educator) explains the theory of teaching and lesson planning.

(ii) He gives a demonstration of some lessons, and allows the pupil-teacher to observe.

(iii) The only feed back is the comments he writes on the lesson note-book.

The defects in this system are :

1. A particular lesson involves a good number of basic kills. Some lesson may involve all the 15 basic skills listed above. It is impossible to give guidance about all the skills in one lesson.

2. The contents of a lesson cover one full period of 40 minutes. The pupil-teacher may be, on the whole, doing justice to the whole lesson, but may be faltering in one small unit. Each unit in the content is important.

3. The pupil-teacher is teaching a big class, and inspite of his best efforts, he may not be able to maintain discipline or evoke participation of all.

4. The supervisor himself has to jot down a lot of things during his observation, and he cannot do justice to each skill. Actually speaking when we supervise the whole big lesson, we call it MACRO-APPROACH. This macro-approach dilutes the attention of the pupil-teacher and the supervisor.

There is, therefore, a specific need for creating some situation where the pupil-teacher could get training in one basic skill at a time. This is possible only when the conditions are controlled. Let us follow the Motto—one competence at a time, and reduce the complexity of the problem. The complexity of the problem could be considerably reduced, if we have a small number of pupils (in place the full size of the class), have a short duration time of only 5 minutes) for paying full attention to a particular unit and shall reduce the content to one unit with a single concept. This would be the MICRO-APPROACH, in contrast, to MACRO-APPROACH. Such an approach has already been followed by **D.W. Allen** and **A.W. Eve,** and the have devised a new system called MICRO-TEACHING.

CONCEPT OF MICRO-TEACHING

As is clear from above, micro-teaching is a miniature class-room teaching. The time selected for teaching a particular unit is reduced to 5 to 10 minutes. The size of the class is reduced to 5 to 10 pupils. The content is reduced to one unit. Only one skill is taken up at one time.

Allen makes a very precise definition as Micro Teaching is a scaled down teaching encounter in class, size and time. He elaborates it further by saying,

Micro-teaching is a system of controlled practice that makes it possible to concentrate on specific teaching behaviour and to practice teaching under controlled conditions.

The conditions controlled are time, content and size of the class.

Bush defines micro-teaching as "A teacher education technique which allows teachers to apply clearly defined teaching skills to carefully prepared lessons in a planned series of five to ten minutes encounter with a small group of real students often with an opportunity to observe the results on video tape."

It may be clarified that after the micro-teaching lesson is over, if it is video-taped the pupil-teacher can himself see and listen how he fared in the class-room. Even a closed Circuit Television can be used for post-lesson observations.

A similar definition is given by **Clift**: "Micro-teaching is a teacher trainee procedure which reduces the teaching situation to a simple and more controlled encounter achieved by limiting the practice teaching to a specific skill and reducing teaching time and class size."

Steps in Micro-teaching

The five major steps suggested by **Allen** (the founder of this system) are Teach, Feed-back, Replan, Reteach and Refeed-back.

After a particular micro lesson is given, the supervisor discussed the same with the pupil-teacher and gives feed-back. The pupil-teacher thereupon, replans the same lesson and reteaches it to another small group, and finally he gets another feed-back from the supervisor. Thus the pupil-teacher gets an opportunity of correcting himself till he becomes more or less perfect in the particular skill.

The major step out of the above is the first step 'Teach'. Here also, a detailed strategy is to be followed.

1. Orientation lectures are to be given on each skill followed by discussion with pupil-teacher.

A model presentation of one of the skills at a time is given by the supervisor. The pupil-teachers are given opportunity to criticise the model.

2. A time-schedule of micro lessons is prepared for each pupil-teacher.

3. Each pupil-teacher prepares a plan for micro lesson with the help of his supervisor.

4. Each pupil-teacher then delivers the micro lesson under controlled conditions. The controlled conditions have already been explained above.

5. The lesson delivered by the pupil-teacher is supervised by the supervisor. If the college possesses a video tape recorder, it is video-taped or televised at close circuit television (CCTV).

6. The lesson is then discussed, and the supervisor gives feed back, i.e., suggested improvements.

7. Each trainee incorporates the suggestions and prepares again to reteach the lesson.

8. The trainee (pupil-teacher) teaches after an interval of time the same lesson to another small group of students.

9. The lesson is again discussed and feed-back given.

10. In micro-teaching the pupil-teacher tries to complete the following 5 R's.

(i) RECORDING, (ii) REVIEWING, (iii) RESPONDING, (iv) REFINING, and (v) REDOING.

Diagrammatic Representation

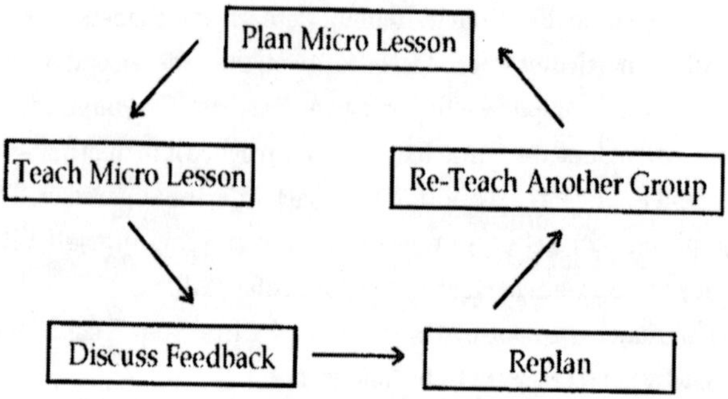

Micro teaching cycle

Principles underlying Micro-teaching

1. Psychological theory of Reinforcement. In the chapter on 'Programmed Learning ; the principle of reinforcement as explained by Shinner and applied to teaching-learning situations has been elucidated. In micro-teaching lessons, the pupil-teacher is given encouragement from time to time for his better performance with the feedback, he is able to perform better and get self-satisfaction. As a result of teaching reinforcement, feedback and reteaching, he becomes perfect. This is what is found in 'operant conditioning' as explained by Shinner.

2. The pedagogic principle of practice and drill. Practice makes a man perfect. How does a successful surgeon attain mastery over surgery ? He practices in the beginning, each minute skill task, beginning from intra-muscular injection to intravenous injection, to dressing a small wound to effecting a small incision, and finally conducting a complex operation like heart operation. He practises each small task, and the use of each small surgical instrument. Like surgery, teaching also is a complex skill, which needs constant drill and practice. Micro-teaching affords practice in each small task or rule-skill enumerated above (list of basic skills), and thereby the pupil-teacher gains mastery.

3. The principle of evaluation. Each micro lesson is supervised and evaluated by supervisor. Besides, with the help of video tape recorder the pupil-teacher is able to self-evaluate his own performance, and thus make improvement.

4. The principle of experimentation. Many aspects of micro-teaching render it significant as a research tool. The supervisor and the teacher trainee conduct experiment on teaching skill under specially controlled conditions. Experimentation in pedagogy is not possible without controlled conditions, which are provided in micro-teaching.

5. The principle of microscopic supervision. Supervision of a lesson can be effective only if the supervisor has a microscopic vision and sees through the lesson all the important points, paying full attention to one point at a time. In routine type supervision, the supervisor cannot do justice to the supervisory task. Micro-teaching involves supervision with minute precision. The supervisor has an Observation Schedule which he fills up while supervising, and makes assessment on a rating scale.

6. The principle of continuity. Micro teaching is a continuous process. Teaching-feedback-reteaching-feedback till perfection is attained in its special feature. The teacher learns and learns continuously the art and skill of teaching.

Role of the Supervisor

1. The supervisor plays a very active role. First of all he gives a demonstration of a particular skill. Suppose the particular skill is black-board writing. He will choose a particular topic which involves a lot of blackboard writing, say lesson in geometry or physics, or English grammar.

2. He prepares a special schedule of micro-teaching lessons in the practising schools. This involves special arrangements. The group of pupils is less than 10. The time is only 5 to 10 minutes. After the lesson, the group is to go, and the pupil-trainees discuss with the supervisor.

3. He supervises the lesson, and makes note of all the improvements that are to be made in presentation by the pupil-teacher.

4. He discusses with the pupil-teacher in the group of other pupil-teachers. He completes evaluation schedule, and gives feedback.

Experiments conducted (even in India) on micro-teaching have proved that this system had a great effect on the supervisor himself. The supervisor (a staff member of the College of Education, who has specialised in the subject) has to make a lot of preparation himself, so, as to be a model for the pupil-teachers. He perspires even at the time of supervising the lesson.

Aids in Micro Teaching

Micro-teaching needs a number of aids, verbal, visual, audio or audio-visual.

1. Observation Schedule. The observation schedule will be in the hands of the supervisor. It is to be used at the time of supervising the lesson. It may be in the form of check list including all items to be observed or a questionnaire. A check list is common. Let us take up the lesson involving one of the basic skills, viz, skill of introducing a lesson. The schedule will have in the beginning preliminary data like Name of the pupil-teacher, topic, class, data, time, lesson etc. Then it may have statement (to be assessed) like the following :

1. The pupil-teacher used previous knowledge of the pupils.
2. The teacher used the correct device for introducing the lesson.
3. The questions were followed by correct responses.
4. The introducing was effective.

Numerical marks also can be given ranging from 0 to 4 on a 5 point scale.

2. Tape-recorder. A cassette tape-recorder can be used for recording the entire conversation in the class-room. It can be listened, again and again for self-appraisal and appraisal by supervisor.

3. Video-tape recorder (VTR). This has the double facility of sight and sound. The pupil-teacher can view the entire class-room transaction again and again, and note especially his own gesticulations, mannerisms and facial expression.

4. Close Circuit Television (CCTV). Through CCTV, the entire class-room event can be viewed in another room and shown to other groups, simultaneously when the class work is going on. In this way, the entire pupil-teacher class, and all the staff-members can see the lesson going on in the hall, without disturbing the actual class-room atmosphere where the conditions are deliberately controlled.

5. A Movie Film. CCTV has a limitation that it is to be used simultaneously, when the class work is going on. A movie film can record and exhibit the entire scene over and over again.

6. One-way Glasses. The class-room as well as another hall or room for observation ran have an intermediatory wall of glasses which are one-way opaque. The observers can see the class work, but the pupils in the class cannot view the observers.

Advantages of Micro-Teaching

D. Allen the founder of the system has advocated five essential propositions :

1. Micro-teaching is real teaching. Although the teaching situation is structured, yet bonafide teaching does take place.

2. Micro-teaching lessens the complexities of normal class room teaching ; size of the class, time and subject matter are all reduced.

3. Micro-teaching focuses on training for accomplishment of specific tasks. These tasks may be instructional skills, practice of techniques of teaching, demonstration of teaching methods and mastery of certain curricular materials, etc.

4. Micro-teaching allows for increased control of practice. In the practice setting of micro-teaching the rituals of time, students, methods of feedback and supervision, etc., can be manipulated. As a result high degree of control can be built in a trained programme.

5. Micro-teaching greatly expands the normal knowledge of results of feedback dimension in teaching. To give a trainee a maximum insight into his performance, several sources of feedback are at his disposal.

Limitations of Micro-Teaching

Inspite of the wide popularity of micro-teaching in the recent years, we cannot equate micro-teaching with the entire internship programme. It is not a substitute, but a first supplement. We must understand its limitations :

1. In micro-teaching 15 or 20 specific skills are focussed. But these skills do not mean all sorts of problems to be encountered in a lesson. The total skill of teaching is greater than the 20 skills put together.

2. In 5 to 10 minutes a very small content is presented, which fragments the lesson.

3. In a small group of 4 to 10 pupils, the pupil-teacher gets a lot of confidence in teaching. But he my fail, when in actual practice he has to face class of 50 or 60.

4. It may not be possible to disturb the existing time-table of practising schools, by calling small groups for 5 to 10 minutes, and learning them after 10 minutes' teaching.

5. An effective micro-teaching system needs tape-records, video-tape, and CCTV. These are extremely expensive for Indian Schools. This is one of the reasons, Micro-teaching could not make headway so far.

CONCLUSION

Micro-teaching is a system of very recent origin. It originated at Stanford University in 1961 as a part of an experimental research project financed by Ford Foundation and Kettering Foundation. The project under the charge of **Prof. D.W. Allen**, resulted in the development of 14 basic skills of class-room teaching under controlled conditions.

The technique became popular in U.S.A. By 1969, more than, 150 colleges used it for secondary-teacher-training. Many more scholars and researches gave further impetus to it. The idea was further extended by **Borg, Kelley, Langer** and **Gall**.

In India, a modest attempt was made at Technical Teachers Training College, Madras (1970), Calcutta (1974) and Chandigarh (1974). **Dr. M.L. Dosajh** made a thorough experiment with the help of Video-tape and CCTV at Technical Teachers Training Institute, Chandigarh.

Micro-teaching has become a full-fledged research project at Centre, of Advanced Studies in Education (CASE), Baroda. **Dr. B.K. Dass**, and his colleagues completed a research project at Baroda.

NCERT took a major project in collaboration with CASE, and conducted a number of workshops at Colleges of Education.

A number of works have been written on this subject by Indian authors also.

Bibliography

Adams, John—Modern Developments in Educational Practice.

Basu, A.N.—Education in Modern India.

Boyles—The Theory and Practice of Teaching.

Bertrand Russel—1. On Education; 2. Education and Social Order; 3. Education and Good of Life.

Bode—Modern Educational Theories.

Brown, Francis J.—Educational Sociology.

Brubacher, John S.—1. Modern Philosophies of Education; 2. A History of Problems of Education.

Bureau of Publication, C.U. -Readings in the Foundations of Education, Volumes I and II.

Clark —Education and Social Change.

Cole, William E. —Sociology in Educational Practice.

Crow and Crow.—1. Education in Secondary School.

Cunningham, William F.—Pivotal Problems in Education.

Dewey, John—1. Democracy and Education; 2. Schools and Society; 3. Schools of Tomorrow.

Dhiman, O.P.—Gandhian Philosophy—A Critical and Comprehensive Study.

Findley—The Foundations of Education, Volumes I & II.

Hambridge—New Aims in Education.

Henderson, Stela V.—Introduction to the Philosophy of Education.

Home, Herman H.—1. Philosophy of Education; 2. Democratic Philosophy of Education.

International Comparison on the Development of Education—Learning to Be.

—do—Education on the Move.

Joad—Return to Philosophy-Review of Philosophies.

Jacks—Total Education

Keatings—Studies in Education.

Kilpatrick, William H.—Source Book in the Philosophy of Education.

Kandel—Conflicting Theories of Education.

MacIver, R.M.—Society.

Mani, R.S.—Educational Ideas and Ideals of Gandhi and Tagore.

Massani, R.P.—Education for World Understanding.

Ministry of Education—1. Report of the Secondary Education Commission; 2. Report of Indian Education Commission; 3. Report of the University Commission.

Monroe—1. A Text Book in the History of Education; 2. Encyclopaedia of Education (New York, 1956).

Neill—That Dreadful School.

Nunn, Sir, Percy—Education-its Data and First Principles.

Philips—Edacation-A Search for New Principles.

Radhakrishnan—Reffirion and Culture.

Rama Krishna Mission. Teaching of Swami Vivekananda.

Ranganathananda, Swami—Eternal Values, in a Changing Society.

Robert Wich—Fundamentals of Democratic Education.

Ross, James S.——Ground Work of Educational Theory.

Rusk, Robert R.—1. The Doctrines of-the Great; Educators; 2. The Philosophical Basis of Education.

Russel, Bertrand—Education and the Social Order.

Saiyidain, K.G.—1. Education for International Understanding; 2. Educational Reconstruction; 3. Man in the New World; 4. Humanist Tradition in Indian Educational Thought; 5. Education, Culture and the Social Order.

Strong C.F.—Teaching for International Understanding.

Tara Singh, Dr.—An Outline of the Philosophy of Creative Education.

Thomson, Godfrey H. —A Modern Philosophy of Education.

Thomson and Long —Principles of Modern Education.

Thomson Hapkins —Interaction-The Democratic Process.

Whitehead —The Aims of Education.

Will Durant —The Story of Philosophy.

W.P. Alexander—The Educational Needs of Democracy.

William, James—Pragmation.

Index

C

D

R

S